D1611283

The Gulf of Mexico

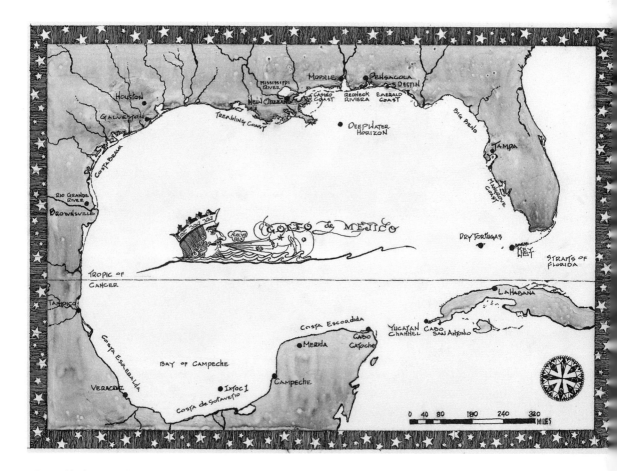

The Gulf of Mexico by Nicholas Holmes III, 2017.

The Gulf of

Mexico
A Maritime History

John S. Sledge

THE UNIVERSITY OF
SOUTH CAROLINA PRESS

NEW HANOVER COUNTY
PUBLIC LIBRARY
201 CHESTNUT STREET
WILMINGTON, NC 28401

© 2019 University of South Carolina
The Gulf of Mexico map by Nicholas H. Holmes III © 2017

Published by the University of South Carolina Press
Columbia, South Carolina 29208

www.sc.edu/uscpress

Manufactured in the United States of America

28 27 26 25 24 23 22 21 20 19   10 9 8 7 6 5 4 3 2 1

Library of Congress Cataloging-in-Publication Data
can be found at http://catalog.loc.gov/.

Publication of this book was made possible through
the generosity of the A. S. Mitchell Foundation, Mobile, Alabama.

isbn: 978-1-64336-014-0 (cloth)
isbn: 978-1-64336-015-7 (ebook)

In memory of my cousins:

Mack Clarke, who fell off a shrimp boat and drowned in the Gulf, 1986

Terry Clarke, who died of a heart attack during Hurricane Georges, 1998

Shadows lengthen; and at last the woods dwindle behind you into thin bluish lines;—land and water alike take more luminous color;—lakes link themselves with sea-bays;—and the ocean-wind bursts upon you,—keen, cool, and full of light.

Lafcadio Hearn,
Chita, 1889

Contents

Illustrations

Acknowledgments

First, my profoundest thanks go to Joseph Meaher and the trustees of the A. S. Mitchell Foundation, whose generous support made this book possible. When I told Cap'n Joe that I wanted to write a maritime history of the Gulf, he immediately asked how the Foundation could help further the project. He also asked if I planned to cover Cabeza de Vaca's epic odyssey along our shores, and I assured him that I did!

I am grateful as well to the many people who expressed their sincere interest during my research phase and shared their rich tidbits of Gulf lore. Jody Kamins Harper made available her extensive interviews with family member Charlie Bodden, whom she had the foresight to record as he recalled working some of the Gulf's last lumber schooners. Retired Orange Beach charter boat captain Earl Callaway graciously spent an entire day taking me around the Alabama shore and regaling me with the most wonderful stories. He is a man of parts. Former Destin History and Fishing Museum executive director Kathy Marler Blue provided valuable insight into charter fishing's early days, and John Ray Nelson of Bon Secour Fisheries told me about his century-plus-old company and life on board Mobile Bay sailing luggers. John Dindo showed me around the Dauphin Island Sea Lab, and his wife, Charlene Dindo, thoughtfully gave a copy of my earlier book on the Mobile River to the legendary naturalist E. O. Wilson, who knows the central Gulf Coast well. I am also indebted to Greg Anderson, Dave Berault, Jack E. Davis, Hardy Jackson, Mike Feore, Watt Key, John Hunter, David Smithweck, Jim Delgado, Ken Cooper, Margaret Long, and Michael Shipler for much good information. Lincoln Paine's thoughts on maritime history in general and its pursuit as a field of study helped me stay focused during many long months of composition.

Among the individuals and institutions to which I am indebted are retired director Greg Waselkov, Bonnie Gums, and Sarah Mattics of the Center for Archaeological Studies, University of South Alabama; past director Tony Zodrow and former chair E. B. Peebles III at GulfQuest National Maritime Museum of the Gulf of Mexico; Amy Raley, education manager at GulfQuest; Jocko Potts, Stephen Potts, Anita Miller, Maggie Lacey, Lawren Largue, Chelsea (Capability) Adams, and Breck Pappas of *Mobile Bay* magazine; director Jimmy Lyons, Judy Adams, harbormaster Terry Gilbreath, and Maria Conchita Mendez at the Alabama Port Authority; Kelly Barfoot at the Mobile Bay National Estuarine Program; Mike Bunn at Blakeley State Park; Gail Walker Graham at the Orange Beach Indian and Sea Museum; Siva Blake at the Civil District Court, Orleans Parish; Germaine Bienvenu,

LSU Libraries; Rebecca Smith, Historic New Orleans Collection; Katie Barry at the Stark Museum of Art in Orange, Texas; Barbara Howard at the Harte Research Institute for Gulf of Mexico Studies in Corpus Christie; Julio Larramendi, Honors College, University of Alabama; Melinda Rose, photographer; Michael Mastro, photographer; Tina McDowell at the Carnegie Institution of Science in Washington, D.C.; and Emerson Hunton and John Powell at the Newberry Library, Chicago. All of these wonderful people took time out of their busy schedules to help me on my way. If I can ever return the favor, I certainly will.

As always, I hold my friends dear. Eugene LeVert was a wonderful sounding board on nautical matters. Scotty Kirkland was never too busy to discuss the finer points of reading and writing history. Nick Beeson was a rock, obtaining high-resolution photographs from a dozen sources and remaining good-humored throughout what must have been far too many intrusions. Grey Redditt Jr. was always ready to talk about Havana, David and Simona Newell took my wife, Lynn, and me on several unforgettable trips up coastal rivers, across choppy bays, and even out onto the heaving Gulf itself on board their handsome Stauter-Built boat, Roy Hoffman never failed with sage literary advice, Nick Holmes III happily agreed to draw the very fine Gulf of Mexico map to go with this book, and his secretary, Margaret Davis, helped facilitate.

I feel fortunate indeed to have a publishing home with the University of South Carolina Press. Former director Jonathan Haupt pounced on this book the minute I inquired, and incoming director Richard Brown was equally enthusiastic. A writer doesn't get that every day. Assistant Director for Operations Linda Haines Fogle (recently retired) and Marketing and Sales Director Suzanne Axland were always generous with their time and never failed to make me laugh. Their professionalism is exceeded only by their good cheer. I am also grateful for the anonymous readers' close attention to the manuscript.

Lastly, my family has been terrific. My mother, Jeanne Sledge, read the manuscript as I wrote each chapter and offered encouragement as well as suggested improvements. Lynn edited it with her usual nuance and care, while our children, Matthew and Elena, both grown and living in Birmingham, were admirably patient with a father who was often preoccupied by the past. My younger brother, Henry, his wife, Andrea, and their son, Jack, all love the Gulf and go there frequently, and their early enthusiasm was much appreciated. It should go without saying, but I will say it, nonetheless—any errors of fact found herein are to be laid solely at my door.

Prologue
Small Craft Advisory

O ur first view of Destin, Florida, came as we raced east across the bridge from Okaloosa Island. The year was 1974, and there wasn't much to the town then—a few high-rise condos, some scattered beach houses, a thinly developed harbor, and about three thousand residents plopped down amid some of the most gorgeous scenery on the entire northern Gulf Coast. The occasion was our annual family vacation. We lived in a little college town called Montevallo, just south of Birmingham, Alabama, where Dad had taught biology since 1962 and Mom was a homemaker. Despite our inland address, we proudly owned deep coastal roots. Dad was a native Mobilian, Mom had spent part of her childhood in New Orleans's famed Pontalba Building, and I was born in Gainesville, where Dad attended the University of Florida before working a stint at a Winter Haven plant nursery and then moving us north. Given this family history, as well as the Florida Panhandle's abundant distractions and drivable distance from home, we regularly vacationed there during the 1970s, though usually farther east at Panama City Beach. Why we chose Destin during this particular year I don't recall, but neither I, at seventeen, nor my brother Henry, ten, complained. We had a close relationship with our parents, and it was good to get away together.

The 1970s were the apogee of the so-called Redneck Riviera, when cheap roadside kitsch, the "Miracle Strip," honky-tonks, the Trashy White Band, piratical land transactions, and minimal to nonexistent environmental protections defined the Florida and Alabama coasts. It was a world where, according to one local, "You can holler 'Bubba' and 15 people will respond." Foley, Alabama, native Kenny Stabler, a former University of Alabama quarterback and soon-to-be Super Bowl–winning NFL star, was the area's beau ideal, proudly announcing: "I live the way I want to live, and I don't give a damn if anybody likes it or not. I run hard as hell and don't sleep. I'm just here for the beer." Paradoxically, the Redneck Riviera was also family friendly, at least during daylight and away from the crowded watering holes like the Green Knight and the Flora-Bama. The beaches were and are some of the world's prettiest, featuring sugar-white sand that squeaks when you walk on it. In fact, this powdery heavenly stuff is quartz washed out of the Appalachian Mountains eons ago and ground to fundamental perfection. The Panhandle is also famous for its crystal-clear waters, unspoiled by large sediment-bearing rivers like the Mobile or the Mississippi to the west. Where shallow, especially right along the beach, over sandbars, and in the passes, it's bathtub warm in summer and a beautiful emerald color, the result of sunlight hitting the sandy bottom and reflecting off copious microscopic algae. Farther away as the depth increases, the water shades into turquoise and then deep blue, all of the colors subtly modulated by conditions of light and cloud. It was and is a delightful place to unwind, listen to laughing gulls, and splash about in the surf.[1]

Destin was still unincorporated in 1974, and nearby resorts like Sandestin and Miramar Beach were yet in their infancy. But despite being lightly settled, it had a long history, and thanks to the proximity of the one hundred-fathom curve, boosters proudly proclaimed it "The World's Luckiest Fishing Village." Just ten miles off Destin, the northern Gulf's broad continental shelf narrows dramatically and the bottom falls precipitously away. Within minutes of the harbor, boat captains can position anglers over a water column where deep-sea fishing of nearly every variety is possible.[2]

Native Americans were in the vicinity first, of course, and left a ceremonial mound in what is now downtown Fort Walton, just west of Destin, to prove it. Then came a few European explorers and the occasional pirate or smuggler, none of whom stayed very long. The area's earliest white settlers arrived during the 1830s. They knew about the fishing, but they also made do with a little farming, hunting, turpentining, logging, and whatever else would turn a dollar or fill the larder. In those pre-sun-worshipping days, the Gulf Coast's windswept barrier islands were considered deserts, likely to wreck a ship in a storm and unable to support more than the occasional hermit or malcontent. People of good sense put down stakes well back from the beach, behind the lakes and lagoons and along the bays among the magnolias and moss-hung live oaks. The closer one got to the beach, the scrubbier the vegetation and the harder the living. A Connecticut Yankee named Leonard Destin decided to try his luck nonetheless and, bucking received wisdom, settled on the south shore of Choctawhatchee Bay, a large body of water fed by several small streams and linked to the Gulf through East Pass. What would become Destin was situated at the western end of a barrier island (since reconnected to the mainland by shifting landforms and so now a peninsula) sandwiched between the bay and the Gulf. The very tip of the island made a small lobster claw, which provided a decent natural harbor. This would become Destin's heart, and home to the largest recreational fishing fleet in the entire Gulf basin.[3]

Soon a few other hardy souls joined Destin in this isolated spot. Elisha Marler and his wife moved down from Georgia and started building boats and fashioning nets, and the little settlement became a bona fide fishing community, regularly sending forth its sons in wooden boats to reap the sea's bounty—red snapper,

Destin Harbor, 1974, viewed from the East Pass. COURTESY STATE ARCHIVES OF FLORIDA.

grouper, scamp, king mackerel, wahoo, and tuna. It was strictly a commercial enterprise then, with the fish kept in live wells amidships and taken to market at Pensacola, where they sold for pennies a pound. By the 1930s Highway 98 and the Destin Bridge were built, and a trickle of tourists began to filter into the area. Ever alert to new opportunities, the descendants of Destin and Marler hit upon the idea of recreational charter fishing and started charging guests for an unforgettable few hours off shore reeling in the big ones. Eager to spread the good word and strengthen the fishery, the Destin Businessmen's Club and some local captains started a fishing rodeo in 1948, and the enthusiasm only grew from there. By the time my family and I arrived in Destin for our vacation, charter fishing was a fully established industry, though the town proper offered few amusements other than some unremarkable restaurants, bars, and stores.[4]

We stayed across the highway from the beach, and after a couple of days trudging over hot asphalt and battling traffic, sandspurs, and sunburn, Henry and I became bored. In an effort to vary the menu, Dad decided that a short fishing trip might be just the ticket. The next morning we had a light breakfast and headed to the harbor where Dad had already made arrangements for a four-hour trawling trip.

Our boat was the *Calypso II,* which Henry and I thought was neat since Dad was a biologist and we loved *The Undersea World of Jacques Cousteau* television series, then in its heyday, featuring the French explorer and his research vessel, *Calypso.* Our conveyance that day was no scientific research ship but rather a deep-sea fishing boat roughly forty feet long with a flybridge, cabin below, and open stern. It was captained by Howard Marler Jr., a navy vet, a descendent of old Elisha, and one of several family members in the charter boat business. He wore a trucker cap and untucked short-sleeve shirt, was deeply tanned, and didn't have much to say. The mate was a wiry young fellow with a ball cap and a Jimmy Buffet–like moustache. Both captain and mate smoked like steam engines. Besides us, a newlywed couple had also booked a trip. After brief introductions, we all got on board, Capt. Marler ascended the ladder to his perch, where he took the wheel, and we motored out of the smooth harbor, rounded a sandspit, and headed south through the pass. It was mostly cloudy and very windy.[5]

Out in the pass a strong southerly gust hit us and whisked Dad's straw hat well astern, where it bobbed jauntily on its crown. Dad just shrugged, but the captain immediately turned us around and deftly maneuvered as close to the hat as he could get. The mate snagged it with a boat hook and courteously handed it back to Dad, none the worse for wear. Clearly, Destin's charter captains and crews prided themselves on superb boat-handling skills and customer service. We then headed south again, and large rollers funneling into the pass made *Calypso II* ride like Six Flags Over Georgia's Great American Scream Machine, growling up and over the big waves. Beyond the rock jetties we could see that it was very rough, and the mate remarked that there was a small craft advisory, with seas running five to eight feet. From an early age, Dad had instilled in us a healthy respect for the Gulf—the ferocity of its sun on unprotected skin, the dangers of its riptides and currents and sea life. Now we were embarking on it in less than ideal conditions. Once out in open water, we were rocking with the green waves lifting and dropping the boat and shoving it in all directions. Dad, a World War II Marine Corps combat veteran whose sea experience included riding out a typhoon on board a supply ship, said it reminded him of being in the Pacific. Henry recently recalled in an email: "I was very worried about getting seasick even though I felt fine. Dad told me not to think about it too much and slipped me a Rolaid. I also believe I asked him if he was ever seasick, and he said it had never bothered him."[6]

About five miles out Capt. Marler paralleled the shore, and the mate got to work. In fact over the next four hours he hardly paused, tending the gear, baiting the hooks, and handling the fish as we reeled them in over the stern. I had done more than my fair share of fishing—from muddy creek banks to placid lakes, murky bayous, Mobile Bay, and the Gulf Shores, Alabama, pier—but this was an entirely new undertaking. And strange to say, it didn't particularly interest me. Happy to let the mate do the hard work, I was more intrigued by the scenery and the seas. To begin with, the shore was just visible, and in fact exactly matched how the colonial explorers had described it. In 1699 for example, Pierre LeMoyne d'Iberville wrote, "The mainland, which I see beyond this lake [Choctawhatchee Bay], looks very fine, quite level, covered with tall trees, the ground elevated enough to be visible from the deck 6 leagues out."[7]

Five- to eight-foot seas wouldn't have been much noticed by Iberville and his compatriots, with their larger vessels and extensive time afloat, but Henry and I were mightily impressed and soon enough left the fishing to Dad, the newlyweds, and the mate in order to explore the *Calypso II*. Henry recalls: "I climbed up to the top where the captain was nonchalantly at the wheel. I could hear the other mariners talking on the radio about the rough seas. He seemed completely unconcerned and was smoking a cigarette. I remember he was knocking the ashes into a Meister Brau can that had the top cut out of it to act as a makeshift ash tray." While Henry was aloft, I decided to go below into the cabin, accessed by a couple of small steps. What in the harbor would have been a simple thing was anything but in those conditions. As I stepped down the boat dropped away from me into a trough, and I tumbled into a heap on the cabin floor. Picking myself up and grabbing something for support, I reeled and lurched with the craft's wild motion. It was like a carnival ride out of control, and I quickly scrambled back on deck, but as I lifted my foot to plant it the boat violently rose, slamming my foot just before I put my weight on it and sending a painful shiver all the way to my lower back. Done with my little foray, I staggered unceremoniously into the others at the stern.[8]

Throughout our trip we watched other boats pitching and yawing in the waves. I vividly recall a small motorboat that had an older couple on board. Despite the relentless tossing, they looked unconcerned, but had the seas been any higher, it is difficult to believe that anyone would have been out there. Through it all our mate kept busy at the fishing lines, at one point scrambling aloft and grabbing a rod to reel in something. Henry and I stared wide-eyed as he leaned against an aluminum rail visibly bending under the strain. Happily, it held, and he wasn't yanked overboard by whatever leviathan was on the other end of the line.

By the end of the trip we had about a dozen large king mackerel to show for our adventure. Back in the harbor the mate swiftly filleted the catch and parceled it out. Dad remarked on his good cheer and phenomenal work ethic. Affixed to the stern was a white sign with red letters: "If you had a good time $ay $omething to the mate." Neither Dad nor the newlyweds needed the encouragement to tip the man generously. He had certainly earned it that day.

Back at the condo Mom cooked up the fish, and we talked about the trip. But as I quickly learned, getting my land legs again would take a little time. No sooner did my head hit the pillow that night than I felt like I was on board *Calypso II* again, lifting and falling and tossing. My mind's eye saw an agitated green sea, nothing but waves in constant motion. Maybe I never really got my land legs back, because ever since I have been haunted by the Gulf, its climate and moods, pleasures and terrors. I have read and wondered about its history and secrets; trembled at the legend of Hurakan, the Mayan storm deity believed to whip the Gulf into a vengeful fury; studied ancient Indian pottery alongside a coastal river; sailed on board a large schooner down Mobile Bay; and clambered over the skeletal timbers of an old shipwreck to the accompaniment of the seagull's cry. I have been absorbed by timeworn charts and thrilled to a newly discovered account of colonial New Orleans. For much of my adult life I have lived within an hour's drive of Alabama's beaches, and my wife and I frequently scoot down there during the off-season for quiet seafood dinners backgrounded by fiery sunsets, or to ride the Fort Morgan Ferry across the mouth of Mobile Bay, staring past Sand Island Lighthouse into a profound and mysterious immensity. I find myself falling into a trance on such occasions, beguiled by the colorful figures and famous ships that have coursed what the writer Lafcadio Hearn called, during his New Orleans sojourn, that "grand blaze of blue open water"—Ponce de León on board *Santa de María de la Consolación,* Francis Drake on the *Judith,* Laurens de Graaf on the *François,* Tyrone Power on the *Shakespeare,* Alexander Agassiz on board the *Blake,* Raphael Semmes and the fearsome *Alabama,* and Charles Dwight Sigsbee at the helm of the doomed *Maine.* I admire the ingenuity of Gulf Coast residents who have developed new vessels and technologies over the centuries, including high-sided, sail-driven barges suitable to both open seas and shallow bays; Biloxi's graceful "white winged queens"; New Orleans's boxy Higgins boats, the plywood amphibious landing craft that helped carry U.S. troops to victory in World War II; and shipping containers, a world-changing concept perfected at Mobile by a former truck driver frustrated with antiquated loading practices.[9] And then there are the exotic cities and ports—La Habana, way station for conquistadores and treasure-filled galleons, a stunning collection of Spanish colonial architecture awaiting reintroduction to the free world; New Orleans, the Big Easy, famous for its beautiful French Quarter, Mardi Gras, and relaxed morals; and Mexico's oldest city, Veracruz, founded by Hernán Cortés and reverently known as Heróica Veracruz, an oft-besieged wonderland of fortresses, churches, a palace, and the impressive Faro Venustiano Carranza, an early twentieth-century lighthouse overlooking the harbor. Throughout history, the residents of these cities and their neighbors along the littoral have struggled with challenges both natural and manmade—devastating hurricanes, frightening epidemics, catastrophic oil spills, and conflicts ranging from dockside brawls and labor riots to pirate raids, foreign invasion, civil war, and revolution. These are the things that have fed my thoughts and dreams for more than half a century. Now it is time to write about them.

Introduction
"The ungovernable Gulf"

On a balmy winter's day in 1866, a young army wife stood at the Galveston wharves amid nervous horses, bustling roustabouts, and burdened, crowding soldiers. Elizabeth Bacon Custer, or Libbie, as she was familiarly known, would have shone in any setting, but did so especially on that rough waterfront with its smelly men and animals. Trim and petite with porcelain skin and wavy, chestnut-brown hair gathered into a knot at the nape of her neck, she was married to Capt. George Armstrong Custer, famous for his golden locks, battlefield valor, and colossal ego, whose fortunes and rank were both sinking in post–Civil War America. Nonetheless, Libbie and the General, as she called him in deference to his last Civil War rank, were hopeful about their transfer from dusty Texas to cosmopolitan New Orleans and then points north and who knew what adventures. Still, she would miss Galveston's charms—"the rose-pink of the oleander, the blue of the sky, the luminous beach, with the long, ultramarine waves sweeping in over the shore." Together with an entourage that included her father-in-law, a jockey, and a cook named Eliza, she and the General boarded their conveyance, a former blockade runner converted into a passenger steamer by two added tiers of cabins. "Our staterooms were tiny," she later recalled, "and though they were on the upper deck, the odor of bilge water and the untidiness of the boat made us uncomfortable from the first." Worse was to come.[1]

Barely out of the harbor, their vessel was struck by a strong cold front, or norther in Gulf maritime parlance, and commenced to wallowing in a heavy swell. "The Gulf of Mexico is almost always a tempest in a teapot," Libbie groused. "The waves seem to lash themselves from shore to shore, and after speeding with tornado fleetness toward the borders of Mexico, back they rush to the Florida peninsula." Worried that the ship might sink, Libbie watched the light fade over "a sea that was lashed to white foam about us." Darkness compounded her fear. While she and her fellow passengers braced themselves in their tight berths, the wind howled, and the vessel creaked and groaned, sounding like it would come apart at the seams. At one point Libbie managed to drift into a fitful sleep but was soon awakened by a "fearful crash" and a violent "rolling from side to side." Desperately clutching the sides of her berth, she was doused by a tumbling water pitcher and thrown into a near panic. The ship's engines had stopped, and the passengers could hear the crew shouting on deck, "followed by the creaking of chains, the strain of the cordage, and the mad thrashing to and fro of the canvas." They were now under sail power alone. What had been confusion became chaos. "The furniture broke from its fastenings," Libbie later recalled, "and slipped to and fro; the smashing of lamps in our cabin was followed by the crash of crockery in the adjoining room; while above all these sounds rose the cries and wails of the women." The men, white faced and vomiting, weren't in much better shape. In an effort to reassure everyone, the General gamely struggled outside, where he observed the decks awash and the machinery wrecked. The captain remained confident, however, and reassured the young officer that the storm was nothing he and his vessel couldn't handle. The General returned to convey the optimistic report and then clambered into his berth, where he succumbed to mal de mer. Morning light further lessened the terror, and Libbie ventured to peek outside. "The waves were mountains high," she wrote, "and we still plunged into what appeared to be solid banks of green, glittering crystal, only to drop down into seemingly hopeless gulfs." An "opportune glass of champagne" helped even more than daylight, as did their reaching the Mississippi River, but only when finally ashore at New Orleans did Libbie feel fully secure. Her short voyage on the "ungovernable Gulf" had been a nightmare. Father Custer expressed her feelings perfectly when he accosted his son: "Next time I follow you to Texas, it will be when this pond is bridged over."[2]

More than a century and a half later, despite technological advances that would have astonished the Custer clan, the Gulf has yet to be tamed, much less bridged. Happily, notwithstanding rampant development, pollution, and neglect, nor have its scenic, culinary, and recreational delights been entirely lost. On any given day, thousands of residents and tourists from Havana's Malecón to Captiva Island to Campeche's seawall enjoy the same sorts of painterly sunsets, vivid floral displays, and breathtaking water views that delighted Libbie Custer so long ago. Patrons at New Orleans restaurants savor steaming platters of royal red shrimp, and little boys eagerly dive for coins at Veracruz. Offshore, roughnecks wrestle pipe atop towering oil rigs while fishermen hopefully cast their lines below, and blue-water mariners nonchalantly ride their steel-hulled behemoths to or from any one of a dozen ports. For those who live, work, and play beside its waters or on them, the Gulf is by turns beautiful, bountiful, frightening, and destructive. But it is never dull.

Incredibly, despite recent high-profile events like Hurricane Katrina and the *Deepwater Horizon* oil spill, the Gulf of Mexico remains underappreciated by many in the United States. This is all the more surprising given that this country gets a quarter of its natural gas and one sixth of its oil from the Gulf, claims fourteen of the basin's nineteen major ports, harvests 1.4 billion pounds of seafood annually from its waters (20 percent of the total U.S. commercial fishery), and logs over twenty million recreational fishing trips a year, and its five Gulf coastal states (Florida, Alabama, Mississippi, Louisiana, and Texas) boast surging beach tourism and overall growth rates two and a half times the national average. Unfortunately, as one pundit quipped, when the region does get noticed it's usually "for its humid climate, conservative political traditions and vulnerability to natural disasters." This contemporary myopia extends to the Gulf's historical record as well, prompting University of Florida historian Jack E. Davis to write, in his Pulitzer Prize–winning 2017 book, *The Gulf: The Making of an American Sea,* that the basin has been "wholly excluded from the central narrative of the American experience." This despite a long and colorful history featuring more rogues, derring-do, and pivotal events than a 1940s Hollywood B movie.[3]

There are to be sure many books about specific aspects of the Gulf's sprawling history, including Jerald T. Milanich's *Florida Indians and the Invasion from Europe* (1995); Robert Weddle's superb trilogy of exploration and early settlement, *Spanish Sea* (1985), *The French Thorn* (1991), and *Changing Tides* (1995); Douglas Brinkley's *The Great Deluge: Hurricane Katrina, New Orleans, and the Mississippi Gulf Coast* (2006); William C. Davis's *The Pirates Laffite: The Treacherous World of the Corsairs of the Gulf* (2005); Robert M. Browning Jr.'s *Lincoln's Trident: The West Gulf Blockading Squadron during the Civil War* (2015); and Mark Kurlansky's *Havana: A Subtropical Delirium* (2018), to name only a few. Considerably less abundant are broad historical overviews, with Davis's *The Gulf,* itself primarily an environmental history, standing virtually alone. The few other books like Robert H. Gore's *The Gulf of Mexico: A Treasury of Resources in the American Mediterranean* (1992), the Harte Research Institute for Gulf of Mexico Studies Series *Gulf of Mexico Origin, Waters and Biota* (2009–present, four volumes so far), and Rezneat Darnell's *The American Sea: A Natural History of the Gulf of Mexico* (2015) all include some history but are principally scientific reference works. Heretofore completely lacking has been a popular maritime history of the Gulf from dugout canoe to shipping container, featuring narrative drive and attention to personality. Boats and ships have always been central to the Gulf's story, of course, but maritime history entails more than the quaint details of fifteenth-century caravels or nineteenth-century oyster luggers, important as those are. As Lincoln Paine noted in his monumental *The Sea and Civilization* (2013), maritime history is also about what vessels carried—"people and their culture, their material creations, their crops and flocks, their conflicts and prejudices, their expectations for the future, and their memories of the past." In order to gain a fuller historical understanding of the Gulf, the rich cultural cross-pollination manifested in its blended populations, foodways, music, architecture, and language must be explored, as well as the ships, voyages, battles, sieges, and treaties that have shaped the political development of three nations. Only then will what it means to be a Gulf Coast resident of Cuba, Mexico, or the United States become intelligible in both its commonalities and its differences. If this book has a bias, it reflects my perch—the north-central Gulf Coast. As a limited-fluency Spanish speaker, I have consulted Spanish-language references along the way, mostly to confirm certain facts from a Hispanic perspective or to see how episodes were handled. But in no sense should this work be construed as based on any thorough reference to the contemporary Spanish-language literature.[4]

To begin we must first make acquaintance with that watery realm—its formation, amplitude, bathymetry, climate, flora, fauna, reefs, and coasts—where our story will unfold. It has gone by many names—Mare Cathaynum (Chinese Sea), Sinus Magnus Antillarum (Great Gulf of the Antilles), Golfo de Cortés, Golfo de Nueva España, Mar del Norte, Ensenada Mexicana (Mexican Cove), Seno Mexicano (Mexican Breast), the Sea in the Midst of the Earth, the American Mediterranean, the American Sea, but most widely and consistently since 1550 el Golfo de Mexico, or the Gulf of Mexico. Appropriately enough, on a contour map it looks like a giant sea creature arching down into aquamarine depths. Defined by the surrounding continental shelf, the head and Veracruz Tongue are wrapped by Mexico and the Yucatán Peninsula (a portion of the Gulf also known as the Bay of Campeche), the body is formed by the Sigsbee Deep (2,393 fathoms), with a broad

The Gulf's seafloor features a wide continental shelf off the United States and the Yucatán and a deep central basin shaped like an ocean creature. COURTESY NATIONAL OCEANIC AND ATMOSPHERIC ADMINISTRATION.

hump off the Texas coast, a slanted dorsal fin at Desoto Canyon (off the Florida Panhandle), a curving lower back traced by the West Florida Escarpment, and the flukes formed by the Yucatán and Florida channels.[5]

The Gulf of Mexico's origins date to the breakup of the megacontinent Pangaea approximately two hundred million years ago. What would become South America and Africa tore away from what is now North America, the Florida Block broke from Africa and the Yucatán Block pulled away from Florida, and in the midst of all the tearing and stretching a large basin opened. Across epochs the spreading and shaping continued, accompanied by periods of flooding from the early Pacific Ocean and then evaporation that left significant salt deposits thousands of feet thick. Drainage from numerous North American rivers, including the early Mississippi, deposited tons of silt atop the salt, adding so much weight that the basin sank still lower. Mixed with all that silt and continually buried beneath its eternal flow was enough organic matter to eventually transform into rich petroleum deposits, fuel for future heaters and cars. And still big pieces of the puzzle were moving. The Yucatán Block—alternately submerged and exposed—joined with Mexico and swung up to its present location, mountain ranges were thrust skyward, and the Pacific's waters were dammed, but not those of the early Atlantic, which streamed across a submerged Florida Block. During their diluvian periods Florida and Yucatán steadily accumulated billions of tiny marine creatures' skeletal remains. Down and down these seemingly insignificant little things drifted through murky ocean light, falling and clumping and forming the limestone that distinguishes those landforms and their accompanying islands and reefs today.[6]

Extraterrestrial forces were not absent in this great dynamic. Sixty-five million years ago a large meteor slammed into the Yucatán's tip, shaking the planet like a giant bell, generating furious winds and massive waves, and shrouding the surface in a cool pall that wiped out uncounted life forms, including the dinosaurs. There followed the Rocky Mountains and Colorado Plateau uplift and, roughly one to two million years ago, glaciation sequences with concomitant sea level changes. Ice sheets thickened to a mile in height and extended all the way to Kentucky, locking up seawater and lowering the early Gulf's depth by over two hundred feet. When the ice melted, the liberated waters gushed down the Mississippi River valley, refilling the basin and bringing its northern shoreline as far as modern Oklahoma. Again and again this happened. Finally, between five thousand and ten thousand years ago the Gulf of Mexico assumed its present character and dimensions with all the attendant rivers, estuaries, deltas, bays, lakes, lagoons, and barrier islands essentially in place. Though its young shores are now vulnerable to slowly rising sea levels and are continually resculpted by wind and tide, the modern Gulf is, fortunately for humankind, considered a geologically stable ocean basin.[7]

The International Hydrographic Organization (IHO), which sets the limits of oceans and seas for scientific study, considers the Gulf of Mexico a subdivision of the North Atlantic. Even at that, it is the tenth largest body of water on the planet, a giant oval roughly one thousand miles wide and five hundred miles north to south, covering six hundred thousand square miles and containing 643 quadrillion gallons of water. The IHO places its eastern limit at longitude 80° 30′ west, which encompasses "all the narrow waters between the Dry Tortugas and the eastern end of Florida Bay." While the IHO then sharply angles the boundary southwest to a point well west of Havana, most sailors and writers across the centuries have considered a due north-south rhumb at longitude 81° west to be the de facto boundary, which includes most of the Florida Straits (ninety-three miles wide and the basin's only direct Atlantic link) and makes Havana a Gulf city. In his 1994 voyage around the littoral, travel writer Peter Jenkins found the Gulf/Atlantic border to be a changeable one. "The waters mingle," he wrote, "one dominating the other depending on the tides and winds. Sometimes the Gulf's water is smoothed by the Atlantic. Sometimes the Atlantic water is pushed back, overwhelmed by the green waters of Florida Bay." On the southwest, the IHO (and common usage) runs the boundary from the western tip of Cuba (Cabo San Antonio) 125 miles across the Yucatán Channel to Cabo Catoche. This is the basin's only direct Caribbean link. For the rest there is curving shore, much of it in the form of barrier islands—3,600 miles from the Yucatán to Florida, with another 240 along Cuba's northwestern coast. Appropriately enough, Mexico has the most frontage—1,743 miles spread among the states of Tamaulipas, Veracruz, Tabasco, Campeche, Yucatán, and Quintana Roo. But if the shorelines of all the numerous bays, harbors, inlets, lagoons, marshes, and so forth are thrown into the calculus the U.S. total balloons from 1,631 miles to a staggering 17,000.[8]

There are, in fact, many coasts around the basin. Every one of them has its own aspect, yet each also communicates an undeniable Gulf spirit. Proceeding counterclockwise, they include Cuba's northern shore from Cabo San Antonio to Varadero, the Florida Keys, the Mangrove Coast (southwest Florida), the Big Bend Marsh Coast (Cedar Key to Apalachicola), the Emerald Coast (Destin), the Redneck Riviera (Alabama and northwest Florida), the Casino Coast (Mississippi), the Trembling Coast (Louisiana), Costa Brava (Texas), the Costa Esmeralda (Veracruz), the Costa Sotavento or Leeward Coast (Veracruz and Tabasco), and the Costa Escondida or Hidden Coast (Quintana Roo). As visitors to any of these diverse Gulf Coasts can testify, there are still further variations and subtleties to be discovered within each. The northern estuarine reaches of Mobile Bay, for example, with mudflats, marsh, swamp, and swaying moss, are profoundly different from the sugar-white dunes and pounding surf only thirty miles south at Gulf Shores.

If one had to choose a single iconic symbol for the entire basin, however, it would be difficult to do better than the palm tree. Various species are found all around the littoral, from Tampa to Tampico and Galveston to Matanzas. They are beautiful and exotic—redolent of parrots and pirates. On a visit to Havana during

Coconut palm photographed beside the Tampico, Mexico, lighthouse, ca. 1890.
COURTESY LIBRARY OF CONGRESS.

the 1850s, the Mobile socialite and author Madame Octavia LeVert thought the palm tree the closest thing to poetry in the natural world. "The trunk rises smooth as a marble column," she wrote, "to about the height of seventy or eighty feet. Then branch out the great leaves, falling one over the other like plumes of feathers in a field marshal's hat. The sea breeze, sighing through them, calls forth a sound as soft as the tone of an Aeolian harp, thrilling the soul with sweet joy." On his tours of the Texas and Mexican Gulf coasts during the early 2000s, the photographer Geoff Winningham saw palms everywhere. In Galveston hundreds were planted throughout an exclusive development tended by a pair of Mexican gardeners, and in La Antigua, Mexico, a cluster of "tall palm trees" swayed over a small plaza and its scattered concrete benches. Less picturesquely, at the thirty-mile marker on Padre Island, Texas, Winningham stumbled onto the spot where two Gulf currents converge and found himself clambering over flotsam and jetsam deposited from hundreds of miles away, including busted plastic chairs, dented oil drums, soggy mattresses, and "whole palm trees" complete with their root balls.[9]

The Dry Tortugas, a system of isolated coral reefs and islands well out from Key West and the farthest flung Gulf holding of the United States, certainly have their share of palm trees, but a *Harper's New Monthly Magazine* correspondent who visited in 1868 was more taken by the ethereal red mangroves. He was intrigued by the tree's fruit, which he initially believed "were Cuban cheroots that had floated across the Gulf Stream from Havana." The writer thought it a wonder how the roots found a footing in the shallows and grew into strong trees with curious "flying buttresses" sticking out at all angles to strengthen and brace the tree, and ultimately build land as they trapped floating debris and sand. Appropriately enough, mangroves give their name to that stretch of the Sunshine State from Florida Bay to Tampa Bay. They are most heavily concentrated at Ten Thousand Islands just south of Naples, where the Everglades spill into the sea. The Spanish found their roots and branches virtually impossible to hack through and once inland cursed the razor-sharp saw grass they encountered. Hugh Willoughby, a naval reservist who canoed across the Everglades in the early 1900s, had a healthy respect for the latter plant. "If you get a blade between your hand and the pole," he declared, "it will cut you to the bone, with a jagged gash that will take long to heal."[10]

Along the northern littoral mangroves are less prevalent, but pine, cypress, and live oak are common and were heavily logged as naval stores. The naturalist Bernard Romans enthused in his 1776 guide to the region, "the grand manufacture to be made of timber here, is SHIPPING, for the purpose no country affords more or better wood; live oak, cedar, cypress, yellow pine, are adapted by nature to this." During the nineteenth century, loggers cut longleaf pine with a vengeance, nearly wiping it out, while casual visitors delighted in its "aromatic perfume." Cypress dominated the swamps and lowlands around Mobile and New Orleans and proved its utility for everything from dugout canoes to house sills and roof shingles. It also excited notice for its knobby knees, dangerous to mounted travelers, and festoons of Spanish moss, which one observer thought lent "a sombre hue to the forests." But most magnificent of all is the live oak, or *Quercus virginiana*. It flourishes along a coastal arc running from Virginia to Texas, and its dark, gnarled limbs, waxy green leaves, and spreading crown grace and shade the streets of coastal cities like Pensacola, Mobile, New Orleans, and Galveston. If the palm tree may be said to best represent the entire Gulf basin, the live oak is suitably emblematic of the northern littoral. In 1859 a writer for *Harper's* pronounced it the most remarkable tree in the South, "leading the arboreous beauty of the country no less universally, and even

Mangrove trees are common in south Florida and the Yucatán. Due to climate change, some have recently been found as far north as the Chandeleur Islands. PHOTOGRAPH BY CHARLES BARRON, COURTESY STATE ARCHIVES OF FLORIDA.

more charmingly, than the elm that of the New England landscape, and with the additional value of its perpetual freshness."[11]

Along the lower reaches of the Texas coast, approaching Mexico, there are fewer trees, and the landscape is more forbidding. This is where the sixteenth-century Spanish castaway Cabeza de Vaca nearly met his end, and it long acted as a natural defensive buffer for New Spain's northern frontier. In the main, few people then had much interest in grasses, cacti, or chaparral, all ubiquitous along that stretch.

One antebellum American traveler who did remarked on the wide-open vista that greeted him there. "It is difficult for the imagination to conceive a more beautiful sight than an extensive prairie covered with new grass after a burn," he wrote. "The grass, when only six or eight inches high, is tender and delicate, and is moved in waves by the gentlest breeze."[12]

Farther south, yucca is among the most notable plants and, according to some, inspired the Yucatán Peninsula's name. The story goes that when Spanish conquistadores showed the plant to some Mayan captives, the Indians called it *yucca tlati*. While this is disputed by some scholars, there can be no doubt that yucca was cultivated by the Indians and the Spanish and proved to be useful for food and for making rope, sandals, and soap.[13]

Of far more immediate economic utility to Europeans was the peninsula's ready stock of logwood, or Campeche wood, as it was often called. The seventeenth-century sailor, naturalist, and writer extraordinaire William Dampier described it as being "much like our white thorns in England; but generally a great deal bigger: the Rind of the young growing branches is white and smooth with some Prickles shooting forth here and there." This tree grows on the coast and inland, and prior to the twentieth century it was an excellent source of washable red, blue, purple, and black dyes, theretofore only obtainable from India at great expense. Merchants at Rouen and Antwerp bought all they could get. Ship crews cut and hauled it home as valuable ballast, and it soon became an attractive way for buccaneers to make a quick profit when they weren't pillaging.[14]

Whether Indians fashioning a dugout canoe; mestizos farming yucca; loggers cutting cypress; or tourists wandering a waterfront park; people have always had plenty of critters for company around the Gulf. Foremost among them in population and aggravation is the mosquito, a plague to everyone throughout the centuries no matter the color of their skin. Cabeza de Vaca found the whining insects "abundant" on the Texas coast. For protection, he and his comrades burned rotten wet wood around their camp, but soon the smoke became as annoying as the mosquitoes. According to Romans more than two centuries later, they were "intolerable" all along the coast. Even sailors off shore could be pestered by them. During the American Civil War, one Federal webfoot on blockade duty jokingly recorded that mosquitoes "in millions made a most desperate attack on all hands in which we defeated after a most fearful contest lasting all night. No one *killed* on our side, and yet—strange to say every one of us was most desperately wounded."[15]

Running a close second are the multitudes of tiny biting midges known to generations of American beach goers as "no-see-ums." Small enough to pass through the mesh of a screen door, these little bloodsuckers have been many a tourist's most lasting coastal memory. According to one expert, "While the amount of blood no-see-ums take is insignificant, many people have an allergic reaction to the anticoagulant these insects inject into their victim to prevent the blood from clotting and gumming up their microscopic beaks. It's the reaction to these chemicals that causes the itchy, painful welts that can last for days."[16]

More pleasing to visitors and coastal dwellers alike are the clouds of orange and black monarch butterflies that migrate through every fall. They gracefully flutter along, dipping and weaving, driven by a mysterious and inexorable urge far south to the Yucatán. There continues to be scientific debate about whether or not these delicate creatures actually cross the Gulf or take land routes, but anecdotal evidence is compelling that many do go by sea. Passing cold fronts provide powerful tailwinds, and monarchs have been spied thousands of feet high riding the blast. Oil rig workers and mariners routinely see them alight on equipment or rigging to rest. "Rough as seamen can be," a retired Alabama charter boat captain recalled in an interview, "I never saw one be mean to 'em." On at least one occasion, oil rig workers were not so restrained, according to a female supply boat cook. She told a scientist she once saw thousands of monarchs descend on every surface of an oil rig, even landing on top of one another. They were so thick that the roughnecks resorted to hosing them off the equipment.[17]

There are other winged creatures in the basin. Birds of magnificent variety inhabit the woods, jungles, marsh, and shore and have long excited attention. One eighteenth-century planter in French Louisiana was surprised by the "prodigious quantities" and "hideous noise" of waterfowl on Lake Pontchartrain. The famous naturalist John James Audubon loved watching brown pelicans in the Florida Keys. "They move in an undulated line," he wrote, "passing at one time high, at another low, over the water or land, for they do not deviate from their course on coming upon a key or a point of land. When the waves run high, you may see them 'troughing,' as the sailors say, or directing their course along the hollows." While rambling south of Veracruz in 1676, Dampier was intrigued by the brilliant parrots. "Their colour was yellow and red," he wrote, "very coarsely mixt; and they would prate very prettily; and there was scarce a Man but what sent aboard one or two of them." Loquacious parrots perched on sea rovers' shoulders were apparently no uncommon thing. Score one for Hollywood.[18]

Reptiles and mammals have also occasioned much comment over the centuries. The Indians knew them all, and they worshipped, hunted, or avoided them as prudence dictated. Alligators (the United States) and crocodiles (Mexico), numerous again thanks to protective laws, awed the first Europeans to see them and remain a source of healthy interest today. While visiting the Campeche shore, Dampier heard about an Irishman who went night hunting and stumbled over a large one. The beast "seized him by the knee," Dampier explained, "at which the Man cries out, '*Help! Help!*'" There ensued a desperate struggle, and when the reptile opened its mouth to clamp down again the man jerked his knee away and clobbered the creature with the butt of his musket. The crocodile then seized the weapon and swam off with it. Dampier related that the man was in "deplorable Condition" but eventually recovered and limped ever afterward. The musket was later found nearby "with two large Holes in the Butt-end of it, one on each side, near an Inch deep." Incredibly, alligators were sometimes kept as pets by antebellum Americans. In 1854, a New Orleans woman named Nell Gary complained to municipal officials that her neighbor "kept in his yard an alligator of immense size and ferocity; and that, as she was frequently obliged to go through the yard, she considered herself in great bodily fear and danger." The owner was arrested but argued that he kept the reptile to guard his property and that unless provoked it was perfectly peaceful. He told the court that unfortunately Miss Gary repeatedly poked the alligator with sticks and threw bricks at it. Convinced, the court released him and ordered Gary to "keep the peace toward 'the pet' and its excellent owner."[19]

All sorts of furry animals crowd the Gulf rim, and to read the colonial era descriptions of the countless deer, bear, fox, buffalo, beaver, opossum, and wildcat is to believe it once a veritable Eden. Deer sustained the Indian tribes along the northern Gulf for centuries and during the eighteenth and nineteenth centuries were the basis of a robust skin trade. Down in the Yucatán monkeys are common. The Maya worshipped a powerful howler monkey god as a patron of the arts, but the creatures were less endearing to Europeans. Dampier was aggravated by them on a jungle walk. "They were a great company dancing from Tree to Tree," he wrote, "over my Head; chattering and making a terrible Noise; and a great many grim Faces, and shewing antick Gestures. Some broke down dry Sticks and threw at me; others scattered their Urine and Dung about my Ears."[20]

Sea captains are more concerned with navigation and safe harbor than interesting, dangerous, or useful plants and animals, however. Rocking offshore and contemplating how best to make a good anchorage, their most common impression of the Gulf Coast is of low white sandy barrier islands or muddy marsh backed by a wall of green, and more shoal water than is comfortable. In fact fully 38 percent of the Gulf's total area is classified as continental shelf at less than ten fathoms. The shelf is quite wide from the Keys to Texas and off the Yucatán Peninsula (the so-called Campeche Banks). Scanning the descriptions in the U.S. government's 1902 edition of *The Navigation of the Gulf of Mexico and the Caribbean Sea,* it is clear that even in an era of reliable dredging, captains had to keep a sharp eye. Of the Florida coast from Charlotte Harbor to Tampa Bay, the guide cautioned, "Much of the shore is bordered by a chain of outlying islets having many shallow passes between them leading into enclosed sounds of considerable extent, but shallow, full of dangers, and of little importance for shipping." The northern Gulf features many large bays and inlets, but few are suitable for blue-water sailors. Tampa, Choctawhatchee, Mobile, and Galveston Bays all average less than twelve feet deep and were historically compromised by shallow bars at their mouths. Only Pensacola Bay, at thirty feet, was inviting for large sailing ships, which could draw as much as twenty-five feet, and even it was tricky to enter without a good pilot familiar with local currents and shoals.[21]

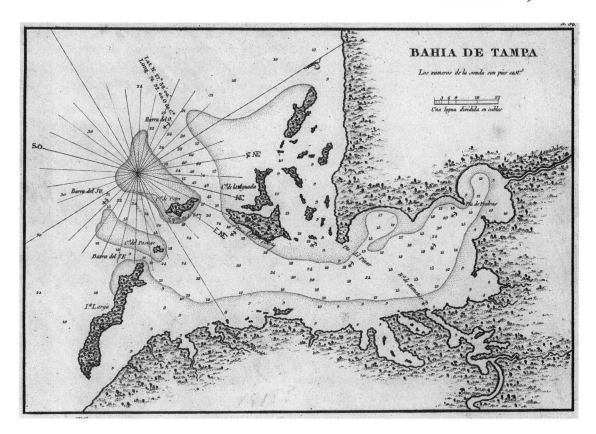

Bahía de Tampa, 1809. Knowledge of the islands, shoals, and soundings was critical to mariners seeking to navigate the tricky harbor entrance. COURTESY LIBRARY OF CONGRESS.

The basin's three most important ports traditionally have been Havana, Veracruz, and New Orleans. Havana is a mariner's dream, pocketed, deep, and snug. In good weather Veracruz is easy to spot from the sea, being right on shore and backed by snowcapped mountains and a volcano. New Orleans, situated almost a hundred miles from the Gulf, is another matter, and simply finding the mouth of the enormous river that leads to it was extraordinarily difficult before modern navigational improvements. To look at the Mississippi River's statistics, one would think that it would be obvious from the sea. It is by far the most important of the 116 streams that empty into the Gulf, discharging trillions of gallons a year, or 65 percent of the basin's total freshwater inflow. Suspended in its brown waters are hundreds of millions of tons of sediment, continually tumbling off the edge of the continental shelf onto the broad Mississippi Fan. One scientist estimates that if things continue at the present rate, Mississippi mud will fill the entire basin in seven million years. Given its huge volume and load, the Mississippi's presence can be traced by distinct rip lines and chocolate color for dozens of miles seaward. Auguste Levasseur, the Marquis de Lafayette's secretary during his 1825 New Orleans visit, did not exaggerate when he declared that the river "announced rather a conqueror than a tributary to the ocean." *The American Coast Pilot,* published in 1827, urged ship captains not to be alarmed when they met the river's "great force" and "appearance altogether singular and alarming" off shore. "On coming into it," the guidebook noted, "it ripples like shoal breakers, but your soundings are regular."[22]

The river's delta projects far out into the Gulf and from above looks like a bird foot with three splayed channels—Southwest Pass, Pass a Loutre, and South Pass—divided by a confusing wilderness of mud, marsh, driftwood, shallow bays, and labyrinthine meanders, consequence of all that continental discharge. In 1699 Iberville searched for the mouth in a long boat and was amazed by the mud lumps, some up to ten feet in height, which he at first took for rocks. "These rocks are logs petrified by the mud and changed into black rocks which withstand the sea," he wrote in his journal. Steering between them, he "found fresh water with a very strong current." With good pilots and channel markers, nineteenth-century captains could make one of the various channels alright (usually the Southwest), but their passengers were frequently sobered by the vast and desolate stretches that greeted their curious gaze. "At the break of day I ascended to the deck, from whence I beheld the most imposing and awful spectacle," remembered Levasseur. Low islands were heaped with "thousands of immense trunks of trees," which "after having flourished for ages under the polar circle, were now decaying under the burning sky of Mexico." Ten years later, the Irish actor Tyrone Power recoiled when he saw "rank growing reeds," muddy water, and rafts of driftwood. "Heaven send us well into blue water!" he cried.[23]

Power's prayer was understandable. When it behaves, the open Gulf can be a beguiling place and is certainly far prettier than the Mississippi's cluttered, dirty mouth. It is a warm sea compelling the body to shuck clothes and the mind to wander. The Tropic of Cancer slices across it at Latitude 23° 26′ N and bisects Mexico just above Tampico. This marks the northernmost latitude at which the sun appears directly overhead at noon on the summer solstice. That is when the northern hemisphere most directly faces the sun, and months of hot weather must be endured. This important geographical delineation is rather prosaically commemorated on Mexico Highway 180 by a much-vandalized big yellow sphere with the Tropic depicted by a painted black line.[24]

Some eighty million gallons of seawater per second are injected into the Gulf through the Yucatán Channel. Once inside, this water forms the Loop Current, a meandering torrent as much as fifteen hundred feet deep. Generally speaking, the Loop Current flows north northwest and then east and south before hooking around and exiting through the Florida Straits. There are numerous permutations to this pattern, however, with eddies and gyres breaking off, spinning counterclockwise, and trending west toward Mexican shores. Many other factors influence and contribute to the Loop Current, including the east-west Trade Winds, the Coriolis

A chart of the Gulf Stream, Benjamin Franklin, 1769. COURTESY NEW YORK PUBLIC LIBRARY.

effect (eastward motion induced by the Earth's rotation), deepwater upwelling, and freshwater inflows. The Loop Current finally blasts out of the Gulf at an astonishing four knots, one of the world's fastest ocean currents. Thus is born the "Blue God," or Gulf Stream, first discovered by the Spanish in the sixteenth century and utilized as an efficient superhighway to Europe ever since. "There is a river in the ocean," Matthew Fontaine Murray, the Pathfinder of the Seas, declared in 1855. "In the severest droughts it never fails and in the mightiest floods it never overflows; its banks and bottom are of cold water, while its current is of warm, the Gulf of Mexico is its fountain, and its mouth is the Arctic Sea." The Gulf Stream made a dramatic impression during sailing-ship days when its force could arrest a southbound caravel or speed a frigate through a headwind. "To a person who has not seen it, it is scarce possible to conceive an Idea," explained a British naval officer in 1764, "of the Strength and velocity of the Current, you meet here, which runs ever to the Northward, and in that degree, that altho' the Wind should be right ahead, the Stream will nevertheless hurry you thro', in a most amazing Manner." During his 1994 trip, Jenkins admired the Stream's dash "of iridescent aqua blue" invading the Atlantic's "deep purple depths."[25]

Fishermen love the Gulf Stream, and little wonder. Warm and nutrient filled, it is a veritable seafood market speeding beneath their hulls. But anglers needn't cruise the Stream's Eastern Seaboard course to have a productive fishing day. The Gulf proper teems with sea life from microscopic phytoplankton to forty-foot whale sharks and everything in between. The most popular sport fish species include red snapper, grouper, amberjack, sheepshead, king mackerel, sea trout, red drum, black drum, bluefish, tarpon, blue marlin, and sailfish. Additionally, there are 25 species of marine mammals (including blue whale, humpback whale, minke whale, sperm whale, killer whale, Atlantic bottlenose dolphin, rough-toothed dolphin, striped dolphin, West Indian manatee, West Indian Monk seal), 49 shark species (bull, thresher, nurse, hammerhead, white tip, black tip, lemon, sandbar, and tiger, to name a few), 5 sea turtle species (loggerhead, green, Kemp's ridley, Atlantic hawksbill, leatherback), 450 species of mollusks (including snails, slugs, squid, octopus, mussels, scallops, oysters), 1,500 species of crustaceans (that is, krill, barnacles, crab, shrimp), and 400 species of echinoderms (sea urchins, sea cucumbers, sea stars, sea lilies, sand dollars). Little wonder that almost anywhere one dips a net or throws a hook, the Gulf delivers.[26]

The phytoplankton are at the bottom of the food chain but can manifest themselves in lovely ways, as in Destin's emerald waters, or nocturnal phosphorescence. On a scientific expedition in 1869, Elizabeth Cabot Agassiz, wife of the famed naturalist Louis, was arrested by the latter phenomena in Havana harbor. "So luminous was the water that every living thing within it was visible," she wrote. "We could count the rhythmical pulsations of the jelly-fishes by the rise and fall of a dim silvery glow which surrounded them; we could track the swift dart and whirl of the shrimps by sudden flashes of light; and every now and then a large fish coming to the surface would scatter a glittering foam for a yard around him." In late September 2008, a reporter for the *Sarasota Herald Tribune* took an evening plunge at Cayo Costa State Park. "The surf at night is always spooky," he wrote, "who knows what's under those waves?—but I shamed myself into swimming in the Gulf of Mexico. Then I noticed something, little points of light in the water. With every stroke, they sparkled. Phosphorescence."[27]

Of all the creatures that inhabit the Gulf, dolphins and manatees are by far the public favorites, though fishermen are not so high on the former due to their thieving ways. The Atlantic bottlenose dolphins include near-shore groups that tolerate brackish water and are routinely sighted in the Gulf's many bayous, bays, inlets, and estuaries. Dolphin-watching cruises are popular attractions, and Fort Walton Beach's Gulfarium has sponsored a dolphin show for decades. During the fall of 1997 an Illinois man described a fairly typical dolphin sighting off Mobile Bay's Eastern Shore. "As we closed in on them they turned and came straight towards the boat," wrote Ron Arbizzani. "They came right up to us. Some disappeared under the bow while others ran along beside us. They seemed to move effortlessly with us at our nine-knot speed and the ones running along beside us would leap completely out of the water and come down with a loud smack." Far less agile in the water, manatees are revered for their slow-motion grace and gentle nature, and watch programs and sanctuaries have been set up along the coast.[28]

Not all of the Gulf's sea life is benign, and seasoned beachgoers have long known to exercise caution lest sea lice, jellyfish, or a stingray ruin a vacation. Even at that, painful encounters are not uncommon. Sea lice are actually jellyfish larvae. Trapped between human skin and tight bathing suits, they deliver little stings that cause itching and an ugly rash. More serious are encounters with the jellyfish-like Portuguese man-of-war. One Alabama resident recalled a ten-year-old relative who once got a man-of-war wrapped around his neck while swimming in a lagoon. The child began "to scream and cry," and the family quickly got him on shore. Back at the beach house, none of their home remedies—alcohol, baking soda, ammonia— seemed to help, and the child "had welts on his body like he had been whipped with a belt and they were there the next day." Stingrays, or stingarees as some northern Gulf Coast residents call them, sport vicious-looking barbs that can inflict serious wounds requiring an emergency room visit. Most local children learn early to shuffle their feet when they walk through the surf, lest they step on one and provoke an unforgettable response.[29]

Sharks, of which there are multitudes in the Gulf, generate the most fascination and fear among the public, but documented attacks have been the exception rather than the rule. Nonetheless, they do happen. By far the basin's most famous occurred in 1749 when Brook Watson, a fourteen-year-old British cabin boy, decided to strip and go for a swim in Havana harbor. Almost immediately he was struck by a large tiger shark. Twice the shark bit his lower calf, shredding flesh from bone and severing the foot. Before it could hit him a third time some sailors in a longboat jabbed the fish with a boat hook, driving it off. Watson was rescued and later in life became lord mayor of London. He told his story to the American painter John Singleton Copley, who in 1778 produced a spectacular oil of the incident. The painting was unveiled at the Royal Academy, where it created a sensation. It was the "*Jaws*" of its day, with crowds lined up around the block.[30]

Bull sharks are one of the most aggressive species and have been implicated in a number of attacks. They can grow up to six feet in length, weigh over two hundred pounds, and are brackish- and fresh-water tolerant. Individuals have been caught in Lake Pontchartrain, Mobile Bay, and miles up coastal rivers. During the 1870s one traveler on the Mississippi coast learned how swimmers there protected themselves. "Upon the end of almost every pier was the bath-house of the owner of some cottage," he wrote while at Pass Christian. "The bathers descended a ladder placed under the bath-house to the salt water below. The area beneath each house was enclosed by slats, or poles, nailed to the piling, to secure the bathers from the sharks, which are numerous in these waters." Modern marine scientists are quick to reassure people that sharks are not evil and like any wild creature should be respected. Not swimming when purple flags, which denote dangerous marine life, are flying; staying out of the water during dawn and dusk feeding times; avoiding bright watches or jewelry; and not splashing about too much are all considered prudent measures for beachgoers.[31]

As if there weren't enough curiosities beneath the Gulf's waters, people have regularly conjured even stranger notions of sea monsters and mermaids. In late summer 1856 a Louisiana angler reported catching "a monster of the finny tribe." While fishing "off the mouth of the Lafourche in the breakers," he hooked a large creature fourteen feet long and twenty feet wide, with a three-and-a-half-foot mouth and "horns on either side." The fisherman killed it with a gunshot and towed it to shore. "Its liver was the size of a rice cask," the *Thibodaux Minerva* reported. "The exterior of this fish was covered with a skin resembling more that of an elephant than anything else to which we can compare it." The paper pleaded for naturalists to write and advise what kind of creature this could be. The answer came soon enough from an Eastern Seaboard journal. "We have not a doubt but this is the veritable devil fish," it responded, "so common on the shores of our southern Atlantic states." In short, it was a manta ray most likely swept into the Gulf and onto the Louisiana shore by a recent hurricane. Stranger still, in the summer of 2014 social media posts from Veracruz reported "a scaly humanoid being with translucent skin, the top half of a human and bottom half of a fish on the beaches." The photographs certainly looked convincing and created much excitement before it was revealed that the "creature" was a movie prop, "a siren created by the special effects team for *Pirates of the Caribbean.*"[32]

As the poor "devil fish" learned to its cost at the mouth of Bayou Lafourche, sea creatures are no more immune than humans from the Gulf's active weather. The basin's climate is dominated during the spring and summer by a permanent Atlantic feature known as the Bermuda High, which circulates air into the Gulf from the east and southeast. Humidity is high, and afternoon and evening thunderstorms are common. From June to November tropical cyclones can gin up anywhere in the basin or move in from the Atlantic or Caribbean, causing widespread disruption and loss of life. In fall and winter the Bermuda High drifts farther north and shrinks, and Gulf humidity and rainfall decrease. From October to April the basin's climate is defined by regular cold fronts dropping down from the northern plains or the Arctic. Snow and ice are rare but do occur periodically. Annual rainfall amounts are high. Mobile is the wettest city in the United States with an average annual total of sixty-seven inches. New Orleans is not far behind, at sixty inches, while Tampico and Merida in Mexico average somewhat less at forty-three and thirty-nine inches respectively. Despite these broadly consistent patterns and scientific forecasting advances, the Gulf's weather can still be frighteningly unpredictable. "If you don't like the weather, wait fifteen minutes" is a refrain often heard on the northern coast.[33]

High summertime temperatures and humidity have long made negative impressions and proven a health hazard and a trial for even longtime residents. In 1769 a British army surgeon reported unfavorably on Mobile's "very considerable" moisture and damp. "Nay this is evident from viewing the sun in the evenings, which about five o'clock begins to be a deeper hue and before he sets is nearly the color of claret. If one leaves off his shoes for one day they are quite mouldy." Almost a century later, a sea captain complained of "fogs and damp moving mists" on the northern littoral that "rust and putrify things." In 1915 a United States assistant naval surgeon cited "terrific and depressing" heat and humidity at Tampico from May until November. And in Havana, "where rescue efforts cannot take place fast enough," the heat and humidity have accelerated the decay of the city's magnificent architecture.[34]

The Gulf's summer afternoon torpor is routinely exploded by afternoon and evening thunderstorms that douse isolated areas with rain and drop temperatures twenty degrees, heaven- sent relief in pre-air-conditioning days. Lightning is usually part of these cloudbursts and can be deadly to people on the beach. But lightning at sea is a singularly terrifying experience. In 1857 sixteen-year-old Sarah Jane Girdler was on board her uncle's clipper ship the *Robert H. Dixey* heading for Mobile Bay when a nighttime thunderstorm rolled over them. "The lightning was very different from any I had seen before," young Girdler wrote in her diary. "There would be a flash in one place, and before the light of that had gone, there would be another so that the sky looked like a perfect sheet of flames all the time." Ships carried lightning rods with chains trailing into the water, but they were often struck with violent results nonetheless. On June 25, 1720, a French vessel was hit off Dauphin Island.

"Lightning struck our topmast, split it in two, cut an iron ring and two wood rings and caused several small splinters in the main mast without damaging it," one of the officers later wrote. Even more spectacularly, twenty-one years later a bolt hit the HMS *Invincible* while she was at anchor in Havana harbor, knocking her mainmast onto the roof of a nearby church and demolishing it.[35]

Isolated afternoon and evening thunderstorms are trifles compared to tropical cyclones that can cover hundreds of miles. Uncounted numbers of these systems have raked the coast through time. Some years are more active than others, but anybody living anywhere around the basin for any length of time will sooner or later face one. Hurricanes begin as low-pressure systems, feeding off warm water. When the rotating winds reach thirty-nine miles per hour the system is classified as a tropical storm. If conditions are right—warm water, abundant atmospheric moisture, minimal wind shear—the winds accelerate around the eye and when they reach seventy-four mph the system becomes a hurricane. Since the early 1970s hurricane intensity has been measured by the Saffir-Simpson Scale. The weakest storms on the scale, classified as Category 1, clock winds between 74 and 95 mph, whereas Category 5 storms, the most powerful, have winds over 155 mph. Hurricanes are highly individual but always scary. They bring drenching rainfall, flooding, damaging tornadoes, and monstrous offshore waves that can wreck ships. During Hurricane Ivan in 2004, the U.S. Navy recorded a phenomenal ninety-one-foot-high wave, the equivalent of a ten-story building. Of extreme concern are the storm surges hurricanes push ahead of them, great heaps of water bunched up along the leading northeast quadrant, the proverbial bad side. The Louisiana, Mississippi, and Alabama coasts were on Hurricane Katrina's leading edge in 2005, and surges ranged from seven feet in Lake Pontchartrain to a staggering twenty-eight feet on the Mississippi coast and twelve feet in Mobile Bay. Sturdy homes that had stood for decades were wiped clean off their foundations, leaving forlornly empty lots. Hundreds of people perished. Not surprisingly, hurricanes have altered the Gulf's human history on several occasions. The Galveston storm of 1900, which still stands as the worst natural disaster in United States history, killed over eight thousand people. There have been many other grimly memorable ones since, though improved forecasting and evacuation procedures have significantly dinted the death tolls. The Labor Day Storm of 1935 (hurricanes were not named until the late 1940s) was particularly severe, killing over four hundred in the Florida Keys. Many of these unfortunate victims were World War I army veterans working on a highway project. The writer Marjory Stoneman Douglas described this storm over twenty years later in her book *Hurricane.* "The hurricane smashed down on a narrow ten miles of Keys from Tavernier to Key Vaca," she wrote. "The wind was flung like knives, 150 to 200 miles an hour with unbelievable gusts at nearly 250 miles that took everything. The people in the small houses saw black water bubble up over floor boards as roofs were sliced off and chaos crashed down on them."[36]

Hurricane Ivan's awesome waves batter the Navarre Beach Pier, 2004. PHOTOGRAPH BY CHRIS DUVAL, COURTESY STATE ARCHIVES OF FLORIDA.

Occasioning almost as much respect and comment as hurricanes are the continental and polar cold fronts that regularly sweep over the Gulf during the winter months—northers, or *nortes* in Spanish, "blue northers" in Texan. Old-timers on both sides of the border know how to recognize the signs—a falling barometer, an oppressive atmosphere, choppy seas, watery clouds, red sunrises, a south wind. As the Spanish proverb goes, "Sur duro, Norte seguro" (A south wind strong, the Norther ere long). When the front finally blasts through the wind positively howls, dropping temperatures by as much as thirty or forty degrees in a matter of hours. Libbie Custer called it "a fury indescribable." The linguist John Russell Bartlett endured one at Corpus Christi on January 3, 1853. "When in the house, we were seated by fires," he wrote, "and when outside the door, wrapped in our overcoats." Buckets of water were frozen, water from the shallow lagoons blown out into the Gulf, and great quantities of fish killed. "At these times people go to the bar with their wagons," he recorded, "and with a spear or fork pick up the finest fish, weighing from ten to a hundred pounds." Any vessels that can find safe harbor do so. During a Veracruz norther in the 1820s, British warships were secured to great bronze rings embedded in the castle walls of San Juan de Ulúa. Sailors and passengers caught at sea are in for an unpleasant time. "Such a wind I had till then never even imagined," declared one British traveler off Tampico during the 1830s. "The sea was apparently leveled under its pressure; and far and near seemed like a carpet of driving snow, from the sleet and foam which were raised and hurried along its surface." For those safely standing on a lee shore, that is, land onto which the wind is blowing, northers can be mesmerizing, as Madame LeVert discovered at Havana during the 1850s. When a front blew through one evening, she and some friends "enveloped ourselves in the largest mantles we could find, and ran to shore." All the clouds had been swept away and the moon shone brightly. "It was really a fearful sight to watch the enormous waves as they came rolling in, breaking against the Punta and the lofty battlements of the Moro," she wrote, "while a booming sound, as of distant cannon, met the ear. The white spray darted up high in the air, and often seemed like a cloud around the *farola* (light-house)." Yet another unforgettable sight was to come. Early the next morning the winds diminished enough for the British fleet to enter the harbor. LeVert stood with "multitudes of people" to watch the large vessels glide by, their towering white sails and colorful flags catching the sunlight.[37]

Wonder. Beauty. Exhilaration. These things have always accompanied the human experience of the Gulf of Mexico. In 1853 the Swedish novelist Fredrika Bremer was taken by the deep Gulf's blue waters: "The heavens, with their soft white summer clouds, arched themselves over the dark blue sea, which heaved and roared joyfully before the fresh, warm summer wind. Oh, how beautiful it was!" Almost a decade later, the Confederate sea raider Raphael Semmes almost forgot there was a war on when he became entranced by the scenes below the *Alabama*'s hull off a Yucatán reef. The water was so "pellucid," he wrote, "that not only her anchor, which lies in seven fathoms, is visible, from stock to fluke, but all the wonders of the coral world . . . lie open to inspection; with the turtle groping about amid the seafern, the little fishes feeding, or sporting, and madrepore and sponges lying about in profusion." And lastly, during the 1990s, an old man living on the Alabama shore recalled a boyhood voyage with his father on board their schooner *Sehome* many decades before. The wind was on their quarter, and they were barreling along. "We were making knots," he recalled, "and the damn *Sehome* could sail—she was going like a bat outa hell probably making 14, 15 knots. And all the tackle, the damn mast and the booms were squeaking and grunting and bending. And we hit a great big wave and she went way up in the air and came back down." His father stood at the wheel, shirt tail out laughing for pure free joy. "And it was just blowing to beat hell, it was a squall and we were making knots and everything was straining, and I never will forget." Many a mariner has no doubt had similar feelings on the Gulf's broad back. Its siren call is irresistible and has been since men and women first glimpsed its viridian waters thousands of years ago.[38]

Chapter One

Indian Shore

Someone looking and idly turning his head, saw the low lines of
the whole world—pale horizon, vapory sky, wide-shadowed green
sea, the mist-white shore . . . and the powdery browns of the
people moving at what they did.

Paul Horgan,
Great River, 1954

On the eve of the American Revolution, a Philadelphia-born naturalist named William Bartram entered British East Florida and made his way toward the Gulf Coast. This was Seminole country, and Bartram dutifully met with one of their chiefs to ask if he could travel the area freely and gather plant specimens. The chief was bemused at the thought of this thirty-five-year-old white man struggling through swamps and bogs in search of harmless botanical wonders, and promptly dubbed him "Pug Puggy," meaning "flower hunter." Happily, permission was granted, and Bartram subsequently wrote almost as much about the Seminoles he encountered as the otherworldly flora and fauna.[1]

Their name comes from the Spanish word *cimarrón,* meaning "untamed" or "wild." They were mostly Creek Indians who had moved south from Georgia and made a new life in Florida's swamps and woods. Bartram liked them at once. "The visage, action, and deportment of the Siminoles," he wrote admiringly, "form the most striking pictures of happiness in this life; joy, contentment, love, and friendship, without guile or affectation." The young men were colorful to behold, "all dressed and painted with singular elegance, and richly ornamented with silver plates, chains, &c. after the Siminole mode, with waving plumes of feathers on their crests." They warmly welcomed this peculiar stranger into their midst, clasping his hand, laughing frequently, sharing game, and exchanging stories around crackling campfires.[2]

Bartram established himself at Talahasochte, a small village on the banks of the Suwannee River twenty miles from the Gulf. It consisted of a trading house, several dozen log cabins, and a large council house. The cabins were roofed with cypress bark, measured about thirty by twelve feet, and had two rooms, one a kitchen and the other a bedroom. Twenty yards distant from every dwelling stood a "chickee," a covered platform reached by a short ladder, "a pleasant, cool, airy situation," where the owner generally received guests. Despite its small size, Talahasochte was a busy place, and while there Bartram observed steady river traffic. The Seminoles traveled by "large handsome canoes," he wrote, "which they form out of the trunks of Cypress trees, some of them commodious enough to accommodate twenty or thirty warriors." Typical journeys included forays to the seacoast and, amazingly, all the way "to the point of Florida, and sometimes across the gulph, extending their navigations to the Bahama islands and even to Cuba." Few Europeans at the time would have dared venture into the open Gulf without a vessel featuring a keel as well as more beam and freeboard than a narrow log canoe. Yet the Seminoles did so routinely. During his short stay Bartram witnessed "a crew of these adventurers" glide upstream and nose into the bank, their cargo "spirituous liquors, Coffee, Sugar, and Tobacco." One of the paddlers gave the naturalist a tobacco plug reportedly from the Cuban governor himself and explained that in exchange they had taken deer hides, dried fish, honey, and bear oil.[3]

Clearly Bartram had encountered a people who had perfectly adapted to their part of the world. Despite the colonies' unsettled political situation and white encroachment, the Seminoles were prospering. Even without European trade goods, which had thoroughly penetrated the local culture in the form of flintlock muskets, iron hatchets, pots, and tools, glass beads, bright cloth, and cotton hunting shirts, there were more than enough natural resources to maintain their existence. The woods were thick with deer, bear, opossum, and rabbit, and cultivated fields of corn, beans, squash, and melon ringed the village. The Suwannee, broad and deep at Talahasochte, was an especially productive larder. Its muddy banks were populated by crawfish, turtles, and frogs sheltered by scuppernong, persimmon, laurel oak, and blueberry. The water immediately next to the banks, Bartram noted, was "turbid" and swarming with "amphibious insects," providing an ideal nursery for small fry, which in turn became food for the larger fish. Midstream the water was startlingly clear and teeming with "finny inhabitants." On one short expedition, Bartram delighted in hooking trout so large they actually pulled the canoe "over the floods before we got them in." After catching several he was hailed by a canoe of Indians, "cheerful merry fellows," who traded a mess of bream, "my favorite fish," for some of the trout. Down on the Gulf, the Seminoles heavily fished the marshy river mouth's tidal creeks and passes, smoking their catch and sometimes trading with Cuban fishermen. They also harvested mollusks and killed the occasional manatee, a bountiful source of fat.[4]

Like every other Indian tribe in the Americas, the Seminoles were descendants of a small East Asian founder group who migrated across the Bering Land Bridge some twenty thousand years earlier. By 12000 B.C.E. these peoples had advanced to the very ends of South America and were probably roaming the northern Gulf rim into Florida as well. By about 4000 B.C.E. they had filtered into Cuba, either from other Caribbean islands, Florida or both. All of these early Gulf inhabitants were Paleo-Indians, small bands of hunter-gatherers who moved constantly in search of the best game. Sea levels were much lower during the earliest phases of this period, and these Indians stalked megafauna such as mastodon, mammoth, bison, and sloths well out onto what is today submerged continental shelf. Those people closest to the ancient seashores learned to exploit the plenteous marine resources. Women and children foraged for mollusks and crustaceans while lithe adolescent boys probably indulged in a little hand fishing to test their skill. The men spearfished and killed manatee and sea turtles, butchering the large carcasses with beautifully faceted stone knives.[5]

Over succeeding millennia the climate warmed, sea levels rose, and the megafauna disappeared or were hunted to extinction. In response the Indians adjusted their habits and improved their tools, entering what modern archaeologists refer to as the Archaic Period (7500–1000 B.C.E.). Groups became more settled and threw refuse like mussel shells, turtle bones, potsherds, and stone flakes onto small piles that eventually grew into larger middens, valuable sources of archaeological data. Increasingly skilled potters learned to temper their clay with Spanish moss and shredded palmetto leaves for additional strength before firing it. Women handwove natural materials into cloth, mats, and baskets. Hunters made smaller spear points and like their ancestors multiplied their throwing power with the atlatl, a small stick with a hooked base. When he wanted to throw his spear, a hunter simply fitted the base of his dart against the atlatl's base, gripped it at the opposite end, and retaining his hold on the device hurled the spear. The atlatl acted as an extension of the thrower's arm, essentially providing an extra elbow and significantly multiplying the throw's force. No one knows exactly when, but it was also likely during this era that people first looked at the multitudinous waters of their world—rivers, streams, lakes, bays, bayous, and lagoons, as well as the blue-green Gulf itself—and decided to embark upon them.[6]

Simple dugout canoes were their means. The basics of making a good dugout probably changed little over the millennia, and an eyewitness description by the naturalist Antoine-Simon Le Page du Pratz in 1700s Louisiana may safely be considered the Indian standard until European trade goods changed everything. The builders' first task was to select a likely tree—cedar, ceiba, or even mahogany in the Yucatán; cypress or poplar along the northern shore; or yellow pine in south Florida. Then they had to bring it down. Fire was the best method, since as du Pratz noted, stone axes "could not cut wood, but only bruise it." After a small fire was set at the tree base the Indians let the flames do their work, perhaps chopping a bit here and there, until the great trunk fell with a crash. They then burned off the top, hacked off the limbs, and placed the trunk onto a large wooden frame. Hot coals were laid along the top of the log and, according to du Pratz, "when the wood is consumed it is scraped so that the insides may catch fire better and may be hollowed out more

How They Build Boats, Theodor de Bry, 1590. Indians fashion a dugout canoe using fire and hand tools. COURTESY LIBRARY OF CONGRESS.

easily, and they continue thus until the fire has consumed all of the wood in the inside of the tree." In order to control the burn and keep it from eating too deeply into the sides, ends, or bottom of the intended vessel, Indians carefully packed wet clay against the wood, thinning it or slathering on more as needed. The boat was finished off using scrapers and even shark skin as sandpaper. Canoe lengths varied, from short craft that could carry two or three people to large war canoes capable of holding dozens. "I have seen some 40 feet long by 3 broad," du Pratz wrote. "They are about 3 inches thick which makes them very heavy." Du Pratz claimed that the labor required to finish a good dugout was "infinite," but steady effort could usually turn one out in a few weeks.[7]

Dugout canoes proved highly serviceable on inland waterways and protected bays. Modern tourists and museumgoers are often surprised to learn this, since the vessels look so unstable. But the Indians were expert handlers, using paddles or poles to deftly propel and steer their craft toward another village or to check a fish trap. Even an unexpected capsize was no problem, according to one sixteenth-century Spaniard. If a canoe flipped, he explained, the Indians "take their vessel between them and turn it so as to have its mouth straight downward." When it comes up full of water, "all simultaneously give it a shake, and when the water in falling is collected on one side, they immediately give it a shake in the opposite direction.

After two such shakes, not a drop of water remains in the canoe, and the Indians reenter it." It was all done in a twinkling. The numerous streams emptying into the Gulf, especially along the northern shore, were natural highways and far preferable to difficult overland routes through broken terrain, jungle, swamps, or thorny thickets. One careful student of the matter has calculated that water routes generally cut travel times to important points in half, and that four Indians paddling a canoe for fifty miles conserved twenty-five thousand calories over a comparable land journey.[8]

Unfortunately, dugouts possessed none of the qualities desired in a good sea boat. Their low ends lacked enough buoyancy to breast oncoming waves or manage a following sea, and the meager freeboard was dangerous in a heavy chop, though the gunwales could be augmented by plank strakes to reduce over wash and spray. Furthermore, their lack of tillers or keels meant poor stability and susceptibility to inefficient lateral movement while under way. Even so, as Bartram observed, American Indians were not afraid to venture into blue water when the occasion warranted. But it was not for the fainthearted. The Gulf's frequent calms were an advantage, but the weather had to be watched closely, and one wonders how many Indian crews were lost to sudden squalls or rogue waves. There would be refinements to and variations among dugouts depending on the tribe and the era including different bow designs and, among the Calusa of southwest Florida, possible sail use and the development of catamarans, but the dugout was never to be a good ocean vessel.[9]

Rafts are easier to make than dugout canoes, as any schoolboy living near a creek knows, and the early Indians frequently resorted to them, especially when traveling overland and confronted by a stream to be crossed. Du Pratz wrote that the Louisiana Indians made rafts out of "bundles of canes bound side by side then crossed double (i.e., a second tier being placed at right angles crosswise)." This made a workable ferry that could be either broken up or left on the bank for future use. Down in Mexico, the enigmatic Olmecs (ca. 1200 to 400 B.C.E.) used big rafts to ferry giant sculpted basalt heads. Some of these heads weighed up to forty tons and were quarried and carved miles from their intended destinations. Gangs of Indian laborers rolled the heads across the ground on logs and maneuvered them onto rafts consisting of balsa trunks resting atop canoes. Once positioned on the raft, the fantastic assembly was towed by hundreds of Indians straining against long yucca lines.[10]

Over time some of the Gulf's native inhabitants developed increasingly sophisticated cultures that at their apogee featured highly stratified city-states, monumental architecture, astronomical and mathematical knowledge, literacy, elaborate myth and ritual, organized warfare, extensive agricultural production, trade routes, and an ongoing dependence on and exploitation of the sea. There were far too many tribes over the centuries to adequately cover in a survey such as this, but by the eve of European contact several native groups were notable for their cultural and maritime achievements. They included the Maya in southern Mexico, the Indians around Mobile Bay, and the Calusa of Florida's Mangrove Coast.

The Maya emerged out of the Mesoamerican Archaic era and by 500 B.C.E. had established themselves in Central America and Mexico. Scholars divide their civilization into preclassic, classic, and postclassic periods, with significant achievements occurring during each of these. When the Spanish first encountered the Maya during the late postclassic period, they were in decline but still formidable. Even at their peak they were never a unified people, settling rather into small city-states that shared a common culture and alternatively warred and traded with one another. Their greatest cities, such as Tikal and El Mirador (in Guatemala) and Uxmal and Chichén Itzá (in northern Yucatán) are now popular tourist destinations, famous for their awe-inspiring stepped pyramids as much as two hundred feet in height, paved plazas, palaces, temples, ball courts, and elaborate sculpture. Each city-state had a king and royal family, a warrior elite, noble priests who conducted frequent and bloody human sacrifices, and tens of thousands of commoners who labored in town and tilled the nearby fields.[11]

The Maya's physical geography included highlands to the south and the Yucatán's broad flat lowlands to the north where the bordering Gulf and Caribbean provided plentiful food, and meaning, to their society. The Spanish priest Diego de Landa wondered that the Maya had been able to survive on the stony Yucatán Peninsula at all, calling it the "country with the least earth that I have ever seen, since all of it is one living rock." Yet the Maya carved out their cities amid the dense forests and improved their prospects by draining swamps, building up fields, constructing irrigation canals to deal with the long dry season, and maintaining household garden patches of maize, beans, squash, and peppers. In the surrounding country they practiced conservation techniques to preserve deer stocks. Along the Peninsula's northern margin, just off the Gulf, stretched a large saline marsh that yielded what Landa called "the finest salt I have seen in my life." During the rainy season clumps of the highly desirable mineral appeared on the surface so thickly that, according to Landa, it looked just like "sugar candy." The natives regularly harvested this bounty, trading it far and wide. Lastly, impressive natural limestone cenotes, or sinkholes, dot the northern third of the Peninsula and served the Maya as sacred shrines and reliable freshwater wells.[12]

Water was important to the Maya for several reasons. They needed it to live, of course, but it also physically linked them together via streams and the sea, and metaphorically defined their spiritual horizons and bounded their underworld. The Mayan pantheon was crowded by dozens of deities, but among the most important were the founder gods Kukulkán (the feathered serpent known as Quetzalcoatl to the Aztecs) and Hurakan. Scholars surmise that Kukulkán was based on an actual warrior prince who arrived at Chichén Itzá around 1000 C.E. and was deified. His cult soon spread, and the Maya came to believe that when he left them he went east over the sea, promising to return. This myth was eventually to bear disastrous fruit for all the Mesoamerican peoples, but prior to that it gave daring and ambitious warriors a powerful motivation to journey offshore. Hurakan, by contrast, was a fearsome storm god who could summon howling winds and lashing rains to knock down trees and destroy villages. Hurakan had conjured the very earth from beneath the ocean, the Maya believed, and populated it with sluggish mud men, whom he subsequently destroyed with water. When Hurakan wasn't visiting ruinous floods on people, the god Chaak was in charge of the rain, and the deeper cenotes were thought to be portals into his realm. If these gods wanted to travel through the watery underworld themselves, they depended on a pair of paddler gods and, what else but a dugout canoe.[13]

Frighteningly, the diverse Maya pantheon had to be continually placated by human sacrifice and bloodletting. Sacrifice usually involved battle captives or losing ballplayers. The victims were marched to the pyramid tops, held down upon stone altars, and their chests ripped open by longhaired priests wielding obsidian knives. Their hearts were displayed to throngs below and offered to the gods, their bodies unceremoniously thrown down the steps. During droughts, Chaak was placated by painting victims blue and hurling them into the cenotes to drown. The ruling elites were important for their supposed ability to communicate directly with these ruthless deities and as such indulged in less drastic but still ghastly personal bloodletting ceremonies in propitiation. Landa described how they would do this by drawing items through their lips, tongues, penises, and cheeks "in a slanting direction from side to side . . . with horrible suffering." The best tools for these tasks were items from the sea like stingray spines and shark teeth. According to Landa, the priests had large stocks of these on hand at all times, the spines "curiously formed in the shape of a saw, so sharp and fine that it cuts like a knife." In order to obtain them, the Maya depended upon well-developed trade networks with their Caribbean and Gulf neighbors.[14]

There were a number of coastal settlements that were vital to this network, including Isla Cerritos and Vista Alegre in what is now Quintana Roo on the Peninsula's northern coast, and Champotón on the Campeche shore. Isla Cerritos and Vista Alegre served as Chichén Itzá's most critical maritime links, with goods carried the roughly seventy miles between capital and seaports by porters on foot, typically a three-day trek each way. Isla Cerritos is a small island situated just offshore, whereas Vista Alegre is positioned atop a slight rise in the middle of an estuary and protected from *nortes* by Holbox Island and Yalahau Lagoon. During recent surveys and excavations at both sites, archaeologists discovered an astonishing range of ruins and artifacts related to the Mayan maritime endeavor. Both feature small pyramids, which probably did double duty as observational platforms to spy incoming canoes; temple ruins; stone causeways; docks and piers; and seawalls, the latter constructed by sinking tall flat slabs in parallel lines and infilling with rubble. At Isla Cerritos the seawall features a center gap as a protected passage with flanking stone platforms. These platforms originally held wattle and daub towers with thatch roofs. Champotón was by far the largest of these three ports, containing eight thousand stone houses surrounded by a rock wall and moats. Just offshore stood a stone tower reached by a dozen or so steps where fishermen left offerings to the necessary gods. Since Champotón sheltered a fleet of two thousand canoes it was likely a busy place.[15]

Trade in the northern Yucatán was dominated by powerful merchant families who, like the well-heeled residents of most Gulf Coast cities throughout history, considered themselves more cosmopolitan than their inland neighbors. Salt was their most valuable commodity, and they strictly controlled access to the coveted pans. Their trade routes webbed across the region, running inland to Chichén Itzá and by sea around the Peninsula and down into Central America and west across the Bay of Campeche into Tabasco and thence the Mexican highlands where the emerging Aztecs were building an empire. A dizzying array of goods would have been constantly coming and going through these port towns—salt, enslaved people, chocolate, purple dyes, pottery, obsidian, chert, jade, gold, copper, pearls, corals, conch shells, turtle shells, fish, shellfish, and the highly prized stingray spines and shark teeth. The favored currency was cocoa beans, a wonder to the Spanish with so much gold and silver in Mexico.[16]

Of all the indigenous peoples who lived around the Gulf, the Maya were probably the most adroit at managing long-distance voyages. To begin with, their canoes featured several improvements for saltwater travel—upswept raking ends with high platform-like prows and sterns pegged onto the main log, flat as opposed to round bottoms for better stability, pointed paddles, and a long steering oar. There is no evidence that the Maya used sails, however. On his fourth voyage in 1502, Columbus famously encountered a canoe full of seagoing Maya in the Gulf of Honduras. By the description of the compassionate scholar-priest Bartolomé de las Casas, these Indians sound like an extended family on a work holiday frolic. Their canoe was enormous, "as long as a galley" and fully eight feet wide with over two dozen men, women, and children on board, the latter comfortably ensconced under palm mat awnings amidships. The vessel carried "cotton blankets, painted in many colors and designs, and sleeveless shirts, also painted and worked," no doubt for trade. Additionally there were wooden swords with inset obsidian edges, copper hatchets, and "many cacao nuts." For sustenance the passengers and crew had corn bread, edible roots, and fermented liquor that the Spanish thought tasted like beer. These Indians were so surprised at the apparition of high-walled wooden caravels with stained sails and bearded white men that they made no resistance. Columbus kept the canoe's head man as a hostage to guide him through the unfamiliar waters but let the rest of them go with a few trinkets as souvenirs of their most unusual day.

Such blue-water trips, even short ones, would have been fraught with peril for the Maya (beyond the theretofore completely unanticipated new one of European interference!), and they made what accommodations they could. Sea travelers mostly hugged the coast or made short fair-weather dashes between the mainland and nearby islands. When stopped along a riverbank or in a protected harbor such as at Isla Cerritos, they tied off their boats with yucca lines to prevent drift or damage from neighboring vessels. Coastal dwellers helped crews navigate by erecting stone lighthouses aligned with passes and channels, visible at night by torches and by day by colorful banners.[17]

The question is, just how far did the Mayans go in their large dugout canoes? Did they visit the Indians of Cuba or what is now the southeastern United States? Scholars have speculated for over a century about the obvious Mesoamerican influences manifest in the Mississippian cultures in particular. It is known, for example, that the agricultural triad of corn, beans, and squash filtered into the southeast from Mesoamerica, but how? Just as compelling, if not more so, are the large flat-topped, four-sided earthen mounds erected by the Mississippian peoples; their comparable burial customs and religious totems, such as a winged rattlesnake motif; and the similarities in the two regions' depictions of human ceremonial adornment—topknots, ear spools, necklaces, tasseled belts, and pointed pouches. Unfortunately,

A Mayan lighthouse. From John L. Stephens, *Incidents of Travel in Yucatan, vol. 2*. London: Murray, 1843.

direct evidence of a trade route or prominent visits that would explain these influences has yet to emerge. A vast and forbidding landscape stretched between the Mesoamerican peoples and the Southeast (as Cabeza de Vaca discovered in the sixteenth century), and tribes like the Karankawa that lived there were free of such influences. Some scholars have speculated that itinerant Aztec traders known as *pochtecas,* who reached the Pueblo Indians in the American Southwest, could have been occasional visitors to the mound peoples as well, bringing distant greetings from their powerful lords along with chocolate, exotic dress, and trinkets to delight the women and children. Such visits would have been a high occasion for all, the lighthearted strains of a flute through field and forest announcing a gust of cosmopolitanism from a far-off empire. One can imagine laughing children dashing to meet the guest with his wonderful backpack, women smiling as they paused at their tasks, and the men brightening at the prospect of news. Alternatively, a canoe of seagoing Maya Indians might have been swept off course and landed on a distant shore where their dress, customs, and routine cargo became a source of inspiration and fascination to a theretofore unfamiliar people. Until definitive proof emerges, one can only wonder.[18]

What is known is that by about 1000 C.E. the Mississippian culture had fully emerged out of the Archaic and Woodland eras. The Indians of this period settled in fertile river valleys or along creeks where they could cultivate large quantities of grains and vegetables. Corn was planted in small mounded patches that made it easier to harvest by hand than if planted in long rows. The Mississippians prospered in the mild climate and settled large towns, built wattle-and-daub houses, erected huge temple mounds, and developed a hierarchical social organization and ritualistic belief system weighted with symbolic content. Like the Maya they divided into competing city-states, or as archaeologists call them, chiefdoms. When these chiefdoms weren't trading or competing with one another on athletic fields they were warring for dominance. Pitched battles were rare, ambush preferred. High-ranking captives were prized, but rather than having their hearts ripped out by longhaired priests atop the mounds, they were tortured to death. The eighteenth-century southeastern tribes burned captives alive, though that might have been a borrowing from the Spanish who had ravaged the region several centuries earlier.[19]

The Mississippians beautifully adapted to their lush environment and used stone, bone, clay, and wood to fashion an incredible variety of utilitarian objects including axes, scrapers, chisels, beads, bowls, trumpets, knives, torches, boxes, cradles, fences, fish traps, shields, rafts and canoes, litters, pipes, and shell inlaid masks. Women skillfully wove animal hair and plant fiber, employing a wood frame to separate the strands and practiced fingers to create the pattern. They carefully dyed their handiwork, applying wax to mark the design on the cloth, dying it, and then melting the wax off the covered portions. The resulting moccasins, shirts, capes, and loincloths must have been lovely.[20]

The northern Gulf Coast's most important chiefdom was situated deep in the heart of the Mobile River delta, an awesome place of labyrinthine swamps, towering moss-choked cypress and gum trees, waving marsh grass, and hundreds of species of mammals, birds, fish, and reptiles. Sometime around 1200 c.e. the Indians moved onto a small island there, reached by what is today called Bottle Creek. Then as now, the site floods part of every year, negating permanent residence, but the location was almost certainly considered sacred and was frequently visited for extended periods. These Indians worshipped the sun and wanted a big mound with a temple atop housing a continual fire. Like the Maya, they also enjoyed games. In order to achieve these things, they had to prepare their chosen place. First all the trees and vegetation were cut down and burned. Then over a dozen mounds were erected surrounding a large plaza. The work must have taken years and indeed was probably ongoing for much of the town's existence. Day after day laborers (some of them enslaved people, perhaps) trudged back and forth between nearby borrow pits and the mound sites bent under woven baskets full of black earth. The largest mound towers forty-five feet over the delta and like its smaller neighbors once featured a wooden structure at the top. To build that, Indians sank large poles, wove cane walls between them, and slathered the walls with mud, then roofed it with cane, mud, and palmetto fronds for a remarkably tight and waterproof shelter. These choice mound-top accommodations were reserved for the tribe's chiefs and priests, who were attended by numerous servants. Bones from superior cuts of meat and larger oyster shells excavated there prove that these individuals also ate better than their underlings.[21]

The Bottle Creek settlement may have represented a colonization effort of sorts by the more powerful Moundville Chiefdom in the Black Warrior River Valley hundreds of miles to the north. As it developed and grew, Bottle Creek in turn came to influence and dominate its surroundings. Included in its sphere of influence was a group of Indians who erected the small mound in what is today downtown Fort Walton. Somewhat misleadingly for the layperson, scholars refer to the Bottle Creek Chiefdom as part of the Pensacola Culture, so called because earlier archaeologists first noticed a preponderance of similar pottery clustered around that city. Further research has since demonstrated that Bottle Creek was in fact the locus of a chiefdom that stretched from Florida's Choctawhatchee Bay to the eastern margins of Louisiana's Mississippi River delta.[22]

Bottle Creek drew its sustenance from the bounteous estuarine environment. To be sure, crops were grown in the boggy delta and along its higher banks, and the people foraged for nuts and hunted game, as the presence of seeds, nutshells, and animal bones at the site attest. But far more common are discarded fish bones and mussel shells from an incredible variety of species. Situated where they were, the Bottle Creek Indians could harvest from fresh, brackish, or salt water, and their diet reflected catches from all three. Among the fish caught with weirs, nets, traps, or spears were mullet, bass, bluegill, sea trout, croaker, red drum, gar, menhaden, shiner, catfish, flounder, and sheepshead. Fish could either be cooked and eaten relatively quickly or smoked to keep for later. Women and children wading in the shallows contributed nutrient-rich mussels, clams, and oysters, which they scooped up by hand and dropped into open-weave bags or baskets. Later their take was cooked on little wooden grills. Researchers tabulating the variety of such remains at Bottle Creek have determined that fish and shellfish constituted over 80 percent of the local meat diet. Reptiles such as turtle and snake, waterfowl like duck and coot, small animals like opossum and squirrel, and bigger game like white-tailed deer and bear constituted the balance. There were no starving times at Bottle Creek.[23]

All of that food meant that the Mississippian Indians were well formed and energetic. The sixteenth-century Spanish respected their physical size and strength. Hernando de Soto's men routinely described them as giants, and one hidalgo declared that their six-foot-long bows were made of such strong wood that "no Spaniard, however much he tried, was able to pull the cord back so that his hand touched his face." Many of the women were pretty, some positively stunning. One chronicler thought that a woman taken at Mauvila "could compete in beauty with the most elegant from Spain who were in all Mexico." In fact, most Europeans frankly admired the appearance of both sexes. Their skin resembled cinnamon "with a copperish cast," Romans wrote two hundred years later of the Mississippians' descendants. The men and women were "of good stature, and neatly limbed," he continued, and their hair "lank, strong, black, and long." The men were beardless, plucking out facial hair with mussel shells as tweezers.[24]

The Indians of Bottle Creek enjoyed an extensive trade network. While their best runners traveled along a well-worn trail system that crisscrossed the landscape from the Great Lakes to the Atlantic, water routes were much preferred. The mighty Mississippi River was a busy artery and easily reachable from the Mobile River delta via a protected water route that included the Mississippi Sound, Lake Borgne, Lake Pontchartrain, Lake Maurepas, and the Iberville River. Popular coastal trade items included salt, dried fish, yaupon leaves (used to make a strong tea for ritual purging), and seashells. Hundreds of mollusk shells like the queen conch and lightning whelk from Florida and Alabama waters have been found far away at the massive Cahokia mound complex, opposite modern St. Louis, Missouri. The Indians there fashioned these prized objects into beads, pendants, nose ornaments, gorgets, and even dippers from the shell's body whorl. In return they would have sent the coastal traders home with feather cloaks, animal hides, and hard cane.[25]

Protected or no, coastal water bodies can quickly get worked into a nasty chop, and the Mississippi at full flood is intimidating even from a big workboat's deck. The central Gulf Coast's Indians were as subject to these vicissitudes as modern mariners, and their dugout canoes were highly vulnerable always. They made various adjustments to compensate. A dugout recently excavated near Tampa Bay displays several innovations, including a raised bow and holes drilled along the vessel's sides. The unusual bow design is not as dramatic as that of the Maya, but it would have improved open-water paddling. A pine pole found underneath caused archaeologists to speculate that it and others like it might have been thrust through the holes to fasten two boats together catamaran fashion. There is no evidence that the Mobile River delta's inhabitants used catamarans, but saltwater barnacle species there likely arrived on dugout hulls, compelling evidence of longer voyages. In fact, the first European explorers routinely sighted Indians scooting across the area's bays, and during the ill-fated Narváez expedition, the hapless Spaniards were pursued beyond Dauphin Island by agitated warriors in long war canoes until rising wind and waves forced the Indians to retreat.[26]

The Maya and Bottle Creek Indians depended upon the Gulf and canoed it in limited fashion, but the most unabashedly saltwater people in orientation and life ways were the Calusa of southwest Florida. Nestled among the multitudinous islands and keys between Tampa and land's end, the Calusa grew no crops but fed almost exclusively on their world's marine bounty. The Caloosahatchee River spilled into the sea midway on their coast, providing them an estuarine artery into a country of lakes and swamps where deer, small game, nuts, and berries were readily obtained. They navigated their marine world in dugout canoes, some fastened together in catamaran fashion with woven mats and thatch shelters between the hulls, and they might have employed sails (there is no conclusive evidence), the only Gulf Indians to do so. Men fished with spears or hooks while women and children waded through the clear waters swirling sabal palm-leaf nets weighted by shells and floated by gourds. Mollusks, crustaceans, fish, eels, turtles, manatee, and even the occasional whale kept them nourished and healthy. The sixteenth-century Spanish castaway Hernando de Escalante Fontaneda described the Calusa as large and "well proportioned." "They go naked," he continued, "except only some breechcloths woven of palm, with which the men cover themselves; the women do the like with certain grass that grows on trees [Spanish moss]." Despite their physical attractiveness, the Calusa were renowned for their bellicosity. Fontaneda thought them mean, and in fact their very name meant fierce in their language. They employed shields, bows, and razor-sharp shell-tipped spears in fighting and delighted in tormenting their captives. Fontaneda firmly believed that the only way to make them was to deceive and enslave them. "Let the Indians be taken in hand gently," he counseled Spanish authorities, "inviting them to peace; then putting them under deck, husbands and wives together, sell them among the Islands, and even on Terra-Firma for money, as some old nobles of Spain buy vassals of the king."

Before the Spanish ruined their world, the Calusa flourished. Their population grew to match their resources and stabilized somewhere around ten thousand individuals. Like the Maya and Bottle Creek Indians, they lived in chiefdoms with varying spheres of influence depending upon their size and power. Their chiefs took multiple wives and on formal occasions could be gotten up magnificently, in one recorded case with an elaborate headdress and beaded leg bands. Like most other native peoples around the Gulf rim, the Calusa were driven to erect mounds that they used for both residential and ritual purposes. Because they did not have stone or mud, however, they built with sand and shell. In order to make a typical mound the Calusa first burned a patch of ground, then placed a layer of sand over it, then a six-foot layer of shell, and then alternating layers of sand and shell. One example at Key Marco near modern Naples measured almost two thousand feet square and rose fifteen feet. During the late nineteenth century the anthropoogist Frank Hamilton Cushing dug into these mounds and explored native cultural remains all along Florida's Mangrove Coast. While mucking about a shallow pond on Key Marco, he spotted structural remains just beneath the water's surface With the help of local laborers he cleaned out the "*débris* and vegetal growth" to reveal a "veritable haven of ancient wharves and pile-dwellings, safe alike from tida wave and hurricanes within these gigantic ramparts of shell, where, through the cannel gateways to the sea, canoes might readily come and go." The Calusa had nt only erected mounds, he learned, but actively engineered their environment for eautifully functional living. Their improvements included shelters on stilts, coutyards bound by conch shells, plazas, ridges, shell rings, ramps, and miles of canals hat facilitated travel and communication. One canal was four feet deep, twenty fe wide, and three miles long. Another traversed the two-and-a-half-mile width of ine Island (near modern Fort Myers), connecting Pine Island Sound with Matlaa Pass, thus negating a laborious ten-mile canoe trip around either end of the islar.[28]

And then there are the artifacts. Exquisitely carved masks and anim figures representing pelicans, sea turtles, crabs, deer, and owls have all been unrthed, further illuminating the Calusa's religious beliefs and ritualistic practic Early Spanish accounts describe large temples screened by reed mats and liney long benches and painted masks, grand processions of masked men and chang women descending a mound, human sacrifice, and ceremonial dances. Intstingly, masks and animal or fish carvings have sometimes been found together, iicating they were part of an elaborate ritual in which a dancer meant to transforn imself into the creature represented. One can imagine the power of such a perfnance, the dancer eerily lit by a flickering fire as he gracefully enacted his pantome before a rapt audience backgrounded by inky darkness. Faith in such transfoations would certainly fit with what one Calusa told a Spanish priest. They beled that when someone died, his spirit merged with that of some aquatic or terrial animal, and that when people in turn ate those creatures, the spirit passedck into human form. All life, in other words, was an interconnected spirit wor Toledo steel and black-robed priests would soon have something to say about th[9]

Chapter Two

Spanish Sea

What a troublesome thing it is to discover new lands.
The risks we took, it is hardly possible to exaggerate.

Bernal Díaz del Castillo,
*The True History of the
Conquest of New Spain,*
1632

C hristopher Columbus stood at the rail of the *Niña* and scanned the forbidding coast, all mangrove, marsh, and shallow sea. It was his second voyage to the New World, but he still firmly believed he was skirting the southern coast of Cathay, a region of fantastical monkey-men and prodigious wealth, rather than previously unknown lands. Indians encountered along the way were mostly happy to indulge the Admiral of the Ocean Sea's bizarre convictions, but some were candid in insisting that this land, Cuba, was actually an island. Unfortunately geographical fact did not fit into Columbus's medieval frame of reference, and he refused to accept it. By June 12, 1494, he had reached Bahía Cortés, less than a hundred miles from Cuba's western tip where lay incontrovertible proof of its insularity. But the coast was still trending southwest, and though his vessels were already feeling the tug of the Yucatán Current "rushing westward like torrents from the mountains," the admiral decided to turn back. Doubtless he was fearful of what he might learn if he pressed on, as evidenced by his insistence that the crew sign a statement that Cuba was indeed a peninsula and not an island. Failure to abide by the document, he warned them, carried a fine of ten thousand maravedis and the forcible removal of one's tongue. And so on June 13, with the coerced testimony safely tucked in his doublet, he brought the *Niña* and his other ships about and headed for Jamaica. The Gulf of Mexico, glittering, vast, beautiful, and bordered by lands and peoples beyond Columbus's wildest imaginings, lay as yet undiscovered by European seafarers.[1]

Spain's Atlantic explorations and eventual conquest of the Gulf's Indian shores were the result of an extraordinary intersection of circumstances—political, military, technological, religious, and intellectual—which Columbus was able to successfully exploit. During the late fifteenth century, the Iberian kingdoms of Castile and Léon were unified under Ferdinand and Isabella, who expelled the Moors in 1492 and forced the Jews to convert to Christianity or leave shortly thereafter. That same year, a Spanish pope was elected, and a learned humanist published a Castilian grammar, which he presented to Isabella with the remark that language was the "perfect instrument of empire." Fired by these developments, ambitious young hidalgos (lesser nobles) were eager to prove their devotion to God and king and, not incidentally, to make a little profit. And where better to direct their energies than toward the exciting goal of opening a reliable trade route to the East, converting or killing infidels in the process? Columbus shared their fervor but believed that rather than pursuing the logical and direct land corridor, plagued by exasperating tolls and banditry, an easier route beckoned to the west, across the Ocean Sea. Brave Portuguese and Spanish captains had already probed the eastern Atlantic, sailing among the Azores, Canary, and Cape Verde Islands, and farther still, returning to tell of extensive seaweed mats, circling birds, abandoned dugouts, and bloated brown bodies. After much delay and uncertainty, Columbus convinced the Spanish monarchs to support the endeavor and thus crossed the Atlantic entire. But despite four voyages and careful Caribbean explorations, he never grasped that he had discovered a new world, *between* Europe and the East, and he never saw the Gulf.[2]

Others soon did, among them men who had accompanied Columbus on one or another of his voyages and several who had actually signed the ridiculous pledge. They included Juan de la Cosa, the *Santa María*'s owner and a chart maker who, Columbus's threat notwithstanding, listened to the Indians and depicted Cuba as an island on his 1500 map; Juan Ponce de Léon, a robust redhead who loved bullying Indians; Antón de Alaminos, a careful pilot "adept in the art of navigation"; and Sebastián de Ocampo, a former servant of Queen Isabella who offended a powerful nobleman and was permanently exiled. It was Ocampo, impatiently biding his time in the Indies, who first discovered the Gulf.[3]

By the early sixteenth century, islands like Hispaniola and Jamaica were being systematically and thoroughly altered. Forests were cleared, cattle and hogs introduced, sugar mills erected, tobacco planted, and the Indians enslaved. These poor souls died in droves by hard use and disease. The islands were so rapidly depopulated that officials worried about a reliable labor source. Given all of that, added to the disappointing facts that neither a convenient passage to the Orient had been found nor gold discovered in exciting quantities, and the impetus for further New World exploration was firmly in place. In 1508, the governor of Hispaniola commissioned Ocampo to take some ships and finally learn whether Cuba was a peninsula or an island and how it might be settled and plundered.[4]

Ocampo was a good choice. Despite the terms of his exile—never to leave Hispaniola on pain of death—he had become a successful trader throughout the Caribbean, traveling among the islands in his own ships and hobnobbing with local officials. For his Cuban voyage he chose two caravels, hardy little craft that were the workhorses of the Spanish Main. Modern observers profess amazement when examining reproduction caravels like Columbus's *Niña* or *Pinta*. The very idea of striking out across uncharted waters in such tiny boats seems at best scary and at worst suicidal. Yet they were seaworthy vessels, officered and crewed by men who knew their every plank, rope, and quirk.[5]

Developed from medieval antecedents like the cog, caravels were distinguished by long, graceful lines, slightly upswept bows, quarterdecks, axial stern rudders, and two masts. The earliest examples were lateen rigged, making them highly maneuverable into the wind and on coastal rivers. When running west on transatlantic voyages with the Trades they were converted into square riggers and called *caravelas redondas* (round caravels) for their bellying canvas. Among the islands and coastlines of the Caribbean and Gulf, the Spanish found the most useful and versatile sail plan to be a square-rigged mainmast with a lateen-rigged mizzen. No two caravels were exactly alike, but a typical example would have been seventy feet long with a fifty-foot keel, twenty-three-foot beam, and nine-foot depth of hold, the vessel drawing only six feet. Caravels were classified according to tonnage, with fifty to sixty being a common range. During the sixteenth century, tonnage meant a vessel capacity in wine tuns, large wooden casks that held roughly 250 gallons each. Fifty or sixty of these wedged into a hold wasn't an especially impressive figure, which meant that caravels were more important as reconnaissance vessels than cargo carriers. Galleons were better suited to hauling the New World's bounty away, but more of them anon.[6]

Navigating caravels was far from an exact science, though for Ocampo's Cuba mission he simply had to hug the shore and see where it trended. That didn't mean coastal piloting, as it was called, couldn't be dangerous. None of the land forms were familiar, and the locations of reefs, shoals, and harbors were likewise a mystery. Ocampo probably kept far enough out to avoid hazards, tacking in more closely when the occasion seemed to require it, such as to investigate a river or to land and take on provisions. When approaching the coast, he would have placed a sailor in the anchor chains with a sounding lead to determine how deep the water was. This simple tool consisted of a lead bar with a slightly hollowed end attached to a knotted rope. The knots were located at regular lengths, usually every six feet (a fathom) which allowed the leadsman to quickly sound the depth and announce it to the pilot. A little tallow was placed in the lead's cavity, and examining it after each throw was helpful in knowing whether the bottom was sand, mud, crushed shell, or rock. In open water, the Spanish generally relied on dead reckoning (Columbus's tried-and-true method) or latitude sailing. Neither was especially accurate, and many a ship was lost during the age of exploration as a result. As the name implied, dead reckoning simply meant pointing the vessel in the general direction where its destination was thought to lie and launching forth. In order to hold a course, caravels carried a simple compass, consisting of a circular card marked with thirty-two directional points (commonly known as a compass rose) balanced atop a magnetized needle on a pivot within a circular bowl. This vital apparatus was housed in the binnacle, a wooden box fixed to the deck and regularly consulted by helmsman and pilot. Latitude sailing involved fixing one's distance from the equator by measuring the height of the sun or the North Star above the horizon. In order to do this, a plain but functional wooden cross-staff was aimed at the horizon, and a sliding vane was moved until it touched the horizon at bottom and the target object at top, allowing the angle to be read off a scale on the staff. Wooden quadrants were also employed to figure latitude. These were quarter-circular instruments with sights along one edge and a plumb bob attached to the apex that would line up with a scale notched along the arc. These aids were imprecise at best (the most accurate sextant was not invented until 1759), and obtaining useful readings from pitching deck was an exercise in frustration. Calculating longitude, which combined with latitude allowed for an exact knowledge of one's location on the plane was not possible at sea until the eighteenth century. All in all, the sixteenth-century mariner's tools weren't much and would probably give modern sailors the willies, but they served their purpose and, combined with much trial and error, helped make known the Gulf.[7]

A typical caravel crew consisted of fifteen to twenty men, most young, uneducated, Catholic, sun bronzed, barefooted, and tough. In warm tropical and semitropical waters they wore baggy trousers, loose linen shirts, and perhaps a Monmouth cap. Their days were regulated by strict routine and regular religious observances. They were divided into two watches of four hours each, set three, seven, and eleven o'clock morning and evening, with an officer in charge. The work itself involved endless hauling on lines and sheets, splicing rope, mending sails, scrambling aloft, scouring the decks with salt water and stiff brushes, and anything else occasion or captain required. They were frequently assembled for prayers and hymns and during their off-hours told tall tales and obscene stories, played cards, or just idled. They slept rough, either on deck with a hawser for a pillow beneath a lifeboat or tarpaulin in foul weather. Their daily rations included one and a half pounds of bread, two pints drinking water, two pints of wine, plus whatever supplemental fare was available, usually cheese, rice, peas, olives, and fish caught over the side or fruit, nuts, and small game gotten by shore parties.[8]

The most important man on board was the pilot, tasked with guiding the ship through unfamiliar waters. Spanish pilots were typically older with much sea time. Everything depended upon their knowledge and ability, and their power, duties, and punishments were starkly stated. According to one dictate, an impetent pilot "should be immediately decapitated, and no mercy or leniency would be given him." If the record is any indication, pilots were not shy about their abilities, but of course none knew the Gulf well at first, and if at least one comporary observer is to be believed they didn't know much else either. "Why do we put up with these pilots," a Portuguese mathematician groused, "with their bad language and barbarous manners; they know neither sun, moon nor stars, nor their courses, movements or declinations; . . . nor astrolabes, quadrants, cross staffs or watches, nor years common or bissextile, equinoxes or solstices?" The reason was because, the occasional cloistered land-based egghead aside, nobody else was any better. In fairness, pilots didn't have much beyond instinct and experience to benefit their efforts. What maps existed were crude approximations based on legend, fancy, and, ever so gradually, painstakingly accumulated direct knowledge. Usually the only way to learn a treacherous reef was to suddenly come upon it. If the pilot was vigilant, regular soundings and a keen eye for color changes and surface disturbances would avert disaster. Knowledge came by doing, and soon enough good and capable Gulf pilots emerged.[9]

Equipped, provisioned, and crewed, Ocampo departed Hispaniola late in 1508. It never behooved a captain to travel the Indies during hurricane season. Sailing carefully west, the caravels probed the Cuban coast as close as the pilots dared to avoid the surging Gulf Stream. As it turned out, the vessels weren't particularly shipshape because they began leaking and giving trouble immediately. Luckily for Ocampo, a perfect stopping place soon presented itself, a deep sheltered harbor easily accessed from the sea. Las Casas, who visited the site shortly thereafter, declared, "There are few harbors in Spain, and perhaps not in any other parts of the world, that may equal it." For his part, Ocampo was delighted, and promptly dubbed it Puerto de Carenas, because it was there that he careened his boats. Careening was a laborious process in which the crew hauled a vessel onto a beach, emptied and washed her ballast, and then cleaned her hull. This was nasty work that involved scraping off wet, stinking barnacles and long slimy ribbons of seaweed; replacing any rotten strakes; and then recaulking and sealing the hull with tar. Happily for the Spaniard plenty of the latter was available from natural petroleum springs in the nearby rocks. While the sailors went about their messy task, a few curious Indians gathered to watch. They were gentle Taínos, who went naked as jaybirds and lived in simple round thatch *bohíos* (huts) beneath the spreading ceiba trees. They called their land "Cuba," probably meaning something like "great place." One of their local chiefs, Haguanex, would give his name to the important city destined to develop there.[10]

The careening done, Ocampo refloated his caravels and tacked out of the harbor. Still hugging the shore, he followed it all the way to Cabo San Antonio. Now verily in the Gulf of Mexico, the first European who can be definitively so documented, he steered around the stony cape and again faced the rising sun. There was no longer any doubt; Cuba was an island. Not only that, but there was gold (at least some), and the natives were lightly armed and docile unless provoked. None of this augured well for them. Ocampo's entire voyage took eight months, and when he returned to Hispaniola he reported his findings to the governor. The conquest of Cuba quickly followed, accomplished by ruthless men like Pánfilo de Narváez (whom Las Casas considered "cruel and stupid"), Juan de Grijalva (the governor's nephew), and Hernán Cortés (a force of nature such as appears but once a millennium), all of whom would go on to further Gulf adventures. Those Indians not slaughtered were forced into slavery. They spent most of their time piling up little earthen mounds to grow yucca plants and, as on the other conquered islands, died in large numbers. As for Ocampo, he appears to have been caught violating his terms of exile and was recalled to Spain, where he was presumably executed, an ignominious end for the Gulf's intrepid discoverer.[11]

Entradas now followed one after the other as the Spaniards explored this previously unknown sea and conquered its shores. They sought gold, people to enslave, lands, knowledge, and new converts to Christianity. But the romantic notion that one of them sought a legendary Fountain of Youth is, alas, false. Juan Ponce de León had already proven himself an effective conquistador by battling the Moors and subjugating Puerto Rico with only a hundred men in 1506. He subsequently governed the island several years before being ousted in a power struggle and replaced by Columbus's son Diego. King Ferdinand, interested in keeping violent men busy, offered Ponce a consolation prize of sorts, a royal patent (at Ponce's own expense) to find and conquer the storied land of Bímini. Once that was accomplished, Ponce would have the sweeping powers of an *adelantado* (a military governor), a juicy prospect indeed. The first mention of the Fountain of Youth as his voyage's motivation dates from a dozen years after his death. The story immediately captured people's fancy, including historians, and endures yet, especially in Florida where tourists and retirees seek their own versions in the warm sand and sunshine.[12]

Cherished legend aside, Ponce set forth on March 4, 1513, in two caravels and a smaller, lateen-rigged *bergantina* equipped with oars for inshore maneuvers. He was thirty-nine years old and itching for action after his Puerto Rico demotion. To ensure success he carefully provisioned his vessels and enlisted the best people available. The latter included Diego Bermúdez, master of the caravel *Santiago*, whose brother had discovered Bermuda; Antón de Alaminos as pilot; Juan Bono de Quejo, a hardy Basque in command of the caravel *Santa María da Consolación*; and several dozen soldiers. Two sisters, Beatriz and Juana Jiméz, also accompanied the entrada, the first European women to gaze on Gulf waters, plus a young black man named Jorge Negro. And so, loaded to the gunnels with people, barrels, boxes, bags, and beef on the hoof, the fleet sailed northwest with the Bahamas on the larboard (left) beam, for that was the direction where Bímini was thought to lie. Several weeks out, storms loomed, and Alaminos steered west to avoid them, making landfall somewhere near present-day Cape Canaveral. It was Easter Sunday, known by the Spanish as Pascua de Flores. Catholic custom was to name discoveries after the closest holy day, and Ponce duly designated the new find, which he believed to be an island, La Florida. The story that he was so inspired because of abundant wildflowers is, like that of the Fountain of Youth, an after-the-fact fabrication. The coast these Spaniards saw was no scented Eden but rather desolate beach backed by wild vegetative tangles.[13]

After several days probing the shore, Ponce ordered the fleet south. As the vessels headed into the Bahama Channel they were walloped by the Gulf Stream's full force. Despite beautiful weather and a north wind, the *Santiago* and the *Santa de María de la Consolación* struggled against the rushing current, dropping anchor and then being whisked out to their cables' lengths where they barely held. The lighter *bergantina* was swept beyond sight and spent several days working her way back toward the caravels. Alaminos studied the situation, and by taking advantage of the north wind and a southerly inshore current, was able to guide the vessels down to Florida's tip, though it took almost a month to do so. But the Gulf Stream's potential was not lost on the observant pilot, who guessed that it could act as a mighty slingshot, speeding Spanish ships back to the mother country.[14]

During early May the fleet rounded southern Florida and on the fifteenth skirted the Keys, which Ponce called Los Mártires (the Martyrs) "because the high rocks at a distance look like men that are suffering." Alaminos had to employ all his tools and skills to safely navigate this shoal- and reef-studded stretch. In order to make the job easier, Ponce ordered his captains to sail only by day and anchor at night. Small groups of Indians canoed out to the vessels near some of the islands, and on one occasion "laid hold of the cable" to commandeer a caravel. This wasn't the kind of behavior Ponce was used to from the gentle Taínos, and his response was predictable. He dispatched a shore party to wreck a few canoes and capture some women. It was a harbinger of what was to come on Florida's Gulf side. Ponce, of course, paid no attention.[15]

There has been much scholarly debate about just where on Florida's west coast Ponce landed, with some researchers arguing as far north as Pensacola Bay, others saying Tampa Bay, still others Charlotte Harbor or Cape Romano closer to the Keys. It was likely somewhere on the Mangrove Coast, because the Indians Ponce encountered were the fierce Calusa, led by a formidable chief called Carlos. The ships anchored between some low islands and the mainland in early June to fill water barrels and otherwise acquire provisions. The *bergantina* was dragged onto a beach and careened. An Indian approached who could speak Spanish, which delighted the men. More Indians appeared, offering to trade pelts. They also claimed that Carlos had gold. For some reason, the negotiations quickly soured, followed by violence. Several Indians seized the anchor cables, apparently a favorite tactic, and tried to board. There followed two sustained assaults, twenty canoes in the first one and over eighty several days later. The Calusa hunkered behind large turtle-shell shields and loosed gusts of fishbone-tipped arrows. Plunging paddles into the water, they dexterously maneuvered their dugouts among the anchored caravels to grab the anchor cables again, but the Spaniards put them to flight with crossbow bolts and musket balls. Still in need of fresh water, Ponce moved his fleet farther up the coast until he could finish provisioning in peace and then sailed west. Well out from the Keys, he discovered eleven small islands that he named the Dry Tortugas for the sea turtles thronging the beaches. There being no Indians, the Spaniards made war on nature instead. Men roamed the beach and crisscrossed the islands, clobbering everything in sight. By the time they left a few days later their take was 160 turtles, 14 seals, and 7,000 birds. Ponce got his comeuppance shortly afterward, when he returned to Florida's Mangrove Coast with two ships in an ill-considered colonization effort. Neither the Spanish nor the Indians were any more tolerant than they had been before, and the expedition immediately came to grief amid fearful attacks. Ponce took a poisoned arrow in the thigh and was ferried to Cuba, where he succumbed to his wound. He had clearly learned nothing from his Florida adventures, but Antón de Alaminos had, and those lessons would soon bear golden fruit.[16]

Throughout the early sixteenth century labor shortages continued to dominate official agendas. Overwork and epidemics steadily reduced the native populations. To compensate Spanish slavers began importing Africans, who brought diseases native to that continent with them to the Indies. But there was creation as well as destruction. Frequent intermixing, some of it forcible and some consensual, produced a new human palette. One historian has quipped, with justification, that the Spanish "left more pregnancies in their camps than they did casualties on the field of battle." The offspring of a European and an Indian was called a mestizo; that of a white and a black, a mulatto; and that of an Indian and a black a zambo. Few of these births were considered legitimate by the Church, and the children of enslaved women were enslaved too unless freed by the white father. Down the generations there would be further blending among these variations, making for a warm range of skin tones around the Gulf.[17]

All of which took time. After Ponce's first voyage the need for labor became especially acute when 110 restless soldiers left Darién (modern Panama) and landed in Cuba looking for land and Indians to enslave in order to establish their fortunes. Among these men was Bernal Díaz del Castillo, a gifted wordsmith and the Cuban governor's nephew. There being no Indians available, Governor Diego Velázquez de Cuéllar cut a deal with the soldiers and a trio of local planters to get their own labor supply. The slave raid was to target the Bahamas, and the financing would be split between the planters and the governor. Command was given to Francisco Hernández de Córdoba, "very able at kidnapping and killing Indians," and the esteemed Alaminos was appointed chief pilot. The fleet included two caravels and a *bergantina,* the soldiers, and some Levantine sailors. But when the expedition set sail, on February 8, 1517, it had evolved from a slave raid into a voyage of discovery.

This was probably due to Alaminos's influence. He had seen the Gulf and surmised there must be undiscovered lands beyond. He doubtlessly convinced the greedy men that they stood to gain greater profit by conquering this new territory than simply kidnapping a few Indians and returning to Cuba, where numerous Spanish planters were already established. Apparently they did not need much convincing. "We sailed toward the west," Díaz wrote much later, "knowing nothing of shoals, currents or the winds at that latitude."[18]

On February 20 the fleet passed Cabo San Antonio and entered the Yucatán Channel. Then a storm hit. According to Díaz it raged two days, "and we were almost lost." The sailors kept their heads and let the vessels do the work, riding the wave crests under reduced sails, wallowing in the swells, laboring onward while breaking seas poured over them and cascaded off the decks. Alaminos and the sailors had seen worse on the Atlantic, but Díaz was a landsman with a lower tolerance for rough weather. His business lay ashore. At last the lookout espied a low line of green. "This land had never been discovered," Díaz claimed, "nor was there any knowledge of it until then." Alaminos believed their discovery was an island. In actuality it was the Yucatán Peninsula.[19]

Greater wonders were to come. As the fleet approached shore the men could see a large town dotted by pyramidal stone temples and threaded by paved streets. It was like nothing else encountered in the New World, and falling back on more familiar references, they dubbed it Gran Cairo. Several large dugouts approached filled with Mayans, "forty to a canoe." The Spaniards made "signs of peace," and the Indians fearlessly clambered on board the caravels. The two groups studied one another open mouthed. "These Indians were dressed in cotton shirts like jackets," Díaz later wrote, "and their private parts were covered with some narrow cloths they called *mosteles*." The Spaniards gave the caciques a few strands of green beads, and the Indians invited them to visit their town.[20]

So far so good as far as New World encounters went, but the following day Hernández armed his men for their shore visit. The conquistadores were a mixed lot, and their appearance was anything but uniform. The officers and wealthier among them sported fine iron helmets and breastplates, but the soldiery wore sandals, knee breeches, quilted cotton jackets or leather jerkins—perhaps a chain-mail vest—and plainer conical helmets. Some carried round shields of wood, metal, or animal hide. Their weapons were well-made and fearsome. These included bright metal swords fashioned of Toledo steel, best in the world; matchlock muskets, capable of throwing a heavy ball over a hundred yards but slow to load and fire; and crossbows, medieval holdovers that were nonetheless effective for their ease of operation and the force of their bolts. Thus attired and equipped, the Spaniards went ashore and walked right into an ambush. The Indians were less heavily armed and protected than their foes but were energetic and brave. "They wore cotton armor which reached to the knees," Díaz explained, "carried lances, shields, bows and arrows, and slings and stones." Accompanied by a racket of shell rattles and turtle drums, the Mayans attacked under bright banners and clouds of arrows. Meso-american warfare was highly ritualized, generally consisting of raids meant to capture sacrificial victims. A knockdown fight with trained opponents who possessed gunpowder was an entirely new experience. The conquistadores may have looked like a rabble, but they did not fight like one, and they turned to their profession with discipline and skill. Díaz proudly noted that the Indians "soon fled when they found out how well our swords cut and about the crossbows and muskets." Fifteen Mayans were dead, no Spaniards. After repulsing the attack, the conquistadores entered the town, awed by its plaza and stone houses. A cleric ducked into a temple and returned with "clay idols, some like faces of devils, some of women, and others of evil figures which appeared to be Indians practicing sodomy with other Indians." The men entered the houses where they found wooden chests filled with carefully fashioned objects, "some small medallions of half-gold, mostly copper, some pendants and diadems, and other small figures of little fish and ducks of the country, all of low grade gold." Things looked promising, more so when they captured two cross-eyed Indian boys whom they planned to use as interpreters.[21]

The Indians gone and the village plundered, Hernández returned his force to the ships and departed. Sailing during the day and coming to at night, the fleet traveled west along the Peninsula's northern end and then rounded it and bore south. On March 29, a large town near a bay came into view. This was Campeche, and the men stopped to take on water. According to Díaz, they were approached by some caciques, who demanded to know "what we were looking for." Then the Indians pointed to the east, asking if the Spaniards came "from where the sun rises and said 'Castilian, Castilian.'" Obviously these Mayans had some familiarity with the Spanish already, most likely shipwreck survivors. Whatever the case, both sides were on their guard as the Spaniards accompanied the caciques back to the town. There, amid "very large buildings, well built of masonry, which were the temples of their idols," they saw unmistakable evidence of human sacrifice, "drops of blood" and grim priests with "great long hair all matted with blood." The priests began waving braziers filled with incense about their unwelcome guests, telling them by signs to "leave their country" before the incense was all burned. The conquistadores were in no mood for another fight against long odds. They quickly returned to their ships and sailed away, still short of water.[22]

Six days later they came to Champotón, where the Peninsula begins bending to the west. At this point Alaminos had to be aware that if the Yucatán was an island, it was an enormous one. Desperate to replenish their water, the men hauled the casks ashore and were soon threatened by Indians, "their faces painted white and black and with ochre." Díaz estimated that there were "two hundred . . . to one of us." Rather than retreat as before, the Spaniards opted to keep provisioning. Not surprisingly, they were attacked the next morning. Arrows rained down, wounding eighty, and then the Mayans closed "and brought us to a bad pass even though we gave them a very good fight with sword and knife thrusts. The crossbows and muskets never stopped playing." Two Spaniards were dragged away screaming, bloody sacrifice or slavery their fate. The others formed a human wedge and smashed through to the ships. Arrows hissed into the water as the soldiers frantically splashed toward the small boats hurrying to retrieve them. Fifty were left dead. The bloodied survivors collapsed on board the caravels, cursing "the pilot Antón de Alaminos, and his voyage and discovery of an island, because he always insisted that it was not mainland." They dubbed their disastrous stop the Costa de la Mala Pelea (Coast of the Bad Fight).[23]

Ill favor or no, Alaminos remained pilot. He declared that their surest deliverance lay in crossing the Gulf to Florida, "because he found from his chart and the latitude that he was only some seventy leagues from there." From Florida, Alaminos reassured the men, "there was a better route and more certain navigation to Havana than the route by which we had come." He knew whereof he spoke. In four days the little fleet hove into the very bay where Ponce had anchored just a few years previously. Good water was there, but Alaminos recalled the belligerent Calusa and warned the men to be ready for trouble. It came almost at once. The Indians assaulted the invaders by land and water, yelling and shaking their weapons. "They were large men," Díaz remembered, "dressed in deerskins and armed with very large bows and good arrows, and lances and something like swords." Six Spaniards went down, including Hernández and Alaminos, the latter grasping at an arrow in his throat. Per usual, the Calusa grabbed the anchor cables and tried to climb onto the caravels. Deeper inside the estuary warriors wrestled a small boat away from some sailors. "We attacked them in water above our waists," said Díaz, "and made them turn loose the boat." Deadly accurate crossbow and musket volleys stopped the Indians at the caravels, and the Spaniards escaped yet another catastrophe. Unfortunately, their return home was further complicated when one of the caravels scraped bottom in the Keys. The men were equal to the moment, however. Díaz proudly stated that despite their depleted condition, "we worked the pumps and managed the sails until our Lord carried us to the town of Havana." There Hernández soon died, but Alaminos recovered, and the voyage's revelations were "extolled" throughout the Indies and Spain. As for the common soldiers like Díaz, who had now battled Indians on two sides of the Gulf, there were no lands or riches, only wounds and debt.[24]

Anxious to exploit events, Gov. Diego Velázquez immediately took credit for the discovery—it helped that Hernández was dead—and ordered another trip "to trade with the natives for gold, pearls, and precious stones." Critical as ever, Las Casas grumbled about the conquistadores' thin interest in spreading the Gospel. Their driving motivation was always gold, he argued, and the Indians understood that very well. Twenty-eight-year-old Juan de Grijalva was appointed captain general, and the ubiquitous Alaminos pilot, "as there was no other so skilled as he." His lust for loot as yet unfulfilled, Díaz signed on board with his weapons. The two hundred-man expedition departed Cuba on May 1, 1518, in four caravels and reached the Yucatán's Caribbean coast in only two days. They then sailed north, discovering Cozumel and Isla Mujeres in the process. The latter place was named for the many women seen gathered about a stone temple, no doubt begging their gods' intercession against the Spaniards. Grijalva's voyage resembled that of Hernández in several ways—wondrous stone towns were encountered, sharp fights took place (Grijalva lost two front teeth in one of them), water supplies dwindled, and tantalizing gifts of gold artifacts kept the enthusiasm alive. With Alaminos at the helm, the fleet probed the Mexican coast, gingerly entering the Río de Tabasco (now the Grijalva), landing at the Isla de Sacrificios (off the coast of Veracruz)—so named for the bloody temples there—and meeting an emissary from the mighty Aztec ruler Moctezuma, who sent a beautiful maiden to Grijalva. The Spaniards endured pesky northers and contrary Gulf currents on the return voyage, all carefully noted by Alaminos, but finally hailed Cuba in October. In the meantime, Gov. Velázquez had commissioned another voyage, destined to be the most consequential of all. It was commanded by Hernán Cortés.[25]

He was thirty-three years old, lean, fit, and above average height, a pale man among the swarthy but possessed of dark, arresting eyes. He was devout, and

Hernán Cortés. COURTESY LIBRARY OF CONGRESS.

friendly to all classes, but a notorious manipulator and womanizer. Above all he owned an unshakeable courage and a burning thirst for gold. Cortés departed Cuba on February 10, 1519, with eleven ships and six hundred men, many of whom were Hernández or Grijalva veterans. They included Alaminos as a pilot and Díaz among the soldiery. The expedition also brought sixteen horses, non-native to the New World and a significant force multiplier in the battles to come. Years later, Cortés claimed that he told his men, "we shall take vast and wealthy lands, peoples such as have never before been seen, and kingdoms greater than those of our monarchs." This may have been invention informed by hindsight, but the statement's confidence is certainly consistent with Cortés's personality. The fleet made Cozumel within days, and then worked its way up, around, and down the Peninsula, landing at various places. A brisk fight took place at Tabasco, but the heavily armed Spaniards defeated the Indians, smashed their idols, and forcibly converted them to Christianity. Grateful to be spared, the caciques swore fealty to an unknown and distant king and promised much gold. Opposite the Isla de Sacrificios, backgrounded by Mount Orizaba's snowy summit, Cortés established a seaport base that he called La Villa Rica de Vera Cruz (the Rich Town of the True Cross). "We first of all marked out the ground for the church," Díaz recalled, "the market, magazines and other public buildings belonging to a town." Then came the fortress. "Cortes himself put the first hand to it, carried a basket filled with stones and earth on his shoulders and worked at the foundations." Thus began Veracruz.[26]

Cortés enjoyed several advantages in his audacious endeavor. Besides the luxuries of gunpowder, armor, and horses, he quickly learned that the Gulf Coast's Totonac Indians were aggrieved vassals of Moctezuma, who frequently collected their children for sacrificial occasions. The Totonac readily switched their loyalty to the formidable conquistador. And formidable he was, never to be turned by doubt. As he later wrote to King Charles, when he wanted to prevent his men from deserting his inland march, he "decided to beach the ships on the pretext that they were no longer seaworthy." But most significantly, the superstitious Moctezuma was convinced that the white-skinned visitor with a beard and awesome powers—who appeared on an important day in the Aztec spiritual calendar no less—was the long-awaited god Quetzalcoatl. The dramatic and complicated story of how Cortés accomplished the conquest of New Spain (as he called it) is too well-known to need retelling here. Suffice it to say that he succeeded, opening Mexico's incredible wealth to the mother country. Getting that wealth safely away depended on the Gulf of Mexico. And no one knew its powerful currents and moods better than Alaminos.[27]

Stately. So they must have appeared, strung across the northern Gulf in an extended crescent-moon formation, heeled over in the wind, sunlight illuminating their sail stacks. Evoking visions of gold bars and romance, the great and graceful galleons hauled Spain's New World winnings home. They were bigger than caravels—140 feet long, 300-plus tons, multidecked, and four-masted with project-ing beaks, low forecastles, and soaring sterns. Well-armed, well-manned, and fully loaded, their speed was at best eight knots. Alaminos had perfected their route, sailing it himself in 1519 when Cortés ordered him to hurriedly ferry royal gifts from Veracruz to the king. He obeyed, but rather than heading directly east, he recalled his experience and guided the *Santa María de la Concepción* on a roundabout but more efficient route that took advantage of the Loop Current and local winds. Feet astride the quarterdeck, he steered his vessel along the northern continental shelf toward Florida, then due south for Cuba, through the Florida Straits, up the Ba-hama Channel, and across the wide Atlantic atop the Blue God.[28]

By the mid-sixteenth century, Spanish sea power and martial success meant that valuable goods and treasure were coming from Mexico, Peru, and the distant Philippines, while the growing colonies in those places needed steady support and supply. In order to manage this empire, Queen Isabella had established the Casa de Contratación (House of Commerce) in Seville in 1503. The Casa proved to be a well-conceived administrative office, overseeing pilot licensing, tax collection, emi-gration, trade laws, and the *padrón real,* or master chart. This carefully guarded doc-ument was continually updated to keep track of New World discoveries, and copies were provided "only to such persons as the monarch or the *Casa de la Contratación* may order." To keep things flowing as smoothly as possible and insure security, the Casa dictated that all maritime traffic to the New World had to sail in one of two annual fleets. The Tierra Firme (mainland) convoy departed Seville, usually in Au-gust, sailed down to Africa and then across the Atlantic and into the Caribbean, where it called at ports like Cartagena in Colombia and Porto Bello, Panama, to load up on Peruvian silver. The Flota de Nueva España, or New Spain Fleet, sailed in spring and called at Veracruz, where it unloaded supplies and took on pearls, hardwoods, chocolate, and bullion as well as spices, porcelain, lacquerware, and silver from the Orient. The latter goods arrived via the Philippines in Acapulco, Mexico, and were then carried overland in mule trains to Veracruz. After spending weeks at their various ports of call, the two Indies fleets reunited in Havana, and returned to Spain together. Havana was not the architectural wonderland then that it is now, of course. The regular population stood at about a thousand people of all hues, and the town consisted of four dirty streets, some scantling board shacks with thatch roofs, and an adobe church. Things bustled when the fleets were there, however, and a spicy maritime sexual slang emerged to go with the excitement. A prostitute, for example, was called a *fletera,* meaning a "rented ship," and the sex act was termed *singar,* that is, to row with an oar sticking from the stern. Rowdy sailor behavior aside, the fleet system was extraordinarily successful, given the frightening vagaries of weather, corruption, and piracy. During the 1550s alone Spain imported some sixteen thousand pounds of gold and silver worth over two million ducats. Most of it was squandered in European wars.[29]

Sophisticated Havana. This late seventeenth-century engraving captures Havana's wealth and culture at the height of its power and influence. Note the chain blocking the harbor in the background. COURTESY NEW YORK PUBLIC LIBRARY.

All that wealth emboldened pirates and adventurers to trespass the hitherto exclusively Spanish Gulf. French corsairs sacked Havana in 1538 and again in 1555. Eventually a watchtower was erected on one side of its channel and a fortress on the other, with a massive chain stretched between. Campeche was taken in 1561, the pirates surprising the complacent residents in their beds. Before the raiders were driven away, they robbed people, burned houses, and desecrated the church, "making it understood that they were Lutherans and enemies of our holy Catholic faith." Occasionally, sea rovers reconnoitered their targets disguised as merchants. The Crown forbade business to any but Spanish ships, but goods-hungry residents around the basin proved eager to barter. Nor were some colonial officials above participating. Labor remained an urgent need, and when the Englishman John Hawkins entered the Caribbean with five hundred enslaved blacks in the summer of 1568, he was able to sell many of them at several ports before reaching the Yucatán Channel. No Englishman had been so far, but with slaves still to sell, he decided to push his luck and entered the Gulf. Hawkins's fleet was small but strong, consisting of the *Jesus of Lubeck,* the *Minion,* the *Judith* (fifty tons, captained by the redoubtable Francis Drake), and three smaller vessels, all carrying four hundred soldiers and sailors. As if in rebuke, a hurricane slammed the English fleet and battered it for three days. The *Jesus of Lubeck* fared the worst, rolling so terribly that breaking seas filled her hold with live fish. Before the sailors could fully assess the damage, another storm raked them, and Hawkins made the decision to "take our succor" at Veracruz. This was a bold move. Like Havana, Veracruz was a small colonial town, but its harbor was defended by a stone fortress located just offshore, known as San Juan de Ulúa. This citadel held eleven brass cannons and bronze wall-mooring rings that allowed ships protection from both pirates and barreling northers.[30]

When Hawkins's weathered fleet materialized off Veracruz, locals thought it was the long-awaited *flota*. Enjoying the element of surprise, he took the port's inspection officers hostage—they were "greatly dismayed"—and bloodlessly seized the fortress, securing his ships to its walls. Consternation spread ashore, turning into fascinated anticipation the very next day when the *flota*, "13 great ships," appeared at the harbor mouth. Unable to enter because of Hawkins's fleet, the Spanish were forced to bargain. Hawkins was shrewd and sensibly feared treachery but struck a deal, allowing the *flota* into the harbor and the English to hold the castle until they could trade for provisions and repairs. Ten hostages on each side sealed the agreement. Within days, however, Hawkins noticed suspicious activity among the Spaniards—"shifting of weapon from ship to ship" and "passing to and fro of companies of men"—that put him on the alert. The attack came quickly. A trumpet blew and Hawkins declared "all sides set upon us." A vicious harbor fight followed, with the cumbersome ships blundering for advantage and loosing thundering broadsides at one another. Hawkins directed the guns on board the *Jesus of Lubeck*, a beer-filled silver cup in his resolute hand. The Spanish launched a fireship, and Hawkins and his gunners had to scramble onto the *Minion*. By the time the battle ended, the *Minion* and the *Judith* were the only vessels Hawkins had left. His strength was further reduced during the night, when Drake "forsook us in our great misery" and sailed off in the *Judith*. A norther blew the damaged *Minion* well away, and the burdened *flota* let her go. Still in danger, Hawkins wandered the Gulf two weeks until putting ashore somewhere near the Río Grande. This was a godforsaken stretch of coast, and half the men were left to fend for themselves. Hawkins later claimed they "desired" it. Critics said he marooned them. All but a few were doomed to perish after suffering thirst, hunger, fatigue, and Indian harassment. As for Hawkins and the others (including some enslaved people), they recrossed the Atlantic. Many died of hunger and privation before the remnant finally kissed English soil in January 1569.[31]

The difficulties of Hawkins's castaways pale beside those of the Gulf's most extraordinary wanderer, Álvar Núñez Cabeza de Vaca. This decent, modest man's incredible coastal odyssey is one of the great narratives of American history, the equal of Lewis and Clark, and deserves to be better known. But first a little background. Even as the Spanish explored, conquered, and settled the Yucatán and south-central Mexico, they sent ships to the north. Ponce thought Florida an island, but Alaminos suspected it might be a larger land mass and convinced the governor of Jamaica, Francisco de Garay, to investigate. In the spring of 1519, Garay dispatched Alonso Álvarez de Pineda with 270 men and four ships to see. Besides settling the issue of Florida's insularity, Álvarez de Pineda also hoped to discover a viable sea passage to the Pacific. Almost nothing is known of this adventurer beyond his name, but he executed his charge admirably. He took his little squadron from Jamaica through the Yucatán Channel and steered north until sighting the Florida Panhandle. Unfortunately, he could not draw upon the expertise of Alaminos, who was away with Cortés, but he did have pilots on board. They carefully guided the vessels along the shore in both directions, discovering Mobile Bay, experiencing the Mississippi River's prodigious outflow (Álvarez de Pineda named it the Río de Espírito Santo), and spending forty days on the Río Pánuco, careening ships and trading with the natives. By the time Álvarez de Pineda returned to Jamaica in the fall, he had sailed the northern littoral from roughly Tampa to Tampico. His pilots presented the governor a crudely sketched map that proved the Spanish Sea to be a bona fide gulf, nearly surrounded by land. Most important, the captain brought optimistic news—the natives were affectionate, wore gold, and desired "indoctrination to our Holy Catholic Faith." None of which was true.[32]

Four years later, Garay himself landed on the Mexican coast and attempted to establish a settlement on the Pánuco. It was a cursed endeavor. "We have come to the land of misery," one Spaniard wrote, "where there is no order whatsoever but everlasting toil and all the calamities that treat us so cruelly: hunger, the heat, malignant mosquitoes, foul bedbugs, vicious bats, arrows, vines that encircle, mudholes and swamps that swallow us." Furthermore, Cortés would brook no encroachment on what he saw as his turf. Garay suspiciously died just days after sharing a meal with the Mexican conqueror. If another entrada was to take place, it had better not be there.[33]

Pánfilo de Narváez understood this better than anyone. He had tried to overthrow Cortés in 1520, losing an eye and several years' freedom as a result. Las Casas hadn't called him stupid for nothing. Back in Spain, he used his wife's carefully saved gold to cultivate influence. After much lobbying, Charles V appointed him Garay's successor with an allotment abutting that of Cortés at the Pánuco and encompassing the territory to the north and east, all of which the Spanish referred to as Florida. Narváez at once determined to settle his new lands and made for the Indies. Fortunately, the touchy Cortés was in trouble with the Crown and preoccupied trying to restore good graces. Free of that worry and fully provisioned, Narváez's expedition departed Cuba in March of 1528, headed for the Pánuco. It included five ships, four hundred seamen and soldiers, a few friars, ten women, and eighty horses. The chief treasurer and scribe was Cabeza de Vaca, whose unusual name, "Cow's Head," derived from a medieval ancestor who marked a critical mountain pass with a cow skull to guide Spanish forces against the Moors. The treasurer was slender, about thirty-eight years old, and expected to be busier with the pen than the sword. And so he was. The chief pilot, Diego de Miruelo, claimed to know the Gulf well but was no Alaminos, as events quickly proved. Hardly out of port, the fleet ran on shoals, and the crews spent two weeks getting the vessels freed. Afloat again, Miruelo was baffled by the Gulf's currents and winds. He landed them somewhere near Tampa Bay, over a thousand miles east of the intended destination. In an unbelievably foolhardy move, Narváez then divided his force. He ordered the pilots, sailors, and women to continue northward with the ships, where the incompetent Miruelo claimed there was a good anchorage. What the pilot had in mind was Apalachee Bay, which he visited during the Álvarez de Pineda expedition. While the fleet waited there, Narváez would march the men and horses by land. Completely absent from this calculus was any appreciation of Florida geography. Apalachee Bay is almost two hundred miles north of Tampa Bay by sea with the entire Big Bend between, a low-energy coast of marsh, swamps, rivers, shoals, and tangles even in modern times. One of the soldier's wives thought it a bad plan and said so to Narváez's face. She predicted, rightly, that the haughty leader would never see his ships again. Cabeza de Vaca agreed, for which Narváez accused him of cowardice.[34]

So it was that on May 1 Narváez, the soldiers, the friars, and the royal treasurer started their march, each supplied with two pounds of biscuit and half a pound of bacon. The food lasted two weeks. "In all that time," Cabeza wrote, "we saw not an Indian, and found neither village nor house." When they did encounter natives Narváez ordered them seized. Like Ponce, he was a big-boned redhead who loved to play the bully. The unhappy captives showed the Spaniards some maize fields, where they were able to abate their hunger. Once the Indians understood these violent newcomers wanted gold above all else, of which they had none, they ingeniously said there was plenty up north in the Apalachee country. The force was already miles inland, and this worried Cabeza. When he suggested they get closer to the coast, Narváez told him to "go and look for it." Cabeza broke away with forty men to do so and became even more intimately familiar with Florida. His party struggled through deep sands and swamps with "water half way up the leg, treading on oysters, which cut our feet badly." At least one modern environmental historian has highlighted the irony of the Spaniards' difficulties and hunger in a rich estuarine landscape that supported thousands of healthy Indians. The conquistadores certainly knew about shellfish and ate them when they could. But it entailed risk. Cabeza reported two attacks on men harvesting the shallows, and ten were killed. The oysters sliced their feet but did not nourish their bodies. The scouting party concluded its quest at a large bay, not worth the effort to reach.[35]

They rejoined Narváez and continued the epic trek, eventually reaching the Apalachee country. There the badly depleted Spaniards found maize fields, abundant game, and a small village, but no gold. The Indians, whom Cabeza described as "like giants" from a distance, avoided open confrontation. Instead they melted into the piney woods, creeping up occasionally to zing an arrow through an exposed neck. Proceeding westward to no one knew where, the conquistadores passed awestruck through towering longleaf pine savannahs carpeted in grasses and wildflowers, sucking bogs haunted by cottonmouths, and sand-bottomed freshwater lakes choked by storm-felled timber. All the while, men and valuable horses were lost to ambush, disease, hunger, and bad thinking. The Suwannee River, wide, dark, and beautiful, was notable because it was there that an impatient hidalgo spurred his mount into the water, where both promptly drowned. Even Narváez conceded they should find the coast. They blundered into it at Ochlockonee Bay, south and east of present-day Tallahassee. The fleet was nowhere in sight, and the situation was dire.[36]

The Spaniards responded with a burst of spontaneous ingenuity such as the Gulf sometimes demands of those who would survive it. Narváez consulted his officers, and they agreed the only hope was to build boats and cast their fortune upon the water. "This appeared impossible to everyone," Cabeza confessed, "we knew not how to construct, nor were there tools, nor iron, nor forge, nor tow, nor resin, nor rigging; finally no one thing of so many that are necessary; nor any man who had any knowledge of their manufacture." After a sleepless night spent puzzling the problem, a soldier said he could make a bellows with sticks and deerskins and thus work iron with fire. The men gathered any metal they could find—stirrups, spurs, musket fittings, crossbow parts—and these were refashioned into "nails, saws, axes and other tools of which there was much need." They labored from early August to late September, felling trees in high humidity and splitting the trunks for planking, stripping the limbs for masts and oars, sewing their shirts together into crazy patchwork sails, caulking the planks with shredded palmetto fronds, sealing the hulls with pine tar, and killing the horses for food, braiding the manes and tails into serviceable rope, and tanning the hides to make water bottles. At last they surveyed the fruits of their prodigious effort—five heavy thirty-foot boats. It was time to launch. Narváez, Cabeza, and three surviving officers each took command of a boat. The men clambered on board, fifty to a vessel, with hardly room to move. Their freeboard was only nine inches, woefully inadequate in open water. According to Cabeza none of them knew anything about navigation. Ochlockonee Bay is a tight cove opening off Apalachee Bay, the broad sheet of water nestled within the Big Bend. This had been their original destination, but they could not wait to get away. They named it the Bahía de los Caballos, the Bay of Horses.[37]

The forlorn fleet moved westward through coastal shallows until reaching Dog Island opposite Carrabelle on September 27. The men were alternately baked by the autumn sun and drenched by showers before a serious storm forced them ashore at Santa Rosa Island. Local Indians knew about the invaders and attacked them, killing three and slightly wounding Narváez and Cabeza. In the Gulf again, the flotilla reached Mobile Bay in only four days, where it sought shelter on the western shore. Large numbers of Indians approached in canoes, and two men offered to go with them to their village. One was black, the other a Greek. Two Indian hostages were exchanged, and the men climbed into a dugout. When the Indians didn't return them the next day Narváez refused to release his hostages, and the situation deteriorated. The Indians tried to surround the boats with their canoes, and the Spanish were forced to flee without their erstwhile comrades. According to Cabeza, the abandonment profoundly affected the company, and no one talked as the boats dipped and rocked in the swell. So many Spaniards had been lost already to arrows, drowning, fever, and accident. Hope diminished by the day. At the Mississippi River they tried to enter one of the passes. "By no effort could we get there," Cabeza wrote, "so violent was the current on the way, which drove us out, while we contended and strove to gain the land." Their helplessness was compounded when a norther "forced us to sea without our being able to overcome it." The boats were scattered like corks, the men at the brink of collapse. The following day Cabeza sighted Narváez's boat and pulled alongside. After a brief consultation, Narváez said they should make for shore, but Cabeza's crew couldn't keep pace. Exasperated, Narváez abandoned any pretense of military order, telling the treasurer "each should do what he thought best to save his own life." Weeks later, Cabeza would learn the fate of his captain. Somewhere near Matagorda Bay, Narváez became irritable and sent his men ashore for the night. He remained on board the boat anchored just offshore. Wise men do not trifle with the Gulf, and Narváez had done so too many times. Late into the evening a strong norther blew the hapless conquistador over the wide blue horizon and into history. He was never heard from again.[38]

As for Cabeza and his men, chilly November surf slammed their boat ashore at Galveston Island. Indians helped them relaunch, but huge waves inundated the boat, drowning two men. The royal treasurer's maritime adventures were finished, and his odyssey became terrestrial. For eight years he wandered. Indians along the way were both kind and cruel. Some befriended him, others merely tolerated him, while still others enslaved him. But Cabeza never killed any Indians, astonishing for a conquistador, nor did he ever write an unkind thing about them. Together with three surviving companions, including the enigmatic and exotic Moor Estebanico, he traveled as a medicine man, mumbling Catholic prayers and making the sign of the cross over the sick. Incredibly, they got well, and Cabeza's reputation became legendary along the Costa Brava. Rather than follow the shore down into Mexico, where the Indians were known to be difficult, the castaways continued westward, finally meeting a band of Spanish slave raiders in the Mexican state of Sonora. They had almost reached the continent's very ends.[39]

The Spanish made two more concerted attempts to conquer and colonize the Gulf's northern littoral. Hernando de Soto landed at Tampa Bay in 1540 and cut a murderous swath through the southeast before succumbing to fever. His body was deposited in the Father of Waters by his weary veterans. Tristán de Luna landed at Pensacola Bay in 1559 and marched into what is today southern Alabama. A hurricane wrecked his ships, the Indians were hostile, food was scarce, and Luna went mad. The expedition's starving remnants built rafts and floated down the muddy Mobile River to reach the coast. Unbeknownst to Soto and Luna, their entradas' most dramatic consequences were the deadly pathogens left in their wake. During the years that followed, epidemics quietly devastated the sophisticated Mississippian cultures, leaving the northern coast fundamentally changed. As for the Spanish, they realized that Florida was not Mexico. There was no gold. So they decided there would be no more entradas. Instead they limited their efforts to settling New Mexico and founding a few missions on the Florida panhandle. A fortress at St. Augustine was established to guard the Gulf Stream, but overall Ponce's discovery of La Florida seemed singularly unpromising. Strategically, it made more sense to concentrate their efforts to the south. Campeche, Veracruz, and Havana were all prospering, and needed the Crown's attention. Throughout the seventeenth century Dutch and English pirates launched vexing Caribbean incursions and carried out limited raids, but the Gulf of Mexico remained a Spanish Sea. And then came La Salle.

Chapter Three

Colonial Crossroads

Even as commerce abounded in the Gulf Coast, only a careless observer would fail to see evidence of recent wars and fear of war.

Kathleen DuVal,
Independence Lost,
2015

Birchbark. When peeled from the tree and opened out it looks like stylized cardboard, something an art student might fashion into a collage or a beautiful object like a box or a basket. It was the genius of those Indians living around the Great Lakes to stitch this pliable stuff together and insert hickory ribs and white cedar gunwales to make light and efficient yet durable watercraft. Strengthened by cedar planks and sealed by spruce gum, birchbark canoes were anywhere from ten to twenty-four feet long and capable of carrying from one to a dozen men plus cargo. They were vital to the early French explorers and fur traders, and in 1682 a small flotilla of them traversed the North American continent and broached the Spanish Sea.[1]

The leader of this extraordinary expedition was René Robert Cavelier, Sieur de La Salle, a thirty-nine-year-old Frenchman, failed Jesuit, and passionate visionary with a thirst for adventure. His portraits depict a haughty man with an aquiline nose, high forehead, tumbling locks, and a pencil-thin moustache jauntily twisted at the tips. He was beautifully educated and whip-smart, understood larger strategic considerations, and enjoyed bending his considerable energies toward shaping affairs in his sovereign's, and his own, favor. Unfortunately, he suffered occasional debilitating manic-depressive episodes and engaged in frequent spats with rivals. He did not handle men well, preferring to dictate rather than to lead, and he wasn't interested in advice. "No one tells him anything," one of his men later wrote.[2]

In 1667 La Salle sailed for New France, where his brother served as a priest, and spent years around the Great Lakes. Never idle, he founded Fort Frontenac, established Indian alliances, developed a robust fur trade, and chafed at news of Father Jacques Marquette and Louis Joliet's voyage down the great western river, known to the Indians as the Messi-sipi. Marquette and Joliet had only gone as far south as the Arkansas country, but Indians assured them their muddy highway continued all the way to the Gulf. La Salle's active mind was already scheming as to how he could complete what had been started, pushing through and establishing the French in what had theretofore been Spanish territory inviolate. It was a breathtakingly bold ambition to be sure, but the potential benefits were enormous—a base from which to attack the Mexican silver mines and threaten the *flota* on its northern Gulf leg, domination of the continent's fur trade, a still-hoped for link to the Orient, and the opportunity to check the worrisome English on the Eastern Seaboard. King Louis XIV grasped the advantages as well, stating, "Our heart desires nothing more than the exploration of this country, in which it appears that a road may be found for entering Mexico." He gave La Salle a patent to make it so, at the explorer's own expense.[3]

The Sun King said nothing about colonizing the coast, but that was La Salle's ultimate goal. His first step was to reconnoiter the big river, which he called the Colbert (after the French finance minister, Jean-Baptiste Colbert), all the way to its mouth and learn exactly where it disembogued. Available maps and travelers' tales were of little help, being at best muddled conjecture and at worst fantastical romance, and a too-literal dependence on them was to lead to much confusion. The Spanish knew about the Mississippi, which Álvarez de Pineda had named Río de Espírito Santo and Soto's tattered veterans had rafted down to escape certain death, but they had not explored it to any degree. Their maps indicated the river spilling into a large protected bay, or Mar Pequeño. The projecting Birdfoot Delta with its multiple mouths, lagoons, and bayous was yet unknown. To add to the confusion, these maps depicted several other large streams along the northern littoral, among them the Río Escondido (thought to be either the Nueces or the Río Grande), which was much closer to Mexico. Almost from the beginning of his voyage, La Salle was uncertain as to which river he was actually on or what his precise position was at any given time. His only compass broke early, and the seven-inch brass astrolabe he carried was imperfectly calibrated and consistently gave latitude readings that were two degrees—better than 130 miles—in error. He had no way to figure longitude. Puzzling the charts and his measurements after the voyage, La Salle concluded, "all the maps are worthless, or the mouth of the River Colbert is near to Mexico. . . . This Escondido surely is the Mississippi." Of course, the maps were worthless and, combined with La Salle's erroneous computations, doomed his grand colonial enterprise before it properly began.[4]

In early February 1682, La Salle and his reconnaissance party shot out of the Illinois River in their birchbark canoes and onto the mighty Mississippi. Dodging occasional ice chunks, they easily rode the prodigious current southward. They included about fifty people, carefully selected and fully equal to the challenge at hand. Among them were almost two dozen rough French frontiersmen known as *coureurs de bois* (forest runners), and eighteen Mohegan and Abnaki Indians, who brought along a few women and children for cooking and scut work. Père Zénobe Membré was company chaplain, and Henri de Tonti, a colorful and memorable personality, was captain. Tonti, thirty-three at the time, had been reared in northern France, the son of Italian emigrants. He had seen service in both the French army and navy and during the Sicilian Wars lost his right hand in a grenade explosion. Legend asserts that he sawed off the mangled remains himself, which beggars belief, but no one disputes that he wore an iron prosthesis thereafter. This may have been a hook or something plainer. Whatever it was it certainly overawed the Indians. They dubbed him "the iron hand," and he wasn't slow to use it in delicate negotiations, clonking recalcitrant chiefs over the head. He was fearless, tough, resourceful—capable of seemingly anything from building a ship to marching through a blizzard unfazed. Even better for La Salle, he was loyal and avoided gossip and backbiting.[5]

By early March the party had passed Marquette and Jolliet's farthest reach and a month later came to the Birdfoot Delta. Most historians believe La Salle entered Pass a Loutre, where he divided his command to investigate three smaller channels. Membré and Tonti were assigned the middle one and took a few Indians with them. "The water is brackish," Membré later wrote, "after advancing two leagues it became perfectly salt, and advancing on, we discovered the open sea." Tonti, assessing matters with a savvy eye, thought the channel "fine." La Salle, meanwhile, had gone down the right-hand branch with six paddlers, where he soon encountered mud lumps and the expansive Gulf. For a while the men simply wondered at it all—the overarching sky, the muddy water, the treacherous currents, the driftwood, the broad lagoons and tidal flats, the numberless alligators and birds, and the sea's dancing chop beyond. One can imagine La Salle's thoughts, having finally reached his desideratum, but the unruly Gulf was no place for birchbark canoes. Reversing course, the groups reunited just above the passes on April 9, where they nosed their conveyances into the muddy bank and climbed onto the natural levee. There solemn ceremony ensued.[6]

Bronzed and calloused hands seized a likely tree trunk from among the driftwood, expertly shaped and sharpened it with tomahawk and hatchet, and drove it into the muck. A cross and a copper plate engraved with three fleurs-de-lis and some Latin were then mounted upon it, and a lead plaque emblazoned with the arms of Louis XIV was buried at its base. In unison, the men chanted the Te Deum—"We praise thee, o God"—and then, according to Membré, La Salle "took possession of that river, of all rivers that enter it and of all the country watered by them." Three volleys and shouts of "Vive le Roi!," and it was done. In the immortal words of the nineteenth-century American historian Francis Parkman, La Salle had given France "a stupendous accession," stretching from the Mississippi's "frozen northern springs to the sultry borders of the Gulf; from the woody ridges of the Alleghenies to the bare peaks of the Rocky Mountains . . . and all by the virtue of a feeble human voice, inaudible at half a mile."[7]

He returned by sea. On August 1, 1684, a little flotilla of four vessels cast off from the wharves at Rochefort, France, and breasted the gray Atlantic. They included *Le Joly*, a thirty-six-gun warship; *Aimable*, a cargo vessel; *Saint-François*, a small ketch; and *La Belle*, a forty-five-ton bark specially built for brown-water work, fifty-one feet long, fourteen feet in the beam, and drawing only seven feet. On board these vessels were La Salle, sanctioned by a royal commission and backed by significant funds; Henri Joutel, his aide and an old family friend; Taneguy le Gallois de Beaujeu, captain of the *Joly*, a level-headed and competent seaman; three hundred colonists and soldiers, including a few women and children; six priests; cannon; muskets, powder, and lead; hatchets; a blacksmith's forge; four hundred pounds of iron; carpenter's tools; coils of rope; two surgeon's cases and medicines; pigs on the hoof; bread; butter; lard; vinegar; oil; water; wine; religious objects; clothing; crockery; pots; utensils; and trade objects, including colorful beads and bright trinkets. In short, everything La Salle thought he needed to establish a permanent outpost on the Colbert River.[8]

The endeavor was ill-starred from the first. The crossing took two months, many people got sick, and two died. On the northern coast of Saint-Domingue (Haiti), the *Saint-François* lagged and was seized by the Spanish. In port at Petit Goâve, a notorious pirate haven on the island's western side, La Salle descended into a feverish funk, and his men immersed themselves in debauchery, carousing with cutthroats and whores. Several deserted the expedition, opting for a pirate's life. In a quieter setting, perhaps at a little wooden table with some rum and a flickering candle, Beaujeu huddled with two buccaneer captains who knew the Gulf well and listened to their gloomy tales. Only a fool would venture onto the Spanish Sea between September and March because of the frequent northers, they declared. A ship could be driven all the way to the Yucatán. And out of Veracruz was the Armada de Barlovento (Windward Fleet), made up of thirty-gun oared galleys, ever on patrol hunting trespassers. Even if Beaujeu made the northern littoral, they warned, the water was shoal, only ten fathoms ten leagues from shore and "very dangerous." The coast itself wasn't much either—"a flat country where the river covers everything when it overflows." Finally, assuming the French got ashore, they would face a thieving lot of hostile, root-grubbing Indians. None of this was communicable to the depressed La Salle.[9]

Whatever reservations Beaujeu may have nurtured, he wasn't especially worried for himself. The *Joly* was only supposed to help deliver the colonists and then return to France. But he was concerned about the others, who were poorly prepared for what they would likely face. The soldiers were second-rate conscripts, and the colonists included men who had exaggerated their artisanal skills. Worse still, some pirates had signed on board at Petit Goâve, who true to form proved ungovernable. At Cuba's western end, on the eve of its entry into the Gulf, the expedition suffered another setback that proved its luck had not changed. A freak gust drove the *Belle* and the *Aimable* into one another, snarling their rigging, and in the confusion the *Belle* lost one of her anchors. It was therefore with great foreboding that Beaujeu finally led the flotilla around Cabo San Antonio on December 18. It did not help his anxiety that La Salle was secretive about exactly where they were going. Standing on the *Aimable*'s canted deck, Joutel was worried too. "We had among us no one who was knowledgeable of this sea and had navigated it," he later wrote in his journal.[10]

Happily, the crossing was relatively uneventful, and on New Year's Day 1685 a sailor in the *Belle*'s crow's nest sighted land. They were somewhat west of the Mississippi's mouth, but La Salle, in his geographical ignorance, ordered them still farther westward. There were no prominent landmarks ashore to guide them. "All that could be taken notice of was a great quantity of wood," Joutel wrote. And so the vessels jogged off and on all the way to Matagorda Bay in what is now Texas. On February 18 the *Belle* and *Aimable* attempted to thread through Pass Cavallo, between Matagorda Island and Peninsula, while the *Joly* stood offshore. According to Joutel, the pilots sounded the pass in small boats where they found eight feet of water and put out stakes "that the vessels might come safe in. All things seem'd to promise a happy event." It was not to be. At this critical juncture, rather than supervise the passage, La Salle went ashore to chase some Indians who had kidnapped a shore party. According to Joutel, they "heard a cannon shot, the noise whereof struck such a dread among the savages, that they all fell flat upon the ground; but Monsieur de la Sale and we were too sensible it was a signal that our ship was aground, which was confirmed by seeing them furl their sails." *Aimable* was hard on the sand Gulfside, exposed to pounding surf. It was a heartbreaking turn, worsened when heavy waves smashed the stern open overnight and, Joutel mourned, "carried out" much of the cargo.[11]

During the following months, La Salle's brash effort continued to unravel. Beaujeu and the *Joly* departed on March 12, and a number of colonists went along, convinced that the enterprise was doomed. Determined to salvage matters, La Salle anchored the *Belle* in Matagorda Bay and established a little settlement on Garcitas Creek, some thirty miles north. The site was slightly elevated and timbered but unreachable by the *Belle*, forcing the soldiers and colonists to make exhausting small boat trips back and forth. Karankawa Indians haunted their flanks, sometimes attempting to trade, at others loosing arrows or kidnapping the unwary. Colonists died almost daily, not only by Indian attack but also from poison fruit or snakebite or drowning. La Salle meanwhile seemed possessed by a strange restlessness and spent weeks traipsing up and down the coast, seeking his Colbert River or perhaps a trail to Mexico. Never communicative, he became increasingly bellicose and paranoid, blaming everything on others.[12]

The ends were ugly. Her captain dead, the *Belle* was under the command of the mate, an irresponsible drunkard who got into the wine and stayed there. In February 1686, out of water and desperate, the skeleton crew attempted to cross the bay for Garcitas Creek and was caught by a fierce norther. Not knowing how to handle the ship, they threw out their last anchor. It wasn't enough. The *Belle* was driven south dragging her hook and plowed into Matagorda Peninsula stern first. Still some three hundred yards from dry ground, several men drowned when their makeshift raft broke apart heading for shore. The others, including the boozy mate, managed to reach the peninsula, but were stranded three months until a storm tossed an abandoned canoe at their feet. This gave them means to get to Garcitas Creek. The colony beset on all sides, La Salle set off with Joutel and the remaining able-bodied men in an attempt to reach New France and send aid. His party was fed up with him, however, and laid an ambush, drilling him through the head with a heavy musket ball. He "dropp'd down dead on the spot," Joutel wrote, "without speaking one word." As for the pitiful settlers left behind at Garcitas Creek, they died, or were taken by Indians and ransomed to the Spanish.[13]

News of La Salle's venture had already reached Madrid. Indian tales, Caribbean gossip, and the confessions of La Salle deserters captured by the Armada de Barlovento, all made their way back to the court of King Carlos II. Spain's long neglect of the northern Gulf suddenly became a crisis. The nation's efforts had been concentrated in Cuba and Mexico for over a century, and royal officials' geographical knowledge of Florida was as abysmal as La Salle's. Frightened into action, they declared, "His majesty's prompt action is required to pluck out the thorn that has been thrust into America's heart." Finding it was the first step, and that would be no easy task. Numerous attempts were made, but the most consequential was that of Captains Martín de Rivas and Pedro de Iriarte, who in December 1686 sailed out of Veracruz harbor in a pair of specially designed vessels. The Spanish may not have known much about the northern littoral, but they knew enough to send boats suited to shoal waters. To that end, they demonstrated the kind of maritime innovation that has defined the Gulf's residents throughout history. They built two shallow-draft *piraguas,* each roughly sixty feet long and equipped with twenty oars, a single sail, six bronze swivel guns, a few canoes, and plentiful provisions. On board were 130 soldiers, some Indians, and an English pilot who had sailed the Costa Brava. The *Nuestra Señora del Rosario* and the *Nuestra Señora de la Esperanza,* or the Two Ladies as they were called, slowly worked their way up the coast, alternately battered by northers and becalmed, forcing the crews to labor at their oars to inch the vessels onward. On April 4, 1687, they crawled into Matagorda Bay and beheld the forlorn remains of the *Belle.* There was no doubt that she had been a French ship—the three faded fleurs-de-lis on her stern proved that—and she had clearly suffered a disaster. The Spaniards could not know that La Salle was already dead, and his colony nearly so, but they guessed as much and proceeded east, taking coordinates, noting the Mississippi's mouth, sounding harbors like Galveston, Mobile, and Pensacola, and improving their charts at every stage. By July they had coasted down Florida and through the Keys, stopped at Havana, crossed the Yucatán

Channel, and wended their way past Tabasco all the way back to Veracruz. It was an astonishing achievement, the first recorded circumnavigation of the Gulf. Rivas disembarked with logs, reports, and meticulously drawn maps, and took them to the viceroy in Mexico City. Fortunately he could report that La Salle appeared to have failed, but others might not.[14]

Spain continued to reconnoiter the northern shore into the 1690s, and everyone who made the voyage agreed that Pensacola harbor was the best, sheltered and deep. Its lack of large feeder rivers did not matter, since the Spanish preferred good anchorages from which their ships could dominate the Gulf. The French, by contrast, sought river systems that provided canoe access throughout the watersheds. The English too were interested in the basin, especially the Mississippi, where they planned to establish a colony of French Huguenots who had fled their Catholic homeland. By placing them in America, English promoters hoped to solve two problems at once—an overabundance of foreign refugees and France's Mississippi Valley ambitions. Expansionist plans by the three powers were further encouraged after the Treaty of Ryswick was signed in 1697, ending King William's War. With peace in Europe, and Spain conceding France's right to Saint-Domingue, conditions were favorable. And so it was that in October of 1698, all three powers launched Gulf voyages.[15]

The Spanish, with the advantage of proximity and their recent surveys quickly reached Pensacola where they hastily erected a pine-log fort and a gaggle of buildings. The French were next, led by Pierre Le Moyne d'Iberville, his charge to find and settle the Mississippi's mouth. Born in 1661, Iberville was no moody La Salle but rather a gifted administrator and navigator who had earned laurels by defeating the British at Hudson Bay in 1697. He was ably assisted by his much younger brother, Jean-Baptiste Le Moyne de Bienville, who was adept at Indian languages and blessed with a strong constitution. The LeMoyne brothers left France in two thirty-gun frigates with a pair of smaller, coastal craft lashed alongside and reached Saint-Domingue without incident. There they linked with the fifty-gun *François*, under the authority of the Marquis de Châteaumorand. Unlike La Salle, Iberville knew that he needed help if he was to locate the Mississippi. Thus it was that he met forty-six-year-old Laurens de Graff, the notorious buccaneer better known as Lorencillo. As a swashbuckling young man during the 1670s and '80s Lorencillo had made himself the scourge of the Caribbean and Gulf. No less authority than Henry Morgan, governor of Jamaica and a former freebooter himself, called Lorencillo "a great and mischievous pirate." His achievements included sacking the cities of Veracruz and Campeche, defeating a rival captain in a beach duel, and capturing numerous Spanish ships laden with fantastic treasure. The Spanish called him El Griffe, a term connoting mixed racial heritage, but there is no definitive proof of that. Witnesses agreed that he was physically imposing and blond with a bushy moustache. Despite his fighting skills and fearsome demeanor, he was generally merciful to captives and seemed to bear the Spanish no personal animosity.[16]

When Iberville and Châteaumorand learned that Lorencillo had spent time at Pensacola Bay and was familiar with the environs, they asked him to join their enterprise. The buccaneer was surely pleased to be offered legitimate employ, and he cheerfully signed on board. Pirates hadn't done La Salle's expedition any good, however, and in reporting the controversial hire to France, the marquis attempted to justify the move: "M. de Graff, captain of a light frigate, has embarked with me. He has been a great help; more than a perfectly good sailor, he knows all the rocks and all the ports of that country there, toward the entry of the [Gulf of] Mexico, having sailed that course all of his life."[17]

At last, on January 14, 1699, the enlarged French fleet rounded Cuba's eastern coast and hove into the Gulf. Here Lorencillo proved his worth, guiding them past rocky Cabo San Antonio, reassuring them that the Gulf Stream's strong tug was not to be feared and that their course was good. Ten days later, through pesky winter fogs and rains, they made land a bit east of modern Destin. In a description that still holds true today, Iberville noted large "sand dunes . . . very white," backed by soaring pines. Because of shallow inshore waters, Iberville kept his larger vessels well off, using the lighter craft to coast west, taking soundings as they went. On January 26, the vessels reached Pensacola, and discerned the hardscrabble Spanish outpost. When several officials came out to investigate the Gallic interlopers, they immediately recognized Lorencillo and must have feared the worst. Iberville and the marquis quickly reassured them, sending a basket of fine wines ashore and claiming they were merely searching for Canadian deserters. Doubtless the Spanish recognized a potential colonization effort if not a piratical enterprise and politely suggested the French keep moving. The irascible Lorencillo took advantage of the negotiations to brazenly sound the harbor entrance from a small boat and was brusquely ordered to desist by Spanish guards.[18]

The following day the fleet anchored off Mobile Bay, its broad, sheltered expanse no doubt inviting through chilly mist and mizzle. The French lingered several days and tentatively explored the environs. Included in the shore parties was a master ship's carpenter named André Pénicaut. While tramping the elongated island at the bay's mouth he got the shock of his life. "When we disembarked," he wrote, "we became terrified upon finding such a prodigious number of human skeletons that they formed a mountain, there were so many of them." Iberville promptly dubbed the place Massacre Island, though it was later learned the bones were those of Indians lost to an epidemic. Understandably, the earliest colonists were unsettled by this name, and the island was soon called Dauphin instead. Unable to find a good anchorage (that would come later), the French sailed west again, eventually coming to the mouth of the Mississippi. For his part, Lorencillo was growing bored. He told his employers he had no particular knowledge of the unglamorous river mouth. And so, on February 19, when Châteaumorand took the *François* back to Saint-Domingue, Lorencillo eagerly went along. The old pirate's obligations had been well met. As for Iberville, he explored the mouth and expressed exasperation with his vessels' inadequacies. "It is a jolly business indeed," he grumbled, "to explore the seacoasts with longboats that are not big enough to keep the sea either under sail or at anchor and are too big to approach a flat coast, on which they run aground and touch bottom half a league off shore." Soon enough he would apply the lesson to a practical remedy.[19]

While the Spanish established Texas missions and fortified Pensacola, and the French probed the Trembling Coast, the English finally arrived in a single ten-gun corvette. The *Carolina Galley*, commanded by Lewis Banks, was scouting a likely site for the Huguenots, when her pilot found the Mississippi River and guided the vessel upstream. Despite previous Spanish and French explorations, she was the first sailing ship to actually head upriver, but the powerful current and shifting winds made the going slow and difficult. By mid-September 1699 the ship was anchored in a tight hairpin bend, eighty miles above the mouth, when Bienville and some men in two bark canoes glided into view. Both parties were equally startled, and in one of Gulf history's most audacious moments, Bienville clambered on board the corvette and informed Banks that the French king possessed the river and "if he did not leave, he would force him to." It seems too incredible to be true—Bienville, barely nineteen years old, backed by flimsy canoes and fowling pieces, ordering an English captain to take his ten-gun, square-rigged ship and leave or else. For his part, Banks believed Bienville's claim that there was a large settlement upstream—there wasn't yet—and besides, he feared the Le Moynes. Iberville had captured him at Hudson Bay and didn't think much of his courage or ability then. He mumbled a few threats but complied. And at that, the Mississippi Valley's short-term destiny was settled—it would be French—and the bend acquired an enduring moniker—the Détour à l'Anglais, or English Turn.[20]

Because the Birdfoot Delta was unsuitable to permanent settlement, Iberville established an interim outpost to the east on Biloxi Bay. This would allow the French to protect the Mississippi until they could find a better locale. In 1702 a bluff overlooking the Mobile River, twenty-seven miles north of Mobile Bay, was chosen to be the capital, and a fort and town were constructed there, initially called Fort Louis de La Louisiane, subsequently Mobile. Named for a local Indian tribe, the new capital enjoyed a number of advantages—good elevation that promised not to flood (unfortunately, it did!), an extensive river system navigable by canoe, easy access downstream to the resource-rich bay, and a fine natural anchorage off the southeastern end of Dauphin Island. After persistent floods and a pirate attack at Port Dauphin, Mobile was moved south to its present site in 1711. Seven years later Bienville founded New Orleans at an old Indian portage on the Mississippi, and in 1723 the capital was transferred there. During the next several decades French ambitions made progress despite storm, disease, Indian attack, and irregular supply.

Priests were anxious about the *coureurs de bois* cohabiting with Indian women and urged the import of marriageable young white women of good morals. Known as the *Pélican* girls (for one of the ships on which they arrived) and the casket girls (for the small chests that held their clothing), they were landed at Dauphin Island and subsequently taken to Mobile, Biloxi, and later New Orleans. Pénicaut approvingly witnessed the first girls' arrival in 1704 and wrote that they "were quite well behaved, and so had no trouble finding husbands." Other shipments brought former prostitutes and petty criminals, so-called correction girls. Arriving underfed and with shaved heads, they too made marriages. Mobile and New Orleans slowly grew, forts were established on interior rivers, good Indian alliances and trade established, and British expansion challenged. Relations with nearby Spanish Pensacola were neighborly, except during the brief War of the Quadruple Alliance (1718) when Bienville captured it and then lost it again. Overall, the French appeared firmly ensconced.[21]

Fascinating insight into early New Orleans is provided by the journal of Marc-Antoine Caillot, a lowly clerk for the Company of the Indies who was resident there between 1729 and 1731. At that time there were about fifteen hundred inhabitants protected from the river by an earthen levee with a well-worn promenade atop. "First you see the parish church, built of wood and bricked inside," Caillot wrote of his new home. "The company headquarters are also very well built, both grand and spacious, consisting of an apartment for the director, a very proper main hall for hearings, and three offices joining it." There were fourteen streets lined by houses, most "built of wood" but others brick plastered with lime "made with shells." These were modest one-story affairs but featured *galeries,* or porches, and gardens out back growing beans, squash, peppers, asparagus, cucumbers, lettuce, and tomatoes. There were two hospitals with twenty-five beds, a convent for the Ursuline nuns, a prison, and a factory "that never produces any genuine pottery." Lastly, sitting in the river were two brigantines, "used to bring in supplies and merchandise to Mobile," an "eighteen-oar galley," three flatboats, and as many as fifty pirogues.[22]

As those vessels demonstrated, French Louisiana's very existence depended upon a variety of watercraft, some European, others inventive solutions to local conditions. Foremost of all was the humble canoe, occasionally birchbark but usually a dugout, which carried *coureurs de bois* and Indians across lakes and bays and up and down rivers and streams for hundreds of miles. Indomitable men thought nothing of paddling from Canada to New Orleans, trading and hunting all the way. Canoes were sometimes called *pirogues* by the French, but the term also referred to a flat-bottomed wooden craft with tapered ends to which a rudder and even a small sail could be added. These remarkable little boats could be paddled, rowed, or even poled in shallow water. There are numerous official references to *bateaux* and *chaloupes* (shallops), connoting a variety of small, flat-bottomed, or shallow-draft

View of the Camp of the Concession of Monseigneur Law at Nouveau Biloxy, Coast of Louisiana, Jean Baptiste Michel Le Bouteux, 1720. This richly detailed French sketch includes several matters of maritime interest. In the foreground, carpenters fashion a *chaloupe,* oars rest on a tree stump, and the artist depicts himself in a small flat-bottomed *bateau* tied to a piling. The cylindrical fountain at left is a barrel well. COURTESY NEWBERRY LIBRARY, CHICAGO.

open boats. Shortly after directing Bienville to establish Mobile, Iberville recalled his frustrations with the longboats at the Mississippi's mouth and ordered his shipwrights to build a special forty-five-ton vessel "designed so that it will navigate on the sea as well as on the rivers, and will draw no more than 4 ½ feet when loaded." This was essentially a big box with high sides, pointed prow, oars, and a mast that could manage both chop and calm streams. Just a few years later, a Mobile shipwright signed a contract to build a flat-bottomed *bateau* of thirty tons that drew less than a foot when empty. Its intended use was as a "transport boat" between Gulf and river town. Moving up the scale, *felouques* were lateen-rigged boats with oars, something like the little galley that Caillot described, which plied the Mississippi Sound, the deeper streams, and coastal lakes and bays. Brigantines were reliable larger vessels. These were trim, two-masted sailing ships of upward to a hundred tons. Their foremast was square rigged, and the mainmast included a fore-and-aft yard that facilitated tricky inshore or riverine maneuver. As Caillot indicated, brigantines regularly sailed between New Orleans and Mobile. Additionally they could easily cross the Gulf to Havana or Veracruz when relations with the Spanish were friendly. Bigger ships included frigates, transports, and even ships of the line, large warships holding as many as seventy-four guns. None of the latter could do much inshore. Typically they anchored someplace like Port Dauphin, and their people and cargo were lightered upstream in *bateaux*.[23]

Much of the northern Gulf Coast's distinctive culture so celebrated by modern tourist bureaus, writers, filmmakers, and musicians has its roots in the French period. To begin with, the colony's diverse human palette provided the vivacious ingredients necessary for something entirely new. Besides French and Canadians, the early colony included Indians, African blacks (most but not all of them enslaved), Swiss and Germans who settled on a Mississippi River stretch that came to be known as the German Coast, and Acadians (Nova Scotians exiled by the British after 1755), and eventually there was blending among the groups. The terms "Creole" and "Cajun" are often used loosely to describe Louisiana's peoples and culture. Originally a Creole simply designated a child born in the colony to European parents, but the word gradually took on more complex meanings, and in both New Orleans and Mobile was applied to lighter-skinned free blacks born of European fathers and black mothers. It has since come to be applied to Gulf Coast architecture (the Creole cottage), music, and food. Creole cottages were practical and comfortable houses that evolved out of a blending of French, Canadian, and West Indian building traditions. A typical example consisted of two to four or more massed rooms (no hallways) with a steeply pitched gable roof parallel to the street, interior chimneys, two front doors, a full-length porch and in rural examples wraparound galleries. Cantilevered wooden balconies were common on two-story residential and commercial buildings. Bienville's personal quarters had one overlooking the Mobile River, the colony's earliest recorded example of such a delightful appurtenance. But it is in cooking that Creole culture is most manifest and exciting. Rice was an early Louisiana product and became an essential element in many dishes, none more so than the zesty concoction known as gumbo. The word is African, denoting the okra that is fundamental to any authentic preparation of the delicious stuff. Slaves were already familiar with rice, which they had used in their stews, and in the New World this tradition merged with those of Indian soups and European bouillabaisse in contributing to the result. Beginning with a dark, rich simmering roux of fat and flour, colonial cooks added onions, peppers, tomatoes, garlic, basil, bay leaves, oyster stock, shrimp, fish, crab, sausage (a German contribution), chicken, anything, and everything to the pot. The variations and varieties were and are endless, particular to the cook, and everyone has their favorite.[24]

In contrast to the Creoles, the Cajuns are descendants of the early Acadian exiles. Historically they settled south Louisiana's bayou country, generally avoiding the older French and Canadian populations, whom they considered arrogant. Virulently anti-British and staunchly Catholic, they developed an animated and rich culture that included swamp lore, cooking, music (zydeco), and pronounced French and later English dialects. The Cajuns were and are expert fishermen, thoroughly familiar with swamp, marsh, and Gulf. During the eighteenth century they were noted for salting and drying their fish on little wooden grills, which preserved it and enabled them to sell it long distance or keep it for later. Despite the Cajuns' clannishness, they enjoyed considerable understanding and tolerance from French Louisiana's last governor, Charles Philippe Aubry, who promised them land. Spanish failure to keep that commitment would soon bear bitter fruit.[25]

Easily French Louisiana's most famous, recognizable, and enduring tradition is Mardi Gras, or Fat Tuesday, celebrated each year before Ash Wednesday and the Lenten season. During his winter 1699 lower-Mississippi explorations, Iberville was inspired by the calendar and named one of the many streams he encountered Mardi Gras Bayou. Whether or not any formal observation or revelry went with it is unknown, but four years later the holiday was at least minimally observed at Mobile. In his memoir Caillot describes participating in New Orleans's 1730 festivities. Together with almost a dozen colonists, including a violin player and a man with an oboe, he attended a gathering on the nearby Bayou St. John. Everyone was masked and elaborately costumed, some "in red clothing, as Amazons, others in clothes trimmed with braid, others as women." Caillot was among the latter, gotten up as a "shepardess in white." His ruse was so convincing, including "plumped up" breasts and beauty marks, that several men in the party could not "extinguish their fires, which were lit very hotly." Eye-catching costumes, masks, cross-dressing, music, drinking, and sexual excitement have been Mardi Gras constants ever since.[26]

The Gulf basin's uneasy political equilibrium was rudely upended by the Seven Years' War (1756–63). The conflict began with clashes between the French, the

British, Indians, and frontiersmen in the Ohio River Valley, and quickly expanded into an epic global struggle involving multiple antagonists. Throughout the conflict, France and England were the principal opponents, however, and the fate of Gulf Coast communities hung in the balance. The British enjoyed early successes in both Canada and the Caribbean, and the Royal Navy effectively corked the Gulf, seizing French supply vessels. New Orleans and Mobile residents felt the pinch and, though they saw no fighting, worried about the outcome. As if things weren't unsettled and confusing enough, in a surprising twist, Spain's new Bourbon king, Carlos III, signed a family compact allying his country with France and in January 1762 declared war on Britain.[27]

It was a stupid decision. Attracted by Cuba's immense wealth, British planners launched an attack on Havana that very year. A fleet of fifty warships and over a hundred transports carrying fifteen thousand sailors, soldiers, and enslaved laborers left Spithead, England, in March, crossed the Atlantic, threaded the Bahama Channel, and loomed off Havana in late May, completely surprising the Spanish. The "Key to the Indies" had grown considerably since its early days as a conquistador seat. It contained at least fifty thousand people, a quarter of them enslaved, and boasted picturesque streetscapes of soaring churches, imposing government buildings, graceful plazas, elegant homes, squalid hovels, raucous bars, and busy brothels. Above all, Havana was a maritime city, a fact reinforced by the ubiquitous nasty smell of *tasajo*, the salted beef constantly in preparation for departing ships' crews and passengers. Furthermore, traffic in slaves, sugar, tobacco, silver, and rum was continually moving on a dizzying variety of vessels large and small. Spain certainly realized the city's value and provided formidable defenses—Morro Castle at the harbor's eastern entrance and Punta Castle at its western. When the British ships appeared, officials barred the pass with a great boom chain and felt secure. In yet another advantage for them, their local forces were augmented by the veteran crews of the Havana Squadron, trapped in port by the sudden invasion. Recognizing the futility of a direct naval assault, the British commander, George Keppel, the Third Earl of Albemarle, landed soldiers both to the east and west of the city and placed artillery on the surrounding hills which, incredibly, had been left undefended. Albemarle, thirty-eight, was an experienced military and political hand, having served as an ensign in the Coldstream Guards and worked his way up through the ranks. He was handsome, proudly sporting a dark pompadour, and paid close attention to his wardrobe. No less authority than Gen. James Wolfe, killed on the Plains of Abraham (Battle of Quebec) in 1759, had earlier known Albemarle and called him "one of those showy men" who preferred palaces and courts to the regimental tent. During the Battle of Culloden, Albemarle was an aide to the Duke of Cumberland and was nearly killed by a rampaging Highlander who mistook him in all his frippery for the commander. Nonetheless, Albemarle was fully cognizant of his challenge at Havana and equal to it. He knew that he had at best a few

A Plan of the Siege of the Havana, Drawn by an Officer, 15th August 1762.
COURTESY LIBRARY OF CONGRESS.

short weeks in which to reduce the Gulf bastion before yellow fever and autumn hurricanes decimated his forces.[28]

The two sides banged away at each other through the summer. The British ships got as close to the Morro and the Punta as they dared and fired rippling broadsides, but their heavy iron cannonballs had almost no effect on the thick stone walls. One witness referred to the bombardments as "a very grand affair to be seen," but that was from a relatively safe, shady perch outside the city. In town, shells exploded in the narrow streets, slinging mud, holing roofs, and knocking down walls. Officials hastily evacuated as many noncombatants as they could. Civilian authorities ordered those remaining to kill all the dogs and throw them into the sea lest the animals scavenge valuable food. During the course of the siege, the Spaniards counted over twenty-four thousand "bombas" thrown their way, mostly at the Morro, where nine hundred slaves were killed while attempting repairs. Conditions weren't much better at the British batteries afloat and ashore. On the big warships' lower decks, nine-and-a-half-foot-long thirty-two-pounder guns (so called for the weight of the projectile) belched fire and smoke recoiling violently against the restraining tackle. After every shot, barefooted, shirtless seamen reeking of sweat and powder scrambled to reload. Enemy hits showered them with deadly splinters and upended the heavy gun tubes. In the hills outside town, British artillerists labored in scorching sun and high humidity, watching as their shots plunged toward the beleaguered garrison. Because the Morro was surrounded by rocky ground and a ditch, the British could not dig effective siege works, and so they launched sharp and sometimes costly infantry raids instead. By midsummer, just as Albemarle had feared, fever was taking a steady toll among his men. Fortunately for him, timely reinforcements arrived, and at last the Morro's walls were blasted open and the citadel overthrown. The city capitulated days later. It was a glorious prize, but it cost at least five thousand men to take it, and thousands more would die of disease during the ten months' occupation.[29]

Albemarle proved himself an agreeable conqueror, visiting prominent residents' homes and inviting the *señoras* and *señoritas* to fancy dress balls—showy man indeed. The British officers scowled at the open race mixing that distinguished Cuban society, though the common sailors and soldiers happily bedded prostitutes of all colors. Local street urchins had a little fun too, selling the unsuspecting occupiers nausea-inducing tropical treats. Meanwhile, trade boomed, as did farming and manufacturing. Decades later, a Spanish planter-journalist wrote that Havana's surrender "gave [the city] life in two ways: the first was the considerable riches, with the great proportion of Negroes, machinery, and textiles which one year of commerce with Great Britain rained down; the second was demonstrating to our court [in Spain] the importance of this city and calling forth all its attention and care."[30]

In truth, Spain would have traded any city in the basin—certainly wretched Veracruz with its pestilence—and all of mosquito-plagued Florida for the Key to the Indies. In the end, it regained Havana, kept Veracruz, won New Orleans, and gave up Florida. The treaties that ended the Seven Years' War dramatically reshuffled the Gulf's political balance. France was the big loser, ceding Canada, Louisiana (New Orleans, Biloxi, and Mobile), and the entire Mississippi River Valley. The French thorn was gone. To Carlos III's great relief, Spain not only regained Havana but was given Louisiana west of the Mississippi and New Orleans east of it, in Gallic gratitude for the belated alliance. Excluding the latter city, the British took

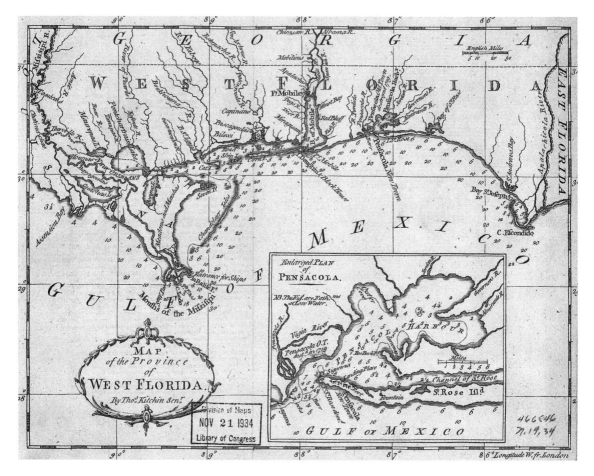

Map of the Province of West Florida, Thomas Kitchin, 1781. The inset shows
Pensacola, the colony's capital. COURTESY LIBRARY OF CONGRESS.

Louisiana east of the Mississippi, which gave them Baton Rouge and Mobile, and
Florida, giving them St. Augustine and Pensacola. Bienville, eighty-six and living
in honorable French retirement, begged the foreign minister not to forsake his beloved Louisiana, where so much had been sacrificed and hard-won. To no avail. It
was done. A regiment of Highlanders occupied Mobile on October 20, 1763, pipes
skirling among the old fort's crumbling ramparts and the town's rotting wooden
galleries. The Francophone Indians camped there were no happier than Bienville
would have been to see kilts and red coats and demanded expensive gifts to assuage
their feelings. Doling out trinkets and surveying his new domain, the British commandant grumbled that it more resembled "a little hamlet formed of Negro huts,
rather than a well-peopled town in Canada." It was considered part of British West
Florida now, a new colony stretching between the Mississippi and Apalachicola
rivers.[31]

For his part, Carlos III was determined to revenge Spain's loss. Anticipating another conflict, he significantly increased military spending at home and in the colonies. The Spanish naval treasury alone consumed seven hundred thousand pesos annually in ship construction and harbor improvements, and thousands of men were recruited. Havana played an important role. Not least among its assets were its bustling shipyards, which went into high gear. The Real Arsenal, or royal shipyard, was located outside the city walls to the southwest. It was the largest such establishment in the world and included construction ways, hoists, open beach for careening vessels, offices, storerooms, workshops, a saw mill, and lumber sheds. Hundreds of skilled and unskilled men worked there and in the twenty years following the war turned out eight ships of the line, two frigates, three brigantines, a dozen schooners, two barges, and two pontoons. The grandest production of all was the 136-gun *Santísima Trinidad,* completed in 1769. Building this behemoth required three thousand trees, and when finished she measured over two hundred feet in length and fifty feet in the beam, drew better than twenty-six feet, and displaced almost five thousand tons. Not surprisingly, given her bulk, the ship sailed poorly, and in light breezes was dead weight. Her primary value however, at least immediately after her construction, was as a forceful statement of Spanish will and ability.[32]

Despite some tension and complaint, most of the Gulf's postwar power transfers went relatively smoothly. Not so at New Orleans. That city's three thousand residents were outraged at the news that they were now to be Spanish subjects. Creoles and Cajuns held mass meetings accompanied by much fulmination and vowed never to lower the French flag. When the incoming Spanish governor arrived in the fall of 1768—backed by only seventy-five soldiers—he didn't help the situation by shunning local society and refusing to honor French promises to the Cajuns. Predictably, he was threatened and then kicked out of town. Humiliated, he established himself at La Balize, the pilot's station at the river mouth, and awaited instructions. Carlos III would have rather concentrated resources on his beloved Havana than a problematical, rebellious swamp settlement. But if he didn't do something the aggressive British would, and then they would be hard on New Spain's border. If nothing else, New Orleans promised to provide a critical buffer. And so he released one of his "wild geese."[33]

Alejandro O'Reilly was not a man to be trifled with. He was one of several native Irishmen who had gone abroad to fight for Catholic countries—hence the colorful designation—with the ultimate hope of wresting his homeland out of British hands. He had attached himself to Spain and seen much service, suffering a leg wound that left him with a permanent limp. Tall, thin, and grave, he was a superb administrator and planner. He listened carefully, kept his own counsel, and acted decisively. On July 6, 1768, grim-faced and determined, O'Reilly left Havana for New Orleans with twenty-seven ships, twenty-seven hundred soldiers (including dragoons, Catalan riflemen, and free black militia), and fifty pieces of field artillery. The fleet must have presented an imposing sight as it glided between the Morro and the Punta, white sails bellying. It consisted of three frigates, two brigs (similar to brigantines but fully square rigged), several sloops and schooners, transports, and a hospital ship. O'Reilly was as good a seaman as a soldier, and carefully orchestrated the potentially perilous Gulf crossing. The vessels sailed in parallel lines with the hospital ship nestled between. Individual ships were less than a thousand feet apart. O'Reilly led the van in one of the frigates. An anonymous report by someone on the flagship tracked their progress. One day out of Havana, winds were from the east-northeast and the ships shortened sail so the slower vessels wouldn't fall behind. "Night fell on this day," the scribe wrote, "with the horizon filled with clouds, and we lit a convoy lamp so that all might follow us." The next day, having passed the Tortugas, O'Reilly ordered soundings, and the leadsman "found 82 fathoms of water with a bottom of fine sand and little brown shells." On the twelfth the weather was changeable, "with waves and lightening which bothered us considerably." Four days later, calculating that they were east and on parallel with the Birdfoot Delta, O'Reilly ordered the fleet due west across roughening seas. On the twentieth the vessels at last reached the river, anchored in forty fathoms, and requested a pilot. In the interim O'Reilly sent an emissary up to the city with a letter. It was brief but courteous in the flowery style of the time, announcing Spain's intention of taking possession. O'Reilly helpfully suggested the French governor initiate "measures which on this occasion you may consider to be necessary for the best service to both Majesties and in keeping with the object of my commission."[34]

Defiance evaporated. The French governor assured cooperation, and the uprising's ringleaders feared for their lives. Anxiety was heightened by the fact that it took the fleet almost a month to work its way upriver. Once arrived, the very elements seemed to conspire in Gallic solidarity, and a terrific thunderstorm lashed the fleet. One of the frigates nearly capsized—men on a nearby ship saw her entire keel swing into view before she righted—other ships lost sails and spars. A small vessel was hit by lightning and burst into flames. Two men were killed and eight hurt. Other ships cut cables, and panicked men jumped overboard. Two drowned. In the peculiar way of the Gulf's summer tempests, skies quickly cleared, and O'Reilly lost no time in marching his men ashore while the sailors cheered the Spanish king from their undamaged spars. According to witnesses, the population stood in stunned silence while the occupying troops formed an open square. Rain-washed pastel skies backgrounded the scene as sunshine sparkled off gun barrels, bayonets, gold buttons, and red cockades. Muskets were lifted to shoulders, and three salutes fired, answered by the flagship's big guns. O'Reilly issued a blanket pardon for the common folk—one witness said it "allowed persons of this city to breathe again"— but arrested twelve of the rebellion's most prominent figures. These men were tried, and six of them were shot, earning the Spanish commander the sobriquet "Bloody

A View of Pensacola in West Florida, by George Gauld, 1770. The vessels represent those Gauld used for his survey work. The insubstantial town hugs the shore.
COURTESY LIBRARY OF CONGRESS.

O'Reilly." As for the others, they swore the mandated oath to Carlos III and went about their business.[35]

Uneasy Gulf neighbors, Spain and England both expected and wanted another war. Or at least the governments did. The people, as ever, stood to lose the most. If and when it came, accurate maps and nautical charts would be critically important. The British were keenly aware of their ignorance of the Gulf and quickly made provision to rectify it. Enter George Gauld, a Scotsman born in 1732 and educated in mathematics, Greek, natural history, French, and Spanish, with a gift for drawing and cartography. At the age of twenty-five, Gauld joined the Royal Navy as a schoolmaster, his charge to instruct boisterous teenage midshipmen in the navigational arts. By 1764, his abilities had attracted attention, and he was sent to Florida as a naval cartographer, with orders to chart the region's rivers, harbors, and coasts. Gauld enjoyed considerable advantages over his earlier brethren in the craft. To begin with, thanks to the invention of the marine chronometer, it was now possible to accurately calculate longitude at sea. Gauld was thoroughly familiar with this revolutionary invention, having sailed with the inventor's son for its sea trials, and he employed one for his Gulf work. The navy also made sure he had plenty of other equipment and supplies at his disposal—two theodolites, half a dozen surveying chains, a reflecting telescope, a quadrant, reams of paper, vellum, lead pencils, and a pantograph for copying drawings at a different scale.[36]

Gauld plied his trade until the eve of the American Revolution, mostly working the eastern half of the basin. He began with a thorough examination of Pensacola Bay, and the resulting chart is a beautiful thing to behold—neat, precise, with shoals and depths indicated, as well as accurate topographic features. The colony's governor was so impressed that he praised Gauld to his superiors as "a treasure not to be lost." The day-to-day work was anything but glamorous, however. Gauld ventured forth for weeks at a time on his support vessel, usually a small, light-draft schooner. This craft would anchor someplace convenient, while Gauld worked the coastlines on board a smaller pinnace with about a dozen jack-tars, their compensation for the tedious duty a double rum ration. Soundings and coordinates were constantly taken, and Gauld painstakingly refined his maps at night on board ship and in his Pensacola abode between trips. The work was not without its trials—from broken equipment to barreling northers and suspicious Spaniards—but Gauld persisted, continually working the coast in either direction to Galveston Bay and all the way down to the Dry Tortugas. As each one of his elegant charts was finished, brushed off, rolled, and dispatched to London, the Gulf became incrementally less a mystery.[37]

War—fire, sword, and the widow's veil—came again in 1775 when the American colonies broke into open revolt against England. In 1777, the French joined the Americans, and two years later Spain followed suit. The British knew they were vulnerable on the Gulf, even though the Floridas were decidedly not in rebellion. Since their takeover, a succession of governors had struggled to make these holdings profitable, with naval stores, deerskins, indigo, cattle, and corn the most common products. One administrator even experimented with grape vines and imported Jamaican pearl divers, with dismal success. Such economic disappointments aside, these colonies were strategically important and had to be defended. Prospects were not good. The overall British general there described Mobile's Fort Charlotte as "a scene of ruin and desolation," and refused to allot more than three hundred men to it. Pensacola, the capital, was a little better off, with a few earthen redoubts, brick Fort George on nearby Gage's Hill, and roughly two thousand men—a mix of regulars, German mercenaries, black militia, and Indians. Three small vessels, the largest with only twenty guns, guarded the harbor. More ships would have guaranteed the Floridas' safety, but the Royal Navy was badly stretched. Conversely, the Spanish were well aware of their enemy's weaknesses and enjoyed a significant strategic advantage with New Orleans, and more important, Havana, close enough to launch attacks.[38]

And attack they did, led by Louisiana's thirty-three-year-old governor Don Bernardo de Gálvez. Despite his youth Gálvez enjoyed formidable political influence because his uncle was on the Council of the Indies, the Spanish king's administrative body for the region. There could be no doubt of his suitability to his post, however.

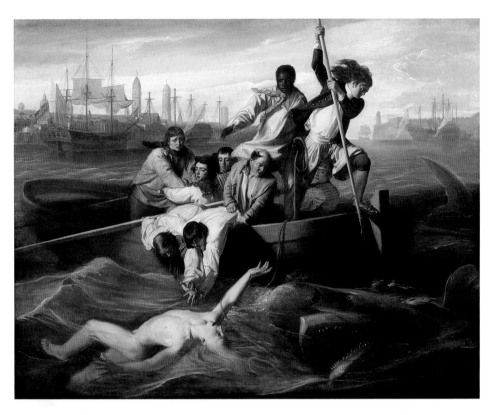

Watson and the Shark, John Singleton Copley, 1778. This dramatic canvas depicts an English sailor's rescue from a tiger shark in Havana Harbor. The victim, Brook Watson, survived and was later lord mayor of London. The painting created a public sensation when first displayed; it was the *Jaws* of its day. COURTESY NATIONAL GALLERY OF ART.

A Norther in the Gulf of Mexico, Thomas Moran, 1884. Northers loom almost as large in Gulf literature as hurricanes. Mariners feared them both. COURTESY STARK MUSEUM OF ART, ORANGE, TEXAS.

A Mayan coastal village from a Chitchén Itzá temple mural. Pictured are distinctive dugout canoes, houses, and marine abundance. Note the fish basket visible through the doorway of the house center left. COURTESY CARNEGIE INSTITUTION FOR SCIENCE.

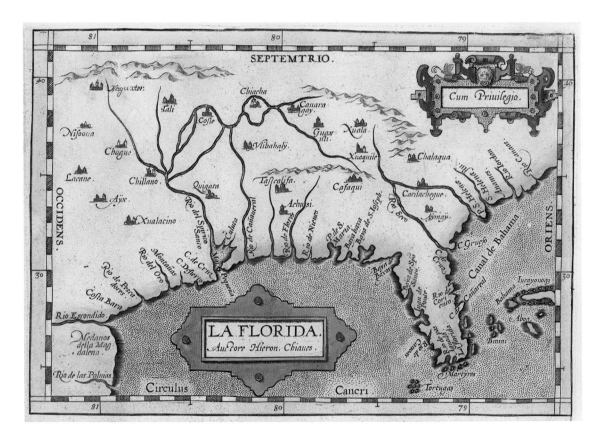

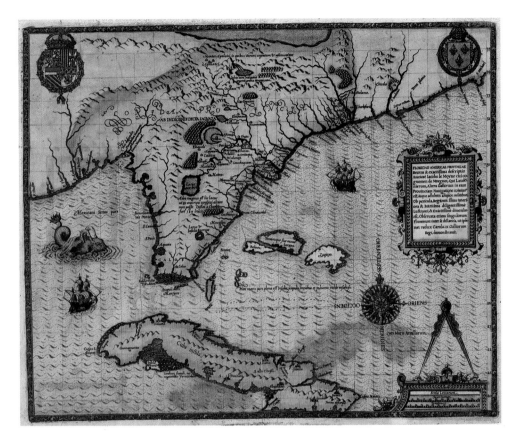

Floridae Americae Provinciae, Jacques Le Moyne de Morgues, 1591. Le Moyne visited Florida, but his map was crude, only roughly illustrating the Keys, the Big Bend, and numerous small bays. The fanciful sea monster probably represents a whale. Knowledge of the Gulf would come slowly. COURTESY LIBRARY OF CONGRESS.

FACING *La Florida,* Hieronymo Chiaves, 1584. Chiaves was royal cosmographer at the Casa de Contratación in Seville. He took information from earlier *entradas* for this map, notable for its representation of rivers and interior Indian villages. The Río Espíritu Santo emptying into the Mar Pequeño, or "Little Sea," is the Mississippi River. There was still no knowledge of the Birdfoot Delta. COURTESY UNIVERSITY OF SOUTH ALABAMA CENTER FOR ARCHAEOLOGICAL STUDIES.

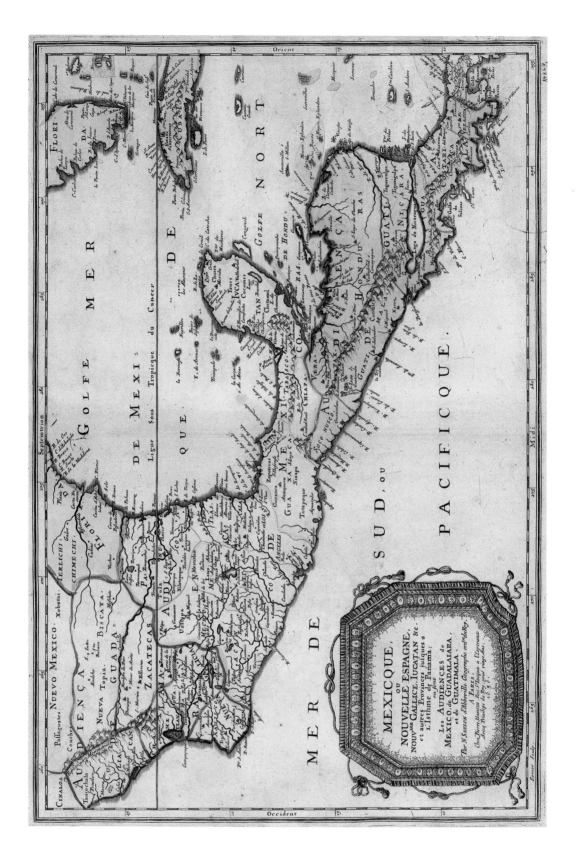

MEXICQUE,
OU
NOUVELLE ESPAGNE,
NOUV.le GALLICE, IUCATAN &c.
et autres Provinces iusques a
L'Isthme de Panama;
ou sont
Les AUDIENCES de
MEXICO, de GUADALAIARA,
et de GUATIMALA.
A PARIS
Chez Pierre Mariette, Rue S.t Iacques a l'Esperance
Avec Privilege du Roy pour vingt ans.
Par N. Sanson d'Abbeville, Geographe ord.re du Roy.

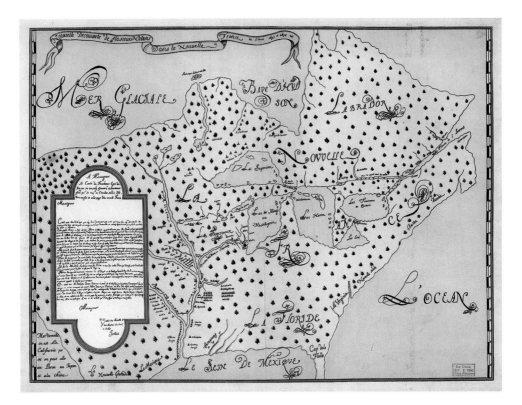

Joliet's map, 1674. Marquette and Joliet traveled the Mississippi River as far south as its juncture with the Arkansas, but Indians assured them it continued all the way to the Gulf. Joliet's portrayal of the river so close to Mexico would have fatal consequences for La Salle.
COURTESY LIBRARY OF CONGRESS.

FACING *Mexicque, ou Nouvelle Espagne, Nouvlle Gallice, Iucatan &c. et autres provinces jusques a l'Isthme de Panama, ou sont les Audiences de Mexico, de Guadalaiara, et de Guatimala,* Nicolas Sanson, 1656. This handsome French chart depicts Central America, Mexico, and portions of Florida and Cuba, collectively known as the Spanish Main. There are relatively few Spanish maps from this period, as the crown forbade their publication.
COURTESY LIBRARY OF CONGRESS.

Carte general de toute la côte de la Louisianne jusqu'a la Baye St. Bernard, coste de la Floride, Baye de la Mobille, Be. de Pansacole, Baye de St. Ioseph, St. Marc des Apalaches. dans l'Amerique septentle, Alexandre de Batz, 1747. At the time this beautiful map was drawn, the boundary between French Louisiana and Spanish Florida was the Perdido River, just east of Mobile Bay. COURTESY LIBRARY OF CONGRESS.

FACING *Carte d'une partie des côtes de la Floride et de la Louisiane, contenant le cours du Missisipi, depuis ses embouchures jusqu'à la Rivière Rouge, l'entrée de la Mobile et les Baies de Pensacola, de Ste. Rose et de S. Joseph,* 1778. When the French Département de la Marine ordered this map, the north central Gulf Coast was part of British West Florida. COURTESY LIBRARY OF CONGRESS.

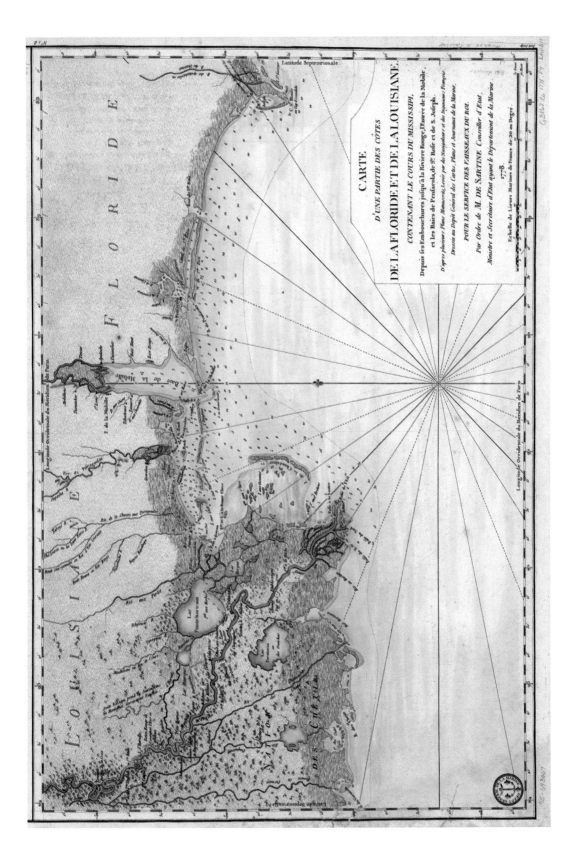

CARTE
D'UNE PARTIE DES CÔTES
DE LA FLORIDE ET DE LA LOUISIANE.
CONTENANT LE COURS DU MISSISSIPI,
Depuis ses Embouchures jusqu'à la Rivière Rouge; l'Entrée de la Mobile,
et les Baies de Pensacola, de S.ᵗ Rose et de S. Joseph.
D'après plusieurs Plans Manuscrits, Levés par les Navigateurs et les Ingenieurs François.
Dressée au Depôt Général des Cartes, Plans et Journaux de la Marine.
POUR LE SERVICE DES VAISSEAUX DU ROI.
Par Ordre de M. DE SARTINE Conseiller d'Etat
Ministre et Secretaire d'Etat ayant le Département de la Marine.
1778.
Echelle de Lieues Marines de France de 20 au Degré.

A new map of North America, shewing the advantages obtain'd therein to England by the peace, London Royal Magazine, May 1763. The thirteen colonies are shown in pink and Britain's gains after the Seven Years' War in tan. Spain's winnings are in green. France was forced from the continent. COURTESY LIBRARY OF CONGRESS.

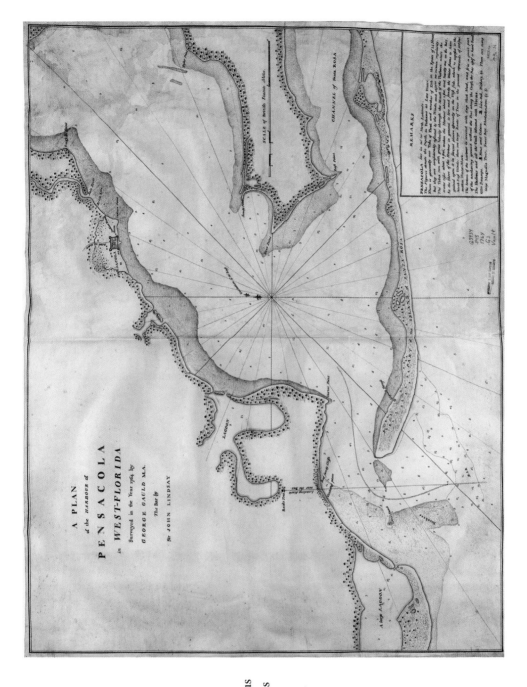

A Plan of the Harbour of Pensacola in West-Florida, George Gauld, 1764. Gauld's meticulous artistry is evident in this superb map. Note the "signal house" on Santa Rosa Island. COURTESY LIBRARY OF CONGRESS.

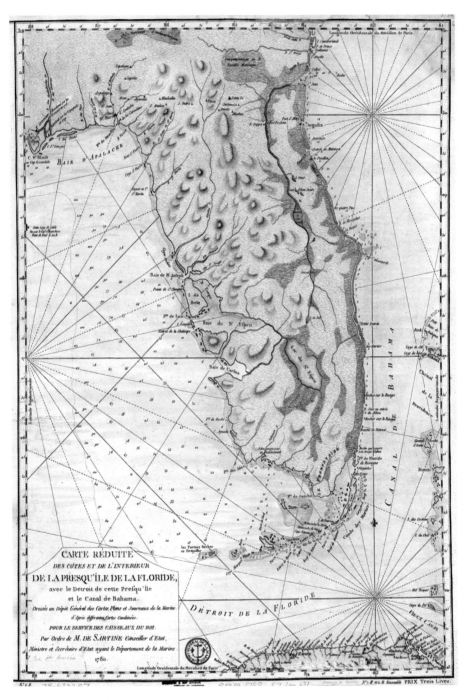

Carte réduite des côtes et de l'interieur de la presqu' île de la Floride, avec le Détroit de cette presqu' île et le Canal de Bahama. Dressée au Dépôt général des cartes, plans, et journaux de la marine, d'après differentes cartes combinées. Pour le service des vaisseaux du roi, 1780. When this map was drawn, Florida was changing from British to Spanish control, but France remained vitally interested. Soundings are indicated to the edge of the continental shelf, and the treacherous Keys are carefully depicted. COURTESY LIBRARY OF CONGRESS.

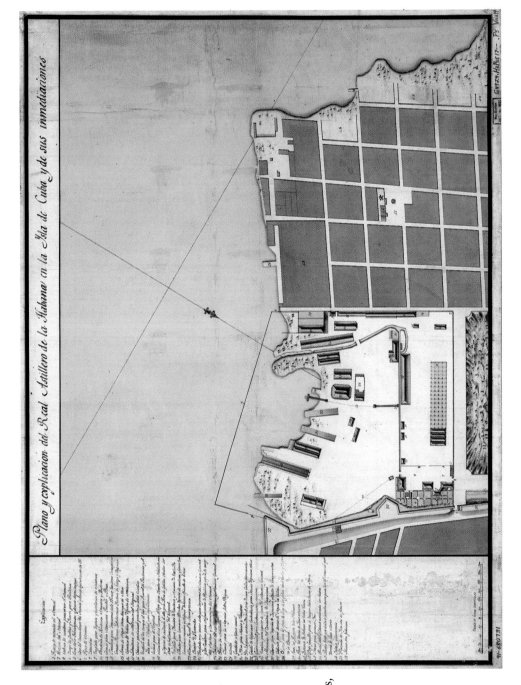

Plano y explicación del Real Astillero de la Habana en la ysla de Cuba y de sus inmediaciones, 1700s. This detailed plan of the Royal Shipyard at Havana shows a protective wall, gates, drainage ditches, a parade ground, piers, ways, a guardhouse, the commandant's quarters, administrative offices, ironworks, carpenters' shop, engineers' offices, a hospital pharmacy, ovens, kitchens, stables, and carriage sheds. COURTESY LIBRARY OF CONGRESS.

Vüe perspective de la Ville de St. François de Campeche dans l'Amerique Septentrionalle, no date. This handsome engraving was originally published in a seventeenth-century Dutch gazetteer. A century later it was hand colored by the French artist Jean François Daumont. The ships in the foreground are not fighting. The vessel at right is hove down for breaming, or burning and scraping off marine growth, while the ship center left fires a salute. Unlike so many other cities around the Gulf rim, Campeche never changed hands until Mexico achieved independence in 1821. COURTESY LIBRARY OF CONGRESS.

Louisiana, Mathew Carey, 1814. Only two years beyond statehood, Louisiana was loosely governed and thinly policed. Its multitudinous bays, bayous, and lakes swarmed with pirates, privateers, and slave runners. COURTESY LIBRARY OF CONGRESS.

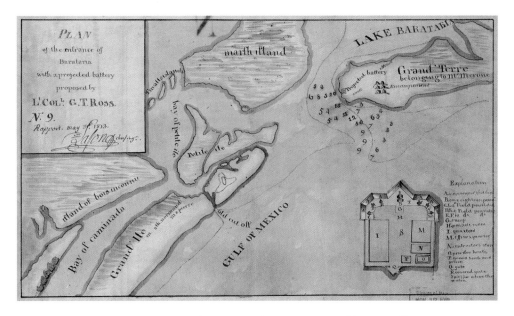

Plan of the entrance of Barataria with a projected battery proposed by Lt. Coll. G.T. Ross. No. 9 Rapport May 3d 1813. The battery, proposed for the west end of Grand Terre, was never built. Instead, Barataria remained a pirate haven for almost two more years. COURTESY LIBRARY OF CONGRESS.

Battle of Lake Borgne, Thomas L. Hornbrook, c. 1838. Five American gunboats, derisively known as "Jeffs," are overwhelmed by British launches on December 14, 1814. One observer thought the gunboats' boarding nets looked like spider webs. COURTESY HISTORIC NEW ORLEANS COLLECTION.

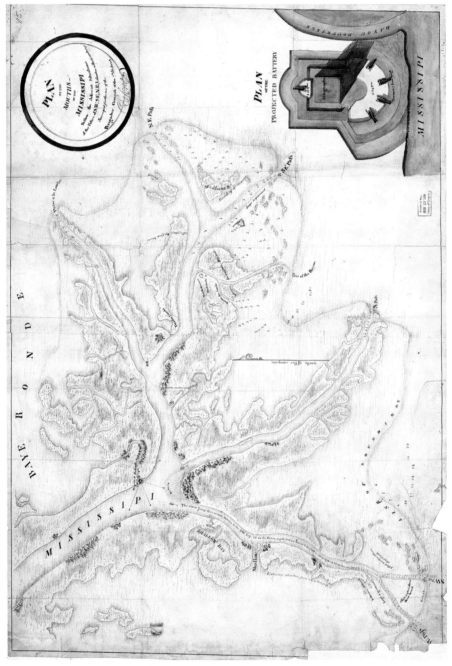

Plan of the mouths of the Mississipi to shew the different situations of the passes of S.W, S.E., N.E., Latoutre & their soundings, Lafon Barthélemy, 1813. The Birdfoot Delta's complexity for navigation and defense is evident in this detailed map.
COURTESY LIBRARY OF CONGRESS.

Die Balize an der Mündung des Missisippi, Paul Wilhelm, Duke of Wüttemberg, 1828–1835. This German print shows the pilot station at La Balize near the Mississippi's Southeast Pass. Among the watercraft are a beached barge, a steamer, what appears to be a brig, and a longboat, at least one of whose oarsmen is black. COURTESY NEW YORK PUBLIC LIBRARY.

Veracruz, 1869. The harbor fortress San Juan de Ulúa and the city's wall helped defend residents through numerous wars across the centuries. Entertainment was not neglected, as the bullring to the right attests. COURTESY NEW YORK PUBLIC LIBRARY.

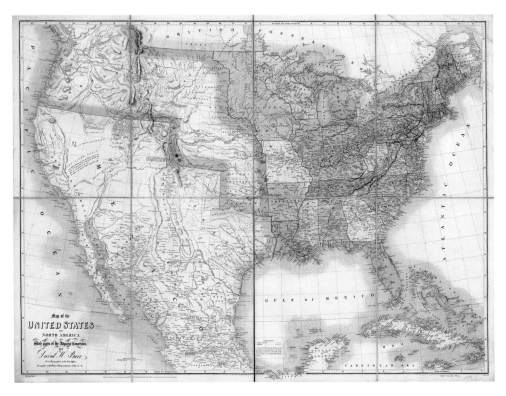

Map of the United States of North America with parts of the adjacent countries, David H. Burr, 1839. Texas and the West belonged to Mexico but beckoned to proponents of "manifest destiny." COURTESY LIBRARY OF CONGRESS.

Landing of the American forces under Genl. Scott, at Vera Cruz, March 9th, 1847, N. Currier. The specially designed surfboats are in the foreground. In reality, the ships would have been much farther offshore. COURTESY LIBRARY OF CONGRESS.

He had been in the military since the age of sixteen, fought Apaches in the American Southwest, and bore several wounds. Unlike O'Reilly, his knowledge of maritime matters was limited, but he was confident, determined, and disinclined to let bureaucratic or petty obstacles deter him. War declared, Gálvez fielded a small force and quickly ousted the British from their thinly held Mississippi River posts at Manchac, Baton Rouge, and Natchez. Mobile was next, besieged in January 1780 by a fleet of warships including shallow-draft row galleys and a polyglot mix of Spanish regulars, Indians, and black troops. Fort Charlotte's garrison sensibly surrendered after a two-week siege, with the loss of only one killed.[39]

Pensacola was a tougher nut, and in October of that year Gálvez set out from Havana with a large invasion fleet. It consisted of fifteen ships under the command of Admiral Don José Solano y Bote Carrasco y Díaz and fifty transports carrying four thousand soldiers. By mid-month the fleet was abreast of the Dry Tortugas headed north. Then disaster struck. A strong hurricane boiled out of the Caribbean, through the Yucatán Channel and into the ships. For eighty hellish hours the storm rocked the fleet, scattering vessels all over the Gulf from Mobile to the Yucatán. Solano's flagship was dismasted, another sunk, and dozens more badly damaged. Half the troops drowned. Solano managed to gather the remnants off Dauphin Island, but after polling his captains decided they were so depleted that the attack had to be canceled. The ships limped back into Havana where the city's legendary dockyard workers went into action to make repairs, and the cautious War Council met to determine a future course. Hurricanes had altered the Gulf's human history more than once before, but Gálvez argued that this one was only a setback and they should proceed. "Have we so little constancy and tenacity that a single tropical storm suffices to halt us?" he passionately asked. The War Council took comfort in the probability that British forces too had been battered and were unlikely to attack Havana. The Council approved another expedition. Solano's Storm, as it came to be called, would be a costly delay, but it would not alter Spanish plans to take Pensacola.[40]

Pensacola's critical moment came the following spring. Gálvez assembled another invasion force of more than twenty vessels, including French ships of the line, and seven thousand men, among them troops of the Regiment of Hibernia, a veritable flock of wild geese. Launching from both Havana and New Orleans, this force converged at Pensacola and quickly compelled the outgunned British ships to retreat. The Spaniards then landed and methodically went about digging their siege works. Robert Farmar, a British officer on the scene, recorded the enemy's progress in his journal. On Saturday, March 17, he wrote: "The enemy attempted to land . . . under cover of two row galleys. The number of Indians in sight prevented them. Three row galleys kept within the bar sounding the channel, at which the Fort at the Clifts fired some shot." Several days later Gálvez sent a surrender demand, which was haughtily refused. Doubtless most redcoats realized they could not hold out long. Throughout the siege, the Spanish enjoyed continual reinforcement, while the British could only watch. On April 19, Farmar described one such occasion, when seven more enemy ships arrived. The hostile vessels "fired several guns, hoisted signals, and stood off and on." On the twenty-fourth news of Lord Cornwallis's victory at Guilford Courthouse, South Carolina, lifted the redcoats' spirits, and they celebrated with an artillery salute, or as Farmar called it a "feu de joy" (fire of joy). But that was only a temporary interlude. Gálvez kept up the pressure, inching his works forward and raining cannonballs onto the enemy. At last, on May 8 at 9 A.M., a lucky shot "was thrown in at the door of the magazine," and there was a terrific explosion. According to Farmar, forty sailors and forty-five soldiers were killed outright, with many more grievously wounded. Demoralized, outnumbered, and without hope of reinforcement, the British capitulated two days later. They were sent to Havana and then New York on Spanish ships. Through persistence, spirit, and enterprise, Gálvez had entirely swept the British from the Gulf Coast. In recognition of his extraordinary services, King Carlos III designated him governor and captain general of Louisiana and West Florida, made him a count, and gave him a coat of arms emblazoned with a brig and the proud motto "Yo Solo" (I alone).[41]

It had been almost exactly a hundred years since La Salle's brazen trespass, but at last, after so much shifting fortune and struggle, the Gulf of Mexico was once again a Spanish Sea. Unfortunately there were clouds—a new nation to the north whose grasping people had little truck with kings, restless Latin American colonies to the south, unruly Indians on the Costa Brava, unscrupulous wreckers in the Keys, and fearless privateers under strange flags, boldly asserting themselves everywhere on the heaving blue-green waters.

Chapter Four

Pirates' Haunt

Over all the modern Gulf there still hangs the uneasy shadow | Harnett T. Kane,
of the pirates and their treasure chests. | *The Bayous of Louisiana*, 1944

On an early January morning in 1813, *La Dorada* lay alongside the Campeche wharf, taking on logwood, cochineal (a red dye), and indigo. Chained below deck, seventy-seven miserable enslaved people awaited a voyage to none of them knew where. If they were lucky it would be short and smooth. Fully loaded at last and ready for sea, the little ship departed without ceremony. Frayed hawsers were cast off weathered pilings, the helmsman took the worn wheel, and small boats pulled the vessel away from the wharf. The Spanish crew called her a *bergantín hermafrodita,* or hermaphrodite brig. As the unusual designation implies, the vessel was two things at once—brig and schooner. Her foremast was square rigged like a brig, with ratlines, yard arms, and blocks, but her mainmast carried a big triangular sail typical of a schooner, easily raised or lowered from the deck and thus manageable by fewer men. Hermaphrodite brigs were the perfect craft for Gulf merchant voyages—small, fast, and safe on the open sea and highly maneuverable among islands or in rivers. *La Dorada* was typical of the type: sixty-nine tons, sixty-two feet long, eighteen in the beam, and drawing a mere fathom. As far as her owner was concerned, the vessel was a reliable workboat, a moneymaker, with no need of fancy appurtenances like dazzling brightwork or a painted figurehead. Only her name, meaning "the Golden One," was extravagant.[1]

Several miles out, a fast schooner intercepted the vessel and ordered her to heave to. The rude interloper was no warship bristling with cannon, but her two small deck guns and fierce ruffians at the rails brandishing muskets, pistols, and cutlasses were more than enough to convince the terrified Spaniards to obey. The desperadoes were led by Jean Jannet, a seasoned pirate sometimes called Janny or Jannetty. With practiced confidence he steered his schooner alongside *La Dorada* and seized her without a fight. Fortunately for the Spaniards, Janny wasn't the murderous variety of sea dog. He was only interested in the cargo and, after assessing the spoils, agreeably landed the crew near town. He then pointed *La Dorada* north and set her sails. Days later the captured craft and her schooner escort approached the Trembling Coast and made a beeline for Barataria Bay, located just west of the Mississippi's mouth and sheltered from the Gulf by two barrier islands, Grand Isle and Grand Terre. Janny's vessels easily negotiated the tricky pass between them and came to anchor in their lee. That they had been observed was evidenced when several small boats approached and hailed. These contained eager agents for back-country planters and New Orleans merchants, and within hours Janny had sold the slaves for $170 each and netted $5,000 for the other cargo. For no more trouble than a quick trip across the Gulf on board a seaworthy schooner, he and his men were much richer, and their leader, or "bos" or *patrón*, had gained a smart new vessel for his fleet.[2]

Freebooters had long been active in the Gulf, of course, going all the way back to John Hawkins and the Yucatán logwood cutters-cum-buccaneers. But during the late eighteenth and early nineteenth centuries a series of political, diplomatic, and economic developments created a more highly favorable environment than ever for them. To begin with, the Spanish Empire was weak and incapable of patrolling so vast a domain. King Carlos IV assumed the throne in 1788 and during his twenty-year reign proved indifferent to matters of state. Indecisive, mentally unbalanced, and obsessed with tinkering and hunting, he left the tedium and stress of rule to his wife and her lover, Prime Minister Manuel Godoy. Unfortunately for Spain, Carlos's ascension coincided with the French Revolution, when a king with a cool head, firm hand, and steady heart was most wanted. He was appalled by the violence, exacerbated when revolutionaries executed his cousin, Louis XVI, and declared war on Spain. Then came Napoleon, and the unwise Godoy masterminded a treaty to ally Spain with France and end the war. Instead of peace, the result was that Britain declared war in 1796.[3]

All of this European maneuvering resulted in a cascade of consequential treaties, laws, and land transfers in the Gulf. By the Treaty of San Lorenzo in 1795, Spain relinquished its exclusive right to navigation on the Mississippi and ceded to the infant United States its claims east of the river (New Orleans excepted) and north of the thirty-first parallel. Congress designated this area the Mississippi Territory three years later. At the time there was some uncertainty about where the thirty-first parallel actually lay, but a 1799 survey by the Pennsylvania clockmaker's son, astronomer Andrew Ellicott, settled the matter. Through careful measurements and calculations in primitive conditions, Ellicott traced the line just north of Mobile and Pensacola. This left those ports in Spanish hands, to the dissatisfaction of back-country Americans dependent on them.

Spain further shrank its colonial holdings in the fall of 1800 when it secretly signed the Treaty of San Ildefonso with Napoleon's France, ceding all of Louisiana, including New Orleans, on condition that the colony not be resold. As far as Carlos

IV and Godoy were concerned, Louisiana's greatest value had been as a buffer between New Spain and the growing United States, but its relinquishment alleviated numerous strains. To begin with, France would assume the expenses and responsibility for the unwieldy colony, while preserving it as a check on American designs. Secondly, the *flota* had made its final voyage in 1778, and consistent with Spain's long-standing Gulf-centric focus, New Orleans no longer mattered as a protective bastion on its northern flank. To be sure, tempting goods aplenty still traversed the Gulf, but in single vessels rather than convoys since the Spanish Crown now endorsed free trade among its colonies. Lastly, other than its government, Louisiana was still only nominally Spanish. The bulk of the population remained French in its composition, culture, and sympathies. As for Napoleon's plans, he envisioned turning the colony into an agricultural cornucopia to support his Caribbean ambitions. News of the transfer badly shook President Thomas Jefferson. "There is on the globe one single spot, the possessor of which is our natural and habitual enemy," he declared. "It is New Orleans, through which the produce of three-fifths of our territory must pass to market, and from its fertility it will ere long yield more than half of our whole produce and contain more than half of our inhabitants. France placing herself in that door assumes to us the attitude of defiance." He needn't have worried. Rebellious Caribbean slaves absorbed Bonaparte's attentions and, combined with yellow fever, decimated the army sent to crush them. With Saint-Domingue lost, Louisiana no longer suited French ends. In an astonishing turn and in defiance of his promises to Spain, Napoleon abruptly sold all of it to the United States—the mighty Mississippi and its tributaries, the vast cypress swamps, the grassy prairies, and the majestic forests. "I renounce Louisiana," he declared. "It is not only New Orleans that I cede; it is the whole colony, without reserve. I know the price of what I abandon." Indeed he did, and at the stroke of a pen the United States doubled in size.[4]

As Americans began to filter into this Eden, they brought a slave economy with them, buttressed by Eli Whitney's newfangled invention, the cotton gin. To the southwest in lower Louisiana, the enslaved people cleared swamps, planted waving fields of cane, and erected sugar mills belching black smoke. Their numbers were nowhere near large enough to satisfy the burgeoning American labor demands. Planters agitated for African blacks but were thwarted when Congress banned the international slave trade in 1808. Not surprisingly, ongoing political disruption led to a way around the problem. The same year as the ban, Napoleon deposed Ferdinand VII, Carlos's son and the new Spanish king, and installed his own brother Joseph on the throne. Indignation was widespread both on the Iberian Peninsula and in the colonies. At home, a determined and violent opposition erupted, supported by Britain. In the colonies, formal separation beckoned as an attractive alternative, one grasped by the city of Cartagena (now part of Colombia) in 1811 when it declared its independence and began issuing letters of marque to privateers. Letters of marque were official documents authorizing sea captains to capture ships and goods belonging to any nation that was at war with the issuing nation. Dozens of adventurers leapt at the opportunity. Officially, Spanish shipping was their prey, but in practice they weren't choosy and seized any vessel that suited them. The most attractive prizes were inbound African slave ships, headed to Gulf and Caribbean ports. The situation was ideal for privateers, pirates, and smugglers—a voracious slave market in the southern United States; abundant, practically defenseless ships packed with chained black bodies; and a thinly spread Spanish navy. By seizing the slavers near their ports of call, sea rovers garnered a profitable cargo without the danger of a transatlantic crossing. It was at precisely this pregnant historical moment that the brothers Laffite made their presence known and became legends of the Gulf.[5]

No other figures in the basin's history have been so obscured by fancy, myth, and salty romance as Pierre and Jean Laffite. It has never been prudent for pirates, scoundrels, or gang kingpins to explain their activities, and the Laffites certainly did what they could during their lifetimes to confuse officials. They told tall tales, took mistresses rather than wives, broke inconvenient laws, evaded authority, and generally spent their days in a shadowy world of conspiracy, corruption, intrigue, and sporadic violence. Ever since, local colorists have embellished their story, filling it with half-truths and untruths. Nonetheless, recent biographers have managed to separate the gold from the dross, and the Laffites' lives have finally emerged with at least some clarity.[6]

They were born of different mothers in late eighteenth-century France, Pierre the elder by ten or so years. Their father was a merchant. Pierre was so inclined himself, but young Jean preferred the sea. Unfortunately, the brothers' prospects were disrupted by the Terror, and they immigrated to Saint-Domingue during the late 1790s. That world was to erupt in bloodshed and disorder as well, and they fled to New Orleans, possibly on board a French privateer. Doubtless they felt right at home on the muddy streets riverside. The city's population was twelve thousand and growing and, despite being a part of the Louisiana Territory, was no more American than it had been Spanish. Most residents were foreigners—French, Creole, German, Acadian, African, Portuguese, Canary Islanders, Italians, and newly arrived Saint-Domingans. Governor William C. C. Claiborne, a polished Virginian, was exasperated by this populace, doubted its loyalty, and had no interest in learning its languages or ways. In short, he didn't like the people, and they didn't like him. Furthermore, he feared the Saint-Domingans' bringing so many "refuse negroes," as he called them, into the city. How did he know some of these people hadn't participated in the revolts?[7]

If Claiborne disapproved of a society in such flux, the Laffites found it very much to their advantage. It was easy for a couple of gregarious Frenchmen like them to frequent taverns and gambling dens, make friends, broker attractive deals, and generally be indispensable. A letter penned in 1809 by an upcountry planter's son makes it clear that they were already dabbling in the black market by that time. Eighteen-year-old Esau Glasscock accompanied his father to New Orleans to buy some slaves, and word of mouth quickly steered them to Pierre Laffite. "He is a strapping man of middle size," Esau wrote home afterward, "with light hair growing low on his forehead. His eyes are dark and his teeth very white. He speaks English with a strong French accent." Pierre assured them he had slaves to sell, and the elder Glasscock traveled down to the brothers' *barracón*—or slave-holding pen—on Grand Isle to make his selections. Upon his successful return to New Orleans, he and Esau celebrated by attending a quadroon ball, something for which the city was quickly becoming famous. It was unlike anything they had ever experienced. Young, racially mixed, free women, called quadroons for being one-quarter black, were arranged along the walls with their seated mothers. European gentlemen circulated, flirting with the daughters and haggling with the mothers. In a practice known as *plaçage* (placement), the men hoped to win a comely mistress, the mothers to secure their daughters' financial futures. Amazed, Esau stepped into a side room where several men were gambling and came face to face with Jean Laffite. "He

Jean Laffite. COURTESY LIBRARY OF CONGRESS.

is tall, with pale skin," the youngster wrote, "and he has large dark eyes. He is clean-shaven except for a beard extending part-way down his cheeks." Esau thought Jean a better dresser than Pierre and noted his small, delicate hands and slippered feet. Dandy or no, Jean wasn't interested in the girls. He was already "in company with a quadroon woman," Esau recalled, "hardly more than a child, with liquid black eyes, such as many of them possess, but somewhat too thin for my taste."[8]

During their short visit, the Glasscocks had glimpsed the Laffites' business model in a nutshell. Pierre handled affairs in town, while Jean managed down at Barataria, its very name derived from a French word connoting illegal maritime barter. It was Jean's responsibility to dispatch his captains, greet them on their return, and divide the spoils. Other pirates and privateers were welcome too—the Laffites' take was half—and eagerly unloaded their captures with nary a United States official in sight. Not surprisingly, given this level of activity, the enterprise was an open secret. American naval officers and Gov. Claiborne wanted to shut it down but were ineffective at first. The navy's ships were weak and slow, and it was difficult to find recruits to man them. Claiborne's underpaid civil officials were corrupt and warned the Laffites of impending searches or raids. And because of the ban on importing enslaved people and wartime embargoes, labor-hungry planters and goods-starved city residents enthusiastically supported smuggling. For those who couldn't make the arduous trip to Barataria, the brothers conveniently established a temporary mart at an old shell midden known as the Temple, located roughly halfway between the city and the Gulf. Word of an impending auction would quickly travel the Crescent City grapevine, and citizens flocked to the site in pirogues and small boats. Dressed in their Sunday best, women wandered amid the boxes, barrels, and makeshift tables set beneath the moss-hung live oaks and browsed the duty-free goods—silk, German linen, stockings, glassware, jewelry, spices, soap, flour, coffee, and candles—while respectful pirates knuckled their foreheads and encouraged offers. The men, including some of the city's most prominent, paused before tools, hardware, naval stores, hides, dry goods, bottles of wine, sherry, and brandy, and fragrant cigars neatly arrayed in boxes. For those eager to get in on the bargains but unable to reach either Barataria or the Temple, the Laffites helpfully ferried their contraband up Bayou Lafourche to Donaldsonville, sixty miles above New Orleans, where inland planters could participate. One bayou resident marveled at the "incredible" volume of goods traveling the stream. "Day and night continually passed Pirogues," he reported. All in all, it was an impressively efficient criminal enterprise, well tuned to the market.[9]

When Janny brought *La Dorada* into Barataria Bay, the Laffites' operation was at its peak. At any given time, at least three hundred smugglers and hangers-on occupied the islands and surrounding oak hammocks, most of them living in primitive lean-tos with palmetto-frond roofs that rattled in the humid wind. Jean occupied a wooden house with a wraparound gallery on Grand Isle's eastern end, next to the pass. Other piratical improvements included log signal towers at strategic points, a flimsy stockade for the *barracón,* and a scattering of small warehouses. Rumors upriver held there was also a fort, but unless a few rusty naval guns propped on a log qualified, that wasn't true. Vessels were constantly coming and going. Sometimes there were as many as two dozen in the bay, the largest flying the new Carthaginian flag. This distinctive banner featured a multipointed white star at the center of a green rectangle nested within a yellow rectangle nested within an orange one. Seizing ships on the open Gulf was only part of these scoundrels' maritime equation, however. In order to cope with the shallow lakes, bayous, and swamps along their northern routes, they improvised an ingenious smuggling barge they called a *piragua* that could be rowed or poled. It was made by cutting a dugout canoe lengthwise and adding planks between the halves. This produced a serviceable flat-bottomed craft that could be partially decked and carry a small mast. In a heavy chop, the crew simply attached leeboards to the gunwales for a more seaworthy vessel.[10]

Daily life at Barataria was generally pleasant for rootless rogues and ne'er-do-wells. A steady sea breeze kept the mosquitoes away, and plentiful seafood and game kept the people fed. Gumbo simmering in iron kettles over red coals was probably a near constant. Jean Laffite's captains, among them Dominique Youx, a Saint-Domingan refugee and expert gunner; Vincent Gambi, an Italian pirate considered the cruelest of the lot; Nat Chigazola, known as "Cut Nose" for a nasty sword scar; and Janny were skilled at their trade and rarely returned empty handed. Their crewmen worked hard and played hard, carousing with lewd women attracted by their freewheeling, spendthrift ways. According to one antebellum magazine article, "The return of the buccaneers to their stronghold . . . after a successful cruise, would be hailed with outrageous joy; the plunder would be divided, the orgies would commence, and, as a retributive finale, would be wound up with an occasional stab, or fatal duel." Still, there were rules. Laffite brooked no challenge to his authority and once shot a man down to prove it. Unlike most other pirates or privateers working the Gulf, he forbade his captains to attack American shipping. One didn't borrow trouble. He was a good neighbor, ordering his men to respect local fishermen and their families. Runaway slaves were immediately returned to their owners. The Laffites certainly felt no qualms about illegal dealing in enslaved people, but they knew better than to harbor or traffic in American runaways. That would have quickly cost them the support of Louisiana's powerful sugar planters.[11]

By 1814 the shenanigans had reached such a pitch that authorities were apoplectic. According to a St. Louis newspaper correspondent, the Laffites had "greatly injured all honest traders" the entire length of the Mississippi Valley. "In consequence of his [Laffite's] piracy and smuggling," he wrote, "a great variety of goods are very cheap here. Flour is 6 dollars per barrel, pork 10, bacon 10 cents per lb., tobacco 5 dollars per cwt [hundredweight, or one hundred pounds]." Not so the slaves, who were marked up over 300 percent between Barataria and the interior markets. Enraged, Claiborne posted a five hundred-dollar reward for "John Lafitte's" arrest. Unintimidated, the brazen pirate printed a proclamation of his own, offering one thousand dollars for Claiborne's apprehension and delivery. At least one observer believed the governor in greater danger. Meanwhile, a U.S. naval captain complained to his superiors in Washington: "The whole of the coast from Vermilion Bay westwardly, round to the Rigolets on the east, appears, in fact, to swarm with pirates,—fitted out, for the most part, at New Orleans." But the Laffites' fortunes were about to change. First Pierre was jailed, and then on September 3, 1814, an armed British brig appeared off Grand Isle, seeking an audience with none other than the notorious Lord of Barataria himself.[12]

Up to that moment, the War of 1812 between the United States and Britain had mostly been fought along the Canadian border and the Atlantic seaboard, far from the glittering Gulf. But Britain had always cast a covetous eye upon New Orleans and by the autumn of 1814 was prepared to wrest it from the Americans. Positioned there, it could choke the young nation's economic potential, thrust northward toward the Canadian border and, just as the French had hoped to do to the thirteen colonies more than a century earlier, block any further westward expansion. In order to achieve these ambitious objectives, British strategy involved acquiring as many allies in the region as possible, including the Spanish (who still held Florida), disaffected Creek Indians, Seminoles, and escaped slaves, or maroons. It was perfectly natural that as part of this effort they should also court the Baratarians. After all, who better to guide them through the swamps and bayous into New Orleans?[13]

One can imagine Laffite's thoughts as he studied the British warship through his brass spyglass. Momentous changes were occurring with unsettling rapidity all around him. Uppermost in his troubled mind was the recent arrest of Pierre in New Orleans "for having knowingly & wittingly aided & assisted, procured, commanded, counselled & advised . . . acts of piracy & robbery on the high seas" and for selling the ill-gotten gains. If convicted, he would hang. The Americans were in earnest. Louisiana had achieved statehood in 1812, and Claiborne was governor. The Laffites were now more of an embarrassment to him than ever, and he was resolved to eliminate them for good. Backgrounding this were stunning developments in the Mississippi Territory, Spanish West Florida, and beyond. Since 1803 U.S. officials had claimed that the Louisiana Purchase included the so-called Florida Parishes, which occupied a narrow strip north of New Orleans and Lake Pontchartrain between the Mississippi and the Pearl River (Louisiana's present eastern border with Mississippi) and the Gulf Coast all the way to the Perdido River (Alabama's present eastern border with Florida). In 1810, frontier rowdies seized the Florida Parishes, raised their bright blue, lone white star flag over Baton Rouge and declared the independent Republic of West Florida. President James Madison quickly accepted their invitation to be annexed into the United States, and Claiborne assumed the area's administration as part of Louisiana. Further asserting themselves, the Americans bloodlessly took Mobile from an underfed Spanish garrison three years later. Practically on the heels of that, a militant Creek faction known as the Redsticks went on the warpath in the Alabama backcountry and was crushed by a rail-thin, tough-as-nails Tennessee general named Andrew Jackson, who then moved down the Alabama River in order to counter a possible British invasion. Jackson was convinced that Mobile would be taken first as a base from which the British could then approach New Orleans overland and furiously prepared his defenses and troops. His challenge became even more daunting after Napoleon abdicated on April 11, 1814, and was shipped to Elba. Of a sudden, the British army and navy were free to concentrate fully on the American war and wasted no time in doing so. To make matters worse, just as Jackson feared, the Spanish gave their powerful allies access to Pensacola's harbor and forts. From there, British officers did everything they could to incite Indians and maroons against American interests, even building a fort for them on the Apalachicola River, issuing them red caps and muskets, and promising the blacks British citizenship. This drove American slave owners, and especially Jackson, into fits and redoubled their determination to obliterate all foreign influences from their southern border. As a sailor, Laffite might have compared the situation to a confused sea, a dangerous circumstance in which tumultuous waves are moving in every direction without a dominant rhythm or direction. He was a master at exploiting uncertainty, but that was with weak players like the Americans, the Spanish, and rival sea rovers. Britain was something else entirely, a major naval power with worldwide reach. What, he must have wondered, do they want of me, and what will it mean for Barataria?[14]

Anxious to know as soon as possible, Laffite ordered four men to row him out in a pirogue. Even as they approached the brig, she dropped a longboat flying a flag of truce. The two craft met halfway. Laffite studied the occupants opposite—hardy British jack-tars at the oars and two officers in the sheets, one clad in a blue coat and the other in resplendent scarlet. They were Capt. Nicholas Lockyer of the HMS *Sophie* and a Capt. McWilliams of the Royal Marines. Lockyer asked if Jean Laffite were ashore and if they might be introduced to him.

Laffite was wary and said he didn't know. Lockyer then handed him an envelope and asked that he deliver it to the famous buccaneer. Ever the gambler, Laffite invited them to his house, where they sat down to his hospitality and he admitted his identity. They had come, as confirmed by the documents, offering friendship, full pardon, and commissions for the pirate captains. According to one contemporary account, Laffite was also promised thirty thousand dollars, a princely sum. If he rejected their overture, Barataria would be destroyed. His mind no doubt racing, Laffite asked for fifteen days to settle his affairs, after which, he pledged, "I would be entirely at your disposal." While these negotiations were transpiring, restless

Baratarians gathered and angrily denounced their visitors. Many of the smugglers were Americans, if not exactly honorable ones, and the thought of cooperating with the British riled them. At Laffite's urging, and under his protection, the officers hurried back to their ship and sailed away to Pensacola.[15]

The British offer might have tempted some men, but not Jean Laffite. He was a Frenchman, after all, and now an American. Earlier writers and romancers have made much, probably too much, of his patriotism, but there was a genuine spark. He always claimed that he had never raised a hand against the young nation, and that was true. America was nothing if not a land of opportunity for him. Life in the king's service with its rules and regimentation was not the least bit attractive. As for the money, Laffite routinely dealt in large sums and hoped to keep doing so. But he did not delude himself. It would not be at Barataria. Happily, Lockyer's packet provided handy negotiating leverage with the Americans.[16]

The following day, Laffite hurriedly penned a note to Claiborne, stuffed it into the envelope with the other documents, and had them delivered by a trusted associate. "This point of Louisiana, which I occupy," he informed the governor, "is of great importance in the present crisis. I tender my services to defend it; and the only reward I ask is that a stop be put to the proscription against me and my adherents, by an act of oblivion for all that has been done hitherto. I am the stray sheep, wishing to return to the sheepfold." As soon as Claiborne got the packet, he called a meeting of local and federal officials. Among the latter was Commodore Daniel Patterson, the American navy's senior officer on the Gulf, who had just received orders from Washington to attack Barataria and clean out the smugglers. In a significant departure from its earlier enforcement efforts, the government made sure he got the necessary resources, including the armed schooner *Carolina* and seventy fully equipped soldiers. This thrilled Patterson because he hated pirates. During blockade duty off Tripoli years earlier, he had been captured and held by Barbary corsairs. He was understandably eager to exact revenge on the lawless brotherhood. That he stood to gain a percentage from the sale of any captured goods further enhanced the raid's attractiveness. Jackson shared Patterson's contempt for the Baratarians, branding them "hellish banditti." Claiborne, who would have wholeheartedly agreed with them earlier, suddenly questioned the attack. "I begin to think it would be advisable, for the present, to postpone it," he mused. Claiborne knew the Laffites well, and realized their swamp knowledge, boats, guns, and fighting spirit would be of inestimable use at underdefended New Orleans. His appreciation for the irascible brothers was considerably heightened by the worrisome indifference among the local Creoles toward military service.[17]

But the die was cast, and during the wee hours of September 11, Patterson's force departed the local wharves and nosed downstream. It consisted of the *Carolina*, six shallow-draft gunboats, and some barges loaded with the soldiers. The little flotilla would have been no match for serious naval opposition but was more than adequate

William C. C.
Claiborne. COURTESY
NEW YORK PUBLIC LIBRARY.

against "banditti." The eighty-five-foot *Carolina* carried a dozen twelve-pounders and three long nines, or nine-pounders, and each gunboat mounted several small cannon. American tars contemptuously referred to the latter vessels as "Jeffs" because they had been commissioned by Thomas Jefferson as a cheap alternative to a blue-water navy. Each was about fifty feet long with a single mast and was meant to guard harbors and bays. They rolled badly in the slightest swell and were barely capable of supporting what little artillery they carried. Still, they were useful in their limited way and, loaded with determined men, were vital to Patterson's raid. The fleet proceeded downriver, exited the southwest pass, and appeared off Barataria at breakfast time on September 16.[18]

Laffite knew about the raid beforehand, of course, but he was in surprisingly good humor. Pierre was free, sprung out of jail earlier and ferried down to Grand Isle, where the brothers were joyfully reunited. Instead of preparing for a fight or running away, they immediately threw a last-minute sale to dispose of as much contraband as possible. When the American fleet hove into view, there were nearly a thousand people at Barataria—smugglers, merchants, factors, agents, associates, and idlers of, Patterson later reported, "all colors." Approaching the pass, Patterson hoisted a large white flag from the *Carolina*'s mainmast with the declaration "Pardon to Deserters." There was no opposition. "I perceived that the pirates were abandoning their vessels, and were flying in all directions," Patterson wrote. "I sent in pursuit of them." While the Laffites escaped in pirogues, troops landed and began tearing apart their lair. Patterson reported "forty houses of different sizes, badly constructed, and thatched with palmetto leaves." They burned beautifully. In the bay, the Americans seized six schooners, one felucca, *La Dorada,* and numerous small boats, many with their crews still on board. "I have captured all their vessels in port," Patterson proudly announced, "dispersed their band, without one of my brave fellows being hurt." The spoils were impressive—dozens of smugglers, including Youx, 163 barrels of flour, 17,200 cigars, 483 pounds of chocolate, 769 gallons of brandy, 10,000 gallons of wine, bolts of linen, boxes of soap, cloves, pepper, Spanish gold coins, naval stores, anything and everything. Patterson and his men had done very well indeed.[19]

Throughout the fall the Laffites skulked in the swamps but made it known via intermediaries that their offer to assist the Americans still stood. They continued to be rebuffed, but with each passing month developments increasingly favored their proposal. Shortly after Lockyer's Barataria visit, four British ships and a contingent of marines and Indians assaulted Fort Bowyer at the mouth of Mobile Bay but were soundly repulsed with the loss of the twenty-gun HMS *Hermes.* Because the attack originated at Pensacola, Jackson acted on his own authority and captured that city in early November, humiliating the Spaniards and forcing seven British vessels to evacuate the harbor. Thanks to American bravery and decisiveness, the British had to abandon their designs on Mobile and coordinate their assault through the Trembling Coast's swamps, bayous, and shallow lakes, the least favorable option, especially without the Baratarians.[20]

They must have been an incredible sight. Fifty vessels, from the eighty-gun leviathan HMS *Tonnant* to frigates, brigs, and transports loaded with over five thousand crack troops fresh from their Napoleonic triumphs, all snugly anchored in Negril Bay, Jamaica. Overall command rested with Vice Admiral Sir Alexander Forrester Inglis Cochrane, a veteran of fights from Egypt to the West Indies and no lover of Americans. "I have it much at heart to give them a complete drubbing before Peace is made," he had written earlier that summer. At last, on November 26 and 27, the fleet departed on its great mission. An eighteen-year-old redcoat described the occasion: "It is impossible to conceive a finer sea-view than the general stir presented. Our fleet amounted now to upwards of fifty sail, many of them vessels of war, which shaking loose their topsails, and lifting their anchors at the same moment, gave to Negril Bay an appearance of bustle such as it has seldom been able to show." Once clear of the harbor, the ships "bounded over the water with the speed of eagles," the youngster proudly remarked, and on December 8 anchored to the north of the Chandeleur Islands at the mouth of Lake Borgne. Flabbergasted Cajun fishermen and awed American scouts quickly spread the word, and soon New Orleans was in an uproar. If as yet unclear in its critical details, Cochrane's preferred route of attack appeared to be through the lakes, landing on the shore of either Borgne or Pontchartrain and marching west into the city across bayou-laced bogs and a dry patch known as the Plains of Gentilly. A direct upriver thrust was fraught with peril. The mouths of the Mississippi were too shallow for the ships of the line, and there were two garrisons besides. Fort St. Philip, situated some forty miles upstream, would hotly contest any passage by smaller vessels. Assuming they successfully ran it, Fort St. Leon at English Turn promised severe punishment at that difficult-to-navigate hairpin.[21]

Looking haggard but resolute, Jackson had arrived in the city on December 1 and begun to coordinate a defense. His resources were decidedly thin—Patterson's meager flotilla, eight hundred army regulars, eighteen hundred buckskin-clad Tennesseans and Kentuckians, some militia, free blacks, and a few dandified Creoles. Bowing at last to repeated entreaties by Claiborne and everyone who was anyone in the city, Jackson finally agreed to accept the Laffites' offer. He and Jean were introduced and briefly conversed on a downtown corner. There is no record of exactly what was said, but they liked each other at once. Though vastly different men, they both hated the British, and each respected the other's daring. If the Baratarians would fight alongside the Americans, they would receive full pardon for their many sins. And so the jailed smugglers were released, including Dominique Youx and his trained gun crews, and those in the swamps returned to the city—Pierre and Jean with their profound local geographic knowledge, and dozens of others clad in pantaloons and billowy shirts with their cutlasses and muskets and a vital cache of gun flints. Cochrane might have scoffed, but soon he would learn what such a cobbled-together, ragtag force could do.[22]

December is a fickle month on the northern Gulf Coast. Short and gloomy overcast days of chilly fog and mizzle alternate with bright, pleasant, balmy ones. Periodic northers plunge temperatures below freezing and push water out of the bayous and bays, limning their margins with ice. Yellows and browns predominate in the swamps, alligators and snakes disappear, and wild ducks descend quacking on the lakes. From an early nineteenth-century military perspective, the season's great advantage was its lack of fevers. Unlike Keppel's experience at Havana in 1762, Cochrane could count on several months of pestilence-free campaigning. Unfortunately, his men had spent weeks in the tropics, and adjusting to periods of cold and wet promised them much discomfort. They endured, by most accounts good-humoredly, because of their officers' promise that "beauty and booty" awaited them in the Crescent City.[23]

Cochrane's first task was to clear Lake Borgne so that he could land his troops unmolested. To do that, he had to capture a small American flotilla consisting of five Jeffs and two small single-gun support vessels. All told, there were less than two hundred men facing him, under the direct command of twenty-five-year-old Thomas ap Catesby Jones, his unusual name a Welsh peculiarity ("ap" meaning "son of"). Cochrane couldn't reach Jones's boats with his deeper-draft vessels, so he dropped forty-five launches loaded with over a thousand sailors and marines. Capt. Lockyer was detached from the *Sophie* to command. Jones tried to withdraw and reposition himself in the narrow pass between Borgne and Pontchartrain, known as the Rigolets. But light winds and a falling tide forced him to anchor and await the attack. It must have taken a particular courage for the Americans to watch the launches steadily approach from miles away, rows of oars rhythmically dipping into the shallow lake water, propelling the enemy ever closer. In preparation they primed their pieces and hoisted boarding nets, which, according to one man, made the gunboats look "as if they were draped in giant spider webs." Faced with such overwhelming odds, prudence would have dictated that Jones destroy his vessels to keep them out of enemy hands and save his men. While probably the militarily smart move, he knew that it would subject him to public opprobrium. Better for a man of honor to hold and fight.[24]

As soon as the launches came within range, "the Americans pounded away," a British officer named John Henry Cooke later wrote, and the "boat crews cried 'Give way!' and cheered loudly." The small launches were now widely spaced and made difficult targets. As they swarmed the Jeffs, "the action became general and destructive on both sides," Jones reported. "The clouds of smoke rolled upwards," Cooke related, "and the splashing of round and grape shot in the water, and the loud exhortations of 'Give way!' presented an animated scene at mid-day." Wielding cutlasses, the British cut through the nets of Jones's boat and clambered onto the deck. After a sharp fight they overwhelmed the crew and quickly turned its guns on the other Jeffs. It was soon finished. The boats were surrendered, the Americans made prisoner, and Borgne was verily a British lake. Cochrane was highly pleased, calling the scuffle a "brilliant affair," and began landing his men.[25]

The Battle of New Orleans took place on January 8, 1815, at a plantation several miles below the city. Jackson's motley men were securely arrayed behind a redoubt of black mud and cotton bales anchored by the Mississippi River on their right and a cypress swamp on their left with a flooded canal in front. Pierre was in the lines helping, as were Youx and a contingent of Baratarians at Battery No. 3, where they gazed along a cannon barrel at the foggy field. Jean was there too, as confirmed by recently discovered pension records at the National Archives in Washington, D.C. According to sworn testimony by five surviving Baratarian veterans, the Laffite brothers each commanded about fifteen men. The British considered them all an undisciplined rabble and launched a full-scale frontal assault with rockets and cannons and three thousand infantrymen. They came on in tightly packed ranks to the accompaniment of snare drums and skirling bagpipes—green-clad light infantry, kilted Highlanders, and red-coated regulars in perfect order beneath colorful banners. The result was one of the most lopsided slaughters in military history. The American line erupted in fire and smoke, and hundreds of British began falling. Cooke suffered cannon and musket fire so intense that it "seemed as if the earth was cracking and tumbling to pieces, or as if the heavens were rent asunder by the most terrific peals of thunder that ever rumbled." Incredibly, he survived, but over two thirds of his comrades were killed, wounded, or captured, including most of the high-ranking officers. American casualties were less than a hundred. Still eager for his spoils, Cochrane wanted to continue, but John Lambert, the general upon whom command devolved, said that it wasn't "prudent" and "recommended re-embarking the army as soon as possible." Cochrane complied, but only sailed as far as Mobile Bay, where he anchored the fleet, captured Fort Bowyer, and began scheming to take Mobile and then march west overland as had originally been planned. It was not to be. News arrived that the Treaty of Ghent had been signed on Christmas Day 1814, and the United States and Britain were again at peace. Despite the fact that the Battle of New Orleans had been fought after the treaty was signed, there is little doubt that the British would have held onto the city if they had taken it. Short of Washington or New York, there was not a more powerful bargaining chip on the continent. Cochrane dashed off a note of congratulations to Jackson and hove away. There would be no "beauty and booty" for him or the defeated men in his ships. Jackson and his dirty-shirt army, including both Laffites and their Baratarians, had saved the day.[26]

As for the Laffites and their men, they were fully pardoned by President Madison on February 6, 1815. According to the proclamation, they richly deserved their reward because they had "abandoned the prosecution of the worst cause for the support of the best." The brothers resumed open city life and filed claims for property taken or destroyed in Patterson's raid. Not surprisingly for such a pair, they proved too restless to settle down as law-abiding citizens. Within a few short years they were up to their old tricks, Jean from a new base on Galveston Island that he called Campeachy and Pierre, as ever, in the city as factotum. Just as Barataria had once done, Galveston perfectly suited the Laffites' methods. The scrubby Texas coast was practically deserted except for a few fishermen and poverty-stricken Indians. Spanish control of the area was lax, the Mexicans were preoccupied with a growing independence movement, and the Americans were powerless to police foreign territory. In 1818 a slave buyer named J. Randall Jones visited Campeachy and found it a booming place. "Lafitte himself had a pretty good house," Jones wrote in a letter, "the balance were made hastily of planks, sails and so on. Lafitte had thrown up an earthen fort and had some cannon mounted on the bay. There was a schooner from Boston there, trading potatoes and groceries." Jones discovered his host to be congenial and the island denizens relaxed. A "Madamoiselle Victoire" ran a bustling bar, dwarfed by infinite water and sky.[27]

Unfortunately for the Laffites, Campeachy could not last. The trouble began, appropriately enough, with an angry sea. It was as if Hurakan had suddenly lost patience and wanted the brothers gone from the Gulf. In the late summer of 1818, a strong hurricane drove four feet of water over the settlement, flattening the fort and all but six houses, scattering the boats, and killing dozens of pirates. One survivor described "unremitting efforts in keeping aloof, with oars and poles, the trunks of uprooted trees and spars of wrecks which the water flung up against our cabin."[28]

Diplomatic hammer blows followed. In 1819 Spain and the United States signed the Adams-Onís Treaty, which gave Florida to the Americans and settled the two nations' southwestern border at the Sabine River (the modern Texas/Louisiana line). Coupled with these events, the Latin American republics were revoking their letters of marque. Anyone caught plundering would be considered a pirate and hanged accordingly. Bowing to the inevitable, Jean burned what was left of Campeachy and sailed away. His and Pierre's ends are wrapped in as much mystery and confusion as nearly everything else to do with their nefarious lives. Some accounts have them perishing of fevers or in battle down in the Yucatán. Others claim that Jean lived years in the United States and even wrote a boastful memoir. Whatever their fates, their stories will long haunt the Trembling Coast's spooky bayous, New Orleans's balconied streets, and Galveston's windswept shores.[29]

The north central Gulf Coast was not the only domain of early nineteenth-century pirates. They flourished down in the Keys and around Cuba's Cabo San Antonio, too, where they were of a decidedly more bloodthirsty nature than the business-oriented and affable Laffites. Their methods were detailed by a captured corsair captain named Gibbs, who prior to his 1831 execution, gave a full confession to an American official. According to Gibbs's statement, he had joined the U.S. Navy at the age of fifteen but didn't like the discipline, jumped ship, and eventually made Havana where he turned pirate. "The crews of the piratical vessels were sometimes 20, 30 or 40 men," he explained, "and the proceeds of a crime were equally divided among them. All the crews of the vessels we captured were put to death; sometimes shot and sometimes thrown overboard. No quarter was given when captures were made." The men then took their prize cargoes into Havana, where rich merchants gave "half the value of them." During his dastardly career, Gibbs estimated that he had killed "about one hundred" people, including half a dozen fellow pirates "whenever my authority was resisted." The only death he mourned was that of a young Dutch girl he had forced to live with him as his mistress at Cabo San Antonio. His mates feared she might escape and reveal their location and convinced him to poison her. "I regret that I did not lose my own life before hers was taken," he reflected sadly, "for I think I loved her."[30]

Any men lucky enough to be spared by pirates were often forced to join them on pain of death. Such a one, he claimed, was Aaron Smith, whose vessel was boarded off Cuba by freebooters "of a most ferocious aspect." The pirates hustled Smith and his comrades into small boats "by repeated blows with the flat part of their cutlasses over our backs, and threatening to shoot us." Casual cruelty was routine among these pirate crews. Theodore Canot, an Italian cabin boy kidnapped in the Keys, described an incident that happened to him. Canot was a good navigator and could read charts, so the pirates made him pilot. But when night fell he feared threading the hidden reefs and recommended they anchor until dawn. The crew complied with much grumbling because the weather was fair. The mate accused him of laziness and forced him to walk the decks instead of going to sleep. Exhausted, Canot sat atop a brass bow gun, where he fell fast asleep. "I know not how long I rested," he later wrote, "but a tremendous shock knocked me from the cannon and laid me flat on the deck, bleeding from mouth, nose and ears." To his incredulity he saw the mate standing over him, "cigar in hand, laughing immoderately, blaspheming like a demon, and kicking me in the ribs with his rough wet-weather boots. He had detected me asleep, and touched off the gun with his *havanna!*"[31]

True to their incorrigible natures, the southeastern Gulf's pirates didn't hesitate to capture American vessels when they got the chance, and they sometimes tortured or murdered the crews. Lurid stories filled the press, business losses mounted, insurance rates doubled, and merchants from New York to New Orleans demanded relief. Editorial outrage grew accordingly. On October 20, 1821, *Niles Weekly Register* fumed, "The *coasting* trade of the United States is almost daily insulted—the voyage to and from New Orleans cannot be made in safety." The paper decried the kind of arrogant boldness demonstrated when a merchant ship bound from Philadelphia to the Crescent City was intercepted by a fourteen-gun corsair off Cabo San Antonio, her cargo confiscated, and an American officer on board given a penciled note by the "chief of the pirates." "Sir," it began, "Between buccaneers, no ceremony; I take your dry goods, and, in return, I send you pimento; therefore we are now even: I entertain no resentment." With a flourish the freebooter's note concluded, "Nothing can intimidate us; we run the same fortune, and our maxim is, 'that the goods of this world belong to the brave and the valiant.'" It was signed "Richard Coeur De Leon." The *Register* demanded immediate action: "We want more strong, but 'flying' schooners to scour the coasts, and cause the property and persons of our citizens to be respected."[32]

The government heard and responded. President James Monroe asked Congress to authorize an antipiracy fleet and generously fund it. In 1822, $160,000 was appropriated and the West India Squadron formed with Commodore David Porter in command. The secretary of the navy stated his four main duties—wipe out the pirates, protect American citizens, suppress the slave trade, and escort Mexican specie headed to the United States. Porter was a sagacious choice. He was in his early forties and, like so many naval officers of the period, had trod wooden decks since his teens and witnessed thundering naval battles. Serious and aggressive, he immediately began assembling a suitable fleet. It eventually consisted of 16 vessels,

133 guns, and 1,100 men. The ships included a decoy merchant vessel with concealed cannon, a steamboat, schooners, and brigs. But the most critical offensive element was the aptly named "Mosquito Fleet." This consisted of five one-gun, shallow-draft, twenty-oar barges—the *Gallinipper, Midge, Mosquito, Sandfly,* and *Gnat.* Like the pests after which they were called, these vessels were to bedevil and harass their victims. Porter established his base at Key West, where he could command the only routes into and out of the Gulf. "The importance of this station appears daily more and more manifest to me," he wrote, "and, in my opinion, it is of but little consequence who possesses Cuba, if we keep a force here." The waters about the Keys were certainly busy. "It is almost incredible the number of vessels that daily pass and repass," he declared.[33]

Porter's officers began patrolling almost at once and enjoyed cooperation by the U.S. Revenue Cutter Service, the Spanish, and the British. The Revenue Cutter Service was something of an all-purpose maritime arm (precursor to the Coast Guard), founded during the eighteenth century to enforce tariffs, monitor trade, supply lighthouses, survey coastlines, save lives at sea, and support the navy in combat efforts. Because of its brown-water work, the Revenue Cutter Service had more shallow-draft vessels than the navy, including two trim fifty- ton cutters that patrolled the Gulf—the *Alabama* and *Louisiana,* homeported at Mobile and New Orleans respectively. Each of these vessels was a topsail schooner with a single-pivot gun amidships. They were bravely manned and scored significant successes down in the Keys and off the Trembling Coast. In one notable episode during the spring of 1819, the crews stormed a "Pirate Island" at the Mississippi's mouth, capturing several reprobates and burning their claptrap shelters.[34]

Such excitement aside, chasing pirates generally meant tedious, weeks-long cruises all around the littoral. The officers and men battled storms, northers, calms, heat, fevers, boredom, and only occasionally pirates. Among their number in Porter's squadron was a young navy lieutenant named David Glasgow Farragut. He later recalled the everyday inconveniences such duty occasioned: "For myself I never owned a bed during my two years and a half in the West Indies, but lay down to rest wherever I found the most comfortable berth." That was usually a hard wooden deck. On July 3, 1823, Lt. Francis H. Gregory, commanding the schooner *Grampus,* sent a fairly typical report detailing his efforts on patrol. His ship had been escorting vessels to and fro among Tabasco, Campeche, and Vera Cruz, he informed Porter, and "scouring the coast up and down." Locals claimed that a nest of scoundrels near Campeche was harassing shipping there. "The pirates issue from their post in barges, small vessels, and in canoes," he related, "hover along the shores, enter the harbors, murder and destroy almost all that fall in their power." Getting to grips with the desperadoes was difficult, however. Whenever the Americans appeared, the pirates sensibly fled and when ashore often posed as simple fishermen. A skilled captain named Stephen Cassin of the USS *Peacock* had better luck off Cabo San

USS *Peacock* (left) overhauls pirates off western Cuba, 1823. Sketched from an illustration in "The United States Navy and West India Piracy, 1821–25," by W. H. Beehler, *Frank Leslie's Popular Monthly*, January 1890. COURTESY NICHOLAS H. HOLMES III.

Antonio. He spied a felucca heading for the *Gallinipper*, but she quickly changed course when the other American vessels appeared. "The barges were ordered in chase, accompanied by all the boats we could muster," Cassin reported. The Americans followed to where the felucca had disappeared into a stream and discovered her covered with bushes. There were several huts nearby. The pirates fired their muskets but missed and then ran. "The officers and men immediately landed," Cassin wrote, "and pursued them through the bushes, when a running fight of more than half a mile took place, the pirates frequently turning, for a moment, and firing." In order to gain ground against their pursuers, the buccaneers "threw off shoes, clothes, and other incumbrances." They escaped, but the Americans burned their houses and took the felucca. Cassin thought her a fine prize "in every respect equal to any of our barges."[35]

The Mosquito Fleet was admirably effective at penetrating shallow coves where pirates liked to hide. As Cassin had done, American sailors frequently landed on foreign soil to give chase, sometimes assisted by local militias or citizens. Any pirates caught were hung. At last, on November 19, 1823, Porter could proudly report to the secretary of the navy: "It will, I hope suffice to say, that at present, I have no knowledge of the existence of any piratical establishment, vessels, or boats, or of a pirate afloat in the West Indies and Gulf of Mexico. They have all been burnt, taken, destroyed, and driven to the shore, where the latter have, in most cases, been speedily captured by the local military."[36]

One pirate Porter never captured was José Gaspar, also called Gasparilla, beloved Tampa icon and the inspiration for a Mardi Gras–style parade in that city and for the Tampa Bay Buccaneers' name. Porter's failure was not due to any shortcoming on his part nor to any skill on Gaspar's. It was because Gaspar never existed. His legend, which is almost as robust as the Laffites', dates to 1900 and the aggressive promotional efforts of a Florida railroad company. Its deepest origin probably rests on the fanciful yarns spun by an old fishing guide and raconteur named John Gómez, who claimed to have been Gaspar's cabin boy. Gómez was unquestionably a good storyteller, and some businessmen on a fishing trip swallowed his lies; the rest, as they, say, is history. Only it's not. Porter never mentioned Gaspar, nor did anybody else prior to 1900. Still, Gómez's renditions of Gaspar's swashbuckling adventures were compelling. The swarthy Spaniard was the Mangrove Coast's scourge, Gómez told rapt listeners around a flickering fire, who kidnapped beautiful women and kept them—where else?—at Captiva Island. When finally cornered by an American ship he wrapped himself in his anchor chain and leapt overboard crying, "Gasparilla dies by his own hand, not the enemy's!" It made great copy, and legends die hard in the Gulf.[37]

Thanks to Porter, the Revenue Cutter Service, and their captains, the real pirates were eradicated and Gulf travel made safer than ever. But until the advent of better charts and reliable lighthouses, the Keys remained notorious for a particular brand of opportunist, who like the Laffites exploited the local circumstances. The Spanish called them Los Wreckers. They were local men—"conchs" in their own slang—some of Bahamian extraction, others Cuban, who made do by fishing, turtling, subsistence gardening, and salvage work. As traffic through the area increased during the early nineteenth century, shipwrecks became frequent occurrences. The Wreckers raced one another to the disaster sites in small schooners and sloops, rescued any survivors, and salvaged whatever they could of cargo and ship. In the early days, some of them were accused of luring ships to their doom with false lights and then ransoming the passengers. But mostly they were not evil men, just salt of the earth struggling to make it. One reporter described them as "waifs on our shores" who were "noted generally for the facility with which they get rid of their money." During the early 1820s, a Mobile businessman named John Simonton who was a frequent traveler through the Straits, grasped wrecking's potential if it was regulated and policed. In an effort to achieve this, he bought the island of Key West from its Spanish owner for two thousand dollars and invited the U.S. Navy to establish a depot there. In a letter to the secretary of the Treasury, he enthused, "If this place was made a Port of Entry it would in all probability become a place of deposit for the productions of other Countries particularly that of Great Britain and France, as it may be termed as a key for the whole Bay of Mexico and the north side of the island of Cuba." The navy had only to build warehouses, he opined, and they would quickly be filled with good and marketable salvage. Officers inspected the island and were impressed by its geographic situation and excellent harbor. Needing no further persuasion, they planted the Stars and Stripes, and true to Simonton's vision, commercial wreckers were soon hauling salvage to the government warehouses. After being carefully recorded, it was then auctioned through the local admiralty court, with all the attendant representation and paperwork. While most Wreckers would have preferred to cut their own deals, they were still making money and keeping busy offshore. During his visit to the area, Audubon witnessed their superior sailing abilities from the deck of a nearby revenue cutter. He watched in wonder "while the unknown vessel leaped as it were, from wave to wave, like the dolphin in eager pursuit of its prey. In a short time we were gliding side by side, and the commander of the strange schooner saluted our captain, who promptly returned the compliment. What a beautiful vessel!" Lost in admiration, Audubon wrote how the schooner "swims like a duck; and now with a broad sheer, off she makes for the reefs a few miles under our lee. There, in that narrow passage, well known to her commander, she rolls, tumbles, and dances, like a giddy thing, her copper sheathing now gleaming and again disappearing under the waves." Of such formidable nautical skill were the Key West Wreckers.[38]

By degrees the North American southeast had been almost completely pacified and folded into the United States. The Laffites were gone from Louisiana and the pirates from the Gulf. British and Spanish threats were removed. Mississippi achieved statehood in 1817, Alabama in 1819, and Florida in 1821. The region's once formidable Indian tribes had been decisively defeated. But for one. The Seminoles remained, still welcomed enslaved people who had run away, and refused to be dominated. Throughout the early nineteenth century the United States government attempted to conquer these people, forcing them ever farther down the Florida peninsula. There were three Seminole Wars between 1816 and the American Civil War. The fighting was never constant, and there were often long quiet periods, but the actions were fierce and bloody. American soldiers mounted frequent patrols through inhospitable swamps, rarely sighting their enemy unless ambushed. The most famous clash occurred in 1835 when two companies of regulars under the command of Maj. Francis L. Dade marched from Tampa into central Florida to reinforce Fort King (now Ocala). The Seminoles attacked them en route and killed all but three soldiers. In later testimony, one of the Seminole leaders, Halpatter-Tustenuggee, or Alligator as the Americans called him, explained the care with which they set their trap: "Just as the day was breaking we moved out of the swamp into the pine-barren. I counted ... one hundred and eighty warriors. Upon approaching the road, each man chose his position on the west side; opposite, on the east side, there was a pond. Every warrior was protected by a tree, or secreted in the high palmettoes."

When the American column came into view, Alligator continued, "every Indian arose and fired." He chuckled at the memory of one Seminole, "a little man," who shook his sword at the soldiers and yelled "God-damn!" After the massacre, the navy invested in canoes with which to better pursue the elusive foe. But in a bureaucratic scandal that will ring familiar to modern ears, an inquiry into the war's high costs revealed that the navy had spent $226 per canoe in contrast to the army's $15. Defeats and scandals aside, the government stayed on the offensive, even employing the already overtaxed Revenue Cutter Service, and eventually most of the surviving Seminoles were shipped to Oklahoma. But a hardy band evaded the army and faded deeper into the Everglades, where their proud descendants still live today.[39]

Even as the Seminole Wars were fought, white Americans flooded into Georgia, Alabama, Mississippi, and Louisiana, passing forlorn slave coffles along the way. Spurred by cheap land, the cotton gin, and legal bondage, planters both rich and mortgaged to the hilt, established farms in a broad swath through the region. Wrote one observer, it was as if "a new El Dorado had been discovered . . . where yesterday the wilderness darkened over the land with her wild forests, today the cotton plantation whitened the earth." There was a new king in the Gulf now, one whose steamboats plied Southern rivers and whose ships crowded the sea lanes, whose greedy courtiers coveted Cuba, Texas, Mexico, and even Central America, and Cotton was his name.[40]

Chapter Five

King Cotton's Pond

Throughout the day, sailing down the outer edges of the Gulf Stream, we see vessels of all forms and sizes, coming in sight and passing away as in dramatic show. There is a heavy cotton droger from the Gulf, of 1200 tons burden, under a cloud of sail, pressing on to the northern seas of New England or Old England.

Richard Henry Dana, *To Cuba and Back: A Vacation Voyage,* 1859

Looking stately and tall, the *Shakespeare* lay alongside New Orleans's levee, her hull even with the adjacent rooftops. She had arrived March 2, 1835, carrying assorted cargo and generating considerable excitement. At 747 tons, she was one of the largest vessels, if not the largest, ever to reach the Crescent City, and her impending departure attracted the interest of several potential passengers. One was the handsome, tousle-headed Irish actor Tyrone Power, at the end of his Southern tour and anxious to return to New York. He examined the *Shakespeare* on March 16, loved her name, pronounced her "noble," and remarked that he was "hugely tempted to take passage."[1]

Power's reaction was understandable. The *Shakespeare* was a brand-new addition to the Louisiana & New York Line, a packet service emphasizing passenger comfort and twice-monthly sailings whether the ship was fully loaded or not. The *Shakespeare* was certainly majestic to look upon—a fully square-rigged, three-masted ship 142 feet long and 34 in the beam, drawing 14 feet. But her most remarkable and innovative characteristic was invisible from the levee. This was her boxy "flat-floor" hull design, which increased her cargo capacity and improved her ability to cross the shallow bar at the Mississippi River's mouth. Dockyard idlers and croakers had predicted that such a design would make the ships clumsy, slow, and uneconomical, but surprisingly, the opposite proved to be the case. Matthew Fontaine Maury explained the design's virtues in 1839. "The buoyancy of the packets," he wrote, "has been obtained by the great length and breadth of their *long, flat* floors, and the lightness of draft has been still further promoted by building them to sail on *even* keels." An old salt who captained some of the early examples was impressed. "They are not only larger but much fuller bodied, caused by less *dead rise,"* he wrote, comparing them to earlier merchant ships. By "dead rise" he meant the angle between the boat's keel and hull—the less dead rise, the less V-shaped the hull. Despite their flat floors, the packets kept "the same sharpness at each end," he continued, were "*faster* sailers, more comfortable, have less motion, and are much better sea boats." Tyrone Power was soon to experience the *Shakespeare*'s performance on each of these claims.[2]

After some annoying delays, Power finally boarded ship on March 22, a day "clear, fresh, and pure." Besides about a dozen passengers, the *Shakespeare* was well stuffed with 674 cotton bales, 125 hogsheads of tobacco, 422 hogsheads of sugar, 50 tons of iron, and almost two hundred crates containing sundry other items. A steamer took the vessel in tow and headed downstream, considerably helped by brisk north winds and a full river. As usual, the English Turn presented a challenge, but the vessels cleared it and were soon rushing "past the fine sugar plantations lying along our course with great velocity." Farther south a spectacular sunset and a roaring marsh fire entertained one and all, before they reached the bar at ten that night and anchored. "The water reported by our pilot to be about eleven feet," Power wrote, "a comfortable hearing, when it is considered that the Shakspeare draws fourteen." Nearby an English merchant ship was hard aground. She had been there forty days.[3]

The following afternoon Power watched as two steamers were lashed to the *Shakespeare,* and "away we went for a dash at the pass." To no one's surprise the *Shakespeare* grounded, and the steamers attempted to work her free. It was not to be. The steamers gave up for the day. Power paced the deck and fretted. "Never go by sea if in any haste," he grumbled. Tides and waves gradually inched them forward, while sailors constantly threw lead lines and chanted the soundings. On March 25 things appeared "a little brighter, a swell setting in from the eastward; the ship evidently working over, as we now have sixteen feet water within half our length ahead." Late that afternoon they finally "launched forward, as though just sent from the stocks," and the still-grounded English crew nearby heartily cheered them. Free at last, the *Shakespeare* drove south and east atop the river's brown, log-choked discharge. Early on March 28 she was well away from shore. Power came on deck "and was delighted to find stun-sails on both sides, a clear blue sky above, reflected on a sea of the same colour, only crested with wreaths of snowy whiteness: wind about west by north." Aided by the Gulf Stream, the journey promised to be an easy one. Power and his fellow passengers agreeably lounged beneath a large canvas awning stretched over the poop deck while the ship proceeded "with just motion enough to be pleasant." By the afternoon of April 7, Power alighted at New York, pleased by his packet ship voyage. It had taken seventeen days, an average run.[4]

When Power crossed the Gulf, its political situation was markedly different from what had obtained just a generation earlier. To begin with, Spain's long dominance was ended. Only Cuba remained beneath the Iberian aegis. Mexico and the South American colonies had all achieved independence, and the burgeoning United States owned a great arc of waterfront real estate from the Dry Tortugas to the Sabine River, over thirteen hundred miles. Texas was part of Mexico, but growing numbers of Anglo-Americans were settling there. Mexican authorities welcomed them provided they became citizens. This was unobjectionable to the Americans, since their designated capital was at Saltillo, seven hundred miles distant in the State of Coahuila. Government of any sort was light on the ground. But then Mexico banned slavery throughout its territories, creating considerable dissatisfaction in Texas. In 1830, largely through the efforts of Gen. Antonio López de Santa Anna, its thirty thousand settlers were further hit with draconian trade regulations and, even worse by their lights, required to become Catholic. Revolution was brewing.[5] In fact, just as in the eighteenth century, the mid- to late-nineteenth-century Gulf was to suffer repeated conflict, much of it with a naval component. There was Spain's attempt to retake Mexico, the Pastry War, the Texas Revolution, the Caste War of the Yucatán, the Mexican War, the War of French Intervention, the American Civil War, and the Spanish-American War. There would be blockades, chases, bombardments, sieges, amphibious landings, brown-water battles, blue-water showdowns, and even an independent Texas navy. But these dramatic episodes must be held in abeyance until the following chapter, in order to more fully concentrate here on the United States' critically important cotton economy, slavery, the packet ships, and the rim's principal cities and towns at mid-century.

Just as Jefferson had predicted, New Orleans quickly became a bustling and prosperous entrepôt. Keelboats, flatboats, pirogues, and chuffing steamboats that could "run on dew" deposited goods on its planked levees from the farthest reaches of the vast Mississippi River basin. Hides, coal, sugar, whiskey, wheat, pork, cheese, onions, potatoes, apples, hemp, beeswax, beans, peas, beer, ale, feathers, honey, lime, white lead, glass, and a thousand other things passed through the city. But the most important antebellum commodity by far was cotton. The United States provided roughly half the world's supply, and 80 percent of that was grown in Georgia, Alabama, Mississippi, and Louisiana. Cotton exports exploded in quantity and value, from 350 million pounds worth $25 million in 1831 to 500 million pounds worth $65 million just four years later, and the Gulf ports of New Orleans and Mobile benefited most. New Orleans passed New York City as the busiest American export town in 1834, and Mobile was not far behind. Beginning in the 1830s at least a million bales of the fluffy stuff passed down the Mississippi River annually and one hundred thousand down the Mobile.[6]

Charles Joseph Latrobe, a British traveler, enthusiastic mountaineer, and soon-to-be Australian official, visited the Crescent City in 1834 and described the shipping, "upwards of two miles," jammed along the riverbank. "Highest up the stream lie the flats, arks, and barges," he wrote, "and below them the tier of steam-boats,

fifty of which may be seen lying here at one time. Then come the brigs ranged in rows, with their bows against the breast of the levee; these are succeeded by the three-masters, lying in tiers of two or three deep, with their broadside to the shore." Latrobe thought the prospect especially breathtaking from his hotel roof "in a sunny morning after a night of storm, when the sails of the whole are exposed to the air, and their signals or national flags abroad." Venturing down onto the levees he found himself immersed in an exotic and animated bazaar. There, "amidst a *melée* of all classes and costumes," he wove his way among fruit, vegetable, and meat stalls interspersed between "piles of timber and bricks, log-wood, coffee, sugar, corn and wheat, beef and pork, and mountains of cotton."[7]

At Mobile, similar scenes, though on a smaller scale, greeted travelers. Cotton was much the most common product in evidence there between October and April. When it arrived from upriver, steamboat roustabouts stacked the four hundred-pound bales so closely wharfside that it was difficult for female passengers to pass with their wide hoopskirts. From there, dock workers trundled the bales into brick warehouses where each one was mechanically compressed by as much as two thirds for more efficient packing on board ship. Because Mobile Bay is so shallow, steamers and barges lightered the pressed cotton down to the bay's deeper southern reaches, where the Lower Fleet lay at anchor. This maritime assemblage

New Orleans waterfront, looking upriver from the Faubourg Marigny, 1852. In the left foreground a packet takes on cotton bales. COURTESY LIBRARY OF CONGRESS.

consisted of large packet ships and barks, sometimes as many as a hundred at a time awaiting their valuable cargoes. Once alongside these vessels, stevedores loaded the bales by swinging tackle into the holds where chanting workers used powerful jackscrews to pack them as tightly against the sides as possible. Little wonder they called Mobile a cotton city. Throughout the busy season, bits of white lint tufted the town and local waters. It littered the wharves and rode bay breezes down narrow streets onto elegant cast-iron balconies and into opened windows where clerks, cotton factors, lawyers, and insurance agents scribbled at their high desks. "Look which way you will see it," wrote one Yankee of the ubiquitous product, "and see it moving; keel boats, steam boats, ships, brigs, schooners, wharves, stores and press houses."[8]

Profits were stupendous, and most of them were captured by shrewd New Yorkers who developed a highly successful triangular trade route. Owned by merchant princes like E. K. Collins, William H. Webb, and Preserved Fish (what a name!) and steered by capable captains like John Collins (E. K.'s brother), Ezra Nye, and Nat Palmer, packet ships laden with cotton traveled from Southern ports directly to spinning mills in Le Havre, France, or Liverpool, England, then recrossed the Atlantic to New York carrying immigrants and sundry merchandise, closing the triangle with a coastal run back south conveying much-needed items like agricultural tools, harnesses, clothing, silks, linens, construction materials like cut stone and marble, ironware, furniture, and the latest European and up-East publications. Many a Southern belle anxiously sent her husband downtown to buy the latest *Godey's Lady's Book* after a ship arrived in port. Energetic Yankee businessmen working for Collins and others moved south and established themselves as vital links in this network—brokering deals, procuring dockside labor, managing financial, legal, and insurance issues, and so on—and eventually succeeded in reorienting the trade, so that the ships were diverted from their direct eastward Atlantic runs and routed hundreds of miles out of the way to New York. The reason for this was that there wasn't enough cargo up East, even with the Erie Canal in service, to fill European-bound ships there. The Gulf South's abundant cotton bales were the perfect solution. New Yorkers became the vital middle men and made their port the lynchpin of the whole endeavor. That held true for many other products as well. Little wonder that one Southerner wrote, "Whatever the country produced for sale, samples of it were brought by the packets to the wharves of New York, and thus the warehouses of that city became an immense variety store, in which is to be found whatever is to be bought or sold in the United States." Many businessmen and planters complained, but the arrangement endured until the Civil War. Truth was, most planters were too busy growing cotton to develop the needed connections. It was easier for them to simply sign an agreement with a cotton factor to sell their crop, even at a profit cut. As an added benefit, planters often presented their Northern agents with lengthy shopping lists for house and farm. In addition to dominating the triangle, Yankee merchants dispatched ships on regular runs to Veracruz and Havana. Newspapers and city directories north and south were filled with advertisements detailing multiple routes and times. "Mexican Packets," read one paid for by E. K. Collins, "Sail from New York on the *fifth,* and Vera Cruz on the *first* of each month. The Ships are the Congress, Mexican." Another announcing New Orleans trips promised "handsome furnished accommodations" at $80, "without wine or liquor but all other stores of the best description will be provided." The Gulf was thus heavily traversed, and the Florida Straits were a busy maritime highway.[9]

Everything in this elaborate enterprise depended upon the packet ships being tough and seaworthy. During a thirty-year lifespan they were constantly at work—braving the stormy North Atlantic, threading the reef-hemmed Florida Straits, and plowing balmy Gulf waters plagued by wood-eating worms. They were built in northern yards where legendary shipwrights could spot sloppy workmanship a hundred feet outside their office windows. A ship's most critical components were the frames (or ribs), structural knees, and planks that made her hull. These had to bear enormous stress and strain, and if they were resistant to rot and pests, so much the better. No wood was better suited than live oak, familiar to Gulf Coast residents from time immemorial. Live oaks are noted for their twisted limbs and gracefully

sculpted trunks that can withstand the worst hurricanes. Skilled antebellum shipwrights could eyeball a sinuous tree and visualize a dozen critical construction elements locked therein. A large ship might require up to five hundred such trees. The
wood itself is dense—seventy pounds per cubic foot—and durable. The navy had
long recognized its usefulness, and in 1828 President John Quincy Adams approved
a live oak naval reservation near what is now Gulf Breeze, Florida. There and at
other Southern tree plantations, busy live-oakers harvested the timber and shipped
it north by schooner, where it was stacked in large sheds with Chesapeake cedar
and Maine-grown white oak.[10]

The wood on hand, construction began. The long keel was laid down first,
its pieces scarfed together by huge bolts. This was followed by the bow and stern
timbers, rudder, frames, and crossbeams for lateral support. Owners sometimes
dropped by the yard at this stage to check on progress and assess the work. One
boasted that he closely inspected the timbers to make sure there were "no flaws,
no knots, no nonsense." The hull's frame was then sheathed in planks attached by
iron bolts or wooden pegs. The bow and stern boards, which had to be curved,
were steamed so as to be more pliable and then hammered into place. The cracks
between the planking were tightly stuffed with oakum and the whole exterior pitch
slathered for waterproofing. Though it was not absolutely necessary, packet owners insisted their vessels be reinforced with an inner skin as well, also caulked and
sealed. This guaranteed that these ships would be safe in all but the most disastrous
circumstances. The hull thus nicely framed atop the ways, two pine decks were laid.
The main decks were flush on packet ships, with topside poop cabins sometimes
added for passenger accommodation. Staterooms included sumptuous fittings like
polished woods, heavy curtains, porcelain sinks, and comfortable beds and linens.
More important to a vessel's sailing ability were the masts, which had to be spaced
correctly for maximum efficiency. The long poles were lowered through deck aper-
tures by wooden cranes and dropped down to the keel. There carpenters fitted them
into their slots, or steps, which were situated adjacent the keelson. Above decks, the
masts and spars were secured by scrambling riggers. These men strung two types
of rigging on every vessel—standing and running. Standing rigging was tarred and
not meant to move. Its purpose was to keep the poles in place. The running rigging
consisted of lighter hemp and was used to maneuver the spars, raise and lower the
sails, and support men working aloft. It soared and crisscrossed above decks, and
ran through blocks, or pulleys, in landsman-confusing fashion. The sails were what
made the ships actually go, of course, and each packet was provided with three sets,
including winter and summer sets. In a service dedicated to speed at all costs, these
saw hard use and were routinely split, torn, or shredded in gales. Every sail had a
name and a purpose, again mysterious to landsmen, but no one denied their beauty
when fully unfurled and bellied out in a breeze. Lastly, the hull was coppered for
protection from worms, and the ship launched amid great fanfare and admiring

press. "The *Queen of the West* is the noblest work of man," a newspaper wrote of one such ship, "and her commander is the noblest work of God."[11]

Those captains and their crewmen who walked with rolling gaits were a common sight in all the major Gulf ports during the early nineteenth century. "Our captain seems a smart hand," Power remarked of John Collins, commanding the *Shakespeare*. Indeed he was. He was also a powerful man who weighed two hundred pounds. Astonished passengers once saw him use only two fingers to tip over a heavy hogshead. Collins was exactly what one observer said a successful packet captain needed to be—a good seaman who possessed "moral courage and physical force." Besides managing rough sailors, he also had to own enough social polish to make the female passengers comfortable. Such rare specimens were altogether a "remarkable type of man, hearty, bluff, and jovial, without coarseness, who would never be mistaken for anything but a gentleman." Nat Palmer, a burly and bearded New Englander who contributed to the flat-floor concept and later designed clipper ships, was another typical example. "Captain Nat," as he was affectionately known in the Crescent City, had rounded Cape Horn, probed icy Antarctic seas, and negotiated with Cuban and South American governmental officials. Impressed, E. K. Collins hired him to sail the New York–New Orleans route, and he quickly distinguished himself there, once completing it in just fourteen days. One writer called him "a rough old sailor. He was very passionate. In calm weather he would come on deck, with an old white beaver hat on, take it off and stomp on it and 'damn' the calm and everything else, but he never abused the men."[12]

That must have taken some restraint. According to one captain, packet crewmen, or "hoosiers" as he called them, were "the hardest kind of men." He elaborated that they could "all sing at their work and were good natured and could work hard, but they did not care much about the officers and would not be humbugged or hazed." Another quipped that they were mostly foreigners and "a husky lot on the topsail yard" who preferred packet work "because it transferred them swiftly from the brothels of one port to another." Captains left routine discipline to savvy mates who were always ready to serve up "'belaying pin soup' and 'handspike hash'" to sluggards and back-talkers. Obedience was critical, according to an article in *Galaxy* magazine, "for the speed and safety of the ship." This made the packet sailor "the fast man of the ocean world" and he took pride in being a "wild packetarian." And wild he was, particularly in port. Gambling, drinking, and whoring were his predictable amusements. One visitor to Mobile during the 1840s decried riverside "dance houses of the lowest order," where loose women "drove decency to cover with their abandoned talk and gestures." Sailors and steamboat men caroused in these bars and brothels, and their revels usually ended in "blood and violence." Authorities preferred to ignore them unless they spilled into respectable neighborhoods or downtown merchants complained. Then police cracked heads and filled the jails.[13]

Black seamen had to walk a more careful line. As late as 1840 they constituted 10 percent of Gulf packet crews—several men per ship—a number that steadily declined as the Civil War approached. In the beginning they attracted little notice along the multiethnic waterfronts of Mobile and New Orleans, both of which had significant free black and Creole populations. In the latter city they frequented brothels at the intersection of Bourbon and Orleans Streets where they could misbehave without fear of prosecution. "When I was a young man in me prime," one of their chanteys went, "I chased them yaller gals two at a time." But as the century progressed, Southern politicians and Caribbean officials worried about the effect free black sailors might have on local enslaved communities. One Cuban slave owner predicted that "the existence of free blacks and mulattoes in the midst of the slavery of their companions is an example which will become very dangerous one day." Legislative restrictions soon followed—Negro Seaman Acts in Alabama, Florida, and Louisiana, and a royal order in Cuba—that prohibited black sailors from setting foot in slave ports. It required the master of any vessel to submit a list of free blacks on board and pay a two thousand-dollar bond. "The condition of the bond is," the Act read, "that such free colored persons shall remain on board the vessel and not leave the same during the stay of the vessel in the waters of this state; and upon its departure, that such free persons will depart with the vessel." Under no circumstances was there to be any communication "between the free colored persons on board the vessel and slaves, or free persons of color within the state." Even more stringent laws required the sheriff to seize and detain black sailors until such time as the ship left. Blacks thrown into Southern jails later reported deprivation and abuse. "They do treat coloured seamen very bad," one black jack complained after he was released from the Crescent City calaboose. Little wonder that fewer and fewer of them signed onto Gulf-bound packets.[14]

Shore troubles aside, sea dangers were equal-opportunity threats to black and white sailors, as well as indomitable captains and well-heeled passengers. Ship owners and captains considered the coastal routes more dangerous than the transatlantic ones. Any sailor worth his salt prefers blue water to muddy rivers, shoals, sandbars, coral reefs, and lee shores. The Gulf included all of the above in addition to irritating calms and autumn hurricanes. Successfully navigating the lower Mississippi River, for example, involved more than just tricky currents and shifting winds at the English Turn or pesky bars at the mouths. During her passage downriver in the early 1840s, the thirty-three-year-old English novelist Matilda Charlotte Houston was unnerved when night fell. Peering into the gloom, she wrote, "the fog became very thick, and we were kept rather in a state of alarm from the number of steamers, which were constantly passing us." In order to avoid a collision, crewmen placed lights at the mastheads. Sailing the Florida Straits was treacherous given the right conditions of winds and tides. In November 1838, the packet ship *Matilda*, out of Mobile with cotton and passengers headed for New

York, was caught "by a strong current" and driven "on a ridge of rocks, about 65 miles from Havana." Fortunately no lives were lost, and the captain went ashore to seek assistance. In his absence, nearby village officials boarded and claimed the cargo as salvage. Exasperated passengers and crew abandoned ship, and a weeks-long diplomatic kerfuffle ensued. In an 1851 letter to the American Light House Board, Capt. George Barker, a Boston merchant captain, enumerated the problems as he saw them. "From 1832 to 1840 I commanded a packet-ship between Boston and New Orleans," he wrote. "The navigation of the Gulf of Mexico through the Gulf of Florida, is very intricate and dangerous. Our first point from the Gulf of Mexico is the Dry Tortugas, on which is a fixed light, but not of sufficient brilliancy and power to be seen over ten miles in very clear weather; then we shape our course through the Gulf." He argued that it was "of the greatest importance" that this light "should be of the first magnitude." The light at Key West he thought adequate as "can be seen fifteen miles," but otherwise the "whole coast . . . is very deficient in lights, beacons, and buoys." In fact, several passes and channels had no lights. Instead, they were poorly marked by stakes driven in muddy bottoms or rotting kegs tethered by slimy ropes invisible in fog, rain, or darkness. Other captains concurred. After careful study, so did the Light House Board. Even well-built brick towers left something to be desired. Of the Pensacola signal, its report noted, "The light is deficient in power . . . Pensacola requires a first-class seacoast light." Mobile's was better. "This is believed to be the best reflector-light on the coast," the report concluded, "being revolving, and fitted with twenty-one lamps and twenty-one inch reflectors." But at a height of only 55 feet its visibility extended 12 miles, not enough, and the study recommended a new tower 125 feet high. The lights at the mouths of the Mississippi were at least carefully maintained, but at great expense and "without commensurate benefits." The report did not mince words: "These lights are of great importance to the commerce of the Gulf of Mexico, and should be rendered the most efficient in the shortest space of time." Until the situation improved, passengers trusted sharp-eyed captains and sailors to bring them safely to port.[15]

Hurricanes were beyond the control of government boards and regulation, and in those pre-satellite days struck with little warning. Sailors preferred to stay out of the Gulf during the worst of the season between August and November, but with cotton crops maturing in the fall that was impossible. A well-captained ship and crew might survive a hurricane in the open Gulf, but if on a lee shore, their prospects were grim at best. In October 1837 a powerful cyclone churned into the Gulf and caught several packets underway. According to one contemporary account, a British ship named the *Seagull* was in the Florida Straits when the storm struck. "She was on a lee shore," it read, "in four and a half fathoms of water, with her sails split and blown out of the bolt-ropes." The quick-thinking captain rove lifelines and dropped the anchor, which rattled out to "one hundred fathoms of chain." Head on to the waves, the vessel breasted the great swells, some of which broke over her deck, cascaded down her length, and sluiced off the stern. Incredibly, both ship and crew survived. Farther into the Gulf, an American packet rode the storm under bare poles, but the howling winds knocked her on her beam-ends—that is, on her side. Desperate crew members hacked away one of the masts, and she slowly righted, all hands alive.[16]

The clipper ship *Robert H. Dixey* was not so lucky. In the late summer of 1860, she delivered a load of cotton to Liverpool, returned to New York where she took on sundries, and was back in the Gulf when a falling barometer and wispy rooster-tail clouds augured doom. Her captain, fifty-one-year-old Richard William Dixey, ordered his black Bahamian crew to make for nearby Mobile Bay with all haste, and they anchored within the bar the evening of September 14. There the *Dixey* was furiously lashed by wind and wave, and her anchor chain parted. At the hurricane's mercy, she was blown first to the north and then south out of the bay and onto a shoal flanking the channel's eastern side. According to a local pilot who had hitched a ride at New York and survived the wreck, "All saw the danger at hand. The mainmast and mizzenmast came up, and everything was going to pieces, when all hands made for the forecastle and lashed themselves on: 24 men all told." The pilot and five men abandoned ship and urged Dixey to do the same, but he refused to desert his brave Bahamians, who could not swim. "Goodbye, I hope we shall meet in heaven," he told the pilot. Capt. Dixey perished with his ship and crew and was buried in Mobile's Magnolia Cemetery.[17]

Unless confronted with a mishap, calms, or bad weather, passengers were generally positive about their packet voyages. Some had a better "undergoing stomach" than others and fared beautifully. Most landlubbers required a little time to get their sea legs, and some took pleasure in the experience's absurdity. One declared: "The bounding of the surges at first occasioned such incessant ludicrous vacillations from a central basis, that I misstepped as one maudled. The ocean boys step wide, and firm, and sway the body to the motion of the ship." The English traveler John W. Oldmixon took a packet out of Mobile during the 1850s. He had to wedge himself into his berth at night to keep from getting pitched onto the deck, but that was expected in heavy seas. Of more concern were the cotton bales stacked everywhere. "Ours is an excellent cabin," he wrote, "but it's full of cotton." Oldmixon adjusted and when the weather was fair set up his little writing desk next to the mizzenmast. During the early 1830s, Latrobe booked a berth on board the Collins packet *Mexican* at Veracruz bound for New York. He thought her a "fine new vessel, clean and well-ordered, a fast sailer, and altogether the most comfortable ship I was ever in. We had our staterooms on deck in a kind of open roundhouse." Their progress was rapid and once in the Gulf Stream they logged five hundred miles in forty-eight hours. Time was money, even in those supposedly less hurried days, and everyone rejoiced in a quick passage.[18]

Those who wrote about their packet trips often described their fellow travelers in great detail, and these mini-sketches make for entertaining reading. Diversity was the rule. In a letter to his brother in 1819, Arthur Singleton enumerated seven passengers on board his ship out of New Orleans—"a Spaniard, a German, a Frenchman, an Englishman, an Irishman, a Missouriman from the lead mines, and myself, a New Englander." Additionally there were ten people in steerage, plus "a yellow steward, and a black cook." On a run to Havana from New York in 1839, Frances Calderón de la Barca, the Scottish-born wife of a Spanish official, wrote that her shipmates "do not appear very remarkable." But then she gave the lie to her statement. There were "Madame A_____," a Mexican prima donna, with her husband and son; "M. B_____ with moustaches like a bird's nest; a pretty widow in deep affliction, at least in deep mourning; a maiden lady going out as a governess, and every variety of Spaniard and Havanero." The most interesting passenger by the Señora's lights was a little deaf-mute girl, "who has been teaching me to speak on my fingers." But for the modern reader, it is surely the bushy "M. B_____, pale, dirty, and much resembling a brigand out of employ," who trod "the deck with uneasy footsteps and a cigar appearing from out his moustaches, like a light in a tangled forest, or a jack-o-lantern in a marshy thicket." On his 1859 trip south, Richard Henry Dana, the Boston lawyer and world-famous author of *Two Years Before the Mast* (1840), noted "Yankee shipmasters going out to join their 'cotton wagons' at New Orleans and Mobile merchants pursuing a commerce that knows no rest and no locality; confirmed invalids advised to go to Cuba to die under mosquito nets and be buried in a Potter's Field . . . and here and there a mere vacation-maker, like myself."[19]

By the mid-nineteenth century, the Gulf basin's cities and towns presented a varied picture of population and prosperity. In Florida, as yet lightly settled and undeveloped, Key West bustled with over two thousand residents and included a naval station, a hospital, a Catholic Church, and a newspaper. Wrecking and fishing provided a sustainable living. Up the peninsula and along the panhandle, Tampa, Cedar Key, St. Marks, and Apalachicola were all little more than villages with a few hundred inhabitants who fished, farmed, cut timber, and at the latter place shipped some cotton. Pensacola had its fine harbor, of course, but the lack of interior rivers kept it small. Mobile and New Orleans were by far the most consequential and wealthy cities on the American coast. With their productive hinterlands and superior river systems, they had 1850 populations of twenty thousand and one hundred thousand respectively. These were the booming cotton ports, their live oak-shaded streets lined by balconied Italianate residences and columned Greek Revival public buildings like Barton Academy at Mobile and the St. Charles Hotel at New Orleans. When Oldmixon toured Alabama's port city in the early 1850s, he found downtown busy and noisy. "Here . . . every corner has its *Exchange*," he wrote, "or great room, with its bar and immense display of bottles, where a Swiss organ or hurdy-gurdy may be heard constantly, and a crowd constantly drinking." One hundred and twenty miles west, the Crescent City was swiftly becoming Americanized, and its older French Quarter was considered a quaint holdover. In 1857, Mary Matthews, daughter of a Massachusetts ship captain, visited the iconic French Market. "Upon arrival there, we found a long, low shed, or perhaps a succession of sheds," she wrote in her diary, "with roofs supported by iron shafts, and beneath a pavement of flagstones. In the immediate vicinity are shops, cafés, sailor boarding houses, and in the rear, the levee and the Mississippi." As she wandered amid a crowd "of all races" and even a mule and two pigs, she browsed "vegetables, fruit, confectionary, clothing, jewelry." Other Vieux Carré first-timers were less enamored. As he was carried by buggy through the Quarter, Frederick Law Olmstead noted "narrow, dirty streets, among grimy old stuccoed walls; high arched windows and doors, balconies and entresols, and French noises and French smells, French signs, ten to one of English, but with funny polygomatic arrangements, sometimes, from which less influential families were not excluded." Oldmixon agreed, citing "the want of care and neatness in everything in-doors and out." He booked a room at the huge Verandah Hotel for three dollars a day where he was overwhelmed by the crowds—"hundreds at table, hundreds at the bar."[20]

Texas, annexed to the United States in 1845, had nothing to compare on its long coastline, though most agreed that Galveston held promise. Over four thousand people lived there, directly facing the Gulf with an expansive bay behind them. Memories of Laffite's Campeachy lent the island a romantic air, but not everyone was impressed by the American town's slapdash look. Matilda Charlotte Houston described rude houses "built of wood, most frequently of planks nailed together, clinker-fashion. The whole affair has, I must say, at present rather a fragile appearance, and it will readily be conjectured, that when viewed from the water, any grandeur of effect must be quite out of the question." All the island's buildings were supported on wooden blocks, and the only bricks Houston saw "were those forming one solitary chimney." Otherwise, where the streets terminated bay side there were several rough piers, a couple of hotels, a few stores, six bars, an oyster house, three warehouses, and, beloved of all Americans, a newspaper office. Despite these primitive beginnings, maritime trade was encouraging—225 annual port calls during the late 1840s—with connections to Tampico, Veracruz, New Orleans, and Havana. In contrast to Mobile and New Orleans, there were few slaves, mostly house servants, dock workers, or shop assistants. A writer for *DeBow's Review* inspected the city in 1847 and painted a more agreeable picture than did Mrs. Houston. He highlighted better dwellings where the wealthier citizens lived and praised Galveston's lush gardens. "Every variety of tropical shrub, flower and tree grow with vigor and rapidity," he wrote, "and are now as green as a bay tree at the north in mid-winter, or any tree with us in June." Especially eye-catching were the towering oleanders "loaded with fresh and beautiful bloom." Foregrounding everything was

Matagorda, Texas, on the eve of the American Civil War. COURTESY LIBRARY OF CONGRESS.

the eternal, booming Gulf. No one worried about what it might do in a wrathful mood.[21]

As for the rest of the Texas coast, there was little to arrest one's attention. The mainland was blocked by long peninsulas and barrier islands, and all the passes had shallow bars. Matagorda and Corpus Christi were lightly settled frontier outposts, and Brownsville, situated on the Mexican border twenty-three miles up the Rio Grande from its modest Gulf outlet, was a crude army town, a stopover for forty-niners, and a cross-border smuggler's haunt. Matamoros stood on the other side of the river in the State of Tamaulipas and was many land-traveling Americans' first exposure to Mexico. "After you get over the ferry, you have an open and picturesque road before you," wrote a correspondent for the *New Orleans Tropic* visiting American soldiers there in 1846. He thought a windowless farmhouse interesting for its woven-reed-and-marsh-grass construction, "not unlike rude basket work." Adobe houses in town were more substantial and betrayed the country's long-running political instability. Wooden doors and blinds were thick, small iron balconies high up, and first stories bare to protect "both male and female from the assaults of sudden revolution, of lawless robbers, of plundering soldiery, and thefts of hungry officials." The reporter entered an unpromising store and found "the stock to consist of an empty claret box, a jug of whiskey, two tin cups, a few pounds of maple sugar, a pail of Rio Grande water, and a Mexican saddle worth one hundred and fifty dollars."[22]

Farther south, below the tropic, Tampico sat upon the Río Pánuco. It was six miles from the Gulf's breakers, and like New Orleans, its commerce was impeded by a shallow bar at the river mouth, with the additional inconvenience of fierce northers. Silver, sugarcane, and dye were its most important exports, and vital agricultural machinery, tools, and manufactured goods from the United States were its imports. The population stood in the low thousands but was regularly purged by cholera and *el vómito,* the graphic local designation for yellow fever. Latrobe, who seems to have been everywhere, visited in 1834 on board a small brig. His first impressions were of the waterfront, crowded by light-draft sailing vessels and "market boats and canoes of the Indians," loaded with fruit, sugarcane, bamboo, hay, and sweet water from farther upstream. Nearby, native women waded "with the Etruscan-shaped water jar of the country." Transfixed, Latrobe stared at their white dresses hiked above glistening brown thighs. They seemed oblivious both of the gawking white man and the alligators "swarming on the neighboring swampy shore." As for the town itself, it was "built in regular squares, upon the narrow and depressed termination of a rocky peninsula." The architecture presented a confused mix of stone, frame, and mud-slathered bamboo, inhabited by European merchants, American traders, and impoverished Indians respectively. Flat roofs, brightly painted walls, and secluded interior courtyards were the better dwellings' common features. Latrobe dismissed the native population as "the most mongrel that can be conceived," but he admired the people's "extremely picturesque" clothing with its "diversity of colour and pattern."[23]

Veracruz was larger and more prosperous with a population of ten thousand, by far Mexico's most important Gulf city. Latrobe approached it from the land and was sobered by the "utterly sterile character of the shore on which it is based" and the "unclean birds" that flocked about it. Once inside its substantial walls, however, he admitted that the city was "regularly and even beautifully built, with fine open streets, a noble spacious square, and many churches." Robert Wilson, an American lawyer who passed through in 1853, contrasted it with New Orleans, which he had just quit four days earlier. "Instead of the noise and bustle of a commercial emporium," he wrote, "all here is as quiet and as cleanly as a church-yard." An open-air marketplace betrayed a little more activity, with people haggling for "meats, and vegetables, and huxter's wares." After morning mass, "bonnetless women of low and high degree" briefly crowded the streets, rubbing elbows with black-gowned priests and the local constabulary "in dirty cotton uniforms." As for the most famous local landmark, the fortress at San Juan de Ulúa, where he went to board his packet ship, Wilson considered it obsolete and worthless but for the "light house which stands upon one of its towers." Good Yankee that he was, Wilson was most interested in trade and reported that the city's exports and imports stood at $26 million each. Cotton was the dominant import, along with American machinery, French silks, and wines. As at Tampico, sugar and silver were shipped out, though

Veracruz appears neat and orderly but somnolent in this 1838 print. The picturesque city had a fearsome reputation for disease and northers. COURTESY NEW YORK PUBLIC LIBRARY.

in far greater quantity. Veracruz enjoyed regular packet service to United States ports except when northers disrupted shipping.[24]

Other than Campeche, a modest old port with stone walls, a beautiful church, and a racially mixed population, fishing villages were the rule around the Yucatán's seagirt margins. Yalahau, practically a stone's throw from Cabo Catoche, was typical. It faced a shallow lagoon protected from northers by Isla Holbox. The island's name means "black hole" in Mayan, a reference to the deep, dark water that fills a small pool on the island's southern tip. During the early 1840s, the American writer and antiquarian John Lloyd Stephens spent a few days there while he explored nearby Indian ruins. He and his entourage traveled by land and beheld "a low, swampy plain, with a grove of coconut trees at a long distance before us." They crossed a slimy stone causeway to the village, "a long, straggling street of huts, elevated a few feet above the washing of the waves." Within an hour, Stephens's company was "completely domesticated" in a little stone house "on the very edge of the bank, so near the sea that the waves had undermined part of the long piazza in front." The village's only distraction was a crumbling fort built to scare off pirates, inhabited by "a little Meztizo tailor" and his wife who "paid no rent, and seemed perfectly happy." Yalahau's sights exhausted, the Americans boarded a canoe the next day to tour Isla Holbox. Their modest conveyance was named *El Sol*. "It was thirty-five feet long and six feet wide at the top," Stephens wrote, "but curving toward bottom. It carried two large sails, with the peaks held up by heavy poles secured at the masts; had a space of eight or ten feet clear in the stern, and all the rest was filled with luggage, provisions, and water-casks." Their "captain" was a middle-aged mestizo, "a fisherman hired for the occasion." Getting to the island was complicated by fickle winds, but eventually the canoe anchored in front of a shack, the only dwelling there. "The fisherman was swinging in his hammock," Stephens observed, "and a handsome Indian boy was making tortillas, the two presenting a fine picture of youth and vigorous old age." Nearby stood several jars of turtle oil, and outside, "rather too near when the wind was in certain quarters, were the skeletons of turtles from which he had extracted it."[25]

Beyond Cabo Catoche, across the Yucatán Channel, and past Cabo San Antonio, Havana was still the Gulf's largest and most important city. When Dana arrived, his salty old sailor's eye immediately assessed the harbor. "What a world of shipping!" he enthused. "The masts make a belt of dense forest along the edge of the city, all the ships lying head in to the street, like horses at their mangers; while the vessels at anchor nearly choke up the passage ways to the deeper bays beyond." When María Mercedes de Santa Cruz y Montalvo, the Countess of Merlín, returned to her native Cuba in 1840 after years living in France, she gloried in the experience. "Here comes the city," she wrote, "here it is, with its balconies, awnings, and rooftops, the delightful single-story houses of the middle class, the doors wide enough to admit a carriage and the tall grated windows, but everything open, so that one can see at a glance the details of domestic life." Her senses nearly overloaded, the Countess wandered narrow, unpaved streets that smelled of coffee, vanilla, and camphor, blessing the shade provided by long, low-slung awnings overhead. Passing shops and apartments, she jostled with throngs of "mulattos and blacks, some in white pants, white jacket, and straw hats, others in torn short trousers and a bright colored bandana tied around their heads." Out of Havana's two hundred thousand residents, whites were a distinct minority. White women generally kept themselves secluded behind thick walls, but women of color were visible everywhere, showing bare shoulders and smoking like sugar mills. "These *negras* show off," the Countess huffed, "rocking their hips in the middle of the street, with their kerchiefs on their heads, their bracelets, and the cigar." A few years later, the Swedish novelist Fredrika Bremer was more charmed than disgusted by the sight of such women, whom she regarded "with great pleasure." Many of their husbands were in trade, she explained, and it was not uncommon to see them "with flowers in their hair, walking with their families on the principal promenades in a manner which denotes freedom and prosperity."[26]

Unfortunately, not all Cuba's people of color enjoyed the fruits of commerce and freedom. Slavery was still legal on the island, and though the international slave trade was not, ships loaded with chained Africans found a friendly reception there. In a letter to the American politician Henry Clay, a British banker and social reformer named Joseph John Gurney lamented the sight of slave ships in Havana's harbor. "They are fitted up with guns," he wrote, "and, like the brigs or schooners, are constructed with consummate art, for the purpose of swift sailing. They are utterly unsuitable for a legitimate commerce. The painful compression of the wretched negroes, in the holds of these vessels . . . is too horrible to be described." The enslavers' successful transatlantic trips meant both high profits and a steady labor supply for the island's plantations and sugar mills. The numbers of enslaved people who landed at Havana varied from year to year, from 10,495 in 1838, to 7,329 fifteen years later. Bremer observed some of these poor souls at work and was appalled by their condition and treatment. "They are regarded altogether as cattle," she fumed. While staying at an outlying sugar plantation, she was "so depressed that I was not able to do much." All around her, enslaved people worked incessantly while an overseer cracked a whip over their heads and gruffly admonished them to go faster. Not surprisingly, there were revolts, including large ones in 1812 and 1844. These were brutally suppressed and the leaders decapitated or beaten and clapped in irons.[27]

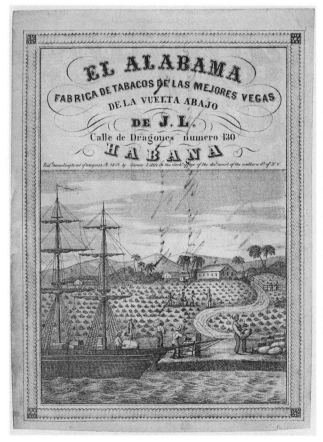

Tobacco label. The nineteenth-century affinity between Cuba and the American South is demonstrated by this 1859 label. It depicts plantation slaves loading tobacco bales onto a waiting ship. Over 110 million Cuban cigars were shipped to the United States that year alone, many to Gulf ports. COURTESY LIBRARY OF CONGRESS.

Americans who were not disturbed by such things found Havana a congenial place of residence and business. Packets regularly ran down from Mobile and New Orleans, insuring close and steady contact. It was no accident that travelers often compared the United States' Gulf ports to Havana and Old World cities. One man felt "a confused remembrance of some of the best Spanish and French West India towns" in New Orleans, while a British correspondent thought Mobile bore a "kinder-sorter" resemblance to Málaga, Spain. In short, the Gulf basin's biggest cities shared a long Latin colonial history, not to mention similarities of climate, flora, and fauna. Southerners certainly felt comfortable in Cuba and owned sugar plantations, operated hotels, and ran businesses there. The president of the New Orleans Gas Light & Banking Company set up a sister operation at Havana, and American mechanics, accountants, and clerks established themselves in a number of enterprises. Little wonder that as the nineteenth century progressed and the theory of Manifest Destiny took hold, more and more Americans coveted the long island to their south. Jefferson himself had said Cuba was "indispensable to the continuance and integrity of the Union," and a Florida senator declared the Gulf "a common basin of expansion." As a slave society, Cuba was also especially attractive to Southerners wishing to add more slave states to the Union. In 1848 President James K. Polk offered Spain $100 million for the island. He was instantly refused. Unwilling to take no for an answer, violent men assembled to the north, filibusters determined to wrest Cuba, Mexico, and the small Latin American republics from their legitimate governments and make them part of a slave empire, a "Golden Circle" round the basin. Truly the Gulf of Mexico would be "simply a Southern lake." It was a ghastly vision, doomed to fail. But it was hardly the first, and would not be the last, to roil the Gulf's beautiful blue waters in that extraordinary century.[28]

Chapter Six

Violent Sea

Kell now sang out, in his powerful clarion voice, through his trumpet, "This is the Confederate States steamer *Alabama!*"

Raphael Semmes,
*Memoirs of Service
Afloat,* 1868

They called it the "Pastry War," and of all the Gulf's nineteenth-century conflicts it was easily the most ridiculous. But it also offered compelling early evidence that a new era of naval warfare was at hand. Ten years in the making, it stemmed from a Mexico City street riot between rival political factions. Such scuffles were common in the capital. Since achieving independence in 1821, Mexico's internal affairs had been marked by disruptive intrigue and frequent leadership changes. It was during one such 1828 power tussle that unruly soldiers looted a local marketplace. Among the ransacked shops was a patisserie whose French owner, M. Remontel, subsequently claimed sixty thousand pesos in damages. This was an astronomical sum at the time, and the Mexican government haughtily rejected his claim. Not easily deterred, Remontel pressed his case for years, and by 1838 had taken it to the French government. Rather than dismiss it as a trivial distraction, King Louis-Philippe saw it as an opportunity to call in past Mexican debts as well as the losses of other French citizens in the riot, all to the tune of six hundred thousand pesos. Unsurprisingly, the sitting Mexican president, Anastasio Bustamante, refused, and Louis-Philippe sent the navy to Veracruz to coerce payment.[1]

The fleet arrived in March, and the Baron Antoine-Louis Deffaudis formally presented a list of demands to Bustamante that included payment of the debt by April 15, the release of any French citizens held in Mexican jails, and the removal of "certain offending officials." Bustamante labeled the demands "un verdadero libelo" (a true libel) and put his trust in *el vomito* and strong northers to drive away the French. In response the French suspended diplomatic relations and blockaded Veracruz. Just as Bustamante had hoped, disease and storm afflicted the fleet, but it did not withdraw, and the standoff remained unresolved into the fall. Eager to force a conclusion, Louis-Philippe sent more ships under Rear Admiral Charles Baudin. By October, two dozen French vessels were offshore. They included transports loaded with four thousand men, three frigates, two bomb ketches, a sloop of war, and two steamers, the *Phaeton* and *Météor,* each boasting 160-horsepower engines. Since the Mexicans were determined not to fire first, Baudin took advantage of the situation and dispatched crews in longboats to take soundings right up to the very walls of San Juan de Ulúa.[2]

Veracruz's venerable harbor fort was no longer as intimidating as it had once been. Its low, soft coral walls, ninety-foot-high square tower, and brick lighthouse were vulnerable to the French navy's thirty-two-pounder guns and exploding shells. To make matters worse, the fort's small cannon were badly mounted, supplied with inferior powder, and poorly served by conscripts who lacked lateral protection from casemates. If there was a fight, it was likely to be a stark demonstration of what would happen when an antiquated fortification faced a modern navy.[3]

On hand to protect American interests was the USS *Erie,* a trim sloop of war commanded by David Glasgow Farragut, promoted to captain since his pirate-chasing days off Cuba. Before any hostilities, the young American officer took the opportunity to visit the French admiral's flagship. He was impressed by Baudin, a balding, fifty-three-year-old, one-armed fighter who had seen service in the Napoleonic Wars. Baudin was a master seaman and strategist who openly shared his plans. After an hour in his company, Farragut opined that he would have been a "*rara avis* in any navy." He approved the admiral's battle-ready decks, everything shipshape and squared away, took particular interest in the thirty-two-pounders equipped with new percussion locks—"no spring, no machinery, in fact, nothing that can become deranged"—and expected the coming contest to be one sided and short. The French had set November 27 as their new deadline, after which "war or peace would immediately follow." Guessing that diplomacy had run its course, Farragut had his bluejackets embark all U.S. citizens and their valuables. As expected, Bustamante was in no mood to concede anything to Baudin. Therefore, on the appointed day Farragut anchored safely off to one side and watched as the *Phaeton* and *Météor* towed the frigates into the most advantageous positions. Steam technology was yet young, but applied to naval warfare, it was even better evidence than the new percussion locks that the old ways were doomed. "Everything was done by them," Farragut wrote of the steamers. "The day was calm, or nearly so, and the ships had no sails to manage. As soon as the anchor was let go, they were ready for action." Still refusing to open hostilities, the Mexicans waited behind their coral walls. "At precisely 2:30 P.M.," Farragut wrote, "the Admiral's ship fired the first gun, and immediately the firing became general."[4]

The French shells were devastating. Farragut was astonished to see them punch a foot deep into the coral and then explode, "tearing out great masses of stone, and in some instances rending the wall from base to top." Inside the fort, gun carriages were upended, men knocked down by growling fragments, magazines exploded, and the square tower blasted to smithereens with its defenders. The Mexicans returned fire desultorily, but most of their rounds splashed short or harmlessly thumped the enemy ships. By sunset it was over, the fort practically pulverized and at least two hundred of its garrison dead. The surviving Mexicans tied weights to their erstwhile comrades and sank them in the harbor. Unfortunately, they did a sloppy job, and in a ghastly coda to the whole affair, Farragut wrote that the deceased "were seen floating about in all directions." For his part, Baudin could only shake his head and curse "the folly" of his brave opponents' leaders for putting them in such an untenable position.[5]

The following afternoon French troops occupied the fort. The defenders were allowed to withdraw, their honor intact. The overall Mexican commander at Veracruz then decided to parley with Baudin in order to avoid a bloody siege. He readily accepted conditions that included letting the French provision and sending all but one thousand of his soldiers at least ten miles away. This news riled the capital. The central government under Bustamante formally declared war and funneled more troops toward the coast. It was at this turbulent moment that Gen. Santa Anna reinserted himself into national affairs, promising to defend the city.[6]

If ever there was a genius at exploiting the main chance, it was Santa Anna. He was forty-four years old, tall, darkly handsome, and brave, though a poor military strategist. Ever since his crushing defeat two years earlier by Sam Houston at San Jacinto, he had been keeping a low profile at his nearby villa. The Pastry War provided him the ideal opportunity to rescue his beloved nation from humiliation and ruin. He thus obtained the government's blessing and appeared in Veracruz's plaza announcing the declaration of war and his intention of throwing the French into the sea. Farragut and several of his officers paid the general a visit on November 29 and were cordially received. Santa Anna assured them that American citizens would be respected. He also appealed to their shared geographic interests, asking them to tell President Martin Van Buren "that we are all one family, and must be united against Europeans obtaining a foothold on this continent." This unusual play on hemispheric solidarity was vintage Santa Anna, as were his parting comments that the recent surrender was an outrage and he would "die rather than yield one point for which they had contended."[7]

Exasperated by this development, Baudin declared that he would not wage war on innocent civilians because of their government's stupidity. In order to avoid a messy siege, he concocted a plan to gut Santa Anna's preparations before they went any further. On the foggy morning of December 5, three French infantry divisions landed on the city's wide waterfront—one to the south, one at the center, and one to the north. "They blew the gates off their hinges with sacks of powder," Farragut wrote. Charging in dense columns, the French rushed Santa Anna's headquarters. The Mexicans fought well, giving the general time to escape "in his shirt and trousers." The farther the French penetrated into town the more obstinate the defense became, and rooftop sharpshooters began taking a toll. Baudin wasn't interested in capturing the city and ordered a withdrawal. True to form, Santa Anna seized the moment when French retreat was certain to sally forth with several hundred men, prancing about in front of them on a white charger. To all appearances he intended to harry the enemy to the water's edge and apprehend Baudin himself. The French knew how to deal with that, with a blast of grapeshot that raked the Mexican line. Over a dozen soldiers were killed or wounded, including Santa Anna, who was hit in the left leg. It was amputated shortly thereafter, but even then the general turned misfortune to advantage, trumpeting his sacrifice and using his new status as the savior of Veracruz to once again ascend to the presidency. In an ironic conclusion to the war, the British, who were alarmed by the blockade's disruptions, sent a small fleet to help broker a treaty. Santa Anna's loud *pronunciamentos* to the contrary, the Mexicans paid the French every peso. The Pastry War was over, Veracruz once again open to commerce, and Santa Anna a hero. And young Capt. Farragut sailed away mulling the lessons he had learned watching steamships pummel an old harbor fort.[8]

Unfortunately for Mexico, the end of the Pastry War did not bring peace. There was trouble north and south. To the north, Texas had been ruling itself as an independent republic since 1836. Santa Anna's attempt at conquest had ended in disaster, but Mexico City still refused to let the province go. The troublesome gringos' cause was helped immeasurably by the Texas Navy. Consisting of a few schooners and brigs, this feisty force effectively blockaded the Mexican coast, harried its shipping, and prevented a maritime invasion or resupply of Santa Anna's troops. Its commodore was twenty-nine-year-old Edwin Ward Moore, a U.S. Navy veteran, aggressive fighter, crack administrator, and fluent Spanish speaker. Moore invested his own funds to keep his ships seaworthy. When they weren't blockading or chasing Mexican fishermen, he had them survey the Texas coast, updating the older, inaccurate charts.[9]

To the south, the residents of the Yucatán Peninsula, many of them native Mayans, grew tired of Mexico City's draconian policies and in 1840 emulated Texas by declaring independence. In response, the central government blockaded Campeche. Alert to an attractive strategic opportunity, not to mention a new revenue stream, Commodore Moore struck an alliance with the Yucatecans, agreeing to protect their coast for eight thousand dollars a month. Back in Texas, incoming President Sam Houston disapproved of the deal and sent two commissioners to New Orleans to seize Moore's ships before they departed. His effort failed when the commissioners sided with Moore. One of them, Col. James Morgan, even joined the expedition. "If I have swerved from my orders or duty," he informed the press, "it was for benefit of my adopted country; for which I have risked my life and am perfectly willing to lose it, provided I can only see her free and at peace with the world." Enthused about his decision, Morgan declared Moore's ships in "apple pie order" and "bully." And so on April 15, 1843, the six hundred-ton flagship *Austin*, with twenty guns, and the four hundred-ton brig *Wharton,* sixteen guns, crossed the Gulf and joined a small fleet of Yucatecan gunboats at Campeche.[10]

Their arrival could not have been timelier. The city was under siege, surrounded by several thousand Mexican soldiers and blockaded by a small fleet that routinely hurled shells into its midst. Moore immediately placed his vessels between the Mexican ships and the town, eliciting wild cheers from residents lining the old stone walls. By any rational calculus, it was an audacious move. Moore's force was lightly armed and undermanned compared to what he was facing. In an effort to buttress their meager navy, the Mexicans had purchased the services of two steamships with British officers and crews. The 775-ton *Guadalupe* was an iron-hulled side-wheeler powered by 180-horsepower engines and armed with formidable sixty-eight-pounder swivel-mounted Paixhans shell guns (named for their French inventor). If properly managed, these weapons promised to smash Moore's flimsy wooden flotilla. Even more intimidating was the 1,100-ton *Moctezuma,* a brigantine-rigged wooden side-wheeler with a pair of 280- horsepower engines, two Paixhans guns, and six big thirty-two-pounders. Undeterred, Moore chose to attack on April 30, only one day after his arrival. The *Austin* and *Wharton* boldly headed out, followed by the diminutive Yucatecan gunboats. For his part, Col. Morgan couldn't wait to challenge the enemy and their "great humbug *Paixhans!*"[11]

Winds were light, making Moore's sailing vessels difficult to maneuver. The steamers kept their distance in order to exploit their longer-range guns, but most of their early shots missed. As the two forces drew closer, each hoisted a medley of flags that would have confused a neutral observer. The *Austin* displayed the Lone Star ensign at her mizzen, British and American banners at her foremast. The *Guadalupe* ran a British flag up her foremast, while the *Moctezuma* hoisted a Union Jack at her main and a Spanish flag at her foremast. That both sides chose to fly British flags was not so surprising if one knew the political background prevalent at the time, which everyone on board those vessels and watching from Campeche did. Britain's first interest was in maintaining commercial dominance. It openly traded with Texas but withheld official recognition because of staunch antislavery policies and significant financial involvement in Mexico. Furthermore, keeping Texas out of the United States and both of those troublesome democracies weak were reasons enough to send the Mexicans two state-of-the-art steamships. As the sun rose over the southwestern Gulf of Mexico, a historic clash between old and new naval technologies loomed.[12]

Situated on board the *Austin,* a young midshipman named Alfred Walke recorded the fight in his journal. "At 7:30 the enemy wore and stood for us," he wrote. "Hauled up the fore sail. At 7:35 the enemy commenced firing at us. Most of their shot passed over us, some fell short but none struck us." Thirty-five minutes later he recorded that his vessel "exchanged broadsides with the enemys steamers, their shot passing over us." Others came frighteningly close: "At 11:05 a sixty-eight pound shot from the Guadaloupe cut the starboard after mizzen shroud about 8 feet above the dead eye (Commodore Moore holding the shroud at the time). Passed between Commodore Moore's and Lt. Gray's head and would have killed both of them but that they inclined their bodies in opposite directions. Passed through the poop deck into the cabin and out the stern about two feet above the transom." By midday both sides broke off the engagement, Moore retiring toward Campeche and the steamers standing offshore several miles. Casualties and damage were light.[13]

Moore wanted to attack again, but fickle winds kept him idle for two weeks. During that time the Yucatecans loaned him several long-range eighteen-pounders from the city walls in order to better his odds. At last on May 16 he sailed, the Yucatecan gunboats prudently choosing to remain closer inshore. The Mexican squadron steamed away, and a sixteen-mile chase ensued. Gently heeled over in the wind, the *Austin* and *Wharton* attempted some shots, but they fell short. At mid-morning the wind abated, leaving Moore's squadron vulnerable, and the steamers reversed their course. The distance closed, both sides' shots began to land. Rigging was cut on board the Texans' ships, bulwarks smashed, decks splintered, and men wounded. One of the *Guadalupe*'s paddle wheels was damaged, and her flagstaff clipped. When her banner fluttered down into the water, according to Walke, the Texans "gave three hearty cheers." In an incredible stroke of good fortune for Moore, the wind abruptly increased, allowing him to drive the *Austin* between the steamers. Of a sudden, he could bring both of his broadsides to bear while the enemy ships dared not fire for fear of missing their foe and hitting each other. The Texans were ecstatic. Walke wrote that they gave "them our broadsides as the guns bore." Tongues of flame darted staccato from the *Austin*'s ports to devastating effect. The *Guadalupe* was "completely riddled by our shot & the *Montezuma* damaged considerably." Casualties on board the steamers were fearful—forty-seven dead and sixty-seven wounded on the *Guadalupe* and forty killed, including the captain, and twenty wounded on the *Moctezuma*. Only three Texans were killed on board the *Austin*. Two were killed on the *Wharton,* one by friendly fire. According to an account in *Niles National Register,* a sailor was "blown to atoms" while loading a gun that was fired before he had a chance to move aside. The steamers limped away, while ashore the Mexican infantry retreated after a series of reverses and steady desertion. Thanks to the Texas Navy, Campeche was saved. It was a stunning victory, not least because for the first and last time in maritime history, a wooden fleet under sail bested heavily armed and armored steamships. Col. Morgan stated it best: "We knocked hell into them."[14]

The consequences of Moore's adventure were significant. The British abandoned their hapless hosts, the Yucatecans negotiated a better arrangement with the central government, and the proud Texas Navy ruled the western Gulf. Considerably less proud was Sam Houston. He was in a blue fury over Moore's disobedience and ordered him arrested as a pirate. Moore was untroubled, labeling the Texas president a "humbug." He knew that patriotic fervor would save him from the gaol. Scholars have spilled considerable ink attempting to understand Houston's motivation. Was it a desire to placate Britain, save money, or something else? To this day no one knows. One contemporary correspondent opined that his proclamations were the result of "insanity." The *Houston Chronicle* argued that Moore was innocent and "cannot be arrested or punished in accordance with the laws of the republic." Galveston's citizens agreed, welcoming Moore as a hero to their wharves. To no one's surprise, he handily won at trial.[15]

In the summer of 1845, not long after Moore's triumphant return, a long essay penned by John L. O'Sullivan appeared in the *United States Magazine and Democratic Review*. The piece celebrated the recent annexation of Texas to the United States and thundered against European powers that would limit or check "our manifest destiny to overspread and to possess the whole of the continent, which Providence has given us for the great experiment of liberty." It was the first use of the term, which O'Sullivan repeated in a more widely read column for the *New York Morning News* at year's end. The coinage perfectly captured the national mood. James K. Polk of Tennessee had been swept into the president's office in 1844 promising to push the nation's borders all the way to the Pacific. Those worried about Texas's addition as a slave state were completely eclipsed by the expansionist fantasies of the masses. Most of this vast landscape belonged to Mexico, of course, and though lightly settled and minimally developed, its people resented the American intrusions. Polk didn't wish to provoke a war if he could help it, however, and offered to buy the lands in question—$5 million for Texas, $5 million for New Mexico (which then encompassed much of the American southwest, including New Mexico, Arizona, and parts of Colorado, Utah, and Nevada), and $25 million for the grandest prize of all, California. The offer was refused. A shooting war looked more likely than ever.[16]

Both sides sent troops to the Río Grande. On the north bank three thousand American regulars under the command of Gen. Zachary Taylor, better known as "Old Rough and Ready," erected an earthen fort opposite Matamoros and drilled beneath the bright Texas sun. Splendidly clad Mexican lancers monitored them from across the river but made no immediate moves. The peace was shattered not long afterward when a small U.S. cavalry patrol was ambushed and many of its men killed or captured. Outrage greeted the news in Washington, and war was declared May 13, 1846. A few newspapers expressed opposition, but throngs of volunteers flocked to the colors, especially in the slaveholding Southern states. American arms enjoyed significant early successes along the Río Grande and by year's end had taken New Mexico and California to boot. The navy mounted an effective blockade along the Gulf and bloodlessly took Tampico, thanks to the work of a female spy.[17]

Despite its losses, the Mexican government refused to make peace. Its internal politics were chaotic, and consensus was difficult to achieve on any point, much

less one so momentous. There were three presidents in 1846 alone, and the ubiquitous Santa Anna would hold the position twice in 1847. Studying the situation from
Washington, Polk knew that Mexico City had to be taken to finish the war. For that
he needed a new strategy and a new general. American troops in northern Mexico
were over five hundred miles away from the enemy capital, with a forbidding landscape between. General Taylor was popular with the army, but some questioned his
military decisions. The general was also a Whig Party favorite, and Polk, a Demo-
crat, feared him as a possible political rival. After much agonizing, the president
decided on his new plan by Thanksgiving. Veracruz would be taken in a combined
army-navy attack, and then the army would march overland the two hundred miles
to Mexico City. Gen. Winfield Scott would command the army, Cmdre. David
Conner the navy. These men were close in age—Scott was sixty-one and Conner
fifty-six—and proud veterans. Each respected the other's knowledge, knew when to
listen, and could yield when necessary.[18]

An amphibious landing is among the most difficult military operations to coordinate and execute, as the British learned to their distress at New Orleans in 1815.
The American effort at Veracruz was to be the largest combined assault the young
nation had ever attempted. The risks were considerable. Scott knew that he had to
take the city and get inland before the dreaded fever season. That meant Conner
would have to manage his fleet during 1847's winter months, when northers were
most prevalent. The commanders marshaled their forces just south of Tampico
at Lobos Island, two hundred miles above Veracruz. The army included roughly
ten thousand men, and the fleet almost fifty ships, among them sloops, a brig, five
schooners, the paddle frigate *Mississippi,* three paddle steamers, the screw sloop
Princeton, numerous transports, and smaller support vessels. Additionally, sixty-five
specially designed surfboats were secured on board the transports. These came in
three different sizes, so as to fit one within another on deck and conserve space.
The boats were contracted in northern Gulf shipyards at a cost of almost eight hundred dollars apiece. Their specifications left nothing to chance or imagination. "The
boats are to be built with both ends alike," they read, "so as to steer with an oar
at each end, and to stow in nests of three each. They are to be built of best well-
seasoned materials, in the most substantial manner, and iron fastened. The keel,
stems, deadwoods, aprons, floors, futtocks, and cap on gunwale to be of white oak."
Each boat was flat bottomed, caulked, painted, and supplied with an anchor and
over a dozen sturdy sixteen-foot ash oars.[19]

There were plenty of petty logistical problems as Scott and Conner attempted
to get everything in order. Bad weather, fumbled orders, and incomplete or inad-
vertently canceled deliveries kept everyone anxious as fever season drew closer. The
forces moved piecemeal south, reuniting at Antón Lizardo, an undefended anchorage several miles south of Veracruz. On March 5, a young American sailor stationed
on board the one thousand-ton sloop of war *Albany* described what happened

when the transports, driven by a strong norther, finally joined the warships. "About noon, General Scott's fleet of transports . . . came like a great cloud bearing down before the storm," he wrote. "The whole eastern horizon looked like a wall of canvas. Vessel after vessel came flying in under reduced sail, until the usually quiet harbor was crowded with them. A perfect wilderness of spars and rigging met the eye at every turn; and for five days all was bustle, activity, and excitement." Scott could now land his troops and take the city.[20]

Early on March 9, smaller gunboats moved toward shore to lay down covering fire, and energetic sailors swung the surfboats over the sides of the transports. Fully kitted out with knapsacks, muskets, and canteens, the soldiers climbed down into their boats. Sailors pulled the oars. All day, back and forth, surfboats kept moving. "It was a grand spectacle!" enthused the young seaman on the *Albany*. "On, on went the long range of boats, loaded down to the gunwales with brave men, the rays of the slowly-departing sun resting upon their uniforms and bristling bayonets and wrapping the far-inland and fantastic mountains of Mexico in robes of gold." Positioned in the bow of a surfboat, Lt. Kirby Smith described the landing. "The entire division reached the shore in good order," he later wrote, "everyone leaping from the boats as their keels grated on the sand, wading the short distance that remained." According to another witness, as soon as the boats landed their men, they returned to the ships for more. "In addition to this," he wrote, "the business of landing the different articles was assigned to different vessels, so that the division of boats belonging to one ship attended to getting the horses ashore, those of another the forage, another the provisions, and so on." It was a model operation that would be studied for years. Incredibly, there was no opposition, and by 10 P.M. the entire army was ashore. Conner and Scott each took justifiable pride in their service's role. Scott even went so far as to express "gratitude and admiration" for the navy's critical work.[21]

Moving quickly, Scott established his troops in a seven-mile arc around the city, cutting off all the roads as well as the fresh water supply. He placed four artillery batteries at strategic points screened by sand hills and chaparral. Each battery contained twenty-four-pounders, mortars, and soon thirty-two-pounders loaned by the navy. An infantry assault was dismissed as needlessly risky. Scott would reduce the city by artillery alone. It was not an unreasonable prospect. Veracruz's old walls were unlikely to be any more effective against heavy ordnance than San Juan de Ulúa's had been during the recent Pastry War. Furthermore, there were less than four thousand defenders, hindered by a large civilian population. Of course, Scott hoped to avoid any kind of fight if possible and first sent a surrender demand. It was refused, and the American guns opened fire March 22. Day and night they thundered. Clinging to the *Albany*'s foretop, the young sailor-chronicler watched in awe. "Bomb-shells were flying like hailstones into Vera Cruz from every quarter," he wrote, "sulphureous flashes, clouds of smoke, and the dull boom of the heavy guns, arose from the walls of the city in return, while ever and anon a red sheet of flame would leap from the great brass mortars on the ramparts of the grim castle, followed by a report which fairly made the earth quake." American shells pulverized the city walls and crashed into buildings, terrifying the populace. It was too much for the Mexicans. They asked for a truce, negotiated surrender terms, and on March 29 capitulated. "The flag of the United States of America floats triumphantly over the walls of this city and the castle of San Juan d'Ulloa," Scott informed the secretary of war.[22]

Just as Cortés had done three centuries earlier, Scott marched on the opulent capital. In June 1847, even as his forces neared their goal, the navy launched an operation against Villahermosa, situated on the Leeward Coast a few miles up the Río de Tabasco. The expedition was led by Commodore Matthew Perry, who had replaced the ailing Conner. It included steamers, schooners, brigs, surfboats, and infantry. The steamers towed the surfboats across the choppy river bar, battling sharpshooters and a small fort. When the Americans finally reached Villahermosa it fell into their hands without a fight. Unfortunately, deadly fever and guerrilla harassment forced them to abandon it after five weeks. Scott had to fight much harder to win Mexico City, but it too finally surrendered on September 14, and the consequences were far more significant. The Mexican War was over at last. The following spring both governments ratified the Treaty of Guadalupe Hidalgo by which Mexico agreed to part with more than half of its territory in exchange for $15 million cash. True to O'Sullivan's vision, "our manifest destiny" had been achieved. The American West lay wide open to eager Anglo pioneers.[23]

The nation's expansionist successes fired the imaginations of Caribbean exiles and restless Southerners who sensed opportunity in a different direction, southward across the Gulf. In the decade after the Mexican War these men agitated, editorialized, plotted, raised money, and even launched ill-fated expeditions. Among the exiled leaders, men like the native Venezuelan and disaffected former Spanish general Narciso López, the motive was to free Cuba; whereas the Southern agitators, or filibusters as they were routinely called, wanted to annex the island as a powerful new slave state. López shrewdly realized that these goals meshed well enough for him to recruit in American cities. Not surprisingly, the Gulf ports were especially receptive. Friendly newspaper coverage, political speeches, and rousing meetings encouraged hundreds to join. In his 1886 memoir, *Reminiscences of the 'Filibuster' War in Nicaragua,* Charles William Doubleday, a youthful champion of "popular liberty," described these excited recruits as "mostly of the class found about the wharves of the Southern cities, with here and there a Northern bank cashier, who had suddenly changed his vocation." Many were veterans who missed the camaraderie they had so recently known. They could fight on land, but few of them were much use on board a ship, and they would need ships to reach their destinations. "Of course they knew nothing of seamanship, not even the names of the commonest ropes," grumbled Doubleday, when he tried to school them on board a vessel in Mobile Bay. Doubleday's solution was to combine the ropes with something the men were thoroughly familiar with—playing cards. He attached various cards to the ropes, "and whenever the order was given to 'haul away on the Ace of Clubs or the Jack of Diamonds,' there was no danger of a mistake being made."[24]

One of the earliest and most ambitious filibustering expeditions gathered just off the Mississippi coast in the summer of 1849, precipitating a blockade by the United States Navy and much fulmination from states' rights advocates. Despite this episode's political, military, and diplomatic importance, it remains surprisingly little known even to locals. The plot's author and chief conspirator was López, aided and abetted by none other than O'Sullivan. Two forces were envisioned—one at New Orleans and one at New York—which would rendezvous off Cabo Catoche and then land on Cuba's southern coast. From there the filibusters would gather discontented islanders to their banner, convince demoralized Spanish soldiers to join them, and seize power. U.S. annexation would follow. It was less harebrained at the time than it appears now, and officials took it seriously. López asked both Jefferson Davis and Robert E. Lee to lead. Each briefly considered before refusing. These men knew such meddling was a violation of the 1818 Neutrality Act, likely

The great naval blockade of Round Island. Showing the immense importance of having an efficient "right arm of the national defence." This 1849 cartoon satirizes the Taylor administration, the navy, the filibusters, and the Cuban government all at once. "Venezuela! St. Domingo! and Yucatan!" declares one of the land-hungry rowdies at the table.

COURTESY LIBRARY OF CONGRESS.

to attract government reprisal. Finally, an Irish immigrant and Mexican War veteran named George William White accepted command of the Southern contingent while López concentrated his efforts in New York. Supplies, weapons, and munitions were purchased and stowed on board two steamers—the *Fanny* at New Orleans and the *Sea Gull* in New York.[25]

Round Island sits in the Mississippi Sound three and a half miles south of Pascagoula and a stone's throw from the Alabama state line. It was somewhat larger 150 years ago than it is today but still small—roughly a mile and a half long by half a mile wide. It was deserted but for a man who kept some cattle and tended the forty-four-foot brick lighthouse on its southwestern shore. Some eight miles farther south lies Horn Island, with Ship Island and Cat Island to the west toward New Orleans. Given Round Island's proximity to both the Crescent City and Mobile, it was a convenient filibuster gathering spot, and in July several hundred unarmed men were deposited there. The plan called for a steamer to transport them to their rendezvous once Colonels White and López completed preparations. In the meantime the recruits pitched tents amid slash pine and palmetto where they drilled during daylight and told tall tales around campfires at night.[26]

American officials had known something was afoot for some time, but the Round Island move convinced them they had to act. At the lowest level, the lighthouse keeper complained to his supervisor in Mobile that the filibusters were slaughtering his cattle and had damaged government property. "I suppose they will be of some trouble," he predicted, "as they seem to do just as they please." The supervisor informed the local U.S. attorney, who wrote to the secretary of state requesting naval intervention. Additional correspondence from the New Orleans U.S. attorney elaborated on the "unholy and illegal" plot and the need for prompt action. It was up to the president to decide whether and how to act. Zachary Taylor now sat in the White House. Just as Polk had earlier feared he would, Taylor had parlayed his wartime popularity into a successful political campaign. Taylor was not in good health, but he was fully cognizant of the risks the filibusters posed to U.S. security and prestige. The politics were dicey at best. Spain was aware of the plot and demanded its immediate suppression. Complicating matters were Southern elected officials and newspaper editors cheering the effort's proslavery impetus. Strong federal action would honor international agreements but was likely to worsen already vexing internal sectional tensions.[27]

Taylor's decision was firm. The filibusters had to be stopped, preferably before they sailed. Their plot was a clear violation of the Neutrality Act, and a war with Spain was to be avoided at all costs, Southern governors be damned. On August 10, the one thousand-ton iron-hulled steamer USS *Allegheny* out of Pensacola dropped anchor off the southwestern tip of Horn Island. Because the vessel drew thirteen feet, and the Mississippi Sound averages ten feet deep, she could get no closer, but the filibusters clearly discerned her masts on their southern horizon. Soon she was joined by lighter-draft gunboats like the *Water Witch, Albany,* and *General Taylor,* which anchored closer to the island, the sunlight reflecting dully off their hulking thirty-two-pounder guns. A few artillery salutes between the vessels had a profound effect on the adventurers. Commodore Victor Randolph followed up the impressive firepower display with a strongly written message. "You are *vagrants* in the eyes of the law," he announced, "and in fact; and therefore cannot be allowed to occupy your present position, and must immediately disperse."[28]

The naval blockade lasted several weeks, during which time conditions on the island deteriorated. Food and supplies were prevented from landing, and the filibusters became increasingly desperate. There was a murder, another man died of disease, and dozens deserted the enterprise to join the navy or take free transport to the mainland. Eventually the navy allowed supplies to land, and even provided provisions to keep the "ignorant dupes" from starving to death. By October it had all unraveled. López's New York operation was disrupted, his steamers seized, and the Round Islanders disbanded. The Southern press erupted. The *New Orleans Delta* decried the blockade as "a clear usurpation of power." The *Mobile Advertiser* complained that Randolph "transcends his powers," and the *Jackson Mississippian* denounced the "outrage committed upon the State of Mississippi." Mississippi governor Joseph Matthews spoke to his legislature in January 1850, fuming: "Our coast was kept, for weeks, in a state of blockade, and our citizens deprived of the exercise of their rights of freemen, in a time of profound peace, by martial law, and in total disregard of the civil authorities of the State." The federal government's actions were clear. Filibustering would not be tolerated, and states' rights would not trump the nation's international obligations.[29]

Despite Taylor's decisiveness, filibustering continued throughout the 1850s. The indefatigable López twice more recruited enthusiastic Southerners for Cuban expeditions and successfully landed on the island both times. The first invasion fell apart from a lack of Cuban support. López fled to Key West just ahead of a pursuing Spanish steamer. He was subsequently tried in New Orleans for violating the neutrality law, but charges were dismissed after three hung juries. On his second invasion, he proudly led his Southern recruits beneath a flag designed by himself and the poet Miguel Teurbe Tolón. Sewn by admiring Crescent City belles, it consisted of a bright red triangle on the left side with a single white star and five alternating blue and white stripes alongside. Inspiring banner or no, the Cubans again refused to join. Spanish troops defeated the filibusters and executed López. His legacy is his flag, officially adopted as the Cuban national banner in 1902.[30]

The most famous filibuster of them all was William Walker, the so-called grey-eyed man of destiny, a Nashville-born doctor and lawyer with visions of grandeur. Just as López had, Walker found his strongest support in the Gulf Coast towns where he promised money, equipment, and land to his recruits. He successfully invaded Nicaragua in 1855, and incredibly, the United States recognized his regime.

Unfortunately for Walker, his experiment fell apart when several Central American armies forced his return to the States. He launched another expedition in 1858. One of his vessels, a schooner named the *Susan,* left from Mobile carrying 120 tough customers armed with "revolvers and bowie knives." The scheme failed when the *Susan* wrecked off the Honduran coast. The crew was ferried back to Mobile by a British warship, where they were treated to an impromptu parade. Walker's plotting was finally ended on September 12, 1860, when Honduran authorities had him shot. Filibustering lost its appeal to proslavery Southrons. Independence became their new mantra.[31]

On April 19, 1861, a week after Fort Sumter's guns ignited the American Civil War, President Abraham Lincoln declared a blockade of the South. This was an enormous task for which the United States Navy was ill prepared. To begin with, 20 percent of its officer corps had resigned to join the Confederacy, and its vessels were mostly deep-draft wooden sailing ships or clumsy paddle-wheel steamers—a poor force to effectively seal a thirty-five hundred-mile coastline that included shoals, bays, estuaries, and multitudinous bayous, sounds, and coves. In order to meet the challenge, the Union high command divided its fleet into four blockading squadrons. The Gulf Coast was split between two of them—the East Gulf Blockading Squadron patrolled from the Florida Keys to St. Andrews Bay (location of modern-day Panama City) and the West Gulf Blockading Squadron (most famously commanded by Farragut) from St. Andrews Bay to the Mexican border. Both fleets saw extensive service, and their stories sprawl with daring blockade runners, exciting chases, thundering forts, brave webfeet, and maritime innovation aplenty that augured the end of traditional navies—ironclads, submarines, mines (or torpedoes as they were called), and more powerful ordnance. The battles were almost exclusively brown-water affairs, such as Farragut's victories at New Orleans in 1862 and Mobile Bay two years later. These have been well covered in numerous books and need no repetition in a broad survey such as this. But during the entire war, there was only one old-style ship-to-ship duel in the open Gulf, a short thirteen-minute slugfest that forcefully demonstrated the importance of guile, big guns, maneuverability, and speed at sea. It is an isolated episode, but an interesting one, and with the reader's indulgence will serve to highlight the Civil War in the Gulf.[32]

By the end of 1862, Mobile was the Confederacy's only remaining Gulf port. But on New Year's Eve a well-led Rebel naval and infantry assault recaptured Galveston, taking six federal ships, sinking one, grounding another, and netting four hundred infantrymen. Six hundred miles to the south, Raphael Semmes did not know any of this. Only days earlier, he had steered his sleek commerce raider, the CSS *Alabama,* into the Gulf and anchored amid the uninhabited Arcas Islands west of Campeche. His intent was to meet a coal tender there and then head to the Texas coast. Recently captured newspapers revealed that Union infantry transports were Galveston bound as part of Gen. Nathaniel Banks's Red River Campaign. Semmes

Raphael Semmes, ca. 1862.
COURTESY LIBRARY OF CONGRESS.

wanted to destroy these ships, but Galveston's recapture had altered the federals' plans. When the *Alabama* reached the Texas coast on January 11, she discovered five enemy steamers dawdling offshore rather than a clutch of helpless transports.[33]

After the war, Semmes described his thinking at that critical moment. "What was best done in this changed condition of affairs?" he asked. "I certainly had not come all the way into the Gulf of Mexico, to fight five ships of war, the least of which was probably my equal." Nonetheless, he relished the prospect of besting an enemy warship after months of capturing helpless merchant vessels. Both he and his ship were equal to the task. Semmes was fifty-three, a native Marylander, lawyer, and U.S. Navy veteran. After the Mexican War he moved to Mobile, which he ever afterward considered home. Physically he was trim and erect with longish iron-gray hair and arresting eyes. His men called him "Old Beeswax" for his elaborately twisted mustachios. In fact, he looked every inch the pirate Northern newspapers labeled him. He was an aloof figure on the quarterdeck, leaving routine command matters to his trusted lieutenant, the burly John McIntosh Kell, known as "First Luff." Semmes loved the *Alabama,* and little wonder. She was a handsome nine hundred-ton, bark-rigged screw steamer constructed in Britain and armed with six 32-pounders, a 110-pounder rifled gun, and a 65-pounder smoothbore. The vessel was fast and powerful, "a very perfect ship of her class." Battle it would be.[34]

Fortunately for Semmes, only one of the federal ships steamed out to investigate. "The *Alabama* had given chase pretty often," he later recalled, "but this was the first time she had been chased. It was just the thing I wanted, however, for I at once conceived the design of drawing this single ship of the enemy far enough away from the remainder of her fleet, to enable me to decide a battle with her before her consorts could come to her relief." As daylight faded, Semmes led his victim farther out, eventually heaving to twenty miles offshore at the ten-fathom curve. His pursuer was the USS *Hatteras,* a sluggish iron-hulled side-wheeler with only six guns. She was commanded by Homer C. Blake, a U.S. Naval Academy graduate and no fool. "Knowing the slow rate of speed of the *Hatteras,* I at once suspected that deception was being practiced," he wrote in his official report. As the distance narrowed he ordered his ship cleared for action. Night fell and the two vessels drifted to within a hundred yards of each other. Blake now realized he was practically alongside the notorious *Alabama.* His only hope was to "board her, and thus rid the seas of this piratical craft." It was not to be.[35]

"The enemy was the first to hail," Semmes wrote. "'What ship is that?' cried he. 'This is her Britannic Majesty's steamer *Petrel,*' we replied." Blake said he would send over a small boat, and Semmes agreed. But the deception had gone far enough. Semmes turned to Kell and ordered him to tell the Yankees who they were. "Kell now sang out, in his powerful clarion voice, through his trumpet, 'This is the Confederate States steamer *Alabama!*'" Instantly the *Alabama*'s broadside shattered the stillness. The *Hatteras* loosed hers in response, and the ships steamed parallel blasting one another. "'Twas a grand though fearful sight to see the guns belching forth in the darkness of the night, sheets of living flame," a Rebel webfoot remembered. Union blockaders fifteen miles away saw lurid orange flashes on the horizon and heard the booming. "My men handled their pieces with great spirit and commendable coolness," Semmes wrote, "and the action was sharp and exciting while it lasted; which, however, was not very long." The *Hatteras* shook as Rebel shot tore off iron sheeting at her waterline and set fires below decks. Her own shots flew high or punched easily repairable holes in the *Alabama*'s wooden sides. His ship on fire and "a hopeless wreck on the water," Blake fired a gun on his opposite side to signal surrender. Amid rousing Rebel cheers, the *Hatteras* began sinking. Two Yankee tars were killed in the fight, a fireman and a coal heaver. The rest were taken on board the *Alabama* and later paroled in Jamaica. When Farragut heard the news, he wrote to a friend that he was "sick of disasters." The *Philadelphia Inquirer* considered the incident "disgraceful." The *Hatteras* was the first steam warship to be sunk by another steam warship in military history. As if that designation was not ignominy enough, she was also the only federal ship sunk by hostile fire in the Gulf during the Civil War. Her wreck still rests on the seafloor off Galveston, a haven for marine life and an intriguing maritime archaeological laboratory.[36]

At the cusp of the twentieth century, the United States was emerging as a maritime power, even less tolerant of Europeans in its hemisphere than seventy-five years earlier when the Monroe Doctrine was announced. Mexican politics remained unstable, but that country's sovereignty was not likely to be challenged since a French intervention there had failed during the 1860s. Cuba was another matter. It was still a Spanish colony, but increasing revolutionary turmoil put its future at risk. Spain was weak, and restless American imperialists sensed opportunity as its empire crumbled from the Philippines to the Antilles. Everything dovetailed perfectly at the end of 1897, when restive Havana mobs caused the U.S. consul to request protection for American citizens and interests.[37]

On Christmas Eve, 1897, the battleship USS *Maine* lay at Key West, her sides, funnels, and superstructure festooned with lights. Locals were charmed, one writing that it "was a picture not often seen in the tropical regions." The twinkling lights only partially softened the *Maine*'s awesome might. She was a steel behemoth—324 feet long and 57 feet in the beam, displacing 6,650 tons and powered by 9,290-horsepower engines. Her armament included a pair of staggered, sponsoned (slightly projecting over the side) gun turrets, each of which sported two ten-inch rifles. Additionally she carried over a dozen breech-loading, rapid-fire rifles. Mean looking, yes, but pretty and neat, too. "Her hull was white to the rail," the *Maine*'s captain later remembered in a magazine article, "the superstructures, funnels, and masts, and all permanent fittings above the rail except the pilot house, were dark straw-color. The boats and bower-anchors were white; the guns and search lights were black."[38]

The captain was Charles Dwight Sigsbee, a native New Yorker who had served under Farragut and was no stranger to the Gulf. Twenty years prior he and Alexander Agassiz had conducted an extensive survey from the Mississippi to Key West to the Yucatán, probing every subaqueous recess and cataloging every creature pulled dripping onto their research ship, but more of that in the next chapter. For his present assignment, Sigsbee knew that he was steaming into a delicate political environment. It was important that he make a good impression when showing the flag. "The crew was required to dress with exceptional neatness in blue," he later explained, "the officers were in frock coats." The *Maine* entered Havana Harbor on the morning of January 25, 1898, and was tied to a mooring buoy. A flurry of formal salutes and visits followed. Sigsbee was complimentary of Spanish officials for their courtesy and professionalism. There was no obvious show of resentment on their part. Popular sentiment was another matter. On his way to a bullfight Sigsbee was handed an insulting circular that referenced "Yankee pigs who meddle in our affairs" and called for "Death to the Americans!" Bemused rather than intimidated, he stuffed it into his coat pocket.[39]

Catastrophe struck at 9:40 P.M. on February 15. Sigsbee was in his commodious quarters aft attending to correspondence. "I was inclosing my letter in its envelope

The USS *Maine* is destroyed in Havana Harbor, February 15, 1898. The explosion's cause was never satisfactorily determined. COURTESY LIBRARY OF CONGRESS.

when the explosion came." Most of the ship's 328 crewmen were asleep in their forward quarters. First Sigsbee heard "bursting, rending, and crashing," followed by "heavy, ominous, metallic sounds." The vessel shook violently and lurched to port. Naval Cadet D. F. Boyd Jr. and a friend were reading in the messroom at the time. Instantly the electric lights went out, and Boyd and his friend scrambled to get on deck. "Together we groped our way out . . . along the bulkhead in the after torpedo-room, where we met a cloud of steam and tremendous rush of water. The force of the water separated us, and as I was lifted off my feet, I caught a steam-heater pipe, and reached for the steerage ladder." Fireman William Gartrell was in the steam-steering room and made for the door. "Everything was dark," he recalled. "I couldn't see nothing; everything was pitch dark." Witnesses around the harbor were horrified. Sigmund Rothschild, a passenger on board a nearby ship, saw the *Maine* lifted fully two feet out of the water by the explosion. "When the ship was going down," he recalled, "there was the cry of a mass of people, but that was a murmur." Rothschild probably heard the 250 men suddenly awakened and doomed to drown. Sigsbee and the other survivors abandoned ship or were rescued by scurrying harbor craft. The Spanish seemed just as surprised as the Americans, offering every aid they could bring to bear. But even as he abandoned ship, Sigsbee thought he heard faint cheering ashore.[40]

The explosion's exact cause has never been definitively determined. A Naval Board of Inquiry concluded that a mine was to blame, whereas a Spanish investigation cited a shipboard accident. Whatever the cause, the *Maine's* destruction inflamed American opinion. Assistant Secretary of the Navy Theodore Roosevelt blamed "dirty treachery by the Spaniards," newspapers agreed, and the public demanded satisfaction. Congress declared Cuba independent on April 19, initiated a naval blockade three days later, and declared war on Spain April 25. The Spanish-American War was a brief, one-sided affair, a "splendid little war" in the words of Secretary of State John Hay. Spain was defeated, and U.S. forces occupied the island for three and a half years. Before withdrawing, they pressured Cuban officials to sign the Platt Amendment. This onerous document stated that "the government of Cuba consents that the United States may exercise the right to intervene for the preservation of Cuban independence." It also allowed the Americans to build a naval base at Guantánamo Bay. These conditions rankled the Cuban people and would lead to future discord between the two governments.[41]

The Gulf's violent nineteenth century was over. Contemplating the grand sweep, an observer could have been forgiven for marveling at the events that had given rise to three independent nations, one of them a colossus. Decades earlier, Matthew Fontaine Maury had compared the Gulf's importance to the United States to that of the Mediterranean to Europe. Now at a new century's cusp the confident Republic was ideally poised to claim its manifest destiny in the watery realm. The Indians, the Spanish, the French, the British, and the freebooters had all been evicted. No longer was the Gulf a Spanish sea or a colonial crossroads or the haunt of bold privateers. It was an American sea, and its American Century was begun.[42]

Chapter Seven

American Sea

There the pirates hid their gold. Today health and happiness | United Fruit Co.
are the treasures sought on the Spanish Main, and the Great White | advertisement,
Fleet Ships, built especially for tropical travel, bear you luxuriously | 1915
to scenes of romance.

Form follows function. As it does in terrestrial architecture, so it does in naval architecture. And so it did with the United States Coast Survey steamer *Blake*. She was a beautiful thing to behold—a 350-ton, 140-by-29-foot, sleek-hulled, two-masted schooner augmented by 270-horsepower steam engines. There was not an inch of wasted space on board. Charles Sigsbee, who commanded the vessel during several important Gulf voyages from 1875 through 1878, detailed her cabins and equipment in a subsequent book. "Aft on the main deck are spacious and well-ventilated quarters for the officers," he wrote. "Forward of the wardroom, on the same deck, is a continuous line of midship houses, reaching nearly to the foremast, and forming the engine-room, boiler-room, galley, pantry, draughting room, lamp-room, and mechanics' sleeping room." A wide gangway punctuated by large portholes ran along each side of these "houses." Below deck were storerooms, a commodious twenty-five hundred-gallon freshwater tank, and enough bunkered coal for a thirty-eight-day cruise.[1]

But the equipment was the main thing. The *Blake*'s mission was to thoroughly sound the Gulf to its profoundest depths and discover what marine life, if any, existed there. To these ends she carried chronometers, compasses, thermometers, sounding rods, a forty-seven-foot-long dredge boom with attendant trawls and tow nets that could be paid out and reeled in by a steam-powered hoisting engine, and, most critically, the newly perfected Sigsbee sounding machine. This contraption looked like a cross between a bicycle and a guillotine, all flywheels and piano wire fitted into a rectangular frame affixed to the *Blake*'s port bow. As the name implies, this machine was Sigsbee's contribution to sounding technology, essentially an improvement to an earlier device invented by the Scottish mathematician Sir William Thompson. The use of flywheels, piano wire, reeling engines, and brakes was as far

Sounding machine and current meter in place, steamer Blake, ca. 1880. Note the sailor positioned on the scaffold below the machine. COURTESY NATIONAL OCEANIC AND ATMOS-PHERIC ADMINISTRATION.

from the tried-and-true method of knotted rope and a lead weight tossed by an old salt in the anchor chains as it was possible to imagine. Piano wire, and later steel cable, proved far stronger and lighter than water-logged hemp lines, making deep-sea sounding a reality. Even more important, the Sigsbee Sounding Machine was operable in heavy weather. Sigsbee boasted that with the *Blake* "hove to in a severe gale in the swift current of the Gulf Stream," his machine's sixty-pound cast-iron sinker had "got bottom in 2,400 fathoms" and been "reeled in by steam without loss."[2]

Sigsbee was a gifted innovator and a more than competent seaman, but he was not a marine scientist. That role was filled during the *Blake*'s 1877 trip by the Swiss-born naturalist Alexander Agassiz. When he boarded the *Blake*, Agassiz was forty-two and owned a solid reputation as a working zoologist. He was the son of the famed naturalist Louis Agassiz and had cowritten the popular *Sea Studies in Natural History* (1866) with his stepmother, Elizabeth Cabot Agassiz. Unusual for a man of science, he was a millionaire to boot, due to savvy management of some Michigan copper mines. "I want to make money; it is impossible to be a working naturalist in this country without money," he wrote to a professor friend before taking on the onerous task of managing the mines. When he was invited on the Gulf survey, Agassiz was excited about expanding oceanographic knowledge. He was passionate about the sea, and even coined a word—thalassography—to describe its study. The term never caught on, but Agassiz's enthusiasm was infectious. "New notions of geological horizons and periods loom up before us," he wrote, "and the problems concerning the formation of continents and oceanic basins now present themselves from a very different standpoint." Agassiz boarded the *Blake* in December at Havana for the voyage, which was expected to last until the following March. This was the season of northers—chapping winds, heaving waves—and a seasick-prone man like Agassiz was likely to have a miserable time. Undeterred, he embraced the opportunity with his characteristic optimism.[3]

Sigsbee and Agassiz formed a quick bond, each respecting the other's accomplishments and expertise. Their working method was to crisscross the Gulf from Havana to Key West to the Yucatán to the Tortugas to the Mississippi and back, taking soundings every six miles and dredging up sea muck so Agassiz could study its composition and any life it contained. It was messy, smelly work. "At great depths, where a light ooze covers the bottom," the scientist explained, "the trawl soon becomes completely filled with the mass of sticky mud which finds its way into it; and when brought to the surface it is found that but little has been washed out through the meshes of the trawl-bag." In order to compensate, Agassiz substituted a net with coarser mesh. Even so, each load of abyssal detritus emptied onto the *Blake*'s well-scrubbed decks was enough to drive an orderly navy man like Sigsbee crazy. Professional that he was, he bore the inconvenience. "At sea, everything had to give way to the work at hand," he wrote. "If the vessel did not look pretty, we concluded that we could not help it, and complacently looked forward to a higher standard on our arrival in port."[4]

Day in and day out through fair weather and foul, the dredge and the Sigsbee sounding machine were deployed. Much of what the nets brought up from the continental shelves and slopes was expected. The Gulf's shallow waters teemed with life—"long stretches of bottom carpeted by the most brilliantly colored animals," Agassiz reported—and where the Mississippi Fan spilled into the basin great mats of dead leaves, bark, bamboo, and dead tree trunks tumbled onto deck. This rotting continental off wash provided ample food sources for numerous sea creatures. But even at the very deepest regions, an icy netherworld that conventional scientific theory considered devoid of biology, the dredge brought up living things. Perhaps just as surprising, some were as eye-catching as their littoral kindred. "We meet highly colored ophiurans [brittle stars] within masses of sponges," Agassiz wrote, "themselves brilliantly colored, at a depth of more than 150 fathoms." Likewise, sea anemones were "orange, red, green, violet, yellow." But most of the deep-sea fishes were "a grayish color, or dull black." Agassiz also collected water samples and recorded temperatures at various depths to better his understanding.[5]

Even as the scientist crouched beneath a bright Gulf sun studying what his trawls brought on board, the seaman kept the ship under way and his sounding machine humming out wire. By voyage's end, Sigsbee reported that the *Blake* had cruised 4,600 miles, burned 163 tons of coal, taken hundreds of soundings, and endured "fifteen gales at sea." No doubt Agassiz was relieved to once again put his feet on solid ground that March when the vessel made New Orleans. Both men would take subsequent Gulf trips, and the sum total of their efforts significantly advanced American knowledge of the southern sea. Sigsbee's soundings allowed him to draw the first accurate bathymetric map of any ocean basin. In honor of his achievement, the Gulf's deepest portion, at over eleven thousand feet, was named the Sigsbee Plain. As for the rest of the seafloor, there were shelves, escarpments, plateaus, reefs, ridges, knolls, and canyons, a watery world theretofore unimagined. Thanks to Agassiz's work, people knew there was life not just on the Gulf's shelves and slopes but in its deepest recesses also.[6]

The ascendant United States was ready to exploit this knowledge. It was the region's dominant political power, its southern shores were populated by capable fishermen, and not least, expanding railroad networks brought previously inaccessible inland markets within practical reach. The *Blake*'s survey had been prompted in part at the urging of the U.S. Fish Commission. Founded in 1871 to promote and improve the country's commercial fisheries, the commission did all it could to assess the industry through its annual reports. Americans had been fishing the Gulf since colonial times, of course, but until the Fish Commission's advent there was no comprehensive effort to record how many people made their living at it, how much they were bringing in at the different ports, and what ancillary businesses benefited. In 1880 the commission launched a comprehensive fishing study of the Gulf Coast from the Florida Keys to the Río Grande. Their man in the field was a twenty-something-year-old native Mainer and amateur ichthyologist turned Pensacola fish-house clerk named Silas Stearns. Despite his youth, Stearns proved to be the perfect choice. He pursued his challenging job with gusto, chatting up fishermen, riding out and returning with them, threading his way along weathered wharves and into noisy canneries and icehouses, notebook always in hand.[7]

He began with the "Bahamian Conchs" and "West Indian Negroes" at Key West. "They know no other profession than fishing, sponging, turtling, and wrecking," he wrote. The most successful were generally Bahamian boat owners whose families lived in "small, comfortable houses in the city." As for the deckhands, they were "dissipated" and "considered a public nuisance." Stearns expressed some optimism that better schooling and the temperance movement were having a positive impact. Farther up the coast at the Cedar Keys, Stearns tallied 260 fishermen, Americans moved down from the East Coast, and some Portuguese immigrants. "Taken as a class," he reported, "they are quite intelligent, industrious, and quick to adopt new methods that will tend to facilitate their work." They lived simply and close to the water. During the 1930s, writer, artist, and botanist Cecile Hulse Matschat provided a description of their village that probably hadn't changed since Stearns's day. "A narrow boardwalk ran from the landing to the settlement squatting beneath the trees," she wrote. The fishermen's wives had lined the little connecting paths with shell-bordered flower beds, and drying nets hung everywhere. The houses had once been brightly painted, but "sun and sea air and time" had faded them. Each dwelling featured glassless windows protected from storms by heavy wooden shutters. Most had only two rooms, "but they were neat and clean." The bunks were covered by homemade quilts. Discarded small-meshed seines had been dyed pink and made into curtains.[8]

Over at Apalachicola on the Panhandle, Stearns found that fishermen were generally Southerners and New Englanders, "good citizens in every way." They lived in houses with little gardens and had large families of ten or twelve children. While Stearns met several "hale and hearty" septuagenarian men who still worked area waters, few of the women lived to see sixty summers. Stearns described them as "broken down" by thirty-five or forty. Over at Mobile, most of the fishermen were of "Spanish, Italian, or Greek descent" and lived "in the same manner as other laboring men and mechanics do." During a good month they could make fifty dollars. Most were Catholic and uneducated, but Stearns reported that their children did receive good schooling. At New Orleans, the fishermen and oystermen were "nearly all descendants of the Mediterranean coast fishermen and sailors." Most were French, Spanish, or Minorcan, with a smattering of Italians, Portuguese, Greeks, Corsicans, and Sicilians. Like all fishermen throughout time, they were superstitious. Stearns described their paralyzing fear at the sight of glowing swamp gas. Conversely, they were savvy weathermen and "will run no risk when the signs are unfavorable." They lived in fish camps and took teenage brides, who like most of their sisters elsewhere along the littoral endured hard lives and died young. The picture was nearly identical along the Texas coast, with more Mexicans in the mix and but few blacks.[9]

Fascinating as their ethnic make-up, religion, lifestyles, houses, and families were to Stearns, Matschat, and a host of later bureaucrats and writers, the most important thing in any Gulf fisherman's existence was his boat. It held the key to his physical safety, his working ease or lack thereof, and his money-making potential. Then came his equipment—lines, hooks, rods, poles, nets, trawls, diving suits, oyster tongs, sponge hooks, and so forth depending on what he was fishing. Just as critical were the dockside people whose services he depended upon—the brokers, fishmongers, icehouse managers, cannery owners, and railroad shipping clerks positioned to turn his catch into ready cash.

Not surprisingly, the variety of American Gulf fishing vessels proved to be just as diverse as the men working them and the manner of catch they sought. The conchs used schooners, skiffs, and small sloops to scour the eastern Gulf for sponge

Tarpon Springs, Florida, 1944. A Greek American deep-sea sponge diver climbing back into the boat, sponge in hand.
COURTESY LIBRARY OF CONGRESS.

beds. They were a tough lot and sometimes got into fisticuffs with Greek sponge divers out of Tarpon Springs. The latter were easy to spot on the water because their boats had a distinctive Mediterranean profile, "like a crescent moon," according to one observer. In 1892 a writer for *Scribner's Magazine* named Kirk Munroe visited Key West and sallied out with the conchs. Their smaller vessels worked the waters to the east, off the very southern tip of Florida. According to Munroe, it was a seascape "filled with low keys, sand-bars, coral-reefs, and mud banks" interlaced by a "bewildering maze of tortuous channels, unsurveyed and uncharted, but known to, and used by the reef-sponger." The conchs' typical method was to find a likely spot and then eyeball the seafloor through a "water glass." This was simply a cedar bucket with a glass bottom that the fishermen could use to pierce the ruffled surface. Some spongers even smoothed the waters with a little bottle that dripped oil over the bow. Sponges appeared as dark blobs on the bottom, difficult to spot amid brilliant sea fans, coral, and "gorgeous anemone." Once he had pinpointed his target, the fisherman used a long sponge hook to retrieve it. The latter tool was typically a thirty-foot wooden pole with a three-pronged, iron business end. Needless to say, it took great dexterity to successfully hit the sponge and lift it on deck. By contrast, farther up the west coast the Greek sponge divers walked the Gulf floor in rubber diving suits breathing pumped air. They usually worked between thirty and one hundred feet down, cutting off the sponges with a special knife. Whether the sponges were speared or cut, once out of the water they soon stank to high heaven. Munroe was revolted by the odor, noting that under a tropical sun, the "mucilaginous animal matter with which the sponge-cells are filled quickly decomposes and emits an odor so powerful and offensive that the presence of a sponge boat can be detected a mile or more from the leeward, and a wise sailor will always pass one to windward if possible." The spongers weren't bothered by the odor at all. They might have said that it smelled like money. In the days before synthetic substitutes, natural sponges were a valuable product, commonly sought by homeowners for their baths, painters for their toolboxes, and doctors for their operating rooms. By 1895, Florida's sponges accounted for $368,871 in profits, or one third of the state's annual seafood industry.[10]

Along the northern littoral, fishermen out of Pensacola, Mobile, Biloxi, and New Orleans used a variety of sailing craft to harvest shrimp, oysters, and red snapper, often traveling as far as the Campeche Banks to hook the latter. Their boats were fashioned out of local woods, including Louisiana cypress and Mississippi longleaf pine, in small shipyards situated beside lazy bayous. The best-known builder of them all was Jacob D. "Jacky Jack" Covacevich of Biloxi, a Croatian immigrant. After an 1893 hurricane smashed the Biloxi schooner fleet, the Covacevich Boatyard worked overtime to replace it. The yard's signature vessels were the two-masted schooners known as "white winged queens" for their graceful canvas spreads. A typical example was sixty feet long with a broad beam and shallow draft. They were admirably adaptable boats. Because of their sail power they could easily drag quarter-mile-long shrimp seines, while their shallow draft and broad beam allowed large crews the ability to work the oyster reefs and pile the catch on deck.[11]

Biloxi's success as a seafood capital was manifested not only by these elegant schooners, but by the plethora of tin shucking sheds, icehouses, canneries, and factories that lined its waterfront. There hundreds of men, women, and children, some as young as three, stood alongside wooden tables shucking and shelling. They were mostly Eastern European migrant workers down from the Chesapeake Bay region. Their working conditions were primitive, and during the winter months cold, numb fingers were the rule. Mississippi outlawed child labor in 1908, but it continued to be a common waterfront practice. As late as 1922 an investigating agent interviewed a seven-year-old girl working on the waterfront who described how "she had cut herself between the thumb and forefinger shucking oysters." She got paid five dollars a week for her trouble and used the money to buy savings stamps.[12]

Profits were considerably better for those higher up the chain. Lazaro Lopez, who had an ownership interest in several canneries, lived in a grand mansion and helped found the Biloxi Bank and a private school known as the Seashore Academy. Cannery owner William K. M. DuKate likewise lived in a spacious Queen Anne mansion. His was designed by a New Orleans architect and featured multiple roof-lines, paneled brick chimney stacks, a turret, and wraparound gingerbread porches. After his death in 1916, his estate was valued at seven hundred thousand dollars, an immense fortune at the time.[13]

The canneries were good for Biloxi too. The population steadily grew, and locals took jobs alongside the migrants. In 1904 there were three hundred boats, twelve hundred fishermen, and over a thousand workers in the factories. Throughout the early 1900s Biloxi's canneries were shipping $1 million worth of oysters annually and fifteen hundred barrels of shrimp. The latter catch was tabulated at sixty thousand dollars in its raw state, and two hundred thousand dollars when cleaned and packed. Cannery owners continually refined their operations to improve their prospects, buying boats, hiring sailors and factory laborers, and erecting frame company bunkhouses. Technological advances like gasoline engines and refrigeration increased their ability to harvest, ship, and market the Gulf's abundant seafood.[14]

Boys tonging oysters, Mobile Bay, 1911. Their wide-waisted boat is a typical lugger, sans pilothouse. Lewis Hines photographer. COURTESY LIBRARY OF CONGRESS.

By the 1920s the white-winged queens were nearly obsolete. Boatbuilders like Covacevich were equal to the challenge, however, and rapidly turned out engine-powered vessels called Biloxi luggers. The typical lugger featured a high prow, low wide waist, a squared stern, the pilothouse aft, and working deck forward. These boats were, of course, completely independent of the wind. Thanks to that, as well as their distinctive otter trawls that spread open under water, they were operable by fewer men. There were numerous variations to this basic design along the coast. Louisiana luggers had rounded sterns, and the so-called Texas trawler placed the pilothouse forward and the working deck aft, but the principles were the same. Of such innovation was born the modern shrimp boat, instantly recognizable by its outriggers, otter boards, and drooping green nets.[15]

Commercial Gulf fishermen who weren't trawling shrimp or tonging oysters were probably seeking red snapper. Even today it is one of the Gulf's most popular fish. Good ones can be up to two feet long and weigh in at forty pounds. Stearns called them "chunky-built," which was another way of saying "good eating." They frequent wrecks and reefs at thirty to several hundred feet deep, feed on crustaceans, and are such greedy guts that they've been known to bite, or snap—hence the name—at bare hooks. Fishermen based out of Tampa, Mobile, and Galveston regularly sailed in search of red snapper, but Pensacola was the fishery's busiest port. In fact, between 1880 and 1930, the small Panhandle town was dubbed "the Red Snapper Capital of the World." Outfits like Saunders and Co. on the Palafox Wharf and the Warren Fish Co. on the Baylen Wharf went into high gear as soon as their boats returned. Scurrying workers offloaded the fish, beheaded and gutted them, stuffed them with ice, and packed them into wooden crates. Each factory had its own railroad spur alongside, and when the crates were ready, men loaded them onto the cars and shipped them north to hungry Yankee restaurant patrons and shoppers. "Snappers should always be boiled or cooked in a chowder," one of the fish commissioners declared in an 1887 report. "Thus treated they are equal to the striped bass, sea bass or turbot, in flavor and texture." Gulf Coast cooks were more broad-minded, stewing, baking, and frying them, throwing some into the gumbo pot, or even making them into a pudding.[16]

But first they had to be caught. And that meant boats. During the 1870s New England–built schooners of twenty to forty-five tons called "well-smacks" were employed. The name derived from the large live wells each vessel had amidships in which seawater smacked against the hull. By the 1880s easily available ice blocks eliminated the need for live wells, and the schooners were made tight bottomed, though they were still sometimes called smacks. On a typical voyage down to the Campeche Banks, a one hundred-foot smack carried twenty tons of ice, and eight to ten crewmen. Once at the fishing grounds, the men were roused at 5 A.M. each day, had breakfast, and then tossed out their lines. Steam-tarred cotton handlines, six-pound lead sinkers, multiple hooks, and salted menhaden bait constituted all the gear needed to pull in copious quantities of snapper. "Sometimes six men will catch a thousand fish in a few hours," one boat owner remarked. During off-hours the men slept, lounged, or played cards. By 1900 there were over fifty schooners and one thousand men sailing out of Pensacola alone, the Gulf's largest working sail fleet. The snapper stocks suffered accordingly. Not surprisingly, the Mexican government took exception to Americans fishing within what it claimed as territorial waters, especially if they didn't have permits. In 1906 it seized three American smacks off Campeche, one each from Galveston, Mobile, and Pensacola, and detained the crews. A diplomatic negotiation ensued before the men were released from what the *Pensacola Journal* called a "vile Mexican prison."[17]

For those fishermen more closely tied to home or unwilling to risk Mexican gunboats, there was an attractive alternative, namely, short one hundred-mile roundtrips lasting three to six days. The fishing wasn't as good as that off the Campeche Banks, but catches of several hundred pounds were possible. These men's vessel of choice was the unusually named "chingamaring," or "ching" for short. Chings were small centerboard sailing craft of less than twenty tons that carried only a few men. There are very few descriptions of them. One old salt recalled "a long, sharp bow, round bilge, fine run, and vertical heart-shaped, square stern, the latter being rather light and very symmetrical." They were rigged as three-masted schooners "without jib." Since the fish factories didn't bother owning small boats the chings allowed independent contractors, many of them black, to garner profits not possible ashore.[18]

Commercial fishermen weren't the only ones nursing nets and lines. All along the American littoral, thousands of residents fished, either for their own dinner tables or to sell to local markets. Many had some kind of small boat or at least access to one, and those who didn't threw cast nets or dropped hooks off bulkheads, piers, jetties, pilings, old logs, and beaches. Catboats, yawls, dories, sloops, and skiffs were ubiquitous, sail power giving way to gasoline engines as the twentieth century progressed. Some of these vessels were homemade, others built by local craftsmen who achieved regional renown. Among the latter was Lawrence Stauter, a gifted boatwright who lived in a little house balanced on pilings at the head of Mobile Bay. Boats were his life, and he used them for crabbing, running trotlines, fishing, duck hunting, and going to town. When he wasn't fishing or working construction, Stauter made twelve-foot plywood boats that he sold for twenty-five dollars. He was exacting about his material. "If there was any sap in the plywood or the frames," he later said, "I'd rip it off, throw it away. That was my rule." By 1946 he was earning enough at his hobby to quit his job and open Stauter Boat Works on the causeway. His mother thought him "a damn fool," but the business did well. Every sportsman on the central Gulf Coast coveted a "Stauter-Built" boat. Stauter adjusted his designs to suit demand, turning out twelve-, fourteen-, fifteen-, and even seventeen-foot models like the "Cedar Point Special" with a vee-shaped hull to manage offshore chop. Other models featured blunt prows and flat bottoms suitable to the Mobile delta's shallow lakes and twisting bayous. In Louisiana men like Stauter were building all kinds of skiffs. Among these small boats were the Mississippi skiff, the Atchafalaya skiff, and most popular of all, the Lafitte skiff. The latter is still popular in south Louisiana and is distinguished by a flat bottom, square stern, and flared, pointed bow.[19]

Enterprising youngsters with salt water in their veins quickly realized they could make money fishing if they catered to the tourists brought by the railroads and improved highways. One such was Barney Farley, a native Floridian born in 1894 who moved with his family to Port Aransas, Texas, when he was sixteen. Port Aransas is located on Mustang Island, opposite Corpus Christi and its namesake bay. It's a beautiful stretch of coast and still a fishing mecca. Farley spent hours "along the docks," he later wrote, "talking to fishing guides and watching as the boats went out to sea and returned, bringing in an array of fish, especially tarpon. I learned that from May to November the boats were booked ahead by wealthy and prominent people from as far away as New York and Chicago." He became a guide himself, taking people out in plain rowboats until those were replaced by inboard motorboats. "A good, strong guide who didn't mind rowing from sunrise to sunset could earn himself three dollars a day," he recalled, "pretty good wages at the time." By 1928 Farley owned a tackle shop, employed six guides, and was a respected figure on the island. Nine years later he was chosen to take President Franklin D. Roosevelt tarpon fishing. He was introduced to the president the day before their planned trip. "We shook hands, and he said simply, 'I've heard lots about you Barney, and I am pleased that you are going to teach me how to fish.'" Barney was impressed by the president's firm handshake and joked that he could catch a whale with a grip like that. The two men hit it off, and Roosevelt thoroughly enjoyed the next day's sport. Universal Newsreel footage depicts Farley and several other men crowded into a small powerboat with the president. Roosevelt hams it up in a floppy fishing hat and reels in tarpon, while a guide gaffs them and lifts them up to admiring photographers bobbing nearby.[20]

Charter fishing proved to be a growth industry. Civic groups all along the coast founded fishing tournaments to promote their areas and the sport. Among the first were the Grand Isle (Louisiana) Tarpon Rodeo (1928) and the Alabama Deep Sea Fishing Rodeo (1929) on Dauphin Island. Literally dozens of others followed, including the Mississippi Deep Sea Fishing Rodeo (1948) at Gulfport and the Pompano Beach Fishing Rodeo (1965) in Florida. Charter boats became more specialized as the century advanced, eventually taking on the classic profile of bow pulpit, foredeck, cabin, flying bridge, and cockpit. In the summer of 2017 retired Orange Beach, Alabama, charter captain Earl Callaway donated his old black cypress fishing boat, the *Sea Duster,* to the town. She was built in 1937 and named for a popular fishing lure of the time. "Even when I was a kid I thought this was the prettiest boat in Orange Beach," Callaway said. "Other ones got newer and faster and stronger and what have you. But I've always loved the *Sea Duster.*"[21]

The American Gulf's smacks, luggers, trawlers, skiffs, and private charters were dwarfed by the oceangoing vessels that routinely crowded its harbors. Four- and five-masted lumber schooners, barks, white-hulled banana steamers, cargo ships, and tankers were all commonly seen moored together until the 1930s, when sail power finally dwindled away. Cotton remained an important commodity, but booming coastal economies significantly diversified export cargoes. Lumber was king. Backcountry loggers harvested thousands of yellow pine and cypress trees and floated them down rivers or railroaded them into cities like Tampa, Pensacola, Mobile, New Orleans, and Galveston. Upon arrival some logs were sawn into planks or made into staves and shingles, the rest simply stacked and shipped as they were. In 1887 Mobile shipped out 30 million board feet of lumber and a staggering 75 million shingles. The Gulf ports also did a healthy business exporting valuable naval stores like turpentine and rosin. In 1914 alone Pensacola shipped 80,000 casks of turpentine and 250,000 barrels of rosin; Mobile 40,000 and 140,000; and New Orleans 25,000 and 100,000. Bananas were among the Gulf South's most popular imports, brought by the United Fruit Company's trim steamers from Central American plantations. United Fruit soon discovered that transporting American tourists south was a profitable sideline to the fruit-hauling business. "There the pirates hid their gold," declared the company's national magazine advertisements of its Caribbean destinations. "Today health and happiness are the treasures sought on the Spanish Main, and the Great White Fleet Ships, built especially for tropical travel, bear you luxuriously to scenes of romance." Besides lumber, bananas, and tourists, a host of other products were shipped in and out of Gulf ports—coal, grain, lead, copper, steel, aluminum, sulfur, phosphate, tobacco, bauxite, and machine parts. Taken in toto all that trade and travel meant bustling wharves and downtowns.[22]

Mobile's stature as an international port was enhanced with the formation of the Waterman Steamship Corporation in 1919. John B. Waterman was a New Orleans native who moved to Alabama's seaport in 1902 as manager for a British steamship company. He was active in local civic and social affairs, and his resume included numerous leadership positions and board memberships, from the Mobile Cotton Exchange, Mobile Rivers and Harbors Committee, and Chamber of Commerce to the Athelstan Club and the Country Club of Mobile. He was nothing if not alert to new business opportunities, and shortly after the First World War he joined with soft drink bottler Walter D. Bellingrath and timber man C. W. Hempstead to form the Waterman Steamship Corporation. The company started modestly with one leased vessel, but steadily grew with advantageous alliances and acquisitions. Benefitting from a national effort to strengthen the American Merchant Marine, the company got more ships, and by the late twenties its network included Tampa,

Key West, Miami, Puerto Rico, and the West Indies. By 1950 Waterman employed almost a thousand mariners who sailed its 125 ships all over the world. It had several strong subsidiaries, including a stevedoring outfit and shipyards in Tampa and Puerto Rico. The firm was headquartered in a handsome downtown skyscraper designed by Texas architect Paul Cret's firm and for years was one of Mobile's most respected corporate citizens.[23]

Tampa, which barely existed during the Civil War, boomed when Henry B. Plant linked it to his South Florida Railroad in 1883. The line ran into downtown and then paralleled the Hillsborough River along Ashley Street where the all-important wharves were. Cigar factories followed, as well as an influx of Cuban immigrants to work there. Phosphates and timber were big industries, and the city's population exploded from 720 to 37,782 by 1910. That same year the British travel writer H. L. Tomlinson arrived on board a tramp steamer and recorded his impressions. Tampa was "a large, hasty, makeshift standing of depots, railway sidings, cigar factories, wharves, and huge elevators which could load I forget how many thousands of tons of bulk cargo into a steamer in twelve hours, as though she were an iron bucket under a pump," he wrote. Overall, he found a "town spontaneous, unexpected, and complete," where everyone was in a hurry "to secure a foothold in life." When the Panama Canal opened four years later, the city was nicely poised to capitalize on its proximity. "The completion of the Panama Canal throws the spotlight on Tampa," crowed a local land company in a 1915 magazine advertisement, and it confidently predicted "the traffic of the whole maritime world will pause at Tampa's door."[24]

Galveston was also doing well. It recovered so nicely from the Civil War that it was dubbed "the New York of the Gulf" in an 1874 Northern newspaper article. That was only a slight exaggeration. The population grew to better than twenty-two thousand, a stimulating mix of Anglos, Germans, French, Spanish, and sundry other nationalities crowding a city graced by elegant brick commercial buildings, three-story Queen Anne mansions, and the magnificent five-story Tremont Hotel with its Italian marble floors and sweeping staircase. Aggressive local boosters worked hard in tandem with the federal government to improve navigation, deepening the ship channel so oceangoing vessels could moor alongside the town. By the turn of the century the channel stood at twenty-seven feet on the outer bar and forty feet along the port's stone-capped waterfront. Swaggering locals derided struggling Houston, fifty miles inland, as "Mudville." Its earnest efforts to dredge little Buffalo Bayou into a serviceable "ditch" to the Gulf in order to compete only provoked their laughter.[25]

Galvestonians' confidence was dealt a terrible blow on September 7, 1900, when a strong hurricane roared across the island. Gulf and bay waters overlapped the town, swirling around the legs of nonchalant businessmen on their lunch hour. By the time the storm's severity became clear, it was too late to evacuate. At least eight thousand people were killed, thirty-six hundred houses swept away, and several big ships driven miles inland. Grim as it all was, locals responded by elevating their entire city approximately twelve feet above sea level from its existing five feet. It was a Herculean task that took six years and badly disrupted daily life. Hundreds of buildings were laboriously jacked up so that sandy fill could be spread beneath them. Streets, water lines, streetcar tracks, and other infrastructure were ripped up, torn out, and rebuilt. Lastly, in an engineering pièce de résistance, a massive concrete seawall was constructed along the Gulf front to blunt future storm surges. The effort paid off handsomely. Trade returned stronger than ever. By 1905 the city bested both Baltimore and Boston on exports, and even threatened New Orleans's dominant cotton totals. As at Tampa, and indeed every American Gulf port, locals were excited about the Panama Canal. One wharf company bragged that the city was "the last port for ships headed south to the canal or the first port for ships headed north." It was true. But Houston owned the future. It had better rail connections and access to inland markets, and by 1920 surpassed Galveston, and then New Orleans. By 1930 it was the nation's third busiest port. The burgeoning petroleum industry had a lot to do with this, but that is a story for the next chapter.[26]

In the days before the shipping container revolution, sailors lent excitement and color to American waterfronts. But even as new technologies transformed ships and shipping, the seafaring life remained hard. Charlie Bodden was an Alabama resident who earned twenty dollars a month as an ordinary seaman during the 1920s. Thankfully, decades later a family member had the foresight to interview him about working some of the Gulf's last commercial windjammers. Bodden sailed on four-masted schooners his father owned, mostly hauling lumber down to the Caribbean. Young Bodden's skin was soon nut brown, his hands rope toughened and tar stained. He thought nothing of climbing the ratlines up a one hundred-foot mast. With admirable frankness, he detailed what it was like in heavy seas. "You cross these waves," he said, "and some of those damn waves were so huge, some were thirty, forty feet high. Sailing ships couldn't go through 'em, had to ride 'em. I've been on there many a time when my feet would go flying out from under me or I'd be hangin' on for dear life." At first this scared him, but soon he "got a certain kick out of it. I learned how to hang on. You didn't fall out but one time." Considerably less thrilling were routine tasks like scraping barnacles off the ship's hull in dry dock. Bodden used an old hoe with the blade bent forward to "bust 'em open." It was revolting work, even to a hardened seaman. "There'd be everything from little oysters to clams and in general there were barnacles, which is some kind of mussel—hell there's millions of them I guess—but all that shit would run down that handle and run up underneath your arm and down your belly and you would smell like fifteen goats and God it was awful, awful." Nasty as the work was, it had to be done periodically lest the ship become slow and unmanageable.[27]

Life on board modern steel-hulled steamers was a little better. In an unpublished manuscript written in 1986, David M. Conwell described what it was like during the 1930s when he was a merchant seaman. One of his ships was the *Ensley City*, a 3,801-ton steamer for Isthmian Lines, Inc. out of New York. According to Conwell, the ship was a "three-island cargo ship with two 'tween decks and five holds." By "three-island," Conwell meant the ship's appearance in profile: "raised forecastle at the bow of the ship, the raised accommodation house, bridge and funnel at the center of the ship, and the raised poop deck at the stern." The crew consisted of a captain, three mates, a radio operator, bosun, carpenter, five able-bodied seamen, a chief engineer, three assistant engineers, three oilers, three firemen, two wipers, a steward, two cooks, and five messboys. In November 1938 the *Ensley City* departed New York for Mobile carrying automobiles destined for Hawaii. The vessel arrived in Alabama's only seaport and loaded cast-iron pipe, pine lumber, and "bundled tin plate for the pineapple and tuna canneries of Hawaii." On November 30 it headed for the Panama Canal. Underway, Conwell found himself "almost constantly engaged in placing the heavy canvas tarpaulins over the weather deck hatches and securing them in place, or else pulling them off in preparation for working cargo on arrival." Cargo was hoisted on board or off-loaded by swing booms and rested in the hold atop rough lumber pallets or boards, referred to as dunnage. Conwell recalled that the Isthmian ships had "mountains of it," all of which had to be removed, "slung up, and hove up on deck for re-use with the cargo to be loaded." Time off was generally spent lounging on "make-shift chairs under the canvas awning on the poop deck" in fine weather, or below if stormy.[28]

Conwell remembered the Gulf ports as "free-wheeling" with "barrooms by the dozen and an abundance of 'business girls' to help seamen pass the fleeting hours in the worst manner possible." In 1929 Galveston had an incredible fifty whorehouses with at least six women per house. Local madams acted as sailors' confidants, notaries, banks, and nurses. One ran a celebrated "French House" that catered to the "pervert trade." Stella, the joint's most popular prostitute, made so much money that the madam gave her a trip to the World Series. During a 1928 visit to New Orleans's French Quarter, the journalist Lyle Saxon found the ladies' names pinned to brothel doors. "As we went along, I read the names aloud," he wrote. "'Laura' and 'Wanda' and 'Annie' and 'Bessie,' and sometimes the names are prefixed by a title such as 'Chicago May' or 'French Marie.'" Prostitution went hand in hand with liquor and drugs like marijuana and opium. Drunken sailors were common in all the Gulf cities and frequently got into fights or were crime victims. Every port had one spot that was worse than any other in town. Mobile's Monkey Wrench corner was just one infamous example known among merchant seamen worldwide during the 1930s.[29]

The United States government wasn't interested, generally, in bad behavior by sailors in domestic seaports. But throughout the twentieth century it proved determined to enforce its power in the Gulf. Dramatic confirmation of this came on April 21, 1914, when U.S. bluejackets and marines stormed ashore at Veracruz in an eerie reprise of 1847. The reason, not surprisingly, was Mexico's continued political instability. The country had been roiled by revolution since 1910 and the elected president executed by the military. His usurper was Victoriano Huerta, whose regime was opposed by Emiliano Zapata in the south and Pancho Villa in the north. This political disorder exasperated the new U.S. president, Woodrow Wilson, a reedy, stoop-shouldered former college president with a moralizing streak. When nine American sailors were seized at Tampico on April 9, 1914, and a German arms shipment was reported bound for Veracruz, Wilson had all the provocation he needed. He ordered dreadnoughts and transports carrying sixty-five hundred men to Veracruz, announcing, "I am going to teach the South American republics to elect good men!"[30]

As American troops flooded into south Texas preparatory to the invasion, a bevy of newspaper reporters and magazine correspondents joined them. Among the latter was thirty-eight-year-old Jack London, on assignment for *Collier's*. At Galveston's wharves, London witnessed fresh-faced young men board their transports. "There was no confusion, no shouting of orders," he admiringly wrote. "So quiet and orderly did the embarking of three thousand men with all their necessary gear proceed that one almost wondered if any orders were being issued. Army wagons, buckboards, motor cars, and reluctant mules streamed steadily on board." Once in the Gulf, London watched the transports form into a moving square "under the direction of destroyers that glide like a long row of shadows out of the gloom . . . talking across the sea to one another in the medium of chimes and lights—red lights and white that flash and disappear in blinding lucidity on the short signal masts." Like everyone else on board, London expected an easy victory against a people whom he considered inferior.[31]

Huerta pulled his troops out of Veracruz ahead of the invasion, but the forty thousand ordinary citizens were a proud lot. They were not interested in Wilson's civics lesson, and furiously resisted the Americans. When the bluejackets and marines stormed ashore, they were met by women hurling bricks and youths sniping from rooftops. A local prostitute nicknamed "America," who should have been looking forward to a brisk business from the occupiers, instead blasted away at them with an ammunition belt beside her. The fight was brief but unexpectedly bloody. Nineteen Americans were killed, and 193 Mexicans. Huerta was ousted, a new leader installed, and the city occupied for seven months, but Mexico's politics remained vexing. Germany avoided the Gulf, though it was perhaps due more to World War I's continental distractions than Wilson's Veracruz adventure. As for the citizens of that city, they celebrated having made it a fourth time heroic.[32]

American Gulf Coast residents have long been famous for their love of frivolity, drink, and abandon. When Congress passed the Volstead Act banning the production, sale, and transport of intoxicating liquors on October 27, 1919, a robust smuggling operation started in the Gulf. Schooners and tramp steamers ran liquor

American ships at Veracruz, 1914. San Juan de Ulúa, historic and obsolete, broods in the background. COURTESY LIBRARY OF CONGRESS.

north out of the Caribbean thousands of cases at a time. Most of these vessels were foreign registered and carried legitimate paperwork showing them bound for Mexican ports. The smugglers' favorite method was to anchor thirty-five miles offshore along an imaginary line called "Rum Row," well out from the three-mile national limit, where the U.S. Coast Guard was powerless to apprehend them. Small motorboats, skiffs, and luggers swarmed these vessels, their occupants shouting up liquor orders and tossing bundles of cash in payment. In order to more efficiently employ their time, the rumrunners took to wrapping the bottles in burlap and suspending them from buoys for pickup. William Faulkner, living in the Crescent City during the 1920s, supplemented his meager writing income by running a lugger out to Rum Row and retrieving these so-called hams for a bootlegger friend. Everyone ashore knew when a fresh liquor supply arrived, and most approved. A reporter for the *New York Times* observed: "Mobile appears to beam pleasantly and to talk a little thickly. Gulfport appears in high spirits. Pensacola, Key West, and Palm beach are mirthful."[33]

U.S. authorities were not mirthful. Their enforcement efforts were overwhelmed. A few Coast Guard cutters were no more capable of sealing the Gulf Coast than Yankee blockaders had been decades earlier. The frustrations came to a head at 6:30 A.M. on March 20, 1929, when the Coast Guard cutter *Wolcott* spotted the rumrunning schooner *I'm Alone* fourteen miles off the Louisiana coast. *I'm Alone* was well known to authorities, having chalked up an impressive record of cargoes delivered and cutters evaded at sea. She was a handsome two-masted vessel with powerful auxiliary engines and a one thousand-mile-range radio the savvy operator of which could intercept Coast Guard communications. She carried Canadian registration papers and flew the Union Jack. The *Wolcott* ordered the smuggler to heave to, but her master, John T. Randell, refused. "Captain, you have no jurisdiction over me," he shouted through a megaphone. "I am on the high seas outside of treaty waters." Repeated warnings were ignored. The two vessels floated alongside one another a while, until *I'm Alone* broke away and a chase south ensued. Increasingly irritated, the Coast Guard captain barked, "Heave to or I fire." Randell was defiant. *I'm Alone* kept sailing, and the *Wolcott*'s skipper made good on his promise. "I do not know the number of shots fired," Randell later told the *New Orleans Times-Picayune.* "Several shots passed through our sails and rigging, and one shell passed through the flag, which was flying from the time the cutter came up first." That it was a foreign flag would be significant in the controversy to come. The chase continued farther into worsening weather. Another cutter named the *Dexter* out of Pascagoula joined the *Wolcott,* both under orders to capture the smuggler no matter what. On March 22, midway across the Gulf, the *Dexter* started blasting the quarry. "Shell after shell came on board smashing our windows, engines and occasionally hitting the hull below the water line," Randell later said. The crew scrambled to abandon their sinking schooner. One man died. They were plucked out of the sea and taken to New Orleans where they were jailed. In a photograph taken shortly after his capture, Capt. Randell smirks for the camera, and little wonder. The illegal attack precipitated an international episode that wasn't resolved until 1935, years after Prohibition went off the books. The U.S. government suffered embarrassment, apologized to Canada, and paid damages to Randell, his crew, and the dead man's widow.[34]

Bullying Mexicans and pummeling rumrunners were mere policing activities in what the United States regarded as its watery backyard. But during World War II the nation faced a dire threat unlike any other theretofore. The war was a transformative experience along the Gulf. Shipyards like Alabama Dry Dock and Shipbuilding Company in Mobile and Ingalls Shipbuilding in Pascagoula employed thousands, including large numbers of women and blacks who rapidly turned out Liberty ships, tankers, destroyers, cruisers, and mine sweepers. In New Orleans, Andrew Jackson Higgins designed a deceptively simple plywood landing craft known as the Higgins boat that became emblematic of American amphibious power. A British visitor described the hard-fisted businessman as "the most outstanding figure I met in America." Others thought him loud and profane. But he knew how to seize the main chance. "I don't wait for opportunity to knock," he once boasted. "I send out a welcoming committee to drag the old harlot in."

Scene in Vera Cruz during the bombardment, March 25, 1847, E. B. and E. C. Kellogg. As usual in war, civilians suffered the most during the American invasion. Today Veracruz touts itself as "cuatro veces heróica" (four times heroic) for battling historic sieges by the Spanish (1821), French (1838), and Americans (1847 and 1914). COURTESY LIBRARY OF CONGRESS.

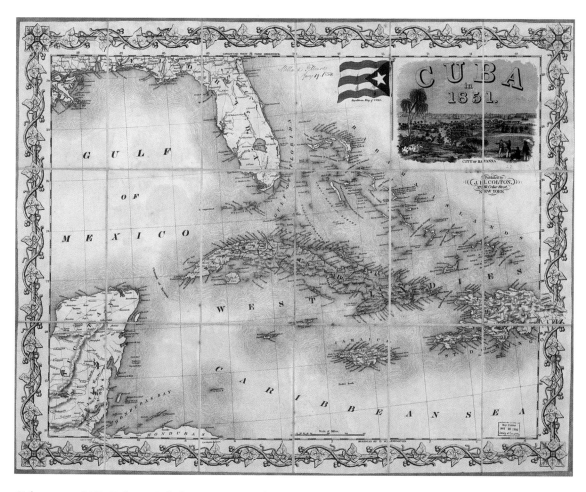

Cuba in 1851, J. H. Colton. Cuba's proximity to the American slave south and unstable politics made it irresistible to filibusters. COURTESY LIBRARY OF CONGRESS.

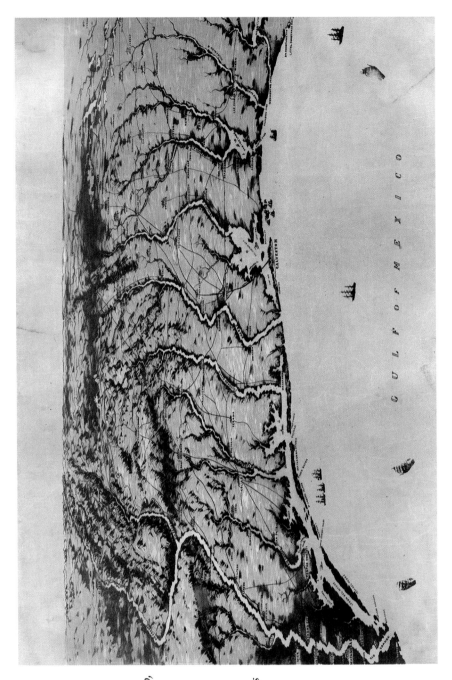

Panorama of the seat of war: Bird's Eye View of Texas and part of Mexico, John Bachmann, 1861. Galveston, right of center, sheltered blockade runners late in the war. The CSS *Alabama* fought the USS *Hatteras* twenty miles to the south in the war's only open-Gulf ship-to-ship duel in 1863. COURTESY LIBRARY OF CONGRESS.

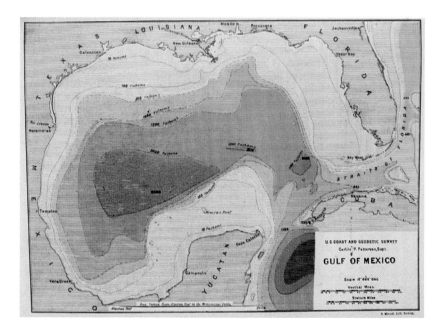

U. S. Coast and Geodetic Survey, Gulf of Mexico. This was the first bathymetric map of any ocean basin. It was compiled by Charles Sigsbee using his sounding machine during the mid 1870s. COURTESY NATIONAL OCEANIC AND ATMOSPHERIC ADMINISTRATION.

Oyster Boat, Mobile Bay, ca. 1905. Thousands of sailing craft worked the American Gulf during the early twentieth century until gasoline engines became the rule. COURTESY JOHN HUNTER.

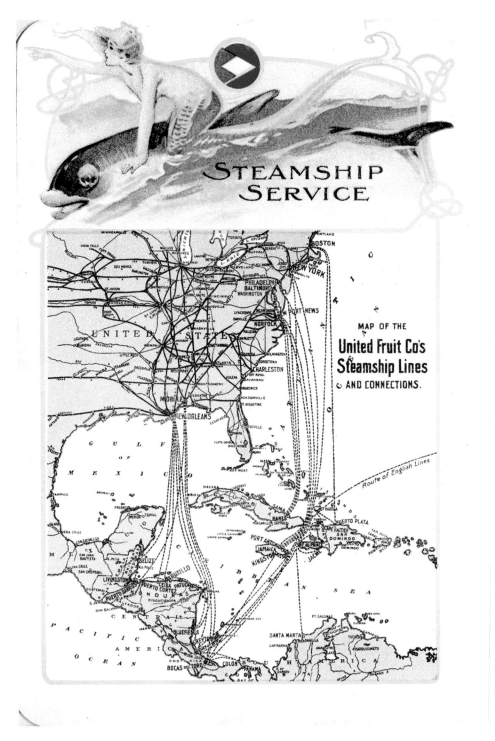

United Fruit Co.'s Steamship Lines and Connections. The proximity of New Orleans and Mobile to the Caribbean and their importance for fruit importation are highlighted by this company map. From *A Short History of the Banana and a Few Recipes for Its Use,* United Fruit Co., 1904.

This happens when you talk to others about ship sailings. Rumors of spies were rampant on the Gulf Coast during World War II. The consequences of loose talk were graphically portrayed by artist John McCrady in this 1942 poster. COURTESY LIBRARY OF CONGRESS.

BELOW Shrimp boats at Bayou La Batre, Alabama, on March 23, 2010. These boats are typical examples of the Texas Trawler type, with the pilothouse forward and the working deck aft. Less than a month after this photograph was taken, the *Deepwater Horizon* oil rig exploded one hundred miles to the south, devastating the Gulf's seafood industry. COURTESY LIBRARY OF CONGRESS.

Container ship at Mobile, Alabama. Gone are the singing work gangs of old with their slings, pallets, and pry bars, replaced by steel boxes, mechanized gantry cranes, computers, and trucks. COURTESY ALABAMA STATE PORT AUTHORITY.

Tanker *Mega Borg* incident, off Galveston, Texas, June 1990. After the vessel exploded, the oil burned out of control for eight days. The cleanup involved some of the first tests of bioremediation. COURTESY NATIONAL OCEANIC AND ATMOSPHERIC ADMINISTRATION.

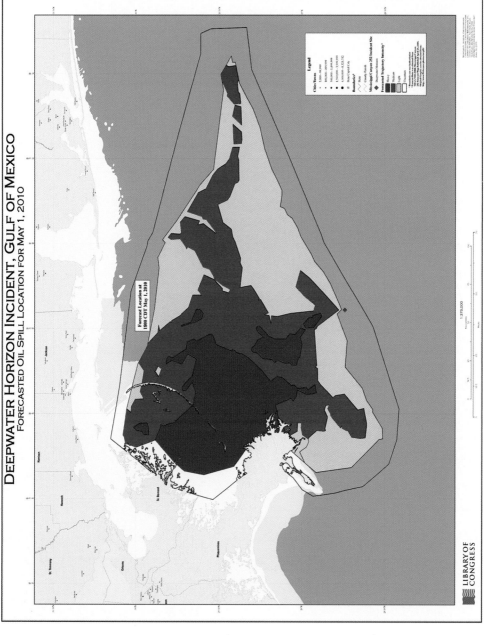

LIBRARY OF CONGRESS

Deepwater Horizon Incident, Gulf of Mexico, Forecasted Oil Spill Location for May 1, 2010. As this map demonstrates, Louisiana's Chandeleur Islands and delicate coastal marshes were first and most heavily impacted during the Deepwater Horizon oil spill. Within weeks, Alabama and Florida beaches were also slathered in oil. COURTESY LIBRARY OF CONGRESS.

OVERLEAF View of Havana from the Morro Castle, Havana Bay. If a nearby port development succeeds, Cuba could once again dominate trade in the Gulf basin. COURTESY JULIO ANGEL LARRAMENDI.

By 1943 Higgins employed more than twenty thousand workers in seven different yards who turned out PT boats and landing craft. Higgins had perfected the latter design during the late 1930s, when oil companies contracted with him for an effective shallow-water vessel. The improved Higgins boat featured a landing ramp and solid pine head log at the bow, a vee section and a reverse curve amidships, and two flat planning sections at the stern. When underway, this arrangement aerated water beneath the hull, efficiently rolling the vessel forward, enhancing its speed and maneuverability.[35]

Despite the Gulf Coast's booming war industries and busy shipping lanes, it was ill prepared for a shooting war. Lights blazed along the shore. Ships sailed unescorted and alone. Germany quickly exploited the situation, sending U-boats ghosting through the Florida Straits early in 1942. The submarine captains called the subsequent six months, during which they had virtual unchallenged sway in the Gulf, the "Happy Times." Cargo ships and tankers were repeatedly torpedoed off the mouths of the Mississippi and along routes leading to Galveston, Mobile, and Tampa. U-boats sank fifty-six ships, totaling three hundred thousand tons. In June 1942 they destroyed more vessels in the Gulf than in all the other theaters of war combined. After U-boats sank several Mexican ships, that nation declared war and joined the allies, coordinating nascent defensive efforts with the United States.[36]

Every submarine attack was unique but there were also similarities, and the story of the sixty-seven hundred-ton *Alcoa Puritan* may be taken as emblematic. On the morning of May 6, 1942, the ship was bound north out of Trinidad for Mobile with a load of bauxite. David Conwell was on board as third mate and later described what happened. He had just come on duty and was carrying "an entire dessert pie" to the bridge when the alarm sounded. He quickly went to his room, deposited the pie, and threw on a life belt. One of the passengers claimed to have seen a torpedo speed just astern, but the sea's surface was calm and unruffled. "While we discussed the possibility of the torpedo's being merely a porpoise," he wrote, "a submarine surfaced astern." What Conwell didn't know at the time was that the enemy craft was U-507, commanded by Harro Schacht, a highly effective officer with the kind of classic Aryan looks Hitler loved. The Germans fired a warning shot but the *Alcoa Puritan*'s captain tried to flee, setting a zigzag course at fourteen knots. To no avail. The U-boat's deck gun opened rapid fire. "These were at a rate of three a minute, for twenty-five minutes," Conwell recalled. The *Alcoa Puritan* was transformed into a smoking wreck, her superstructure and funnel punctured, her anchors shot away, windows smashed, instruments broken, and multiple fires started. The captain ordered abandon ship. Conwell "ran along the port side of the main deck, now covered with heaps of bauxite from our holds, and jumped over the taffrail into the water." He successfully swam for a lifeboat and clambered on board. No sooner was the crew safely bobbing astern the *Alcoa Puritan* than another torpedo sped into her. The vessel was finished. The "sea-green colored submarine" then approached the life rafts, and Schacht, wearing only shorts, apologized for the attack. He shouted that he hoped they "would make it all right," waved, and went back below. Incredibly, none of the *Alcoa Puritan*'s crew had been killed, but they had certainly gotten the fright of their lives.[37]

Always up for a fight, the writer Ernest Hemingway, living in Cuba, wanted to go after the Germans in his thirty-eight-foot wooden fishing boat, *Pilar*. It was an altogether quixotic scheme. The *Pilar* was handsome and fast, but she was no patrol boat. "Papa's" plan was to lure a U-boat to the surface with the prospect of obtaining fresh fish and then attack it by dropping grenades down the hatch or shooting the crew. Cuba had declared war against the Axis powers on December 7, 1941, but Hemingway wanted to fight under the Stars and Stripes. Incredibly, Washington's man on the island, Ambassador Spruille Braden, approved his proposal. That he did so was likely more due to American desperation in the face of the Nazi U-boat campaign than any confidence in Hemingway. Fortunately for the famous writer, he never got the opportunity to test his tactics. If he had, the *Pilar* likely would have been reduced to splinters and the world deprived of its captain's literary genius.[38]

Reeling under the German assault, the Americans quickly ramped up their war efforts in what was designated the "Gulf Sea Frontier." Blackouts were ordered along the coast in an effort to reduce ship silhouettes that might be seen from offshore. Beach patrols even confronted nocturnal flounder fishermen about their spotlights. Fort Morgan at the mouth of Mobile Bay was reactivated, with two 155-mm guns placed on the historic site, sixty-inch searchlights at the ready. A convoy system was implemented for shipping, along with aggressive aerial and seaborne armed patrols. U.S. forces scored their first and only Gulf of Mexico U-boat kill on July 30, 1942. A passenger ship named the *Robert E. Lee* was heading for the Mississippi's Birdfoot Delta with over four hundred people, mostly survivors of previous U-boat attacks, when a torpedo slammed into her. Twenty-five passengers perished. Even as the ship began to sink, her escort vessel, USS *PC 566*, made hard for the submarine's estimated position, dropping depth charges set to explode at different depths. An oil slick bubbled to the surface, suggesting a kill, but credit at the time went to the crew of a Coast Guard seaplane that had dropped some bombs in the vicinity. Only in 2001 when the submarine's wreckage was located by an oil company's remotely operated vehicle (ROV) was the official record corrected. The wreck's location clearly precluded its destruction by the seaplane. ROV footage showed the eerie form of an upright submarine boat, U-166, five thousand feet down, her marine-life-encrusted conning tower and deck gun intact. Her bow displayed catastrophic damage. In recognition of its mistake, the navy posthumously awarded Captain Herbert G. Claudius of *PC 166* a Legion of Merit with a Combat "V" device, for heroism.[39]

By the autumn of 1942, except for sporadic episodes, the U-boat threat was effectively over in the Gulf. Final Allied victory restored peaceful trade, but fundamental changes were brewing. During the latter half of the twentieth century, increasing globalization profoundly impacted maritime trade and seaports. Containerization, flags of convenience, and bland, depersonalized waterfronts became the rule. One of globalization's pioneers coordinated his piece of this sweeping revolution from Mobile. Malcolm McLean was a native North Carolinian who had been a truck driver in the 1930s. During East Coast deliveries he was frustrated by the long delays necessitated by cumbrous ship-loading practices. Stevedores still worked much as they had for decades, using slings, pallets, hand trucks, and winches. Most cargo at the time was break bulk, in other words separate. Boxes, barrels, crates, sacks, and bundles had to be individually managed and stowed. Shippers grumbled that their vessels spent more time dockside than at sea. McLean was struck by the "time and money" wasted and hit upon an idea. He asked himself, "Why couldn't an entire truck be hoisted aboard ship . . . and then used for delivery purposes at the other end of the line?"[40]

In 1955 McLean bought Waterman Steamship Company and went to work. His idea evolved by degrees. At first he used a roll-on/roll-off system whereby cargo was piggybacked onto trucks, which were driven on board ship. Then the truck drivers unhooked their trailers so new drivers could retrieve them at the next port of call and drive them ashore. It was faster than loading break bulk, but McLean was dissatisfied nonetheless. He chafed at the method's inefficiencies—the trailers' space requirements and extra weight. By McLean's lights, the solution was to manufacture a detachable steel container that could be trucked dockside, lifted off the trailer, and dropped into a specially designed hold. On April 26, 1956, he tried it with an altered tanker named the *Ideal X*. McLean loaded her at Newark, New Jersey with fifty-eight containers and sent her to Houston. The voyage took six days. Upon arrival a crane hoisted the containers off the vessel and neatly deposited them on waiting truck trailers. Gone were the work gangs and the frustrating delays. Old-timers dubbed the shipping container "the longshoreman's coffin." Gone too, in time, were the traditional seaport's color and interest. Ships became larger and more automated, requiring fewer crewmen. When they arrived in port, only hours instead of days were required to load or unload. Sailors no longer swaggered down city streets. Dockside, vast concrete expanses meant to facilitate motorized transport and towering cranes operable by only one man replaced the bustle of wooden quays with cargo sheds and their singing roustabouts, exotic products, smells, and piles of cordage. The economic benefits were enormous, offset by cultural impoverishment.[41]

In addition to containerized shipping, the burgeoning cruise industry has had a significant impact on the Gulf ports during the last few decades. Cities like Houston, Galveston, New Orleans, Mobile, and Tampa all hustled to attract cruise ships with their attendant business and wharf fees. For many ordinary Americans, travel across the Gulf to tropical Mexican or Caribbean locales beckoned as an exciting vacation opportunity. This was a profound transformation. Abolished were the discomfort and inconvenience suffered by packet ship or steamer passengers like Tyrone Power and Libbie Custer. While sea sickness can still suddenly take a passenger unawares, modern cruise ships like *Carnival Dream,* which regularly departs Galveston and New Orleans, are efficiently designed with comfort foremost. To begin with, these vessels are huge, accommodating as many as forty-five hundred passengers and crew. The *Dream* is a 1,004-foot, 130,000-ton behemoth with retractable fin stabilizers that dramatically reduce rolling at sea. Cruisers in search of distraction are offered a spa, onboard waterpark, casino, rum bar, theatre, and restaurants. In economic terms the cruise industry has proven to be important for all five of the U.S. Gulf states. In Texas alone, cruise industry direct expenditures were a staggering $1.33 billion in 2014. More than twenty-two thousand jobs were attributed to the industry, or about 6 percent of the U.S. total. Given these kinds of numbers, it is no surprise that cities aggressively compete with one another for vessels and are forced to scramble if a cruise line abandons them for a better deal elsewhere. Cruise terminals have been constructed and port improvements made at considerable public expense, and the advantages are usually to the cruise line. Mobile discovered this in 2011 when Carnival abruptly pulled out and relocated its ship *Elation* to New Orleans, leaving the city holding the debt on a $20-million terminal. Thanks to intensive lobbying by civic officials, the company returned five years later, homeporting the *Fantasy* at Mobile. City leaders made sure they had an ironclad thirteen-month contract in place and, as of this writing, have secured still another one-year extension into 2019.[42]

In the postmillennial world, seaports all around the Gulf are working hard to keep pace with economic change. The challenges are significant. To begin with, like *Carnival Fantasy,* the latest container ships are enormous—up to 1,200 feet long, 150 feet wide, and drawing nearly 50 feet—exceeding the ability of traditional ports to handle their bulk. Indeed, the Gulf's biggest ships of yore like the *Santísima Trinidad,* the *Shakespeare,* and even the 524-foot *Ideal X* would be dwarfed by these supersized vessels. In order to compensate, officials have widened and deepened ship channels and built massive offshore facilities and container ports removed from historic downtowns. American domination is no longer a given. Cuba has pursued a $900-million project in part financed by Brazil at the Port of Mariel, thirty-one miles west of Havana. Improvements to the latter city's famous harbor were impossible because of an automobile tunnel at its mouth. The new site includes concrete aprons, highways, railroads, and a sixty-foot-deep harbor that can accommodate Neo-Panamax vessels specially designed to fit the enlarged Panama Canal (opened 2016). Furthermore, the new port has been designated a Special Economic Development Zone, exempting it from the Cuban government's restrictive socialist policies. Alert to both the threat and the opportunity of a "Cuban Hong Kong," American interests have lobbied hard to improve ports like Tampa, Houston, Mobile, and New Orleans. Politics hasn't helped the situation. "When you're in New Orleans, you're twice as close to Havana as you are to New York City," two Louisiana trade advocates wrote in the *Times-Picayune* in 2016. "Prior to the trade embargo, Louisiana had a flourishing trade relationship with Cuba. . . . It would be beneficial to our state's economy to expand commerce with one of our closest neighbors and historic trading partners. Every day we don't expand trade with Cuba we are leaving money and opportunities on the table."[43]

On the basin's western side, Veracruz has also been effectively expanding its capacities. "We see ourselves as competitors with the Port of Houston," remarked an official there. Owning an already respectable share of trade in automobiles, rice, corn, fertilizers, pig iron, steel, and petroleum, this is no idle fantasy. The current port is already serviced by twenty-seven shipping lines, with routes to North and South America, Europe, and Africa. It is Mexico's most important Gulf port and in 2014 handled 21.8 million tons of cargo, excluding petroleum products. The ambitious expansion is called "Veracruz II" and is located north of the old port. A Mexican shipping manager explained the reasons for a new locale. "The challenge with Veracruz is that the terminal is in the middle of the city," he said, "so anything and everything that goes and comes from the port, it has to go through the city, which leads to a congested city, congested roads in and out of the terminal itself —and it has no room to expand." Veracruz II's key elements are highways, a 2.6-mile break-water, a 1.7-mile wharf with eight berths dredged at fifty-nine feet, and plans for greater container handling ability, two new turning basins, and a logistics center. Easy in, easy out. All very impressive, but removed from the venerable urban back-drops of San Juan de Ulúa and the Faro Venustiano Carranza, not to mention the 444,438 people who now call Veracruz home. Still, one suspects that Cortés would have approved.[44]

Chapter Eight

Blowout!

"It . . . knocked me to the back of the cab. I fell to the floor . . . | Micah Sandell,
put my hands over my head and I just said, 'No, God, no.' | *Deepwater Hori-*
Because I thought that was it." | *zon* survivor, 2010

She was a ship only an oil company executive or stockholder could love—a crude oil tanker with a blunt bow, a wide hull 853 feet long, and a 66-foot draft, registering 141,000 deadweight tons. Every one of her design elements was meant to enhance cargo capacity and efficiency. There were sixteen oil tanks below decks, as well as four pumps for loading/unloading, and big diesel engines capable of driving her slowly but steadily across the world's oceans. Topside she featured a stubby white foremast, pipes, lines, flexible hoses, two derricks, and a multistory bridge astern with projecting wings and an exhaust stack that displayed her Norwegian owner's company logo. Like most modern ships she was coated with red oxide below the waterline to impede marine growth. Topside she was painted a slightly darker brownish red. Overall the effect was comparable to burnt umber, not pretty and, paradoxically, a failure at masking fifteen years' worth of rust, stains, and dings. Even her name was ugly—*Mega Borg*. On the evening of June 8, 1990, the ship anchored fifty-seven miles off Galveston with thirty-eight million gallons of sweet Angolan crude on board. It was just a little over a year since the *Exxon Valdez* had run aground in Prince William Sound, Alaska, precipitating a catastrophic oil spill. As the *Mega Borg*'s hook plunged into the warm Gulf waters, little did her captain or crew suspect that she too would soon come to grief.[1]

Because of her enormous size, the *Mega Borg* could not approach the coast any closer than the ten-fathom curve. In order to overcome this difficulty, she was met by a smaller tanker, the *Fraqmura,* which was to lighter three hundred fifty thousand barrels of her oil up to one of Houston's multitudinous refineries. Since there are forty-two gallons in a barrel, the *Fraqmura* would be taking roughly a third of *Mega Borg*'s cargo. The Norwegian supertanker would then visit several other Texas ports before heading to the Caribbean. As the vessels floated alongside in light winds and calm seas, crews maneuvered derricks and muscled hoses into position to begin transferring the cargo. It was a strictly routine procedure, completed safely multiple times a year. But something went terribly wrong on board the *Mega Borg* that night. First there was a fire in her pump room. Then an explosion ripped the pump room house off the deck, flinging it amidships. Two men were killed instantly, and two others were missing and presumed dead. The blast ruptured the engine room bulkhead, and the fire spread. In an effort to distance themselves from the catastrophe, the *Fraqmura*'s crew quickly decoupled their vessel, spilling ten thousand gallons of oil in the process. A nearby crew boat (common parlance for a "platform supply vessel") evacuated the supertanker's survivors and retreated to a safe distance. Subsequent explosions shot spectacularly skyward, spraying fuel and spreading the fire. As the tanker began settling in the stern, oil flowed freely through her opened pumps into the Gulf, where it burned out of control.[2]

The first Coast Guard cutter arrived shortly after 2 A.M. on June 9 and initiated firefighting efforts. As the sun rose, crews could see a slick drifting northwest toward Corpus Christi. Within days, shifting currents reversed the slick, and it snaked toward Louisiana's Trembling Coast instead. On Sunday morning June 10, Galveston residents retrieved their newspapers to be confronted with the first detailed news of the disaster. "Tanker Blast Kills Two," blared a headline over an image of the burning vessel. Instantly, visions of the recent viscous nightmare at Prince William Sound were conjured—ruined shores, struggling birds, hazmat-suited workers. Readers were further unsettled to learn that the *Mega Borg* carried thrice the oil of the *Exxon Valdez*. Local fishermen and environmentalists feared incalculable damage to Galveston Bay's already much-abused oyster reefs and salt marshes. Municipal officials worried about oiled beaches and an economic body blow. "Tourism is one of Galveston's main industries," one knowledgeable observer told the *New York Times*. "This really couldn't have come at a worse time for the city, economically." But there was no undoing what had happened. Everyone was advised to prepare "for the worst."[3]

Coast Guard officers on the scene were well aware of the risks and consequences attending their subsequent actions. Their overriding concerns were to save the vessel and prevent "a 38 million gallon oil spill." Worldwide interest in the disaster was intense. According to one official, the onshore coordination office "was surrounded by media satellite feed trucks," and the twice-daily press conferences were jammed by "scores of reporters." Spill responders' every move would be reported, second-guessed, and criticized. The various governmental agencies and private contractors involved faced several challenges. To begin with, they did not have the benefit of "standardized radio frequencies," making communication and coordination difficult. Secondly, necessary assets were scattered along the coast. In one case, special fire suppressant foam had to be brought all the way from Europe. A Texas A&M University professor bluntly assessed the situation: "Here again, we were missing an adequate contingency plan and resources on hand to carry it out."[4]

Fortunately, responders also enjoyed some significant advantages that set the *Mega Borg* spill apart from that of the *Exxon Valdez*. Most important, her cargo was light crude, more prone to evaporation than the heavy black oil that had fouled Prince William Sound. Furthermore, because the oil was already on fire in the water, it was decided to let as much of it burn off as possible. Other than light air pollution, this decision effectively turned the disaster on itself. In a further stroke of good luck, the *Mega Borg*'s single hull remained intact—oil was welling up over her burning stern and not through a hull rupture—which meant that if the onboard fire could be doused, the pumps shut off, and the vessel kept afloat, a major spill could be prevented. Responders threw everything they had at the disaster. Two Coast Guard cutters, fifty commercial vessels, fireboats, helicopters, and fixed-wing aircraft all thronged the site. While the fireboats sprayed seawater onto *Mega Borg*'s flaming stern to cool the metal and suppress the fire, crews deployed oil skimmers, bladders, and boom on the calm Gulf waters to capture as much of the oil as possible. At the same time, big C-130 transports lumbered low overhead spraying thousands of gallons of dispersant, meant to break the oil into smaller droplets. It was hoped that this would spread the oil through the water column where it was more likely to dissolve or be consumed by hungry microbes. In order to improve the probability of the latter outcome, one hundred pounds of bacteria were plopped into the water. It was the first time bioremediation had been tried on an oil spill at sea.[5]

The *Mega Borg* burned for eight days before crews finally killed the blaze. Once that was done, the vessel was quickly stabilized and the oil flow stopped. Ultimately, more than four million gallons were spilled, but fire, dispersants, and microbes all helped to blunt a worst-case scenario. Shortly afterward, an overly optimistic pollution report stated, "There is no indication that any product . . . will impact the coastal area in the near future." As if in rebuke, millions of tar balls washed onto the Trembling Coast the following morning. Of the twelve thousand to forty thousand gallons of oil estimated to still be offshore, it was eventually broken down and dispersed by wind and wave. The *Mega Borg*'s remaining cargo was safely lightered, and the stricken vessel towed to Pakistan to be broken into scrap. Thanks to the effective response and considerable good fortune, an even worse disaster had been avoided. No tourist beaches were fouled. But as one scientist glumly wrote shortly thereafter, "the hidden cost in environmental degradation of pelagic organisms, disrupted offshore food webs, and the larvae, the juveniles, and subadults of fishes and invertebrates will never be known."[6]

Oil and the Gulf. They have always gone together. While the *Mega Borg*'s sweet crude arrived from Africa, the basin itself is a prodigious petroleum repository. No one knows exactly how much oil and natural gas are in the Gulf, of course, but even conservative estimates are staggering. According to a 2015 Bureau of Ocean Energy Management report, there are "20.06 billion barrels of oil and 193.8 trillion cubic feet of gas from 1,312 fields" under the U.S. Gulf outer continental shelf alone (defined as the seabed between three and two hundred nautical miles from shore). The fields off Texas and Louisiana are the most enticing, the result of massive primordial salt domes that have pushed through heavier overlying sediments, trapping petroleum in the resultant gaps and faults. Mexican waters also cover rich fields, with one recent exploratory well tapping into a billion-barrel pool only forty-three miles offshore.[7]

The basin's human occupants have known about these riches since the Stone Age. Gulf Coast Indians regularly encountered oil seeps, tar balls, and gas vents and put them to limited use. Oil was thought to have medicinal value and proved especially handy in waterproofing baskets and pottery. It was easily collected from bayous and marshy ponds by brushing the surface with feathers. Tar balls were simply plucked off the beaches. Gas escaping out of the ground was sometimes set afire, the Indians watching as it burned for days. The early Spanish explorers also appreciated petroleum's waterproofing qualities—as when Ocampo's men sealed their hulls at Puerto de Carenas, later Havana, in 1508. But it would not be until the turn of the twentieth century that petroleum would become a bona fide industry, one that would define and defile the Gulf for decades to come.[8]

Spindletop changed everything. For it was there in 1901 that oil roared out of a newly dug well, showering the roughnecks and making Gulf Coast history. That well was twenty-five miles inland on the Texas side of the Sabine River, but prospectors knew that there was plenty of offshore oil too. Getting to it was the challenge. They began carefully, anchoring barges in marshy lakes and erecting derricks with steam-driven drills before moving into the Gulf of Mexico proper. In 1937 Superior Oil and Pure Oil partnered to build a steel strap-reinforced fixed timber platform a mile off Cameron Parish, Louisiana. The rig stood in fourteen feet of water, its platform elevated fifteen feet above the sea's surface. The drill struck oil at a depth of ninety-four hundred feet, and the companies eventually took four million barrels from the site. Shortly thereafter, Humble Oil constructed a drilling platform over a mile out from McFadden Beach, Texas, in fifteen feet of water. Humble used over three hundred yellow pine logs to support its rig. Workers came and went by a long wooden pier with railroad track laid atop. Unfortunately for Humble, the well proved unproductive, and after a hurricane wrecked the platform, the company abandoned it. Despite Humble's disappointing experiment, more rigs followed, springing up off Louisiana and Texas like strange marine growths. The drills changed from steam to diesel-electric, and the workers were housed in converted World War II landing craft anchored alongside the platforms. Chartered shrimp boats ferried the crews, their salty Cajun captains relishing the extra income. "Nobody really knew what they were doing at that time," one early roughneck recalled. "It was blow-by-blow. And it wasn't easy living out there." There were lots of inconveniences, not least bad weather that prevented the men from boarding the platforms. But extremity

The Gulf of Mexico's first offshore oil rig, Cameron Parish, Louisiana. This photograph originally appeared in the *Louisiana Conservation Review* in 1939, two years after the well's construction. The rig stood in fourteen feet of water, and workers were ferried out by shrimp boat. COURTESY LOUISIANA SEA GRANT DIGITAL IMAGES COLLECTION, LOUISIANA STATE UNIVERSITY.

encouraged innovation. Crew quarters were built on the platforms themselves, and supply boats began making regular runs. The oil companies kept reaching out to deeper water—beyond the three-mile limit in 1946 and just a year later beyond the horizon at ten miles.[9]

During the following decades, the U.S. petroleum industry ballooned in the Gulf, dwarfing every other economy that had preceded it—slaves, cotton, lumber. And like those economies, petroleum developed its own vessels, tools, practices, and slang. Wooden barges, converted landing craft, and shrimp boats were replaced by seismic research vessels, drillships, platform supply vessels, anchor-handling ships, cable-laying ships, and well-intervention ships. Rigs likewise became more complex and innovative as companies searched for oil in ever deeper waters. In addition to fixed platforms, engineers designed compliant towers capable of flexing with waves, floating tension leg platforms connected to the seabed by steel tubes, and floating production systems that are semisubmersible and anchored by wire rope. Between 1954 and 1986 alone, the U.S. government leased tens of millions of Gulf seabed acres and permitted over four thousand drilling sites.[10]

Finding and getting offshore petroleum are sustained maritime activities, and the work ranges from tedious to challenging to downright dangerous. In a 2013 article Ryan Carlyle, a field engineer and a Yankee among good ol' boys, described his activities on board an eight hundred-foot-long drillship in the "ultra-deepwater" Gulf. Drillships are used for petroleum exploration at depths between two and ten thousand feet. Because of their maneuverability they are more efficient compared to cumbersome platform rigs. A typical vessel features a helipad at the bow and a moon pool amidships with a towering derrick above. The moon pool is simply an opening in the vessel's hull that allows tools or instrumentation to be raised and lowered in a controlled environment. Once over her target, the vessel drops her equipment to the seafloor. If oil is found, the drillship caps the well. Later, a semisubmersible platform rig may be towed out to fully exploit the resource. Carlyle's vessel was dynamically positioned, meaning that she could use GPS, sonar beacons, propellers, "and six enormous 360-degree thrusters" to hold a position "in any weather short of a hurricane." Her derrick was capable of supporting two million pounds of pipe. None of this awesome capacity came cheap. The ship cost a hefty one million dollars *a day* to lease. When Carlyle arrived on board, he was required to attend a safety briefing, "watch a video, fill out medical paperwork, and then listen to a speech about rig-specific rules like what to do with laundry." Most days were routine, except when they weren't. "When something goes wrong," Carlyle explained, "we work around the clock and we work *hard*. It's pretty nerve-wracking when you're new (every minute of delay literally costs $700) but after a while you get used to the pressure."[11]

Like Carlyle, the 250 men and women who work on board Shell's $1.45-billion tension leg platform *Ursa* fly out on helicopters, but their rig would tower over any drillship. In fact, *Ursa* is one of the largest man-made structures in the Gulf of Mexico, weighing 97,500 tons. It features a semisubmersible ring pontoon hull 38 feet wide and 29 feet high with a quartet of 85-foot diameter yellow steel columns 177 feet high attached. These support the deck modules overhead. The modules are 300 feet square by 50 feet high and within their open-truss frames include the well bay, crew quarters (every room has cable television), and galley, plus areas reserved for power, drilling, and various processing functions. This colossus is held to the seafloor sixty-five miles off the Birdfoot Delta in four thousand feet of water by sixteen (four at each corner) steel tendons. Even though the *Ursa* is technically floating, there is no sea motion discernable on its busy topside. Working offshore two weeks at a time, its crew produces one hundred thousand barrels of oil per day from multiple wells. Captured oil and natural gas are transported via long pipelines to a platform rig closer inshore. The *Ursa*'s crew work extended stretches, but they enjoy good food and services. Shell hired a company to manage the galley, where six people serve up heaping plates of food. "It's not a job to us," caterer Dawn Best, affectionately known as Miss Dawn, told an interviewer. "We're more like family out here. I have three sons who work offshore for other companies, so I treat all of the workers here the way I'd want people to treat my boys."[12]

Not surprisingly, petroleum's economic impact on the coastal communities of Louisiana and Texas has been especially profound. Men and women with high school educations have landed well-paying jobs, and millions of dollars have been pumped into local economies. Shoreside support services have prospered, pumping stations and refineries proliferated, and charter fishermen have discovered the benefits of oil rigs as artificial reefs. Louisiana's petroleum statistics are impressive, hardly surprising since its waters have so many rigs. According to a 2014 report, the Pelican State "is the nation's number two producer of crude oil and the number two producer of natural gas" and ranks "number two among the states in petroleum refining capacity." Texas is number one, of course, with many more wells on land. Once extracted, oil and natural gas are transported through 112,000 miles of pipeline that interlace the bayou country like a dense web. The report is also helpful in illuminating why local politicians are so eager to please Big Oil. In 2011, for example, petroleum "supported $73.8 billion in sales in Louisiana firms, generated over $20.5 billion in household earnings for Louisianans, and supported 287,008 jobs in the state." All of which translates into almost two billion dollars in taxes and fees for revenue-hungry governments.[13]

Besides all the regionally extracted oil and gas, Louisiana imports more foreign petroleum than almost any other state. This is largely because of the Louisiana Offshore Oil Port (LOOP), which opened in 1981. Situated eighteen miles off Grande Isle in 110 feet of water, LOOP consists of three single-point mooring buoys and a large multilevel pumping platform. When supertankers arrive, they moor at one of the buoys, and their oil is pumped through a forty-eight-inch pipe to shore. Once ashore the oil can either be transferred through multiple lines to the Midwest, stored in aboveground tanks, or pumped into vast subterranean salt caverns. LOOP's advantages include the ability to handle large ships without risky maneuver in confined harbors; the elimination of cumbrous lightering operations; and greater speed, efficiency, and capacity.[14]

Mississippi and Alabama are lesser players. Alabama has several natural gas rigs in Mobile Bay that are required to operate under strict environmental regulation. Florida's horizons are clear of rigs, however. Petroleum exploration and drilling have been banned in the eastern Gulf since 1990, when that state's leaders decided clean beaches were more important to their economy than oil. Despite intense pressure from oil companies to overturn the moratorium, it has held and even been extended to 2022 since the recent *Deepwater Horizon* disaster. But industry keeps pushing and has at last found a sympathetic audience in President Donald J. Trump. In the spring of 2017 Trump rolled back decades-long drilling restrictions in the Arctic and Atlantic oceans, giving new hope to Big Oil in the eastern Gulf. What the president will do there is unclear as of this writing, but most Floridians' opposition remains unchanged, including state politicos on both sides of the aisle. Democratic senator Bill Nelson declared, "Ever since I was a young congressman, I've been fighting to keep oil rigs away from Florida's coast, and I'm not going to stop now." Likewise, Francis Rooney, a Republican congressman representing the state's Nineteenth District (Fort Meyers, Naples) opined in the *Pensacola News Journal*, "The industrial infrastructure needed to support offshore drilling, and ultimately offshore production of oil and gas, is wholly incompatible with existing tourist-centric development."[15]

There is certainly no escaping petroleum's visual, and olfactory, imprint on the Texas and Louisiana coasts. During his 1990s tour of the Gulf littoral, journalist Frederick Turner topped a bridge leading into Port Arthur and was dazzled by the nocturnal vista. "Times Square could have had nothing on this place . . . ," he enthused, "its thousands of refinery lights winking and glowing and the smoke from these plants standing out in chilly darkness like great ornamental boas." Despite the industrial vibe it was beautiful, "a sudden and unexpected gift." During the early 2000s, New Yorker Justin Noble and his girlfriend moved to the Crescent City and settled in an industrial suburb known as Arabi because it seemed "gritty and magical." It was also cheap. Unfortunately, there were other costs to living there. Sometimes simply breathing was difficult, thanks to a nearby ExxonMobil refinery, "whose smokestack emissions floated down our street, wrapping around trees and homes, sneaking into our nostrils as we walked the dogs, scraping our eyes and throats." Shortly after settling in, Noble drove his girlfriend down to the Gulf to show her "the machinery that runs the world." At some unnamed point, most probably Port Fourchon, Louisiana, they stopped. The town was a beehive of activity, "heliports and communication towers and control valves and loading docks and offshore support vessels and 1,200 trucks a day, delivering food and materials and men to be ferried out by the helicopters and vessels to the more than 4,000 oil-production rigs and drilling platforms located off the coast of Louisiana. From the beach we watched as, one by one, oil rigs lit up the horizon." And in his elegantly penned book *The Gulf*, Jack Davis describes the scenery along Louisiana State Route 23—the seventy-four-mile-long asphalt ribbon that runs down the Mississippi's western bank from Gretna to Venice—where the "discards of Louisiana's biggest profit makers lie about everywhere: junkyards of rusting equipment, tumbles of rusting pipes, weedy plats of sidelined barges, also rusting."[16]

Unfortunately, Big Oil's negative impacts far exceed unpleasant smells and abandoned pipe. Since the industry's earliest days, environmental damage has been constant. For decades there was practically no environmental regulation other than forbidding ships to dump bilge in busy harbors. During his 1930s merchant seaman days, Conwell spent time on board oil tankers, which frequently cleaned their tanks offshore. "Although no one gave the matter much thought at the time," he wrote half a century later, "it amazes me now to recall that we regularly dumped tons of oil-soaked sludge from the tanks over the side of the ship, often while steaming close to the beaches of south Florida." When under way, "every tanker discharged oil-contaminated water into the sea. Wherever tankers went they were followed by a tell-tale ribbon of discolored water." Then there were the accidental spills caused by overtopping, broken pipes, and vessel collisions. Even in the modern era with more laws and increased governmental oversight, spills happen frequently. According to a 2017 *Houston Chronicle* story, Galveston Bay has had an astonishing 285 oil spills since 1998. While some of these were small, "less than one gallon," experts cautioned that even one gallon is enough "to kill half the fish and shrimp larvae in a million gallons of water, more than it would take to fill up an Olympic-size swimming pool." A local marine scientist quipped, "It's like death by a thousand cuts, especially when you combine the oil spills with all of the other stressors to the bay."[17]

The big events like the *Mega Borg* fire get the headlines, however. Unfortunately, there have been a distressing number of those. And as the residents of the Texas coast learned in 1979, sometimes even a distant mishap can have a direct impact. So it was that summer when a Mexican well in the Bay of Campeche suddenly blew out, spewing oil for months. Ixtoc-I was located sixty-five miles northwest of Ciudad del Carmen, at the time a sleepy Mexican shrimping town of thirty thousand nestled right where the Yucatán Peninsula gracefully sweeps westward toward the state of Tabasco. During the early 1970s a local shrimper had reported unusual oil patches in the area. When Mexico's national oil company, Petróleos Mexicanos (Pemex), investigated it discovered an enormous oil reserve. Pemex was encouraged by its early work at Ixtoc-I. Its rig, known as *Sedco 135*, sat in 150 feet of water and had drilled down more than 11,000 feet below the seafloor when the bit suddenly encountered soft strata. The well immediately lost mud circulation in its pipe. Mud is critical to modern oil drilling because it equalizes the pressures in the shaft and as it returns it can be monitored for gas. Once the drill hit the soft strata, mud began escaping into numerous rock fissures, dropping circulation. Workers tried to raise the drill and pump down material to seal the fissures but the well got ahead of them. Mud came roaring up the shaft and blasted out the top of the rig, closely followed by oil from the blown wellhead. The resulting fumes ignited when they came into contact with the rig's pump motors, and flames leapt into the muggy night air. "It was like the whole area was cast in an orange glow," one fisherman recalled. All seventy-one of the rig crew escaped safely, but tons of equipment collapsed into the Gulf. Meanwhile, an estimated thirty thousand barrels of crude oil were gushing to the surface with each passing day.[18]

Fortunately, the oil was of a light brownish variety, and as the Coast Guard would do eleven years later with the *Mega Borg* fire, Pemex decided to let the flames burn off as much as possible. The company attacked the rest aggressively. Several dozen vessels deployed skimmers, boom, and absorbent rope, while overhead aircraft dropped hundreds of thousands of tons of a chemical dispersant known as Corexit. Meanwhile, coastal dwellers from Ciudad del Carmen all the way to Galveston anxiously tracked the progress of a large slick as it ghosted the Mexican shoreline west and then north. "We all followed it closely," a Mexican shrimp boat captain later told an American journalist. "It was a drag." Efforts to cap the well proved disappointing and the slick kept growing. By August, 165 miles of Texas beachfront were fouled. "Hotels placed temporary walkways over the tar-covered beaches," one eyewitness wrote. "Oiled sand was scraped from beaches. Booms were placed across inlets to prevent the oil from getting into the fragile nursery areas of the Laguna Madre behind the barrier islands." Despite these measures, Ixtoc-I cost the Texas economy an estimated $4.4 million and killed thousands of birds, sea turtles, crabs, and dolphins. An estimated three million barrels of oil flowed into the Gulf before a relief well finally stopped the spill. That September Hurricane Frederic helped break up what was left of Ixtoc-I. Fortunately, its environmental impacts were relatively limited. Worse was to come, however. Though no one knew it at the time, the blowout in the Bay of Campeche was a harbinger.[19]

Blowout preventer. Riser pipe. Top hat. Top kill. Junk shot. Berms. Booming. Americans learned a whole new vocabulary during the spring and summer of 2010 when the *Deepwater Horizon* rig exploded, killing eleven men and sending oil into the Gulf unimpeded for eighty-seven very long days. Television viewers were mesmerized by underwater footage of great, brown billows rolling and tumbling continuously out of the wellhead. No one seemed able to stop it. Many suspected that engineers were making things up as they went along, and British Petroleum (BP) didn't help the situation with its confusing and evasive answers. What was clear to everyone, however, was that an entire way of life on America's Gulf Coast was threatened. From Destin to Port Arthur charter fishermen, tour boat operators, shrimp boat captains, deckhands, seafood distributors, restaurant owners, waiters and waitresses, barkeeps, beachfront hotel owners, t-shirt merchants, gift shop owners, amusement park employees, zoo keepers, automobile salesmen, vacationers, everyone watched anxiously as repeated attempts to stifle the spill failed and the oil inexorably drifted north toward ecologically delicate marshes and some of the world's prettiest beaches. Governors, mayors, and city council members caucused about how best to protect their shores and guard fragile economies. Port authorities pondered how to prevent contamination of vulnerable urban waterfronts from incoming ships with oiled hulls. People stocked up on shrimp and froze it for later, when there would be none safe to eat from their beloved waters. Prayer vigils were held along muddy bayous and on white sandy beaches. When the wind was right there was a diesel reek miles inland, and then the oil hit. Livelihoods were ruined, an Orange Beach charter boat captain committed suicide, New Orleans's famed restaurants suffered a lack of oysters and customers, and cleanup workers complained of adverse health effects because of their exposure to oil and chemical dispersants. It was the worst environmental disaster in American history.

One crewman called it "the well from hell," another "a nightmare." Its origins were typical however. In March 2008, BP leased a portion of the central Gulf seafloor known as Mississippi Canyon Block 252. The Minerals Management Service (MMS) approved its exploration plan a year later. Not long afterward, the company's surveyors found a promising site forty-eight miles off the Birdfoot Delta in five thousand feet of water. The plan called for an exploratory well that could be converted into a production well if enough petroleum was indicated. The MMS approved a drilling permit for the newly christened Macondo Well on May 22, 2009. It was named after the doomed village in Gabriel García Márquez's seminal novel, *One Hundred Years of Solitude,* by a BP employee who won a United Way competition. The choice turned out to be prophetic. That October Hurricane Ida crippled the rig *Marianas* halfway through the job and it had to be towed away. In February 2010 BP leased Transocean Limited's *Deepwater Horizon* to resume drilling. By any measure it was an impressive vessel—semisubmersible and especially equipped for deepwater work. Its defining feature was a centered twenty-five-story derrick, complete with over five thousand pieces of drilling equipment. Its 146 crew members enjoyed state-of-the-art accommodations too—private rooms with baths, a gym, a sauna, a movie theater, laundry facilities, and a cafeteria. Little wonder they called it a "floating Hilton." As for the crew members themselves, one newcomer described them as "maybe a little rough" but "very intelligent." They worked for various companies like BP, Transocean, and Halliburton, at jobs including captain of the rig, safety officer, senior tool pusher, mud logger, mud engineer, cementer, ROV operator, tank cleaner, technician, rig mechanic, welder, crane operator, and floor hand. Despite their expertise and *Deepwater Horizon's* sophisticated capabilities, they were working at the limits of technology in a challenging geological environment. Just like the job at Ixtoc-I, their drill bit encountered porous rock that quickly channeled away critical drilling mud. The resulting pressure drops in the pipe leading up to the rig, known as the riser, led to sharp "kicks" that made the *Deepwater Horizon* difficult to control. Not surprisingly, the job fell weeks behind schedule and soared millions of dollars over budget. To make matters worse, BP had been cutting critical safety corners to save time and money. The well's blowout preventer, for example, a five-story, four hundred-ton device that sat atop the wellhead to monitor pressures and shut down the flow in an emergency, was a decade old and long past due for a check-up.[20]

April 20, 2010, was the fateful day. Having drilled down to an incredible 13,300 feet below the seafloor, it was as if *Deepwater Horizon* had suddenly crossed some forbidden frontier and pricked a primordial Mayan god, stirring its wrath. Subsequent investigations concluded that no one person or event was to blame for the disaster. Rather, as BP put it in its postmortem, "a complex and interlinked series of mechanical failures, human judgments, engineering design, operational implementation and team interfaces came together to allow the initiation and escalation of the accident." Pressure built in the well. At 9:40 that evening oil and gas came rushing up, forcing mud out of the riser pipe and onto the platform. What began as an upwelling suddenly exploded into a geyser that shot higher than the derrick. On board the nearby supply boat *Bankston,* Capt. Alwin J. Landry suddenly saw "mud falling on the back half of my boat, kind of like black rain." A crewman watched amazed as a mud-blasted seagull fell onto the deck. Meanwhile, alarms were going crazy on *Deepwater Horizon.* The mud geyser was followed by "gassy smoke," according to Micah Sandell, a crane operator who had a front-row seat. Then there was an explosion and a great billowing pillar of fire. "It . . . knocked me to the back of the cab," Sandell later recalled. "I fell to the floor . . . put my hands over my head and I just said, 'No, God, no.' Because I thought that was it." Not far away, chief engineer Steve Bertone had just settled into bed to read. He heard a strange noise. "As it progressively got louder, it sounded like a freight train coming through my bedroom and then there was a thumping sound that consecutively got much faster and with each thump, I felt the rig actually shake." Outside in the hallway debris was everywhere and people were in shock. "When I looked out the window, I saw fire from derrick leg to derrick leg and as high as I could see," Bertone said. "At that point, I realized that we had just had a blowout." The *Deepwater Horizon* was blazing like a giant Roman candle. Throughout the ordeal many crew members displayed incredible heroism in rescuing injured comrades and making sure as many as possible evacuated the doomed rig. Bobbing nearby in lifeboats, on board the *Bankston,* or swimming through oily water, they were lucky to be alive and could only watch in horror as the rig burned. It finally listed and sank two days later. The blowout preventer had failed spectacularly. Oil was gushing out of the wellhead, rising to the surface, and spreading.[21]

BP faced an environmental and public relations crisis. No one knew how much oil was flowing out of the wellhead, though corporate and government spokespeople consistently lowballed the figure at between one to five thousand barrels a day. Gimlet-eyed scientists put it much higher, some at as much as seventy thousand barrels a day. Regardless of the amount, it had to be stopped. But by May it was evident that neither industry nor government knew how to do it. Tony Hayward, BP's top man, didn't help matters when an intended apology to Gulf Coast residents went very wrong. "We're sorry for the massive disruption it's caused their lives," he said of the spill. "There's no one who wants this over more than I do. I would like my life back." Christopher Jones, whose brother was one of those killed on the rig, tersely responded at a Washington, D.C., hearing shortly thereafter, "Well, Mr. Hayward, I would like my brother's life back." BP scrambled to stem both the PR fallout and the spill, with no success on either front. Despite his efforts to smooth things over, Hayward continued blind to the situation's optics. On June 19 he was photographed looking relaxed at a yacht race in England. A BP spokeswoman attempted to explain when she said, "He is having some rare private time with his son." White House chief of staff Rahm Emanuel wasn't amused: "To quote Tony Hayward, he's got his life back." Out at the well, things weren't going any better. The company tried an array of solutions during the spring and summer. These included attempting to close off the blowout preventer's valves with ROVs, capping the well with a containment dome (top hat), shooting it full of golf balls (junk shot), and pumping it full of heavy drilling mud (top kill). Nothing worked. The public's anger turned to despair as weeks passed and the oil kept coming.[22]

That July, David Gessner, a nature writer from North Carolina, drove down to the "national sacrifice zone" to see what was happening firsthand. At Pensacola Beach he found tar balls everywhere. "As I looked into these clumps of oily turds I began to suspect that this time we had really done it," he mused. "We have passed a point, and the fact that many of our current actions are suicidal must be becoming obvious to even the most casual observer of the natural world." Several hundred men, hired by BP at $15 an hour, "moved through the mist like a ghostly prison crew in florescent vests, sweeping the sands." Most of the workers were black, "many formerly unemployed," and were supervised by "overweight" white men who "barked orders and drove around in four-wheel-drive ATVs that looked like amped up golf carts." All along the coast Gessner met locals who were "angry or giddy-drunk with the money that BP is handing out to assuage their bile." Boat operators idled by the spill were paid to participate in the "Vessels of Opportunity Program," ferrying supplies, deploying boom, and assisting with wildlife rescue. "One of the small, sad sights down here," Gessner wrote, "is watching the boat captains, seamen who have likely not worn life preservers since they were toddlers, all buckled up in their vests as they putter out to sea each morning." They were taking BP money, which meant they were "beholden" to the company's liability lawyers. A nearby sign tacked to a post reading "do not litter" only heightened the irony.[23]

The Macondo Well was finally capped on July 15. The disaster's extent and consequences continue to be evaluated, but in 2015 the National Oceanic and Atmospheric Administration presented some sobering numbers in its environmental impact statement. "Approximately 3.19 million barrels (134 million gallons) of oil were released into the ocean," the document stated, resulting "in observable slicks that extended over 43,300 square miles (an area about the size of the state of Virginia), affecting water quality and exposing aquatic biota. Oil was deposited onto at least 400 square miles of the sea floor, and washed up onto more than 1,300 miles of shoreline from Texas to Florida." The National Wildlife Federation estimated catastrophic losses to Gulf wildlife—between twenty-seven thousand and sixty-five thousand Kemp's ridley sea turtles, at least one thousand bottlenose dolphins, as much as 12 percent of the brown pelican population, billions of oysters, millions of larval fish, and untold numbers of other species from algae to sperm whales. People living along the Gulf Coast had long taken pride in their beautiful environs and its abundant resources, but the disaster left them reeling and worried.[24]

Epic events like Ixtoc, *Mega Borg,* and Macondo aside, there is an even more consequential catastrophe unfolding along the Trembling Coast, albeit an insidious and less dramatic one. During Category 2 Hurricane Georges in 1998, scientists noticed that its power didn't diminish when it passed over Louisiana's coastal marshes. In the old days there would have been enough marshland to slow the surge, but much of that important defense was going or gone. This meant even less protection for vulnerable coastal fishing villages, not to mention metropolitan New

Orleans. Four years later, the *Times-Picayune* highlighted the increased danger in stark terms. "A major hurricane could decimate the region," it declared, "but flooding from even a moderate storm could kill thousands. It's just a matter of time." The ongoing land loss dates back decades. Much of it has been exacerbated, not surprisingly, by navigational improvements. First, the powerful Mississippi River was channelized between massive levees, depriving the surrounding marshes of its sediment-replenishing floods. Secondly, the Gulf Intracoastal Waterway was cut across lower Louisiana during the 1940s as part of its thirteen hundred-mile run from Carrabelle to Brownsville. In an effort to reach it directly, numerous ancillary businesses dredged short canals, hastening erosion and furthering salt water's inland reach. On an even larger scale, an estimated ten thousand miles of canals each averaging 15 feet deep by 150 feet wide had been dredged arrow-straight throughout the state's southern marshes by oil and gas companies digging wells and seeking more efficient routes for supply boats and pipelines. This ditch maze allowed significant saltwater incursions into what had theretofore been freshwater lakes, killing plants whose roots held the boggy soil together. Dredge spoil dumped as levees along these waterways further threw the region's naturally balanced flow cycles out of whack. Boat wakes sped shoreline collapse, canals merged one with another, and what had been biologically rich marshland was converted into vast expanses of salt water. In fact, a 2011 U.S. Geological Survey study concluded that between 1985 and 2010, Louisiana showed a "wetland loss rate of 16.57 square miles a year" or in terms familiar to the state's sports-crazed populace, "more than a football field every hour." Combined with climate change and rising sea levels, the prognosis was very bad.[25]

In the summer of 2005, Hurricane Katrina had dramatically demonstrated just how bad. The flooding that inundated New Orleans, killing hundreds, was worsened by the Mississippi River Gulf Outlet, or MRGO. Authorized by Congress in 1956 and completed by the Corps of Engineers in 1968, MRGO amounted to a seventy-six-mile watery arrow piercing the heart of the city. Perspicacious locals dubbed it a "superhighway for tidal surge." By the 2000s erosion had tripled its width and decimated the adjacent marshes. During Katrina, the storm surge was efficiently funneled through this broad corridor right into the city. According to one study, MRGO "amplified the waves to 9.2 feet." Had the canal not been there, and had the original "wetland apron" been intact, the wave height would have been half that, easily handled by the existing levees. As the historian Douglas Brinkley said of MRGO after Katrina, "The result was the same as if a team of top-flight engineers had been assigned to build an instrument for the quick and effective flooding of New Orleans." The waterway's obvious role in the city's tragedy prompted its closure by tons of rock in 2006.[26]

Unfortunately for Louisiana's residents most directly facing the Gulf's fury, there are no such solutions. The cultural damage that can accompany land loss was

Song-n-Dance Girl, Isle de Jean Charles, Louisiana, 2005. Despite land loss and rising sea levels, south Louisiana's Biloxi-Chitimacha-Choctaw Indians remain inextricably linked to the waters they have known for centuries. COURTESY MELINDA ROSE, PHOTOGRAPHER.

thrown into relief in 2016 when the residents of Isle de Jean Charles were awarded $48 million by the federal government to resettle on firmer ground forty miles inland. Isle de Jean Charles is a narrow ridge situated deep in Terrebonne Parish. The residents are a proud bunch, Biloxi-Chitimacha-Choctaws, who claim descent from Jean Charles Naquin, a Frenchman, and Pauline Verdin, an Indian woman. Tribal lore relates that Naquin's father had smuggled for the Laffites and knew the bayou country like the back of his hand. Young Naquin was ostracized for marrying an Indian, so he decided to make his own way in his father's old haunts. He and Pauline moved down to what became the Isle de Jean Charles and had five children, all of whom married descendants of Biloxi-Chitimacha and Choctaw Indians living in the area. This became the community nucleus. In 1876 several men bought the ridge and improved their bayou by widening it for easier travel. Pirogues were their universal conveyance until well into the twentieth century. Their earliest houses were traditional huts with raised clay floors, clay walls mixed with moss, and palmetto-frond roofs pierced by smoke holes. The men hunted, fished, and herded cattle while the women reared children and tended garden plots. Shrimp, fish, oysters, squirrel, deer, squash, okra, and rice were just some of the local bounty that went into residents' iron cooking pots. The settlement grew, albeit slowly, before it began its decline. The 1910 census recorded seventy-seven people. It peaked at several hundred residents, but today there are less than a hundred. In 2014 one longtime resident, Edison Dardar, described island life in simple and appealing terms for the filmmaker Emmanuel Vaughan-Lee: "I still do the same thing I was doing when I was ten years old. We talk. We laugh. We catch some shrimp." Another old-timer, Wenceslaus Billiot, told the *Guardian* that when he was a child, "You could walk for a long time. Now, nothing but water." The government's resettlement award is significant because it is the first to address dislocation due to climate change. Billiot said he would likely stay, but others are inclined to pull up stakes. Maryline Naquin told a reporter for the *Times-Picayune:* "I'm sad about it, but it's necessary. I can see water from both sides of my house. The water is getting closer." But at least one younger woman was practically evangelical about what her people were doing. "This community not only signed up to be the guinea pig," she said, "they also signed up to be the teachers." The new 515-acre inland site meets the tribe's main criteria of being rural and accessible by water—St. Louis Bayou bisects it—plus it is much closer to stores and services. Houma, Terrebone Parish's seat, is only twenty minutes away. Contemplating all the profound changes, Brenda Dardar Robichaux, a former chief of the much larger United Houma Nation, remarked: "Louisiana is paying a grave price for what the rest of the country is enjoying, whether it's seafood or what oil and gas can provide. But our tribal citizens are paying the ultimate price."[27] As the Biloxi-Chitimacha-Choctaws know better than anyone, life on the Gulf has always been challenging. Despite being forced to retreat, they are determined to maintain their identity, bound as ever to the warm southern sea on their doorstep.

Epilogue
The Wreck of the Rachel

All around the Gulf, rich cultural legacies remind us of our long relationship with this beautiful, pocketed sea. Whether contemplating a Mayan lighthouse set on a rocky Yucatán promontory; an exquisitely carved pelican figurehead in a Florida museum; a bronze mooring ring at Veracruz; the sea baths below Havana's Malecón; or a nineteenth-century brick fortress off the Mississippi coast, we marvel at the ingenuity and history these things represent. But as wonderful as they are, none matches the romance of a wooden shipwreck half-buried in white sand beside emerald waters. If one is lucky enough to encounter such a rare survival, thoughts turn at once to old salts and peg legs, broadsides and ratlines, exotic ports, and garrulous parrots. One of the Gulf's most famous examples, the *Rachel*, lies on the Alabama coast five miles east of Fort Morgan between a stilted vacation house and the wrack line, easily visible to beachgoers. Children and adults from landlocked states are especially fascinated by this unexpected artifact. As one Kentuckian told an Associated Press reporter, "We don't ever see anything like this." Speculation as to the vessel's identity runs the gamut among these folks. Was she a pirate ship? A Civil War blockade runner? A rumrunner? None of these guesses is unreasonable. All are known to have once coursed these waters.[1]

The truth might seem more prosaic—she was an early twentieth-century lumber schooner, "like the tractor trailers of today," as Mike Bailey, the director at Fort Morgan put it—but therein lies a tale with its own compelling elements. To begin with, the *Rachel* was built not for any practical reason but as an act of filial piety. Capt. John Riley Bliss McIntosh was a Mississippian with a love of the sea who saved and saved but never achieved his dream of owning a ship. After he died, his daughter, Rachel, took the one hundred thousand dollars he'd accumulated to a Moss Point shipbuilder named John De Angelo to fashion a schooner as a memorial to the old man. De Angelo was reluctant, knowing the maritime world's brutal economics, but considering the post–World War I downturn in his business, his sons took the unusual commission. The resulting vessel was large for a three-masted lumber schooner—155 feet stem to stern and 36 feet in the beam, drawing 12 feet loaded—and looked positively boxy from the stern. Christened, appropriately

The Wreck of the *Rachel,* 2015. COURTESY WWW.MICHAELMASTRO.COM.

enough, the *Rachel,* the completed vessel remained docked, the fees paid by McIntosh's daughter until her death in 1922. The De Angelo brothers claimed the schooner for expenses shortly thereafter and then sold her at auction.[2]

So it was that by late 1923 the *Rachel* was owned by one W. B. Patterson, who hired a Mobile outfit to manage the vessel. This was at the height of the Deep South lumber boom, when fast schooners sailed from the Gulf ports down to the West Indies loaded with sawn yellow pine, hewn hardwood, cypress shingles, round logs, and staves. In October the *Rachel*'s new captain and seven-man crew took on a load of yellow pine and made sail for Cuba. They crossed the Gulf in a few days and delivered their cargo without incident, and then headed back home. Rumors that they indulged in a little rum-running could well be true, it being the Prohibition era and Mobilians known for liking their liquor, but there is no way to prove it now.[3]

That autumn was a stormy one in the Gulf, and as the *Rachel* sailed north a massive tropical disturbance extending from Veracruz to the Louisiana coast prompted small craft warnings as far east as Pensacola. By October 16 the system was rated a minimal hurricane with a barometric pressure of 22.22 inches and winds at seventy-four miles per hour. Its center was expected to track over Morgan City, Louisiana between the hours of 4 and 6 A.M. For those ashore, the resulting blow ranked as little more than a gusty thunderstorm. New Orleans reported southeast winds of thirty-six miles an hour, Mobile sixty, and Pensacola sixty-four. Damage was minimal, confined to a few small fishing boats smashed together at Gulfport and about a dozen barges wrecked at Pensacola.[4]

Out on the open water it was a different story. Those ships and their crews dotted across the horizon faced the dreaded prospect of a lee shore. Lumber schooners like the *Rachel,* dependent on sails and low-pressure steam engines, risked being driven aground unless well out to sea. Wallowing in the big swells and unable to beat to windward, they were facing serious trouble. To the east of the *Rachel,* the schooner *Bluefields* was on a run from Tampa to Cuba, when the storm hit. Her captain later reported his vessel "buffeted and battered" for two wretched days before being dashed onto the beach at the Alabama-Florida line. The crew abandoned ship beforehand, but unfortunately four of these brave souls perished trying to swim ashore. The others made the beach exhausted, where they were rolled in the surf until able to claw their way to safety, gasping and grateful to be alive. Meanwhile, the *Rachel* attempted to hold her own by dropping heavy anchors and reducing canvas down to bare poles. One can imagine the terrifying scene—heaving seas, slashing rain, roaring wind, dragging anchors, and land ever closer as the small crew cowered on the pitching deck. Being in ballast—that is, without cargo—the *Rachel* was swept ashore like so much flotsam and grounded "high and dry." Happily, her crew remained on board and was safe.[5]

In the following days the *Rachel*'s owner attempted to have the ship towed off, but she was forty feet from deep water and so firmly planted that even the big tugs that attempted the task were unable to accomplish it. Resigned to the loss, Patterson had her stripped and filed an insurance claim. Soon enough he collected his settlement and then dismissed the guards he'd hired to protect the vessel. Subsequently the *Rachel* was repeatedly scavenged by beachcombers and eventually burned down to the waterline.[6]

And so there she lies to this day, mute testimony to nature's raw power, periodically covered and then exposed by shifting sands. Each time her elegantly tapered outline is revealed to the bright sun, tourists and residents alike gather to see the schooner's bones. Few of them will ever likely know the real story of the *Rachel*—the old captain's dream, the daughter's homage, the peril of a lee shore, or the sailormen's frantic struggle in the face of an October gale. But of such are human endurance and history's weave. Meanwhile the Gulf, breasted, mapped, loved, and fouled, remains ungovernable as ever, heaving to its own infinitely variable rhythms.

Notes

Prologue

1. Jackson, *Rise and Decline of the Redneck Riviera*, 81–95 (on the 1970s), 90 ("you can holler"), 89 (Stabler).
2. Ibid., 13 (one hundred-fathom curve). A fathom is six feet.
3. On Destin history, see "Brief History of Destin Florida," http://www.destinfl.com /history (accessed November 27, 2016).
4. *Fifty Years of Fishing*, 15–18 (early Destin).
5. I am grateful to my brother, Henry, for helping me recall many details of the trip. "My Recollections," email to author, Henry Sledge, December 16, 2015.
6. Ibid. Today, sea states are generally described in two-foot brackets, so conditions that day would have either been seas five to seven feet or six to eight feet. Nonetheless, Henry and I both distinctly recall that five to eight feet was how they talked about them on board *Calypso II*.
7. McWilliams, ed., *Iberville's Gulf Journals*, 32 ("The mainland").
8. "My Recollections," email to author, Henry Sledge, December 16, 2015.
9. Hearn, *Chita*, 5 ("grand blaze").

Introduction

1. Merington, *Custer Story*, 42 (on Libbie); Custer, *Tenting on the Plains*, 173 ("The rose pink"), 174 ("Our staterooms").
2. Custer, *Tenting*, 174 ("The Gulf," "a sea," "ungovernable"), 175 ("fearful crash," "creaking"), 176 ("the furniture broke"), 178 ("mountains high"), 179 ("champagne," "next time").
3. Kotkin, "Rise of the Third Coast" (energy, "derided"); Darnell, *American Sea*, 439

(ports), 450 (fishing); J. E. Davis, *Gulf*, 4 ("wholly excluded").
4. Paine, *Sea and Civilization*, 10 ("people and their culture").
5. Darnell, *American Sea*, 5 (names), 39 (contour map). See also Gore, *Gulf of Mexico*, endpapers, for an excellent contour map.
6. Darnell, *American Sea*, 27–34; Bird et al., "Tectonic Evolution of the Gulf of Mexico Basin," 3 (formation).
7. J. E. Davis, *Gulf*, 13–15.
8. Gore, *Gulf of Mexico*, 52–53 (size, volume, shore length); J. E. Davis, *Gulf*, 17 (size); International Hydrographic Organization, *Names and Limits*, 16 (boundaries); Weddle, *Spanish Sea*, 10 (81° west as eastern limit); Jenkins, *Along the Edge*, 64 ("The waters").
9. LeVert, *Souvenirs of Travel*, 291–92 ("The trunk"); Winningham, *Traveling*, 58 (Galveston), 122 ("whole palm trees"), 245 ("tall").
10. Holden, "Dry Tortugas," 266 ("cheroots," "flying"); Willoughby, *Across the Everglades*, 110 ("If you get").
11. Romans, *Concise Natural History*, 182 ("But the grand"); Oldmixon, *Transatlantic Wanderings*, 162 ("aromatic"); Houston, *Texas and the Gulf of Mexico*, 126 ("sombre"); Richards, "Rice Lands," 738 ("arboreous").
12. Winningham, *Traveling the Shore*, 27 ("It is difficult").
13. Weddle, *Spanish Sea*, 63 (yucca); Lanz, *Compendio de Historia de Campeche*, 12 (etymology of Yucatán).
14. Morison, *European Discovery*, 299 (logwood); Dampier, *Dampier's Voyages*, 159 ("much like").

15. Cabeza de Vaca, *Relation,* 105 ("abundant"); Romans, *Concise Natural History,* 227 ("intolerable"); Browning, *Lincoln's Trident,* 390 ("millions").

16. *Fort Myers Florida Weekly,* June 29, 2011 ("While the amount").

17. *Northwest Florida Daily News,* April 25, 2015 (monarchs); Earl Callaway, personal interview, October 27, 2016 ("rough as seamen"); "Trans-Gulf Migration" (oil rig workers).

18. Krech, *Spirits of the Air,* 17 ("prodigious," "hideous"); Audubon, *Writings and Drawings,* 450 ("They move"); Dampier, *Collection of Voyages,* 128–29 ("Their colour").

19. Dampier, *Collection of Voyages,* 77; "Alligator," 38 (New Orleans story).

20. Dampier, *Collection of Voyages,* 39–40 ("They were a great company").

21. Gore, *Gulf,* 52 (continental shelf); *Navigation of the Gulf,* 70 ("Much of the shore").

22. Darnell, *American Sea,* 39 (Mississippi); Twichell, "Review of Recent Depositional Processes," 141 (Mississippi Fan); J. E. Davis, *Gulf,* 76 (Mississippi sediment); Levasseur, *Lafayette in America,* 88 ("announced"); Blunt, *American Coast Pilot,* 144 (quotes).

23. McWilliams, ed., *Iberville's Gulf Journals,* 51 ("These rocks"); Levasseur, *Lafayette in America,* 88 ("At break of day," "thousands"); Power, *Impressions of America,* 262 (quotes).

24. S. E. Morse, *System of Geography,* 8 (Tropic of Cancer); Winningham, *Traveling the Shore of the Spanish Sea,* 179 (monument).

25. Darnell, *American Sea,* 80–86 (Loop current); Ulanski, *Gulf Stream,* 13–14 (Murray quote); Mereness, *Travels in the American Colonies,* 390 ("To a person"); Jenkins, *Along the Edge,* 94 (quotes).

26. Darnell, *American Sea,* 277–95 (species); Gore, *Gulf of Mexico,* 139–40 (species).

27. Agassiz, "Dredging Excursion," 507 ("So luminous"); *Sarasota Herald Tribune,* November 1, 2010.

28. Schmidly and Würsig, "Mammals (Vertebrata: Mammalia) of the Gulf of Mexico," 1343–46 (dolphins and manatee); Arbizzani, *Living Aboard,* 36–37 ("As we closed").

29. *New Orleans Times-Picayune,* June 13, 2016 (sea lice); Pugh and Gasca, "Siphonophorae (Cnidaria) of the Gulf of Mexico," 395–96 (Portuguese man-of-war); Buskens, *Well, I've Never Met a Native,* 148 ("scream and cry," "had welts," "stingarees").

30. Sletcher, ed., *New England,* 41. Copley was a Bostonian. Appropriately enough, his famous painting got a cameo in the movie *Jaws.*

31. *Mobile Press Register,* July 19, 2016 (bull sharks); Bishop, *Four Months in a Sneak-Box,* 231–32 ("Upon the end").

32. Brasseaux, "Close encounter," 9–10 ("devil fish"); *Latin Times,* August 8, 2014 (Veracruz mermaid).

33. Darnell, *American Sea,* 61–66 (weather), 65 (rainfall totals); Chatelalin, "Gulf Shores Weather" ("If you don't").

34. P. J. Hamilton, *Colonial Mobile,* 266 ("very considerable," "Nay"); Oldmixon, *Transatlantic Wanderings,* 163 ("fogs," "rust"); McDowell, "Sanitary Notes," 350 ("terrific and depressing"); Ruggles, ed., *On Location,* 73 ("rescue efforts").

35. Girdler, *Antebellum Life at Sea,* 75 ("The lightning"); Higginbotham, *Voyage to Dauphin Island,* 56 ("Lightning struck"); Baher, *Moon Havana,* 43 (the *Invincible*).

36. Darnell, *American Sea,* 66–68 (hurricanes); Bush et al., *Living on the Edge of the Gulf,* 51 (Saffir-Simpson Scale); Emanuel, *Divine Wind,* 83 (Galveston storm); FEMA, *Hurricane Katrina* (storm surges, 1–10 to 1–16); Wilkinson, "Marjory Stoneman Douglas."

37. Barca, *Life in Mexico,* 17 (proverb); Custer, *Tenting,* 115 ("a fury indescribable"); Bartlett, *Personal Narrative,* 530 ("When in the house"), 531 ("At these times"); Blunt, *American Coast Pilot,* 447 (bronze rings); Latrobe, *Rambler in Mexico,* 17 ("Such a wind"); LeVert, *Souvenirs,* 296 ("envel-

oped," "It was really"), 297 ("multitudes").

38. Bremer, *Homes of the New World*, 253 ("The heavens"); Vol. 3 Semmes, *Memoirs*, 539 ("pellucid," "not only her anchor"); Harper, *What We Eat*, 111 (*Sehome*).

Chapter One: Indian Shore

1. Wulf, *Founding Gardeners*, 75 ("Pug Puggy").

2. Hatch, *Osceola*, 30 (meaning of Seminole); Van Doren, *Travels of William Bartram*, 182–83 ("The visage"), 206 ("all dressed"). According to scholars, the word *Seminole* made its first appearance in 1765, less than a decade before Bartram encountered the tribe. The Spanish *cimarrón* was combined with a Muscogee word, *semanoli*, to eventually become *Seminole*. See also Dixon, "Black Seminole Involvement and Leadership during the Second Seminole War, 1835–1842," 36.

3. Hudson, *Southeastern Indians*, 216–17 ("chickees"); Van Doren, *Travels of William Bartram*, 168 ("a pleasant"), 193 (quotes on canoes and trade).

4. Van Doren, *Travels of William Bartram*, 195 ("turbid," "amphibious"), 191 ("finny"), 194 ("over the floods," "cheerful," "my favorite").

5. Bridges, *Alabama*, 4 (first Americans); Milanich, *Florida Indians*, 18–19 (Paleo-Indians); Panamerican, "Underwater Remote Sensing Survey," 3 (earliest people on northern rim); Crooker and Pavlovi, *Cuba*, 30 (first Cubans). Ongoing archaeological discoveries are continually pushing back the dates for the first human arrivals in North and South America. The figures provided here are based on the latest estimates, but these will undoubtedly change soon!

6. Milanich, *Florida Indians*, 20–21 (Archaic Period).

7. Swanton, *Indian Tribes of the Lower Mississippi Valley*, 66–67 (du Pratz quotes); Brown, *Bottle Creek*, 196–97 (canoe building).

8. Hartmann, "Development of Watercraft," 126 ("take their vessel," "all simultaneously"), 135 (travel advantages and statistics by water).

9. Paine, *Sea and Civilization*, 29 (strakes); Milanich, *Florida Indians*, 61 (Calusa canoes).

10. Swanton, *Indian Tribes of the Lower Mississippi Valley*, 67 ("bundles"); Bernal, *Olmec World*, 51 (rafts).

11. Burkholder and Johnson, *Colonial Latin America*, 6–7 (the Maya); *Eyewitness Travel Guide: Mexico*, 278–80 (Chichén Itzá).

12. Lockwood, *Yucatán Peninsula*, 1 ("country with the least"); Burkholder and Johnson, *Colonial Latin America*, 6–7 (agriculture); Landa, *Yucatán*, 96 ("finest salt," "sugar").

13. *Eyewitness Travel Guide: Mexico*, 48–51 (religion), 269 (Quetzalcoatl); Lanz, *Compendio de Historia de Campeche*, 3 (Kukulcán); Peck, *Yucatán*, 112 (motivation for sea voyages); Emanuel, *Divine Wind*, 18 (Hurakan).

14. Burkholder and Johnson, *Colonial Latin America*, 8 (bloodletting), 10 (sacrifice); Cunningham-Smith, "Fish from Afar," 16 (stingray spines), 17 ("in a slanting," "curiously formed").

15. Ford, *Archaeology of Maritime Landscapes*, 11 (Vista Alegre); Shatto, "Maritime Trade," 152 (Isla Cerritos); Weddle, *Spanish Sea*, 174 (Champotón).

16. Ford, *Archaeology of Maritime Landscapes*, 198 (attitudes of coastal families); Shatto, "Maritime Trade," 12, 21 (trade goods); "Ancient Trade Routes for Obsidian," 25 (trade routes).

17. Shatto, "Maritime Trade," 238–40 (Mayan canoes), 14 (Columbus's canoe encounter); Peck, *Yucatán*, 114 (canoe improvements); Paine, *Sea and Civilization*, 27 (no sails); Morison, *Admiral of the Ocean Sea*, 594–96 (Columbus's canoe encounter); Canter and Pentecost, "Rocks, Ropes," 6 (tying canoes); McKillop, "Ancient Maya Canoe Navigation," 98–99 (canoe navigation);

Cerrillo, "Navegacion entre lost Antiguos Mayas" (navigation).

18. Hudson, *Southeastern Indians*, 82, 88 (influences and *pochtecas*); Peck, "Case for Prehistoric Cultural Contact," 9–12 (similarities).

19. Bridges, *Alabama*, 13–14 (Mississippian Period); Hudson, *Southeastern Indians*, 77–82 (Mississippians), 255–57 (torture).

20. Walthall, *Prehistoric Indians of the Southeast*, 189 (utilitarian items and dye).

21. Galloway, *Choctaw Genesis*, 61–63; Brown, "Bottle Creek Site," *Encyclopedia of Alabama*, http://www.encyclopediaofalabama .org/article/h-1160 (accessed February 7, 2017).

22. Galloway, *Choctaw Genesis*, 61–63.

23. Brown, *Bottle Creek*, 124–25, 134–38 (food resources).

24. Clayton, Knight, and Moore, *De Soto Chronicles*, 70 ("no Spaniard"), 333 ("could compete"); Romans, *Concise Natural History*, 42 (quotes on appearance); J. E. Davis, *Gulf*, 35 (Gulf ecology as reason for stature).

25. Hudson, *Southeastern Indians*, 313–16 (trade); Moorehead, *Cahokia Mounds*, 150–51 (shells and objects).

26. *Tampa Bay Times*, October 17, 2017 (Tampa canoe); Brown, *Bottle Creek*, 203 (barnacles); Cabeza de Vaca, *Relation*, 35 (Narváez incident).

27. Hudson, *Southeastern Indians*, 8, 76, 281 (the Calusa); B. Smith, *Memoir of Don d'Escalente Fontaneda*, 11 ("well proportioned," "They go naked"), 12 ("Let the Indians").

28. Fowler, "Calusa Indians," 57 (Calusa numbers); Hudson, *Southeastern Indians*, 76 (Calusa); Cushing, "Exploration of Ancient Key Dwellers' Remains on the Gulf of Florida," 334 ("*débris*"), 335 ("veritable haven"); J. E. Davis, *Gulf*, 37 (canals).

29. Fowler, "Calusa Indians," 59 (religion); J. E. Davis, *Gulf*, 39 (Calusa belief).

Chapter Two: Spanish Sea

1. Weddle, *Spanish Sea*, 13 ("rushing westward"); Morison, *Admiral of the Ocean Sea*, 463–66.

2. Kessell, *Spain in the Southwest*, 4; Rafael, *Contracting Colonialism*, 23 ("perfect instrument"). See also Gibson, *Empire's Crossroads*, 13–16.

3. Vascáno, *Ensayo Biográfico del Célebre Navegante y Consumado Cosmógrafo Juan de la Cosa*, 103 (Cosa); Weddle, *Spanish Sea*, 57 ("adept"), 21 (Ocampo); Morison, *European Discovery of America*, 503 (Ponce de Léon). A healthy cottage industry has flourished for years claiming various foreigners penetrated the Gulf before the Spanish. Candidates include the ancient Jews, Greeks, Carthaginians, and Romans; the medieval Welsh; and Africans. Tantalizing archaeological finds (like a purported Roman shipwreck in Galveston Bay) and obscure documentary references are cited to support such theories, none of which reputable, trained historians or archaeologists find sufficiently credible. Nonetheless, it must be admitted that in theory such voyages were possible, no matter how unlikely. Such a journey would certainly provide a compelling basis for the legend of Quetzalcoatl!

4. Gibson, *Empire's Crossroads*, 42–43; Weddle, *Spanish Sea*, 21 (Ocampo).

5. Thomas, *Rivers of Gold*, 311.

6. Paine, *Sea and Civilization*, 384–85; R. C. Smith, "Ships in the Exploration of *La Florida*," 19 (caravels); Morison, *Admiral of the Ocean Sea*, 115 (dimensions and tonnage); Azcue and Vas Mingo, "Riesgo del transporte marítimo del siglo XVI," 584 (sketch of Spanish ship designs), 587–58 (caravels).

7. Morison, *Admiral of the Ocean Sea*, 187–89 (compass), 186 (quadrant); Paine, *Sea and Civilization*, 380–83 (navigation); Azcue

and Vas Mingo, "Riesgo del transporte marítimo del siglo XVI," 590–91 (navigation).

8. Morison, *Admiral of the Ocean Sea*, 168–77; Haring, *Trade and Navigation between Spain and the Indies*, 273, 278 (diet). Most Spanish sailors made between fifty and sixty ducats annually, compared to a peasant landsman's average of forty-four ducats. Bueno, "Oficiales y Marineros de la Carrera de Indias (Siglo XVI)," 34n7.

9. Azcue and Vas Mingo, "Riesgo del transporte marítimo del siglo XVI," 588–90 (pilots); Paine, *Sea and Civilization*, 381 ("should be"); Morison, *Admiral of the Ocean Sea*, 186–87 ("Why do we").

10. Weddle, *Spanish Sea*, 21 (departure), 22 (careening); Caballos, "En torno a la expedición de Sebastián de Ocampo a la isla de Cuba (1506)," 201–2 (trouble with vessels); Humboldt, *Island of Cuba*, 138 (petroleum springs); Cluster and Hernández, *History of Havana*, 2 ("There are few," Habaguanex), 3 (Indians); MacDonald and Maddicks, *Culture Smart! Cuba*, 18 ("great place"). Caballos uses contemporary Spanish accounting documents to claim that Ocampo sailed in 1506 rather than 1508, and that because of trouble with his caravels did not complete the circumnavigation.

11. Estrada, *Havana*, 32 ("cruel and stupid"), 27–29 (conquest of Cuba); Valdés, *Historia de la Isla de Cuba*, 46–49 (Spanish cruelty and Indian mortality).

12. Shaer, "Ponce De Leon Never Searched for the Fountain of Youth." The legend is given considerable ink in both Morison's *European Discovery of America*, 503–5; and Weddle's more scholarly *Spanish Sea*, 38–39. The reader may be assured that having to discard this venerable tale is a source of considerable regret to the author, a Florida native!

13. Weddle, *Spanish Sea*, 40–41; Morison,

European Discovery, 506–7; J. E. Davis, *Gulf*, 45 (shoreline).

14. Kessell, *Spain in the Southwest*, 12; Miller, *Environmental History of Northeast Florida*, 99; Olcina and Olcina Cantos, *Tratado de Climatología*, 177 (the Gulf Stream).

15. Morison, *European Discovery*, 510 (quotes).

16. Miller, *Environmental History of Northeast Florida*, 93–94 (landing spots, fights); Morison, *European Discovery*, 511 (Dry Tortugas).

17. Burkholder and Johnson, *Colonial Latin America*, 121 ("left more"), 122 (mixing); Winters, *Mulatta Concubine*, 3–6 (skin tones, mulattos); Gibson, *Empire's Crossroads*, 79 (zambos).

18. Weddle, *Spanish Sea*, 56–57 ("very able"); Rosen, *Golden Conquistadores*, 74 ("We sailed"). See also Peck, *Yucatán*, 166–67, wherein that author claims the voyage was meant to be a voyage of discovery from the beginning.

19. Rosen, *Golden Conquistadores*, 74 (quotes).

20. Wood, *Conquistadores*, 17 (Gran Cairo); Rosen, *Golden Conquistadores*, 74 ("forty to," "signs of peace"), 75 ("These Indians").

21. Munson, "Conquistador Clothing"; Hassig, *War and Society*, 73 (Mayan warfare); Rosen, *Golden Conquistadores*, 75 (Díaz quotes); Lanz, *Compendio de Historia de Campeche*, 11 (Mayan equipment). Modern archaeology has yet to confirm sodomy in Mayan sculpture.

22. Landa, *Yucatán before and after the Conquest*, 4–6; Rosen, *Golden Conquistadores*, 76 (quotes).

23. Rosen, *Golden Conquistadores*, 77–78 (quotes). Some sources label the location of the Champotón disaster the "Bahía de la Mala Pelea" (Bay of the Bad Fight). See Lanz, *Compendio de Historia de Campeche*, 19.

24. Rosen, *Golden Conquistadores*, 78–80 (quotes).

25. Pagden, *Hernan Cortes*, 5 ("to trade"); Weddle, *Spanish Sea*, 67 ("as there");

Prescott, *History of the Conquest of Mexico,* 124–25 (expedition); Rosen, *Golden Conquistadores,* 83 ("that was the end"); Wood, *Conquistadores,* 17–18 (Isla de Sacrificios); Lanza, *Compendio de Historia de Campeche,* 20–25 (Grijalva voyage).

26. Prescott, *History of the Conquest of Mexico,* 142–43 (physical description); Reed, *Ancient Past of Mexico,* 133 (departure); Rangel, *Historia de México I,* 134 (founding Veracruz); Simpson, *Cortés,* 22 ("we shall take" speech); Lockhart, *Memoirs of the Conquistador Bernal Díaz,* 111–12 ("We first of all"); Chang-Rodríguez, *Latinoamérica,* 47–49 (good basic Spanish overview of Cortés).

27. Rosen, *Golden Conquistadores,* 101 ("decided"). Charles ascended to the Spanish throne in 1516. In popular legend, Cortés is said to have burned his ships, and there are numerous historic paintings depicting the dramatic scene.

28. Paine, *Sea and Civilization,* 432 (galleons); Azcue and Vas Mingo, "Riesgo del transporte marítimo del siglo XVI," 584 (sketch of Spanish ships); Lugo-Fernández et al., "Analysis of the Gulf of Mexico's Veracruz-Havana Route of La Flota de Nueva España," 13–14.

29. Paine, *Sea and Civilization,* 407–9 (Casa and fleets), 407 ("only to such"); Acosta Rodríguez, González Rodríguez, and Vila Vilar, *Casa de Contratación y La Navegación entre España y Las Indias,* 617–18 (*padrón real*); Haring, *Trade and Navigation,* 201–208 (fleets); Hannay, "Galleon," 669 (cargoes); Cluster and Hernández, *History of Havana,* 5 (Havana, import value), 12 (sex slang).

30. Cluster and Hernández, *History of Havana,* 6 (raids on Havana); Weddle, *Spanish Sea,* 288 ("making it understood"), 297 (Hawkins); Plasencia, *Península de Yucatán en el Archivo General de la Nación,* 136 (1561 attack on Campeche); Payne, *Voyages of Hawkins, Frobisher and Drake,* 73 ("take

our succor"); Haring, *Trade and Navigation,* 204n1 (San Juan de Ulúa).

31. Payne, *Voyages of Hawkins, Frobisher and Drake,* 73 ("dismayed"), 74 ("13 great ships"), 76 ("shifting," "passing to and fro"), 77 ("all sides"), 78 ("forsook"), 79 ("desired"); Weddle, *Spanish Sea,* 297–301; Quijano, *Historia de las Fortificaciones en Nueva España,* 9–12 (San Juan de Ulúa and Hawkins).

32. Reséndez, *Land So Strange,* 5–6 (on the lack of attention to the Cabeza de Vaca story in the United States); Fontana, *Entrada,* 17 ("indoctrination"); Weddle, *Spanish Sea,* 99–102 (voyage); Galloway, *Choctaw Genesis,* 81 (map).

33. Weddle, *Spanish Sea,* 133 ("We have come"), 142 (Garay's death suspicious).

34. Reséndez, *Land So Strange,* 48 (Cabeza de Vaca description); Varnum, *Álvar Núñez Cabeza de Vaca,* 64; R. A. Davis, "Beaches, Barrier Islands, and Inlets of the Florida Gulf Coast," 89–90 (nature of coast).

35. Cabeza de Vaca, *Relation,* 29 ("in all that time"), 30 ("to go," "water half way"), 48 (foragers ambushed); J. E. Davis, *Gulf,* 55–56 (marine abundance).

36. Cabeza de Vaca, *Relation,* 36 (the country), 39 ("like giants"); Weddle, *Spanish Sea,* 190–91. The fleet waited for the land force in all the wrong places for a year before returning to New Spain. The women told Narváez they would not wait for doomed husbands, and would remarry as soon as they were able. One presumes they did!

37. Cabeza de Vaca, *Relation,* 46 ("This appeared"), 47 ("nails, saws").

38. Chipman and Joseph, *Spanish Texas,* 29–30; Cabeza de Vaca, *Relation,* 60 ("By no effort"), 62 ("each should"). The black man and the Greek lived with the Indians many years, as Hernando de Soto learned during his 1540 *entrada.*

39. Reséndez, *Land So Strange,* 143–44 (slavery); Varnum, *Álvar Núñez Cabeza de Vaca,* 102 (Cabeza as healer).

Chapter Three: Colonial Crossroads

1. Paine, *Sea and Civilization*, 32–33.

2. Weddle, *Wreck of the* Belle, 25–27 (La Salle's character), 26 (portrait as a young man); Weddle, *French Thorn*, 49 (portrait in middle age), 23 ("No one tells").

3. Schneider, *Old Man River*, 93 (Marquette and Joliet); Weddle, *Wreck of the* Belle, 46–47 ("Our heart"), 66 (strategy).

4. Chipman and Joseph, *Spanish Texas*, 70 (Mississippi River confusion); Brower, *Mississippi River and Its Source*, 84n1 ("all the maps").

5. Weddle, *Wreck of the* Belle, 69; Strand, *Inventing Niagara*, 21 ("the iron hand").

6. De Vorsey, "Impact of the La Salle Expedition of 1682 on European Cartography," 69–70 (the mouth); Cox, *Journeys of Rene Robert Cavelier Sieur de La Salle*, 145 ("The water is brackish"); Tonti, *Relation*, 89 ("fine").

7. Claiborne, *Mississippi, as a Province, Territory, and State*, 14 (ceremony); Henschel, *Te Deum Laudamaus*, 2–3 ("We Praise"); Cox, *Journeys of Rene Robert Cavelier Sieur de La Salle*, 145 ("took possession"); Parkman, *Discovery of the Great West*, 283 ("a stupendous," "frozen"). The ceremony probably took place near modern Venice, Louisiana.

8. Weddle, *French Thorn*, 15 (departure); Weddle, *Wreck of the* Belle, 10–11, 17 (cargo); Bruseth et al., Belle, 27–28 (bills of lading).

9. Weddle, *Wreck of the* Belle, 142 (dangers); Weddle, *French Thorn*, 18 ("very dangerous," "a flat country").

10. Weddle, *Wreck of the* Belle, 146; Weddle, *French Thorn*, 20 ("We had among us").

11. Joutel, *Joutel's Journal*, 68 ("All that could"), 80 ("that the vessels"), 82 ("heard a cannon"), 84 ("carried out").

12. Weddle, *French Thorn*, 25–29.

13. Bruseth and Turner, *From a Watery Grave*, 3 (wreck of the *Belle*); Joutel, *Joutel's Journal*, 134 ("he dropp'd"). The *Belle's* wreck was discovered during the 1990s and thoroughly excavated, revealing much about La Salle's enterprise.

14. Kessel, *Spain in the Southwest*, 137 ("His majesty's"); Weddle, *French Thorn*, 52–53 (*piraguas*), 58–64 (circumnavigation).

15. Weddle, *French Thorn*, 110 (Spanish and French in Gulf); Giraud, *History of French Louisiana*, 1:22 (Huguenots); Weber, *Spanish Frontier*, 115–16 (Treaty of Ryswick).

16. "LeMoyne Brothers," *Encyclopedia of Alabama*, http://www.encyclopediaofalabama.org/article/h-1102 (accessed May 29, 2017); Konstam and Kean, *Pirates*, 118 ("a great"); Weddle, *French Thorn*, 129 (Lorencillo); Plasencia, *Península de Yucatán en el Archivo General de la Nación*, 138–39 (Lorencillo's reputation).

17. Weddle, *French Thorn*, 129 ("M. de Graff").

18. McWilliams, *Iberville's Gulf Journals*, 29 ("sand dunes"), 33–34 (Pensacola Bay).

19. McWilliams, *Fleur de Lys and Calumet*, 10–11 ("When we"); McWilliams, *Iberville's Gulf Journals*, 52 ("It is a jolly").

20. Giraud, *History of French Louisiana*, 1:80 (English Turn Incident); McWilliams, *Iberville's Gulf Journals*, 107 ("if he did not").

21. P. J. Hamilton, *Colonial Mobile*, 51 (Mobile founded), 85 (moved downstream), 100 (New Orleans founded); Higginbotham, *Old Mobile*, 133–34 (*Pélican* girls); McWilliams, *Fleur de Lys and Calumet*, 97 ("quite well behaved"); Gayarré, *History of Louisiana*, 190 (casket and correction girls); Marley, *Wars of the Americas*, 242 (Quadruple Alliance).

22. Greenwald, *Company Man*, 78 ("First you see," "The company headquarters"), 79 ("built of wood," "made with shells"), 80 ("never produces"), 83 ("used to bring," "eighteen-oar").

23. Paine, *Sea and Civilization*, 459 (canoes and bateaux); Surrey, *Commerce of Louisiana*, 58 (pirogues), 59 (bateaux); McWilliams, *Iberville's Gulf Journals*, 162 (Iberville).

24. Kein, *Creole*, 15 (Creoles); Sledge, *Pillared City*, 62–63 (Creole cottages); Gould, *From Fort to Port*, 7–9 (porches); Sledge, *Mobile River*, 41 (Bienville's balcony); Nobles, "Gumbo," 98–102. I hope readers will forgive this brief and overly simplified survey of Creoles and Creole culture, subject of countless books and papers!

25. Hurley, *Surf, Sand, and Post Card Sunsets*, 206 (grillers); DuVal, *Independence Lost*, 68 (Aubry). Ditto the Cajuns!

26. Tallant, *Mardi Gras*, 96; Greenwald, *Company Man*, 135 ("in red clothing," "shepardess"), 136 ("plumped," "extinguish").

27. Gibson, *Empire's Crossroads*, 133–34 (Seven Years' War).

28. Gage, *Nueve Relacion que Contiene Los Viages de Tomas Gage*, 297–98 (tasajo); Cluster and Hernández, *History of Havana*, 22–23 (siege); Lee, *Dictionary of National Biography*, 11:43 ("one of those").

29. Cluster and Hernández, *History of Havana*, 23–25 (siege), 25 ("a very grand"); Pezuela, *Diccionario Georgrafico, Estadistico, Historico, de la Isla de Cuba*, 51 ("bombas," casualties of enslaved people); Whipple, *Seafarers*, 42–43 (British gun crews).

30. Cluster and Hernández, *History of Havana*, 32 ("gave").

31. Gibson, *Empire's Crossroads*, 135 (reshuffling); P. J. Hamilton, *Colonial Mobile*, 216 (Bienville), 217 (Highlanders); Thomason, *Mobile*, 43 ("a little hamlet"); Lafuente, *Historia General de España*, 128–35 (good Spanish account of the Havana siege and subsequent territorial transfers around the basin).

32. Knight and Liss, *Atlantic Port Cities*, 23 (spending); Lapuerta, *La Belle Creole*, 13 (shipyard); Monzote, *From Rainforest to Canefield*, 60 (quantity ships, *Santíssima Trinidad*); "Spanish Ship *Santísima Trinidad*." The *Santísima Trinidad* saw much service during the Napoleonic Wars and was badly damaged at the Battle of Trafalgar in 1805. British attempts to salvage the vessel failed, and she sank.

33. Fraiser, *French Quarter*, 23–24 (rebellion).

34. Chandler, "O'Reilly's Voyage," 203 ("Night"), 204 ("found"), 205 ("waves and lightening"), 206 ("the measures").

35. Weddle, *Changing Tides*, 17 (storm); Fraiser, *French Quarter*, 24 ("Bloody O'Reilly"); Chandler, "Notes and Documents," 324 ("allowed persons"). The site where the men were shot was later named Frenchmen Street in their memory.

36. Ware and Rea, *George Gauld*, 1–3 (background), 15 (tools).

37. Ibid., 37 ("a treasure"). Roughly concurrent with Gauld's work were several other surveys of the colony, most notably by Thomas Hutchins and Bernard Romans, whose work led to books. These men borrowed heavily, and in Hutchins's case, blatantly plagiarized Gauld for their navigational sections. See J. E. Davis, *Gulf*, 84–86; Ware and Rea, *George Gauld*, 198–201.

38. Fabel, "Reflection on Mobile's Loyalism in the American Revolution," 38 ("a scene"); Fabel, *Bombast and Broadsides*, 48 (economy); Simons, "Pensacola Fortifications," 45–50.

39. Lanning, *American Revolution*, 143–44 (Gálvez); P. J. Hamilton, *Colonial Mobile*, 312–15 (Mobile).

40. Ferreiro, *Brothers at Arms*, 143–45; Neely, *Great Hurricane of 1780*, 111 ("Have we so").

41. "Siege of Pensacola," 166 ("The enemy"), 168 ("fired several"), 169 ("*feu*"), 171 ("was thrown"); Dawson, *Louisiana Governors*, 59 ("Yo Solo").

Chapter Four: Pirates' Haunt

1. W. C. Davis, *Pirates Laffite*, 95 (*La Dorada*); Faye, "Types of Privateer Vessels," 120 (hermaphrodite brig).

2. W. C. Davis, *Pirates Laffite*, 60, 95–96; Head, *Privateers of the Americas*, 47, 165–66n32. Head posits that Janny was an

English corruption of the Italian Gianni, and says that his nickname was Barbienfume, or Redbeard, a suitable pirate moniker if ever there was one. However, in the labyrinthine fun house world of Laffite studies, where so much is foggy confusion, Davis asserts that Janny and Barbienfume were in fact separate people.

3. Saul, *Illustrated Encyclopedia of Warfare,* 153.

4. Clark and Guice, *Old Southwest,* 162 (San Lorenzo); Sledge, *Mobile River,* 65–68 (Ellicott); Tarver, *Spanish Empire,* 53 (San Ildefronso); S. E. Morse, *American Universal Geography,* 604 (*flota*'s final voyage); Schneider, *Old Man River,* 187 ("There is on the globe"), 189 ("I renounce").

5. Obadele-Starkes, *Freebooters and Smugglers,* 5 (ban); Head, *Privateers of the Americas,* 15–17 (Cartagena).

6. The finest biography to date is William C. Davis's *Pirates Laffite* (2005), an incredible feat of scholarship. Despite his work some writers continue to repeat the tired old legends, none of which is more enduring than that the Laffites owned a Crescent City blacksmith shop. The existence of Laffite's Blacksmith Shop Bar at 941 Bourbon Street cements the notion in the popular imagination. Though the charming building is certainly old enough to have been associated with the brothers, dating to the eighteenth century, they never owned it. See W. C. Davis, *Pirates Laffite,* 572.

7. W. C. Davis, *Pirates Laffite,* 2–7 (background); Groom, *Patriotic Fire,* 92–93 (New Orleans, Claiborne); Rowland, *Official Letter Books of W. C. C. Claiborne,* 361 ("refuse").

8. Saxon, *Lafitte the Pirate,* 9 ("He is a man"), 11 ("He is tall," "in company"); Winters, *Mulatta Concubine,* 61–62 (quadroon balls); Ward, *Voodoo Queen,* 36–37 (*plaçage*). The name "Laffite" has been spelled different ways by contemporaries and later writers,

as demonstrated by Saxon and Davis in their book titles. Winston Groom has a bit of fun with the multiple spellings, enumerating at least six variants. Groom, *Patriotic Fire,* 272–73. But Pierre and Jean always signed their name "Laffite," and like Davis I follow their lead. See W. C. Davis, *Pirates Laffite,* 1–2.

9. Saxon, *Lafitte the Pirate,* 37 (Barataria meaning); W. C. Davis, *Pirates Laffite,* 51 (brothers' division of labor), 124 (Temple), 17–18 (Bayou Lafourche), 102 (variety of goods); Head, *Privateers of the Americas,* 48 ("incredible," "Day by day").

10. W. C. Davis, *Pirates Laffite,* 196–97 (Barataria); Faye, "Types of Privateer Vessels," 123 (smuggler barges).

11. Fraiser, *French Quarter,* 94–95 ("Cut Nose"); "Life of Jean Lafitte," 436 ("The return"). Dominique Youx is often mentioned as Jean's brother, but they were not blood kin.

12. Vogel, "Jean Laffite, the Baratarians, and the Historical Geography of Piracy in the Gulf of Mexico," 66 ("The smuggling"); Saxon, *Lafitte the Pirate,* 101–3 (rewards); W. C. Davis, *Pirates Laffite,* 82 ("The whole").

13. Stoltz, *Gulf Theater,* 9.

14. W. C. Davis, *Pirates Laffite,* 160 ("for having"); Pickett, *History of Alabama,* 516 (Mobile seized), 592–94 (Creeks crushed); Stoltz, *Gulf Theater,* 13 (Napoleon); Millett, *Maroons of Prospect Bluff,* 48 (British enter Pensacola), 53–57 (fort).

15. Latour, *Historical Memoir of the War in West Florida and Louisiana in 1814–1815,* 19 (thirty thousand dollars offer), xi ("I would be"). Davis doubts the thirty thousand dollars figure, considering it unrealistically high for the resources at Lockyer's command. W. C. Davis, *Pirates Laffite,* 553n66.

16. W. C. Davis, *Pirates Laffite,* 172–74.

17. Latour, *Historical Memoir,* xiv ("This point"); Groom, *Patriotic Fire,* 88 ("hellish

banditti"); W. C. Davis, *Pirates Laffite*, 184 ("I begin").

18. W. C. Davis, *Pirates Laffite*, 186; Groom, *Patriotic Fire*, 110 ("Jeffs").

19. Saxon, *Lafitte the Pirate*, 156 ("all colors"), 157 ("Pardon," "I perceived," "I sent," "forty houses," "I have captured"); W. C. Davis, *Pirates Laffite*, 192 (spoils).

20. Stoltz, *Gulf Theater*, 14–19.

21. Buchanan, *Jackson's Way*, 305 ("I have it"), 313 ("It is impossible"), 314 ("bounded").

22. Groom, *Patriotic Fire*, 103 (American forces); Buchanan, *Jackson's Way*, 323 (Laffite and Jackson).

23. Latour, *Historical Memoir*, 255–56 ("beauty and booty").

24. Buchanan, *Jackson's Way*, 326; Groom, *Patriotic Fire*, 112 ("as if").

25. Cooke, *Narrative of Events*, 180 ("The Americans"), 180–81 ("The clouds"); Buchanan, *Jackson's Way*, 327 ("the action"); *London Gazette*, March 9, 1815 ("brilliant affair").

26. Brown, *Amphibious Campaign*, 136 (map of the battlefield); Keyes, "Eyewitness Pension Record Testimonies Place Jean Laffite at Battle of New Orleans"; Cooke, *Narrative of Events*, 234 ("seemed"); *London Gazette*, March 9, 1815 ("prudent," "recommended"); Buchanan, *Jackson's Way*, 342 (Treaty of Ghent).

27. Saxon, *Lafitte the Pirate*, 195 ("abandoned"), 218 ("Lafitte himself"); W. C. Davis, *Pirates Laffite*, 353 ("Madamoiselle").

28. Girard, *Adventures of a French Captain*, 86 ("unremitting efforts").

29. Buchanan, *Jackson's Way*, 368 (treaty). The Jean Laffite journal has occasioned much scholarly and popular debate. Davis believes it a forgery, whereas Groom is open to its legitimacy. See W. C. Davis, "Journal of Jean Laffite," 2–16; Groom, *Patriotic Fire*, 276–77. Davis's article is fascinating and was to have been the last chapter of his Laffite book, but the publishers cut it.

30. *New York Times*, July 14, 1860 (Gibbs, quotes by).

31. A. Smith, *Atrocities of the Pirates*, 10 ("of a most," "by repeated"); Mayer, *Captain Canot*, 51 ("I know not").

32. *Niles Weekly Register*, October 20, 1821. According to Saxon (*Lafitte the Pirate*, 260) some New Orleanians believed that the author of the arrogant note was none other than Jean Laffite himself. "But there was no proof of it," concluded Saxon. Whoever "Richard Coeur de Leon" was, he certainly had flair.

33. Konstam, *World Atlas of Pirates*, 397 (Squadron); McCarthy, *Twenty Florida Pirates*, 69 (Mosquito Fleet, "The importance").

34. Ostram, *United States Revenue and Coast Guard Cutters in Naval Warfare, 1790–1918*, 81–82 (Revenue Cutter Service).

35. Spears, *David G. Farragut*, 122 ("For myself"); Beehler, "United States Navy and West India Piracy," 8 (Gregory quotes); *American State Papers, Naval Affairs*, 1:1110 (Cassin's quotes).

36. *List of Reports to Be Made to the House of Representatives*, 190 ("It will, I hope").

37. J. E. Davis, *Gulf*, 324–25. Davis is clear-eyed about the Gaspar legend, which Tampa civic promoters and residents have enjoyed embellishing down the decades. Not a bit of it true, but undeniably fun.

38. Cox, *Key West Companion*, 41 (wrecking industry); Viele, *Florida Keys*, 3:73 ("conchs," "noted generally"), 3:72 ("waifs"), 3:33 ("If this place"); Audubon, *Audubon and His Journals*, 345 (quotes).

39. Sprague, *Origin, Progress, and Conclusion of the Florida War*, 90 ("Just as the day"), 91 ("a little man," "God-damn!"); Mahon, *History of the Second Seminole War*, 323 (canoe scandal). As a small boy I visited a Seminole settlement near Miami in 1961. I still vividly recall the chickees, or raised platforms of the same kind that Bartram saw, and distinctive, beautiful shirts. My parents bought me a carved toy canoe as a souvenir. How I wish I still had that treasure!

40. Sparks, *Memories of Fifty Years,* 364 ("new El Dorado").

Chapter Five: King Cotton's Pond

1. *New Orleans Bee,* March 2, 1835 (arrival); Power, *Impressions,* 252 ("noble," "hugely").
2. Albion, *Square-Riggers on Schedule,* 292 (*Shakespeare* dimensions), 58 (flat-floor design), 91 ("They are," "same sharpness," "faster sailers"); Roland et al., *Way of the Ship,* 153 ("pathfinder"); Bluff, "Supplement to the Lucky Bag No. IV," 170 ("The buoyancy"). Harry Bluff was Matthew Fontaine Maury's nom de plume. Any kind of vessel could be a packet, including brigs, schooners, and steamers. But in practice most of them serving the Gulf ports during the early nineteenth century were big ships or barks with the largest cargo capacity.
3. Power, *Impressions,* 256 ("clear, fresh"), 257–58 ("past the fine"), 261 ("The water"); Albion, *Square Riggers on Schedule,* 309 (*Shakespeare*'s cargo).
4. Power, *Impressions,* 263 ("away we went"), 264 ("Never go"), 265 ("a little"), 266 ("launched"), 268 ("and was delighted"), 271 ("with just").
5. Cartwright, *Galveston,* 58–59 (Americans in Mexico).
6. Hunter, *Steamboats on the Western Rivers,* 84 ("run on dew"); DeBow, "New Orleans," 55 (goods); Rothman, *Flush Times and Fever Dreams,* 3–4 (cotton exports); Amos, *Cotton City,* 21 (Mobile number).
7. Latrobe, *Rambler in North America,* 331 ("upwards"), 332 ("Highest," "in a sunny morning," "amidst"), 333 ("piles").
8. Phillips, *Plantation and Frontier Documents,* 286 ("Look which way"). For a thorough treatment of Mobile's cotton business, see Sledge, *Mobile River,* 90–96, and New South Associates, *From Alluvium to Commerce,* 118–19.
9. Sloan, "Roots of a Maritime Fortune," 105–107 (the New Yorkers); Phalen, *Consequences of Cotton in Antebellum America,* 41–42 (Triangle); DeBow, "Direct Foreign Trade of the South," 132 ("Whatever"); *Longworth's American Almanac,* 60 ("Mexican," "Sail"); *New York as It Is,* 175 ("handsome," "without").
10. Albion, *Square-Riggers on Schedule,* 92 (live oaks); Crothers, *American-Built Packets,* 37 (wood weight); Tucker, *Encyclopedia of the War of 1812,* 419 (Gulf Breeze reservation).
11. Oldmixon, *Transatlantic Wanderings,* 169 ("no flaws"); Albion, *Square-Riggers on Schedule,* 93–95 (construction), 96 ("The Queen"); Coggins, *Ships and Seamen of the American Revolution,* 43–48 (shipbuilding).
12. Power, *Impressions,* 266 ("Our captain"); Clark, *Clipper Ship Era,* 44 ("moral courage," "remarkable type"); Spears, *Captain Nathaniel Brown Palmer,* 152 ("Captain Nat"); Laing, *Seafaring America,* 263 ("a rough").
13. Low, *Some Reflections by Captain Charles P. Low,* 34 ("hoosiers," "the hardest," "all sing"); Spears, *Captain Nathaniel Brown Palmer,* 149–50 ("a husky," "because it"); Laing, *Seafaring America,* 218 ("'belaying pin'"); "Packetarians," 725 ("the speed," "the fast man," "wild'"); Morris, *Wanderings of a Vagabond,* 461 ("dance houses," "drove decency," "blood and violence").
14. Bolster, *Black Jacks,* 237 (percentages), 199 ("When I was a young man," "the existence"), 204 ("They do treat"); Mansfield, "Onerous and Unnecessary Burden," 15 (Mobile Harbor Act); Ormond, Bagby, and Goldthwaite, *Code of Alabama,* 243 ("the condition," "between the").
15. Houston, *Texas and the Gulf of Mexico,* 129 ("the fog"); "Disasters at Sea," 164 ("by a strong," "on a ridge"); *Report of the Officers Constituting the Light House Board,* 28 ("From 1832," "The navigation," "of the greatest," "should be," "can be seen," "whole coast"), 141 ("The light,"), 142 ("This is believed," "without commensurate," "These lights").

16. Jennings, *Hints on Sea Risks,* 20 ("She was," "One hundred"); "Hurricanes in 1837," 106 (beam ends).

17. Girdler, *Antebellum Life at Sea,* 157 ("All saw"). Today the wreck site is designated the "Dixey Bar" and is a favorite fishing spot.

18. Knight, *Letters from the South and West,* 140 ("undergoing"), 145 ("bounding"); Oldmixon, *Transatlantic Wanderings,* 168 ("Ours is"); Latrobe, *Rambler in Mexico,* 225 ("fine, new"). Knight's book was originally published under the pseudonym Arthur Singleton, and it is cited both ways in the literature. I have chosen to cite it in the notes and bibliography under the author's actual name, Henry Knight.

19. Knight, *Letters from the South and West,* 139 ("a Spaniard," "a yellow"); Barca, *Life in Mexico,* 2 (all her quotes); Dana, *To Cuba and Back,* 10.

20. Bray, *Sea Trip,* 37 ("Upon arrival," "of all races," "vegetables"); Olmstead, *Cotton Kingdom,* 291 ("narrow, dirty"); Oldmixon, *Transatlantic Wanderings,* 142 ("the want," "hundreds"), 153 ("Here . . . every corner").

21. Houston, *Texas and the Gulf of Mexico,* 256 ("built of wood," "were those"); Cartwright, *Galveston,* 77–78 (the town); DeBow, "American Cities," 349 (*DeBow's* quotes).

22. "Scenes in the Suburbs of Matamoros," 275 ("after you get," "not unlike"), 276 ("both male," "the stock").

23. Latrobe, *Rambler in Mexico,* 29 ("market boats," "the Etruscan-shaped," "swarming"), 23 ("built in regular"), 24 ("most mongrel"), 26 ("extremely picturesque," "diversity").

24. Wasserman, *Everyday Life and Politics in Nineteenth Century Mexico,* 141 (Veracruz population figure for 1856); Latrobe, *Rambler in Mexico,* 221 ("utterly sterile," "unclean birds," "Regularly"); Wilson, *Mexico and Its Religion,* 16 ("instead," "meats," "bonnetless," "dirty cotton"), 18 ("lighthouse").

25. R. Hamilton, *Fly-Fishing the Yucatán,* 9 ("black hole"); Stephens, *Incidents of Travel in Yucatan,* 345 ("a low, swampy"), 346 ("a long straggling"), 347 ("completely domesticated," "on the very edge"), 350 ("a little Meztizo"), 351 ("paid no rent"), 353 ("It was thirty-five," "captain," "a fisherman"), 355 ("A fisherman was swinging," "rather too near").

26. Dana, *To Cuba and Back,* 30 ("What a world"); Cluster and Hernández, *History of Havana,* 39 ("Here comes the city"), 49 ("These *negras*"); Bremer, *Homes of the New World,* 3:220 ("with great," "with flowers").

27. Gurney, *Winter in the West Indies,* 207 ("They are fitted"); Humboldt, *Island of Cuba,* 221 (numbers); Bremer, *Homes of the New World,* 2:309 ("They are regarded"), 311 ("so depressed"); Kurlansky, *Havana: A Subtropical Delirium,* 49–50 (revolts).

28. Guterl, *American Mediterranean,* 31 ("confused"), 20 (Southerners in Havana); Russell, *My Diary North and South,* 190 ("kinder, sorter"); J. E. Davis, *Gulf,* 101 ("indispensable"), 105 ("a common basin"); Richter, *Historical Dictionary of the Old South,* 158 ("Golden Circle"); Jordan, *Tumult and Silence at Second Creek,* 67 ("simply a Southern lake").

Chapter Six: Violent Sea

1. Flank, "Pastry War"; Bancroft, *Works of Hubert Howe Bancroft,* 13:186–87.

2. Bancroft, *Works,* 188 ("certain offending," "*un verdadero*"), 193 (fleet); "Miscellany," 109 (steamships).

3. Bancroft, *Works,* 192.

4. Farragut, *Life of David Glasgow Farragut,* 133 ("*rara avis*"), 135 ("no spring"), 127 ("war or peace"), 134 ("Everything," "The day"), 128 ("at precisely"); Sondhaus, *Navies in Modern World History,* 70–71 (importance of the steamships).

5. Sondhaus, *Navies in Modern World History,* 134 ("tearing out"), 130 ("were seen"), 129 ("the folly").

6. Bancroft, *Works*, 196–97.

7. Clayton and Conniff, *History of Modern Latin America*, 97 (Santa Anna); Farragut, *Life*, 131 (quotes).

8. Farragut, *Life*, 131 ("They blew," "shirt and trousers").

9. Robenalt, *Historic Tales from the Republic of Texas*, 122; McIllvain, *Texas Tales*, 67.

10. *Niles National Register*, June 10, 1843 ("If I have swerved"); Robenalt, *Historic Tales*, 125 ("apple pie," "bully"); McIllvain, *Texas Tales*, 67.

11. *Yucatán Times*, May 5, 2015; *Niles National Register*, June 10, 1843 ("great humbug").

12. "Journal of Alfred Walke" (various flags); Obadele-Starks, *Freebooters and Smugglers*, 88–90 (diplomatic situation).

13. "Journal of Alfred Walke."

14. *Yucatán Times*, May 5, 2015; "Journal of Alfred Walke" ("gave three hearty," "our broadsides," "completely riddled"); *Niles National Register*, June 10, 1843 ("blown to atoms"); Meed, *Fighting Texas Navy*, 214 ("We knocked").

15. *Yucatán Times*, May 5, 2015; Robenalt, *Historic Tales*, 124 ("humbug"); *Niles National Register*, June 3, 1842 ("insanity," "cannot be").

16. Hietala, *Manifest Design*, 255 ("manifest destiny"); Nevin, *Mexican War*, 22 (offer to buy).

17. Nevin, *Mexican War*, 22–23 ("Old Rough and Ready"), 77 (Monterey captured). Ann Chase was the heroine of Tampico. She was a British national married to the U.S. consul there. When he was forced to leave, she remained, protected by her British citizenship. She learned everything she could about the local garrison and its defenses, and then convinced Mexican authorities that an army of twenty-five thousand Americans was approaching. Santa Anna immediately evacuated his troops. When American ships appeared in the harbor, Chase climbed to her rooftop waving the Stars and Stripes. The town fell blood-lessly, and Chase was hailed by the American press. See Nevin, *Mexican War*, 132.

18. Clark and Moseley, "D-Day, Veracruz, 1847," 105–7.

19. Ibid., 107–8 (forces marshaled); Sondhaus, *Naval Warfare, 1815–1914*, 44 (ships); Ohls, "Roots of Tradition," 278 (surfboats); Temple, "Memoir of the Landing of United States Troops at Vera Cruz in 1847," 494 ("The boats").

20. "Capture of Vera Cruz," 1 ("About noon").

21. Ibid., 359 ("It was a grand," "On, on"); Nevin, *Mexican War*, 139 ("The entire division"); Temple, "Memoir of the Landing of United States Troops at Vera Cruz in 1847," 502 ("In addition"), 504 ("gratitude").

22. Nevin, *Mexican War*, 139–41 (siege); "Capture of Vera Cruz," 3 ("Bomb-shells"); *Niles Weekly Register*, April 17, 1847 ("The flag").

23. Nevin, *Mexican War*, 152–61 (Villahermosa expedition), 220 (fall of Mexico City), 222 (Treaty).

24. Gibson, *Empire's Crossroads*, 203 (López); Guterl, *American Mediterranean*, 27 (Southern filibusters); Doubleday, *Reminiscences of the 'Filibuster' War in Nicaragua*, iii ("popular liberty"), 201 ("mostly of the class," "Of course"), 202 ("and whenever").

25. Cova, "Taylor Administration," 297–302; Caldwell, *López Expeditions*, 48–49.

26. Cova, "Taylor Administration," 302. My wife and I toured Round Island during the fall of 2016, courtesy of friends David and Simona Newell. It is an easy boat ride from Pascagoula River Park. The island is uninhabited but frequently visited by every imaginable variety of small craft from kayaks to jet skis, bass boats, sailboats, and motorboats. The water is mostly shoal along its south side, but deeper on the north side, where we landed. The original lighthouse was replaced in 1859 by another, which stood until Hurricane Georges in 1998. A partial reconstruction on site was damaged by Hurricane Katrina in 2005,

after which the lighthouse was fully re-constructed alongside Highway 90 in Pascagoula, where it may be visited free of charge.

27. United States Senate, Executive Document 57, *Message of the President*, 4 ("I suppose"), 4–5 ("unholy and illegal"); Cova, "Taylor Administration," 303–4.

28. Cova, "Taylor Administration," 310 ("You are").

29. Caldwell, *López Expeditions*, 55 (island conditions); United States Senate, Executive Document 57, *Message of the President*, 15 ("ignorant dupes"); Cova, "Taylor Administration," 323 ("a clear," "transcends"), 324 ("an outrage"), 326 ("Our coast").

30. Antón and Hernández, *Cubans in America*, 39–43.

31. Cartwright, *Galveston*, 87–88 (Walker and Galveston); Scroggs, *Filibusters and Financiers*, 345 (Walker), 373–75 (*Susan* episode), 374 ("revolvers"), 390–91 (execution).

32. Tucker, *Civil War Naval Encyclopedia*, 487 (resignation percentage); Paine, *Sea and Civilization*, 550 (Union navy); Browning, *Lincoln's Trident*, 58 (squadrons).

33. Cartwright, *Galveston*, 106–108 (Galveston's recapture); Fox, *Wolf of the Deep*, 84–85 (*Alabama* in Gulf).

34. Semmes, *Memoirs of Service Afloat*, 542 ("What was best"); Wright, *Language of the Civil War*, 210 ("Old Beeswax"); Fox, *Wolf of the Deep*, 62 ("First luff"). *Luff* is a naval term that refers to the forward edge of a fore and aft sail. To "luff" a vessel is to guide her just close enough to windward so that the sails begin to flap, usually preparatory to tacking. Browning, *Lincoln's Trident*, 260 (armament); Francaviglia, *From Sail to Steam*, 204 ("a very perfect").

35. Semmes, *Memoirs*, 542 ("The *Alabama*"); *New York Times*, January 11, 2013 (*Hatteras*); U.S. War Department, *War of the Rebellion*, ser. 1, 2:18 (hereinafter cited as *ORN*; all references are to series 1 unless otherwise noted) ("Knowing," "board her").

36. Semmes, *Memoirs*, 543 ("The enemy," "Kell now"), 544 ("My men"); Browning, *Lincoln's Trident*, 261 ("Twas a grand"); *ORN*, 2:19 ("a hopeless"); *New York Times*, January 11, 2013 ("sick of"); Fox, *Wolf of the Deep*, 87 ("disgraceful," significance of sinking).

37. Cluster and Hernández, *History of Havana*, 100–102.

38. Sigsbee, "Personal Narrative of the 'Maine,' First Paper," 81 ("a picture"), 77 (ship specifications, "Her hull").

39. Dyal, *Historical Dictionary of the Spanish American War*, 306 (Sigsbee); Sigsbee, "Personal Narrative, First Paper," 82 ("the crew"), 87 ("Yankee pigs").

40. Sigsbee, "Personal Narrative, Second Paper," 242 ("I was inclosing," "bursting," "heavy"), 253–54 ("Together"), 254 ("Everything was dark"), 249 ("When the ship").

41. Roland et al., *Way of the Ship*, 259 ("dirty treachery"); Hendrickson, *Spanish-American War*, xix–xx (timeline); Goldstein, *Mine Eyes Have Seen*, 186 ("a splendid"); Cluster and Hernández, *History of Havana*, 111 ("the government").

42. Maury, "Gulf of Mexico," 365.

Chapter Seven: American Sea

1. Sigsbee, *Deep Sea Sounding and Dredging*, 19 ("Aft on the main deck").

2. Sigsbee, "Appliances for Deep Sea Sounding," 580 ("hove to," "got bottom," "reeled in").

3. Sears and Merriman, *Oceanography*, 88 (Agassiz, "I want to make money"); Agassiz, *Letters and Recollections*, 168 ("New notions").

4. Agassiz, *Three Cruises*, 1:27 ("At great depths"); Sigsbee, *Deep Sea Sounding and Dredging*, 21 ("At sea").

5. Agassiz, *Letters and Recollections*, 189 ("long stretches"); Agassiz, *Three Cruises*, 1:310 ("We meet," "a grayish"), 312 ("orange").

6. Sigsbee, *Deep Sea Sounding*, 15 (cruise

statistics, "fifteen gales"); Garrison and Martin, *Geologic Structures in the Gulf of Mexico Basin,* 23 (Sigsbee Plain).

7. J. E. Davis, *Gulf,* 127–28.

8. Goode, *Fisheries and Fishery Industries of the United States,* 24 ("Bahamian Conchs," "West Indian Negroes," "They know no other," "small, comfortable," "dissipated," "considered"), 25 ("taken as a class"); Matschat, *Suwannee River,* 260 ("A narrow boardwalk," "Sun and sea"), 261 ("neat and clean").

9. Goode, *Fisheries and Fishery Industries of the United States,* 25 ("good citizens," "hale and hearty," "broken down"), 27 ("Spanish, Italian," "in the same manner," "nearly all"), 29 ("will run no risk").

10. J. E. Davis, *Gulf,* 139 ("like a crescent"); Munroe, "Sponges and Spongers of the Florida Reef," 640 ("filled with," "bewildering maze"), 642 ("water glass," "gorgeous"), 643 ("mucilaginous"); Snyder, "Gulf Coast Gold," 142 (value).

11. J. E. Davis, *Gulf,* 136 ("Jacky Jack"); Ownbey and Wilson, *Mississippi Encyclopedia,* 101 ("white winged queens").

12. Paradise, *Child Labor and the Work of Mothers in Oyster and Shrimp Canning Communities on the Gulf Coast,* 12 ("She had cut").

13. *Biloxi Daily Herald,* December 21, 1889 (Lopez), February 25, 1918 (DuKate).

14. Rowland, *Mississippi,* 370 (statistics).

15. Edwards and Verton, *Creole Lexicon,* 44 (luggers); J. E. Davis, *Gulf,* 137 (Texas trawler); Mistovich and Knight, "Cultural Resources Survey of Mobile Harbor," 46 (luggers and trawlers).

16. J. E. Davis, *Gulf,* 126–27 ("chunky-built"); Raupp, "Fish On," 325 ("Red Snapper Capital"); Goode, *American Fishes,* 76 ("Snappers should always"); Ladies of St. Francis Street Methodist Church, *Gulf City Cookbook,* 16–26 (for Mobile fish recipes).

17. Raupp, "Fish On," 328 ("well-smacks"), 333 ("Sometimes six men"); Bucchino, "Talking Smack," 33 ("vile").

18. Bucchino, "Talking Smack," 43–44 ("chings," "a long, sharp").

19. "Stauter-Built," 34 ("If there was any," "Cedar Point Special"), 33 ("damn fool"); Evans, *Archaeology of Vernacular Watercraft,* 116 (Lafitte skiff). I can personally testify to the Stauter-Built brand's qualities and toughness. During a 2017 journey up Baldwin County's scenic Magnolia River on board David and Simona Newell's sixteen-foot model, we ran hard into a submerged piling, which left nary a mark. A good-condition vintage Stauter-Built fetches thousands of dollars on today's market, and the boats are still seen all over Mobile Bay.

20. Farley, *Fishing Yesterday's Gulf Coast,* xii ("along the docks," "A good, strong"), 5 ("We shook"); "FDR Fishing, Gulf Port" (newsreel footage).

21. Mason, *Fishing,* 12 (Grand Isle Tarpon Rodeo); Thomason, *Mobile,* 190–91 (Alabama Deep Sea Fishing Rodeo); Beam, *Beam's Directory of International Tourist Events,* 243 (Mississippi Deep Sea Fishing Rodeo); Cavaioli, *Pompano Beach,* 7 (Pompano Beach Fishing Rodeo); Mullen, "Orange Beach Acquires Piece of Charter Fishing History" (Callaway quotes).

22. Morrison, *Mobile,* 47 (1887 figures); "To Make New Orleans Open Lumber Market," 23 (turpentine, rosin figures); *Scribner's Magazine,* 79 ("There pirates").

23. Kirkland, "Waterman Steamship Corporation," *Encyclopedia of Alabama,* http://www.encyclopediaofalabama.org/article/h-1550 (accessed May 27, 2018).

24. Acosta, *Tampa's Hyde Park,* 8 (railroad); Department of Commerce and Labor, Bureau of the Census, *Thirteenth Census of the United States 1910,* 71 (population); Tomlinson, *Sea and the Jungle,* 366 (quotes); North Tampa Land Company Advertisement ("The completion").

25. Cartwright, *Galveston,* 119 ("New York of the Gulf"), 142 ("Mudville"), 232 ("ditch").

26. Ibid., 16–17 (hurricane), 190–92 (raising city), 193 (1905 prosperity), 203 ("the last port"); Feagin, *New Urban Paradigm,* 69 (Houston's growth).

27. Charlie Bodden, audio interview by Jody Kamins Harper, 1994–5 ("You cross," "got a certain kick"); Harper, *What We Eat at 13 Kenneth Street,* 135 ("bust 'em," "There'd be").

28. Conwell, "Sea-Going Days, Part Two," 10 ("Three-island," "raised forecastle"), 13 (crew), 11 ("bundled," "almost constantly"), 12 ("mountains," slung-up"), 14 ("make-shift").

29. Ibid., 7 ("free-wheeling," "barrooms"); Cartwright, *Galveston,* 226 ("French House," "pervert trade"); Boulard, *Huey Long Invades New Orleans,* 127 ("As we went"); Joe Ollinger, personal interview, January 10, 2013 (Monkey Wrench Corner).

30. Quirk, *Affair of Honor,* 2 ("I am going").

31. London, "Red Game of War," 7 (all quotes).

32. Krauze, "April Invasion of Veracruz." Among the American casualties was a young sailor from Mobile, twenty-year-old Esau Frohlichstein, whose funeral became a huge patriotic outpouring in Alabama's port city. Thousands of mourners filed past the casket, including Confederate veterans, Alabama's governor, and local militia. Pres. Wilson sent a smilax wreath. Frohlichstein's headstone in Sha'arai Shomayim Cemetery contains the entire text of his last letter written to his parents the night before the landing. See Sledge, *Cities of Silence,* 85–86.

33. Moss, *Southern Spirits,* 244 (Volstead Act); Sanders, "Delivering Demon Rum," 98 (Faulkner, "hams"), 94 ("Mobile begins").

34. Skoglund, *"I'm Alone* Case," 2 ("Captain, you have," "I am," "Heave to," "I do not know," "Several shots"), 5 ("Shell after shell").

35. Thomas, "Mobile Homefront during the Second World War," 56–57 (Alabama Dry Dock and Shipbuilding); "Gulf Coast Shipbuilding," 90 (Ingalls); Heitmann, "Demagogue and Industrialist," 155 ("the most," "I don't wait"), 153 (design).

36. Cronenberg, "U-Boats in the Gulf," 164 ("Happy Times"), 171 (Mexico declares war). For number of ships sunk, see Church et al., *Archaeological and Biological Analysis.*

37. Conwell, "Sea Going Days, Part Two," 66 ("an entire"), 67 ("While we," "These were"), 69 ("ran along"), 70 ("sea green," "would make it").

38. Mort, *Hemingway Patrols,* 52 (*Pilar*), 81 (plan); Reynolds, *Hemingway,* 66 (ambassador approves).

39. Morison, *History of United States Naval Operations in World War II,* 135 ("Gulf Sea Frontier"); Thomason, *Mobile,* 236–37 (preparations); Church et al., *Archaeological and Biological Analysis,* 122–25, figs. 7.11–17; Howard, "72 Years Later."

40. Paine, *Sea and Civilization,* 583–85; Mayo and Nahira, *In Their Time,* 203 ("time and money"); Cudahy, "Containership Revolution," 6 ("Why couldn't").

41. Cudahy, "Containership Revolution," 6–7; Roland et al., *Way of the Ship,* 362 ("the longshoreman's coffin"); Paine, *Sea and Civilization,* 589 (impact on ports).

42. "Carnival Fantasy" (ship specifications); Business Research and Economic Advisors, *Contribution of the International Cruise Industry to the U.S. Economy in 2014,* 51 (Texas statistics); *Mobile Press-Register,* September 3, 2015 (Carnival's timeline in Mobile), November 9, 2016 (Carnival returns to Mobile), November 26, 2018 (commits into 2019).

43. Cudahy, *Box Boats,* x (*Ideal X* length); Beresford and Pettit, *International Freight Transport,* 146 (Neo-Panamax); *Havana Times,* January 28, 2014 ("Cuban Hong Kong"); *New Orleans Times-Picayune,* April 3, 2016 ("When you're"). Interests in Mobile have argued much the same, and in

1993 established the first American sister city relationship with Havana. See Dominguez and Prevost, *United States–Cuban Relations,* 133.

44. Gallagher, "Veracruz Port Takes Aim at US Competitors with Expansion" ("We see," statistics); Morley, "Veracruz Port Expands to Support Manufacturing Demand" ("The challenge"); "Veracruz, Mexico."

Chapter Eight: Blowout!

1. *New York Times,* June 11, 1990; "Mega Borg—IMO 7388944."

2. Leveille, "*Mega Borg* Fire and Oil Spill," 273.

3. *Galveston Daily News,* June 10, 1990 ("Tanker Blast," "the worst"); *New York Times,* June 11, 1990 ("Tourism").

4. Leveille, "*Mega Borg* Fire and Oil Spill," 274 ("a 38 million"), 275 ("was surrounded," "scores"), 273 ("standardized"); *New York Times,* June 17, 1990 ("Here again").

5. Leveille, "*Mega Borg* Fire and Oil Spill," 273–76; Gore, *Gulf of Mexico,* 283–84.

6. Leveille, "*Mega Borg* Fire and Oil Spill," 276 ("There is no"); *New York Times,* June 17, 1990; Gore, *Gulf of Mexico,* 284 ("the hidden cost").

7. Burgess, Kazanis, and Shepard, *Outer Continental Shelf,* v ("20.06 billion"); *New York Times,* July 12, 2017 (Mexican well).

8. Bureau of Land Management, *Department of the Interior Final Environmental Statement,* 84, 86 (Indians, Spanish, and oil).

9. J. E. Davis, *Gulf,* 265 (Spindletop); Leffler, Pattarozzi, and Sterling, *Deepwater Petroleum Exploration and Production,* 5 (first offshore rigs); Morton, "Beyond Sight of Land," 62 (offshore rigs); National Commission on the BP Deepwater Horizon Oil Spill and Offshore Oil Drilling, *Report to the President,* 22 ("Nobody knew," "It was").

10. Gore, *Gulf of Mexico,* 241–43.

11. Carlyle, "What Does It Feel Like to Work on an Oil Rig?"

12. "Ursa Oil and Gas Field Project" (*Ursa*

specifications); Lieber, "Life on Board a Gulf of Mexico Oil Drilling Platform" ("It's not a job").

13. Scott, *Energy Sector,* iii (report quotes). Other significant U.S. producers include North Dakota, Alaska, and California, their rankings sometimes surpassing Louisiana's. See *USA Today,* July 28, 2015.

14. U.S. Army Corps of Engineers, *Final Feasibility Report for Sabine-Neches Waterway Channel Improvement Project Southeast Texas and Southwest Louisiana,* 1:iv–10, 11; *New Orleans Times-Picayune,* May 24, 2009.

15. *New York Times,* June 27, 1990 (drilling banned off Florida); Henry, "Oil Lobby Pushes for Offshore Drilling in the Eastern Gulf of Mexico" ("Ever since"); *Pensacola News Journal,* December 1, 2017 ("The industrial").

16. Turner, *Border of Blue,* 186 ("Times Square," "a sudden"); Nobel, "Everything Spirals Back Around," 26 ("gritty and magical"), 27–28 ("whose smokestack"), 29 ("machinery"), 30 ("heliports and communication"); J. E. Davis, *Gulf,* 513 ("discards").

17. Conwell, "Sea-Going Days, Part 2," 6 ("Although," "every tanker"); *Houston Chronicle,* April 6, 2014.

18. Ross et al., "Ixtoc-I Oil Blowout," 26–28; *New Orleans Times-Picayune,* July 4, 2010 ("It was like").

19. Ross et al., "Ixtoc-I Oil Blowout," 34–35; Jiménez Cisneros, *Contaminación Ambiental en México,* 655–66 (Ixtoc disaster); *New Orleans Times-Picayune,* July 4, 2010 ("We tracked, "It was"); Macko, "Almost Forgotten Oil Spill" ("Hotels").

20. National Commission on the BP Deepwater Horizon Oil Spill and Offshore Oil Drilling, *Report to the President,* January, 2011, 2 ("well from hell," "nightmare"); *New York Times,* September 9, 2010 (Macondo derivation), December 25, 2010 ("floating Hilton," "rough," "intelligent").

21. BP, Deepwater Horizon *Accident Investigation Report* 11 ("a complex"); National

Commission on the BP Deepwater Horizon Oil Spill and Offshore Oil Drilling, *Report to the President,* 12 ("mud falling"), 9 ("gassy smoke," "It knocked," "I fell," "As it"), 10 ("When I," "At that point").

22. Cavnar, *Disaster on the Horizon,* 116 (flow rates), 122–36 (containment efforts); Farrell, *Gulf of Mexico Oil Spill,* 91 ("We're sorry"), 92 ("Well, Mr. Hayward"); *New York Times,* June 19, 2010 ("He is having," "To quote").

23. Gessner, *Tarball Chronicles,* 4 ("national sacrifice"), 9 ("As I looked," "We have passed"), 6 ("moved through the mist," "many formerly," "overweight," "barked orders"), 17 ("angry"), 21 ("One of the small," "beholden," "do not litter"); Upton, *Deepwater Horizon Oil Spill and the Gulf of Mexico Fishing Industry,* 10 (Vessels of Opportunity). I drove down to Gulf Shores with my family in mid-June of 2010 to see the oiled beaches firsthand. There was almost no traffic, parking lots were empty, and the air smelled strongly of fuel. We walked to the beach and were heartbroken. No one was in the water. There were no children shouting or laughing. Instead, clusters of people in street clothes stood behind the oil-slathered wrack line staring in silence. They were mourning the Gulf. On the horizon, three Vessels of Opportunity—shrimp boats—were anchored cheek by jowl where they had lain boom.

24. National Oceanic and Atmospheric Administration, *Deepwater Horizon Oil Spill,* 1–2 to 1–3 ("Approximately"). Immediately after the disaster some official estimates placed the amount spilled at 4.9 million barrels, and that figure is still widely cited. The exact amount will probably never be known. See National Commission on the BP Deepwater Horizon Oil Spill and Offshore Oil Drilling, *Report to the President,*

346n76; National Wildlife Federation, *Five Years and Counting,* 3 (summary of wildlife loss).

25. Harris, *Pulitzer's Gold,* 7–8 ("A major"); J. E. Davis, *Gulf,* 482 (Gulf Intracoastal Waterway); U.S. Geological Survey, *Wetland Change in Coastal Louisiana, 1932–2010* ("wetland loss," "more than").

26. Zakour, Mock, and Kadetz, *Creating Katrina, Rebuilding Resilience,* 146 ("amplified"), 148 ("wetland apron"); Brinkley, *Great Deluge,* 219 ("The result"); Buuck, *St. Barnard Parish Fire Department in Hurricane Katrina,* 29 ("superhighway").

27. *Guardian,* March 15, 2016 (Isle de Jean Charles, "You could walk," "This community not only"); McQuaid et al., *Path of Destruction,* 89–91 (tribal history); *"Bienvenue, Aiokpanchi,* Welcome to Isle de Jean Charles" (tribal history and federal settlement); *Isle de Jean Charles* ("I still do the same thing"); *New Orleans Times-Picayune,* December 19, 2017 ("I'm sad"); National Commission on the BP Deepwater Horizon Oil Spill and Offshore Oil Drilling, *Report to the President,* 203 ("Louisiana is paying").

Epilogue

1. *Lagniappe,* January 20, 2016 ("We don't ever").

2. Ibid. ("like the tractor trailers"); De Angelo, *Schooner* Rachel, 1–3 (history); *Mississippi Press,* June 13, 2010 (history).

3. *Dallas Morning News,* September 8, 2012 (possible rum-running).

4. "Storms and Weather Warnings," 544 (wind speeds).

5. *Mobile Register,* October 19, 1923 ("buffeted"); October 20, 1923 ("high and dry").

6. *Mobile Register,* October 23, 1923 (distance from water).

Bibliography

Newspapers

Biloxi Daily Herald
Dallas Morning News
Fort Myers Florida Weekly
Galveston Daily News
Guardian
Havana Times
Houston Chronicle
Lagniappe (Mobile)
Latin Times
London Gazette
Mississippi Press
Mobile Press Register
New Orleans Bee
New Orleans Times-Picayune
New York Times
Niles National Register
Niles Weekly Register
Northwest Florida Daily News
Pensacola News Journal
Sarasota Herald Tribune
Tampa Bay Times
USA Today
Yucatán Times

Books, Articles, and Other Sources

Acosta, Delphin. *Tampa's Hyde Park.* Charleston, S.C.: Arcadia, 2012.

Acosta Rodríguez, Antonio, Adolfo González Rodríguez, and Enriqueta Vila Vilar, eds. *La Casa de Contratación y la Navegación entre España y las Indias.* Seville: Universidad de Sevilla, 2003.

Agassiz, Alexander. *Three Cruises of the United States Coast and Geodetic Survey Steamer 'Blake.'* Vol. 1. New York: Houghton, Mifflin, 1888.

Agassiz, Mrs. E. C. "A Dredging Excursion in the Gulf Stream." *Atlantic Monthly,* October 1869, 507–16.

Agassiz, G. R., ed. *Letters and Recollections of Alexander Agassiz with a Sketch of his Life and Work.* New York: Houghton, Mifflin, 1913.

Albion, Robert Greenhalgh. *Square-Riggers on Schedule: The New York Sailing Packets to England, France, and the Cotton Ports.* Princeton, N.J.: Princeton University Press, 1938.

"The Alligator." *Harper's New Monthly Magazine,* December 1854, 37–50.

American State Papers, Naval Affairs. Vol. 1. Washington, D.C.: Gales & Seaton, 1834.

Amos, Harriet. *Cotton City: Urban Development in Antebellum Mobile.* Tuscaloosa: University of Alabama Press, 1985.

"Ancient Trade Routes for Obsidian." *New Scientist,* April 18, 1985, 25.

Antón, Alex and Roger E. Hernández. *Cubans in America: A Vibrant History of a People in Exile.* New York: Kensington Books, 2002.

Arbizzani, Ron. *Living aboard a Boat Named Farfetched: A Couple Tells Their Story of Eight Years Living and Traveling aboard Their Boat.* Bloomington, Ind.: iUniverse, 2008.

Audubon, John James. *Writings and Drawings.* New York: Library of America, 1999.

Audubon, Maria R. *Audubon and His Journals.* 2 vols. New York: Scribner's, 1897.

Azcue, Concepción Navarro, and Marta Milagros del Vas Mingo. "El riesgo del transporte marítimo del siglo XVI." In *Congreso de Historia del Descubrimiento (1492–1596), actas (ponencias y comunicaciones)*, vol. 3, 579–614. Madrid: Real Academica de la Historia, Confederacion Española de Cajas de Ahorros 1992.

Baher, Christopher. *Moon Havana*. Berkeley, Calif.: Avalon Travel, 2015.

Bancroft, Hubert Howe. *The Works of Hubert Howe Bancroft*, vol. 13, *History of Mexico, 1824–1861*. San Francisco: History Company, 1887.

Barca, Madame Calderón de la. *Life in Mexico: During a Residence of Two Years in That Country*. London: Chapman & Hall, 1843.

Bartlett, John Russell. *Personal Narrative of Explorations and Incidents in Texas, New Mexico, California, Sonora, and Chihuahua*. Vol. 2. New York: Appleton, 1856.

Beam, Amy. *Beam's Directory of International Tourist Events*. Washington, D.C.: TTA, 1991.

Beehler, W. H. "The United States Navy and West India Piracy, 1821–25." *Frank Leslie's Popular Monthly*, January 1890, 2–16.

Beresford, Anthony and Stephen Pettit. *International Freight Transport: Cases, Structures, and Prospects*. London: Kogan Page, 2017.

Bernal, Ignacio. *The Olmec World*. Trans. Carolyn B. Czitrom. Berkeley: University of California Press, 1969.

Bird, Dale E., Kevin Burke, Stuart A. Hall, and John F. Casey. "Tectonic Evolution of the Gulf of Mexico Basin." In *Gulf of Mexico Origin, Waters, and Biota*, vol. 3, *Geology*, edited by Noreen A. Buster and Charles W. Holmes, 3–16. College Station: Texas A&M University Press, 2011.

Bishop, Nathaniel H. *Four Months in a Sneak-Box: A Boat Voyage of 2600 Miles down the Ohio and Mississippi Rivers, and along the Gulf of Mexico*. Boston: Lee & Shepard, 1879.

Bluff, Harry. "Supplement to the Lucky Bag No. IV." *Southern Literary Messenger*, February 1841, 169–70.

Blunt, Edmund M. *The American Coast Pilot*. New York: Blunt, 1827.

Bolster, W. Jeffrey. *Black Jacks: African American Seamen in the Age of Sail*. Cambridge, Mass.: Harvard University Press, 1997.

Boulard, Garry. *Huey Long Invades New Orleans: The Siege of a City, 1934–1936*. Gretna, La.: Pelican, 1998.

Brasseaux, Carl A. "Close Encounter with a Creature of the 'Finny Tribe.'" *Gulf Coast Historical Review* 7, no. 1 (1991): 6–17.

Bray, Mary Matthews. *A Sea Trip in Clipper Ship Days*. Boston: Badger, 1920.

Bremer, Fredrika. *The Homes of the New World: Impressions of America*. 2 vols. New York: Harper & Brothers, 1854.

———. *The Homes of the New World: Impressions of America*. Vol. 3. London: Arthur Hall, Virtue, 1853.

Bridges, Edwin C. *Alabama: The Making of an American State*. Tuscaloosa: University of Alabama Press, 2016.

Brinkley, Douglas. *The Great Deluge: Hurricane Katrina, New Orleans, and the Mississippi Gulf Coast*. New York: Morrow, 2006.

Brower, J. V. *The Mississippi River and Its Source*. Minneapolis: Harris & Smith, 1893.

Brown, Ian W., ed. *Bottle Creek: A Pensacola Culture Site in South Alabama*. Tuscaloosa: University of Alabama Press, 2003.

Brown, Wilbur S. *The Amphibious Campaign for West Florida and Louisiana, 1814–1815*. Tuscaloosa: University of Alabama Press, 1969.

Browning, Robert M. *Lincoln's Trident: The West Gulf Blockading Squadron during the Civil War*. Tuscaloosa: University of Alabama Press, 2015.

Bruseth, James E., Amy A. Borgens, Bradford M. Jones, and Eric M. Ray, eds. *The Belle: The Archaeology of a Seventeenth-Century Ship of New World Colonization*. Austin: Texas Historical Commission, 2016.

Bruseth, James E., and Toni S. Turner. *From a Watery Grave: The Discovery and Excavation of La Salle's Shipwreck, La Belle*. College Station: Texas A&M University Press, 2005.

Bucchino, Nicole Rae. "Talking Smack: The Archaeology and History of Pensacola's Red Snapper Fishing Industry." Master's thesis, University of West Florida, 2014.

Buchanan, John. *Jackson's Way: Andrew Jackson and the People of the Western Waters.* New York: Wiley, 2001.

Bueno, Pablo E. Pérez-Mallaína. "Oficiales y Marineros de la Carrera de Indias (Siglo XVI)." In *Congreso de Historia del Descubrimiento (1492–1596), actas (ponencias y comunicaciones),* vol. 3, 27–56. Madrid: Real Academica de la Historia, Confederacion Española de Cajas de Ahorros, 1992.

Bureau of Land Management. *Department of the Interior Final Environmental Statement Proposed 1979 Outer Continental Shelf Oil and Gas Lease Sale, 58A. Western and Central Gulf of Mexico.* Vol. 1. Washington, D.C.: U.S. Government Printing Office, 1979.

Burgess, Grant L., Eric G. Kazanis, and Nancy K. Shepard. *Outer Continental Shelf: Estimated Oil and Gas Reserves Gulf of Mexico OCS Region, December 31, 2015.* New Orleans: U.S. Department of the Interior, December 2016.

Burkholder, Mark A., and Lyman L. Johnson. *Colonial Latin America.* New York: Oxford University Press, 2004.

Bush, David M., Norma J. Longo, William J. Neal, Luciana S. Esteves, Orrin H. Pilkey, Deborah F. Pilkey, and Craig A. Webb. *Living on the Edge of the Gulf: The West Florida and Alabama Coast.* Durham, N.C.: Duke University Press, 2001.

Business Research and Economic Advisors. *The Contribution of the International Cruise Industry to the U.S. Economy in 2014: Prepared for Carnival Cruise Lines International Association, September 2014.* Exton, Pa.: Business Research and Economic Advisors, September 2015.

Buskens, Joy Callaway. *Well, I've Never Met a Native.* Columbus, Ga.: Quill, 1986.

Buuck, Michelle Mahl. *The St. Barnard Fire Department in Hurricane Katrina.* Gretna, La.: Pelican, 2008.

Caballos, Esteban Mira. "Entorno a la expedición de Sebastián de Ocampo a la isla de Cuba (1506)." *Revista de Indias* 56, no. 206 (1996): 199–203.

Cabeza de Vaca, Álvar Núñez. *Relation of Álvar Núñez Cabeza de Vaca.* Edited by Buckingham Smith. New York, 1871.

Caldwell, Robert Granville. *The López Expeditions to Cuba, 1848–1851.* Princeton, N.J.: Princeton University Press, 1915.

Canter, Ronald L. and Dave Pentecost. "Rocks, Ropes, and Maya Boats: Stone Bollards at Ancient Waterfronts along the Rio Usumacinta; Yaxchilan, Mexico to El Porvenir, Guatemala." *PARI Journal* 9, no. 3 (2007): 4–16.

"The Capture of Vera Cruz." *Knickerbocker,* July 1847, 1–5.

Cartwright, Gary. *Galveston: A History of the Island.* Fort Worth: Texas Christian University Press, 1991.

Cavaioli, Frank J. *Pompano Beach.* Charleston, S.C.: Arcadia, 2001.

Cavnar, Bob. *Disaster on the Horizon: High Stakes, High Risks, and the Story behind the Deepwater Well Blowout.* White River Junction, Vt.: Chelsea Green, 2010.

Chandler, R. E. "Notes and Documents: Eyewitness History: O'Reilly's Arrival in Louisiana." *Louisiana History* 20, no. 3 (1979): 317–24.

———. "O'Reilly's Voyage from Havana to the Balize." *Louisiana History* 22, no. 2 (1981): 199–207.

Chang-Rodríguez, Eugenio. *Latinoamérica: Su Civilización y su Cultura.* 4th ed. Boston: Thompson Higher Education, 2008.

Chipman, Donald E., and Harriet Denise Joseph. *Spanish Texas: 1519–1821.* Austin: University of Texas Press, 1992.

Church, R., D. Warren, R. Cullimore, L. Johnston, W. Schroeder, W. Patterson, T. Shirley. M. Kilgour, N. Morris, and J. Moore. *Archaeological and Biological Analysis of World War II Shipwrecks in the Gulf of Mexico: Artificial Reef Effect in Deep Water.* New Orleans: U.S. Dept. of the Interior, Minerals Management Service, Gulf of

Mexico OCS Region, OCS Study, 2007.

Claiborne, J. F. H. *Mississippi, as a Province, Territory, and State with Biographical Notes of Eminent Citizens,* Vol. 1. Jackson, Miss.: Power & Barksdale, 1880.

Clark, Arthur Hamilton. *The Clipper Ship Era: An Epitome of Famous American and British Clipper Ships, Their Owners, Builders, Commanders, and Crews, 1843–1869.* New York: Putnam, 1912.

Clark, Paul C., and Edward H. Moseley. "D-Day Veracruz, 1847—A Grand Design." *Joint Force Quarterly* 10 (1995–96): 102–15.

Clark, Thomas D., and John D. W. Guice. *The Old Southwest, 1795–1830.* 1989. Reprint, Norman: University of Oklahoma Press, 1995.

Clayton, Lawrence A., and Michael L. Conniff. *A History of Modern Latin America.* Belmont, Calif.: Thompson Wadsworth, 2005.

Clayton, Lawrence A., Vernon James Knight Jr., and Edward C. Moore, eds. *The De Soto Chronicles: The Expedition of Hernando De Soto to North America in 1539–1543.* Tuscaloosa: University of Alabama Press, 1993.

Cluster, Dick, and Rafael Hernández. *The History of Havana.* New York: Palgrave Macmillan, 2006.

Coggins, Jack. *Ships and Seamen of the American Revolution.* Harrisburg, Pa.: Promontory, 1969.

Conwell, David M. "Sea-Going Days, Part Two." Unpublished manuscript. Conwell Family Papers. Norfolk Public Library.

Cooke, John Henry. *A Narrative of Events in the South of France, and of the Attack on New Orleans, in 1814 and 1815.* London: Boone, 1835.

Cova, Antonio Rafael de la. "The Taylor Administration Versus Mississippi Sovereignty: The Round Island Expedition of 1849." *Journal of Mississippi History* 62, no. 4 (2000): 295–327.

Cox, Christopher. *A Key West Companion.* New York: St. Martin's, 1983.

Cox, Isaac Joslin, ed. *The Journeys of Rene Robert Cavelier Sieur de La Salle.* Vol. 1. New York: Allerton, 1922.

Cronenberg, Allen. "U-Boats in the Gulf: The Undersea War in 1942." *Gulf Coast Historical Review* 5, no. 2 (1990): 163–78.

Crooker, Richard A., and Zoran Pavlović. *Cuba.* New York: Chelsea House, 2010.

Crothers, William L. *American-Built Packets and Freighters of the 1850s: An Illustrated Study of Their Characteristics and Construction.* Jefferson, N.C.: McFarland, 2013.

Cudahy, Brian J. *Box Boats: How Containerships Changed the World.* New York: Fordham University Press, 2006.

———. "The Containership Revolution: Malcom McLean's 1956 Innovation Goes Global." *TR News,* September–October 2006, 5–9.

Cunningham-Smith, Petra. "Fish from Afar: Marine Resource Use at Caracol, Belize." Master's thesis, University of Central Florida, 2011.

Cushing, Frank Hamilton. "Exploration of Ancient Key Dwellers' Remains on the Gulf Coast of Florida." *Proceedings of the American Philosophical Society* 30 (1896): 329–35.

Custer, B. Elizabeth. *Tenting on the Plains.* New York: Harper & Brothers, 1895.

Dampier, William. *A Collection of Voyages.* Vol. 2. London: Knapton, 1729.

———. *Dampier's Voyages,* vol. 2, edited by John Masefield. London: Richards, 1906.

Dana, Richard Henry. *To Cuba and Back: A Vacation Voyage.* Boston: Ticknor & Fields, 1859.

Darnell, Reaznet M. *The American Sea: A Natural History of the Gulf of Mexico.* College Station: Texas A&M University Press, 2015.

Davis, Jack E. *The Gulf: The Making of an American Sea.* New York: Liveright, 2017.

Davis, Richard A. "Beaches, Barrier Islands, and Inlets of the Florida Gulf Coast." In *Gulf of Mexico Origin, Waters, and Biota,* vol. 3, *Geology,* edited by Noreen A. Buster and Charles W. Holmes, 89–100. College Station: Texas A&M University Press, 2011.

Davis, William C. "The Journal of Jean Laffite."

Laffite Society Chronicles 11, no. 2 (2005): 2–16.

———. *The Pirates Laffite: The Treacherous World of the Corsairs of the Gulf.* New York: Harcourt, 2005.

Dawson, Joseph G. III, ed. *The Louisiana Governors: From Iberville to Edwards.* Baton Rouge: Louisiana State University Press, 1990.

De Angelo, Ken. *The Schooner* Rachel: *Built by the De Angelo Shipyard at Moss Point, Mississippi.* Moss Point, Miss.: Ken De Angelo, 2010.

DeBow, J. D. B. "American Cities: The City of Galveston." *DeBow's Review,* April 1847, 345–50.

———. "Direct Foreign Trade of the South." *DeBow's Review,* January 1852, 126–48.

———. "New Orleans." *DeBow's Review,* July 1846, 53–65.

Department of Commerce and Labor, Bureau of the Census. *Thirteenth Census of the United States 1910.* Washington, D.C.: U.S. Government Printing Office, 1912.

De Vorsey, Louis, Jr. "The Impact of the La Salle Expedition of 1682 on European Cartography." In *La Salle and His Legacy: Frenchmen and Indians in the Mississippi Valley,* edited by Patricia K. Galloway, 60–78. Jackson: University Press of Mississippi, 1982.

"Disasters at Sea." *Sailor's Magazine and Naval Journal,* January 1838, 164–67.

Dixon, Anthony E. "Black Seminole Involvement and Leadership during the Second Seminole War, 1835–1842." Ph.D. diss., Indiana University, 2007.

Dominguez, Esteban Morales, and Gary Prevost. *United States–Cuban Relations: A Critical History.* Lanham, Md.: Lexington Books, 2008.

Doubleday, Charles William. *Reminiscences of the 'Filibuster' War in Nicaragua.* New York: Putnam's, 1886.

DuVal, Kathleen. *Independence Lost: Lives on the Edge of the American Revolution.* New York: Random House, 2015.

Dyal, Donald H. *Historical Dictionary of the Spanish American War.* Westport, Conn.: Greenwood, 1996.

Edwards, Jay Dearborn, and Nicolas Kariouk Pecquet du Bellay de Verton. *A Creole Lexicon: Architecture, Landscape, People.* Baton Rouge: Louisiana State University Press, 2004.

Emanuel, Kerry. *Divine Wind: The History and Science of Hurricanes.* New York: Oxford University Press, 2005.

Estrada, Alfredo José. *Havana: Autobiography of a City.* New York: St. Martin's, 2007.

Evans, Amanda M., ed. *The Archaeology of Vernacular Watercraft.* New York: Springer, 2016.

Eyewitness Travel Guide: Mexico. New York: DK, 2015.

Fabel, Robin F. A. *Bombast and Broadsides: The Lives of George Johnstone.* Tuscaloosa: University of Alabama Press, 1987.

———. "Reflection on Mobile's Loyalism in the American Revolution." *Gulf South Historical Review* 19, no. 1 (2003): 31–45.

Farley, Barney. *Fishing Yesterday's Gulf Coast.* College Station: Texas A&M University Press, 2002.

Farragut, Loyall. *The Life of David Glasgow Farragut, First Admiral of the United States Navy.* New York: Appleton, 1891.

Farrell, Courtney. *The Gulf of Mexico Oil Spill.* Edina, Minn.: ABDO, 2011.

Faye, Stanley. "Types of Privateer Vessels, Their Armament and Flags in the Gulf of Mexico." *Louisiana Historical Quarterly* 23 (1940): 118–30.

Feagin, Joe R. *The New Urban Paradigm: Critical Perspectives on the City.* New York: Rowman & Littlefield, 1998.

FEMA. *Hurricane Katrina in the Gulf Coast: Mitigation Assessment Team Report.* FEMA 549, July 2006.

Ferreiro, Larrie D. *Brothers at Arms: American Independence and the Men of France and Spain Who Saved It.* New York: Random, 2016.

Fifty Years of Fishing: The Destin Fishing Rodeo, a Pictorial History, 1948–1998. Panama City, Fla.: Boyd Brothers, 1998.

Fontana, Bernard L. *Entrada: The Legacy of Spain and Mexico in the United States*. Tucson, Ariz.: Southwest Parks and Monuments Association, 1994.

Ford, B. I., ed. *The Archaeology of Maritime Landscapes: When the Land Meets the Sea*. New York: Springer, 2011.

Fowler, Lucy Williams. "The Calusa Indians: Maritime Peoples of Florida in the Age of Columbus." *Expedition Magazine*, July 1991, 55–60.

Fox, Stephen. *Wolf of the Deep: Raphael Semmes and the Notorious Confederate Raider CSS* Alabama. New York: Knopf, 2007.

Fraiser, Jim. *The French Quarter of New Orleans*. Jackson: University Press of Mississippi, 2003.

Francaviglia, Richard V. *From Sail to Steam: Four Centuries of Texas Maritime History, 1500–1900*. Austin: University of Texas Press, 1998.

Gage, Tomas. *Nueva Relacion que Contiene los Viages de Tomas Gage en la Nueva España*. Tomo Segundo. Paris: Librería de Rosa, 1838.

Galloway, Patricia. *Choctaw Genesis, 1500–1700*. Lincoln: University of Nebraska Press, 1995.

——, ed. *La Salle and His Legacy: Frenchmen and Indians in the Lower Mississippi Valley*. Jackson: University Press of Mississippi, 1982.

Garrison, Louis E., and Ray G. Martin Jr. *Geologic Structures in the Gulf of Mexico Basin*. Geological Survey Professional Paper 773. U.S. Geological Survey. Washington, D.C.: U.S. Government Printing Office, 1973.

Gayareé, Charles. *History of Louisiana*. New York: Widdleton, 1867.

Gessner, David. *The Tarball Chronicles: A Journey beyond the Oiled Pelican and into the Heart of the Gulf Oil Spill*. Minneapolis: Milkweed, 2011.

Gibson, Carrie. *Empire's Crossroads: A History of the Caribbean from Columbus to the Present Day*. New York: Atlantic Monthly Press, 2014.

Girard, Just. *The Adventures of a French Captain*. New York: Benzinger Brothers, 1878.

Giraud, Marcel. *A History of French Louisiana*, vol. 1, *The Reign of Louis XIV, 1698–1715*. Translated by Joseph C. Lambert. Baton Rouge: Louisiana State University Press, 1974.

Girdler, L. Tracy. *An Antebellum Life at Sea: Featuring the Journal of Sarah Jane Girdler Kept Aboard the Clipper Ship 'Robert H. Dixey' from America to Russia and Europe January 1857–December 1858*. Montgomery, Ala.: Black Belt, 1997.

Goldstein, Richard. *Mine Eyes Have Seen the Glory: A First-Person History of the Events That Shaped America*. New York: Touchstone, 1997.

Goode, G. Brown. *American Fishes: A Popular Treatise upon the Game and Food Fishes of North America*. Boston: Page, 1887.

——. *The Fisheries and Fishery Industries of the United States: Section IV: The Fishermen of the United States*. Washington, D.C.: Government Printing Office, 1887.

Gore, Robert H. *The Gulf of Mexico: A Treasury of Resources in the American Mediterranean*. Sarasota, Fla.: Pineapple, 1992.

Gould, Elizabeth B. *From Fort to Port: An Architectural History of Mobile, Alabama, 1711–1918*. Tuscaloosa: University of Alabama Press, 1988.

Greenwald, Erin M., ed. *A Company Man: The Remarkable French-Atlantic Voyage of a Clerk for the Company of the Indies. A Memoir by Marc-Antoine Caillot*. New Orleans: Historic New Orleans Collection, 2013.

Groom, Winston. *Patriotic Fire: Andrew Jackson and Jean Laffite at the Battle of New Orleans*. New York: Vintage, 2007.

"Gulf Coast Shipbuilding: Vital Industry Booms in the South." *Life*, May 26, 1941, 87–95.

Gurney, Joseph John. *A Winter in the West Indies: Described in Familiar Letters to Henry Clay, of Kentucky*. London: Murray, 1840.

Guterl, Matthew Pratt. *American Mediterranean: Southern Slaveholders in the Age of Emancipation*. Cambridge, Mass.: Harvard University Press, 2008.

Hamilton, Peter Joseph. *Colonial Mobile*. Boston: Houghton, 1910.

Hamilton, Rod. *Fly-Fishing the Yucatán*. Guilford, Conn.: LP, 2017.

Hannay, David. "The Galleon." *Blackwood's Magazine*, July 1909, 663–72.

Haring, Clarence Henry. *Trade and Navigation between Spain and the Indies in the Time of the Hapsburgs*. Cambridge, Mass.: Harvard University Press, 1918.

Harper, Jody Kamins. *What We Eat at 13 Kenneth Street*. Mobile, Ala.: Privately printed, 1997.

Harris, Roy J., Jr. *Pulitzer's Gold: Behind the Prize for Public Service Journalism*. Columbia: University of Missouri Press, 2007.

Hartmann, Mark Joseph. "The Development of Watercraft in the Prehistoric Southeastern United States." Ph.D. diss., Texas A&M University, 1996.

Hassig, Ross. *War and Society in Ancient Mesoamerica*. Berkeley: University of California Press, 1992.

Hatch, Thom. *Osceola and the Great Seminole War: A Struggle for Justice and Freedom*. New York: St. Martin's, 2012.

Head, David. *Privateers of the Americas: Spanish American Privateering from the United States in the Early Republic*. Athens: University of Georgia Press, 2015.

Hearn, Lafcadio. *Chita: A Memory of Last Island*. 1889. Reprint, Jackson: University Press of Mississippi, 2003.

Heitmann, John A. "Demagogue and Industrialist: Andrew Jackson Higgins and Higgins Industries." *Gulf Coast Historical Review* 5, no. 2 (1990): 152–62.

Hendrickson, Kenneth E. *The Spanish-American War*. Westport, Conn.: Greenwood, 2003.

Henschel, G. *Te Deum Laudamaus: Set to Music in the Key of C*. London: Novello, Ewer, 1893.

Hietala, Thomas R. *Manifest Design: American Exceptionalism and Empire*. Ithaca, N.Y.: Cornell University Press, 1985.

Higginbotham, Jay. *Old Mobile: Fort Louis de la Louisiane, 1702–1711*. Mobile, Ala.: Museum of the City of Mobile, 1977.

———. *A Voyage to Dauphin Island in 1720: The Journal of Bertet de la Clue*. Mobile, Ala.: Museum of the City of Mobile, 1974.

Holden, J. B. "The Dry Tortugas." *Harper's New Monthly Magazine*, July 1868, 264–67.

Houston, M. C. *Texas and the Gulf of Mexico; or Yachting in the New World*. London: Murray, 1844.

Hudson, Charles. *The Southeastern Indians*. Knoxville: University of Tennessee Press, 1976.

Humboldt, Alexander. *The Island of Cuba*. Translated by J. S. Thraser. New York: Derby & Jackson, 1856.

Hunter, Louis C. *Steamboats on the Western Rivers: An Economic and Technological History*. Cambridge, Mass.: Harvard University Press, 1949.

Hurley, Frank T. *Surf, Sand, and Post Card Sunsets: A History of Pass-a-Grille and the Gulf Beaches*. St. Petersburg, Fla.: Frank T. Hurley, 1977.

"Hurricanes in 1837." *The Nautical Magazine and Naval Chronicle, for 1844. A Journal of Papers on Subjects Connected with Maritime Affairs*. London: Simpkin, Marshall, 1844.

International Hydrographic Organization. *Names and Limits of Oceans and Seas*. Special Publication no. 23, 4th edition. Monaco: IHO, June 2002.

Jackson, Harvey, III. *The Rise and Decline of the Redneck Riviera: An Insider's History of the Florida-Alabama Coast*. Athens: University of Georgia Press, 2012.

Jenkins, Peter. *Along the Edge of America*. Boston: Houghton Mifflin, 1995.

Jennings, Edward. *Hints on Sea Risks Containing*

Some Practical Suggestions for Diminishing Maritime Losses Both of Life and Property; Addressed to Merchants, Ship Owners, and Mariners. London: Bate, 1843.

Jiménez Cisneros, Blanca E. *La Contaminación Ambiental en México: Causas, Efectos y Technología Apropiada.* Mexico City: Limusa, Colegio de Ingenieros Ambientales de México, A. C., Instituto de Ingeniería de la UNAM y FEMISCA, 2001.

Jordan, Winthrop. *Tumult and Silence at Second Creek: An Inquiry into a Civil War Slave Conspiracy.* Baton Rouge: Louisiana State University Press, 1993.

Joutel, Henri. *Joutel's Journal of La Salle's Last Voyage, 1684–7.* Edited by Henry Reed Stiles. Albany, N.Y.: McDonough, 1906.

Kein, Sybil, ed. *Creole: The History and Legacy of Louisiana's Free People of Color.* Baton Rouge: Louisiana State University Press, 2000.

Kessell, John A. *Spain in the Southwest: A Narrative History of Colonial New Mexico, Arizona, Texas, and California.* Norman: University of Oklahoma Press, 2002.

Knight, Franklin W., and Peggy K. Liss, eds. *Atlantic Port Cities: Economy, Culture, and Society in the Atlantic World, 1650–1850.* Knoxville: University of Tennessee Press, 1991.

Knight, Henry. *Letters from the South and West.* Boston: Richardson & Lord, 1824.

Konstam, Angus. *World Atlas of Pirates: Treasure and Treachery on the Seven Seas.* Guilford, Conn.: Lyons, 2017.

Konstam, Angus, and Roger Michael Kean. *Pirates: Predators of the Seas.* New York: Skyhorse, 2007.

Krauze, Enrique. "The April Invasion of Veracruz." *New York Times,* April 20, 2014.

Krech, Shepard, III. *Spirits of the Air: Birds and American Indians in the South.* Athens: University of Georgia Press, 2009.

Kurlansky, Mark. *Cuba: A Subtropical Delirium.* New York: Bloomsbury, 2017.

Ladies of the St. Francis Street Methodist Episcopal Church South, Mobile, Alabama. *Gulf City Cookbook.* Dayton, Ohio: United Brethren, 1878.

Lafuente, Modesto. *Historia General de España: Desde los Tiempos Primitivos Hasta La Muerte de Fernando VII.* Tomo IV. Barcelona: Montaner & Simon, 1879.

Laing, Alexander. *Seafaring America.* New York: American Heritage, 1974.

Landa, Diego de. *Yucatán before and after the Conquest.* New York: Dover, 1937.

Lanning, Michael Lee. *The American Revolution, 100: The People, Battles, and Events of the American War for Independence, Ranked by Their Significance.* Naperville, Ill.: Sourcebooks, 2008.

Lanz, Manuel. *Compendio de Historia de Campeche.* Campeche: Tip. "El Fénix" de Pablo Llovera Marcín, 1905.

Lapuerta, Alina-García. *La Belle Creole: The Cuban Countess Who Captivated Havana, Madrid, and Paris.* Chicago: Chicago Review Press, 2014.

Latour, Arsené Lacarriere. *Historical Memoir of the War in West Florida and Louisiana in 1814–1815.* Philadelphia: Conrad, 1816.

Latrobe, Charles Joseph. *The Rambler in Mexico.* New York: Harper & Brothers, 1834.

———. *The Rambler in North America.* Vol. 2. London: Seeley & Burnside, 1836.

Lee, Sidney, ed. *The Dictionary of National Biography,* vol. 11, *Kennett–Lluelyn.* London: Macmillan, 1909.

Leffler, William L., Richard Pattarozzi, and Gordon Sterling. *Deepwater Petroleum Exploration and Production: A Nontechnical Guide.* Tulsa, Okla.: PennWell, 2003.

Levasseur, A. *Lafayette in America in 1824 and 1825; or Journal of a Voyage to the United States.* Philadelphia: Carey & Lea, 1829.

Leveille, Thomas P. "The *Mega Borg* Fire and Oil Spill: A Case Study." *International Oil Spill Conference Proceedings,* no. 1 (1991): 273–78.

LeVert, Octavia Walton. *Souvenirs of Travel.* Vol. 1. Mobile, Ala.: Goetzel, 1857.

"The Life of Jean Lafitte, The Pirate of the Mexican Gulf," *Littell's Living Age,* March 1852, 433–46.

A List of Reports to Be Made to the House of Representatives at the First Session of the Eighteenth Congress by the Executive Departments. December 1, 1823. Washington, D.C.: Gales & Seaton, 1823.

Lockhart, John Ingram, trans. and ed. *The Memoirs of the Conquistador Bernal Díaz del Castillo Written by Himself Containing a True and Full Account of the Discovery and Conquest of Mexico and New Spain.* Vol. 1. London: Hatchard, 1844.

Lockwood, C. C. *The Yucatán Peninsula.* Baton Rouge: Louisiana State University Press, 1989.

London, Jack. "The Red Game of War." *Collier's,* May 16, 1914, 5–7.

Longworth's American Almanac, New York Register, and City Directory. New York: Longworth, 1834.

Low, Charles Porter. *Some Reflections by Captain Charles P. Low.* Boston: Ellis, 1906.

Lugo-Fernández, A., D. A. Ball, M. Gravois, C. Horrell, and J. B. Irion. "Analysis of the Gulf of Mexico's Veracruz-Havana Route of La Flota de la Nueva España." *Journal of Maritime Archaeology* 2, no. 1 (2007): 24–47.

MacDonald, Mandy, and Russell Maddicks. *Culture Smart! Cuba.* London: Kuperard, 2006.

McCarthy, Kevin M. *Twenty Florida Pirates.* Sarasota, Fla.: Pineapple, 1994.

McDowell, R. W. "Sanitary Notes from the U.S.S. *Ozark*—Malarial Phrophylaxis." *U.S. Naval Medical Bulletin* 9, no. 2 (1915): 347–50.

McQuaid, John, and Mark Schleifstein. *Path of Destruction: The Devastation of New Orleans and the Coming Age of Superstorms.* New York: Little Brown, 2006.

McWilliams, Richebourg Gaillard, trans. and ed. *Fleur de Lys and Calumet: Being the Pénicaut Narrative of French Adventure in Louisiana.* Baton Rouge: Louisiana State University Press, 1953.

———. *Iberville's Gulf Journals.* Tuscaloosa: University of Alabama Press, 1981.

Mahon, John K. *History of the Second Seminole War, 1835–1842.* Gainesville: University Presses of Florida, 1991.

Mansfield, Mike. "An Onerous and Unnecessary Burden: Mobile and the Negro Seaman Acts." *Gulf South Historical Review* 21, no. 1 (2005): 6–28.

Marley, David. *Wars of the Americas: A Chronology of Armed Conflict in the Western Hemisphere from 1492 to the Present.* Santa Barbara, Calif.: ABC-CLIO, 2008.

Mason, Paul. *Fishing: The World's Greatest Fishing Spots and Techniques.* Mankato, Minn.: Capstone, 2011.

Matschat, Cecile Hulse. *Suwannee River: Strange Green Land.* New York: Literary Guild of America, 1938.

Maury, Matthew Fontaine. "The Gulf of Mexico." In *The Resources of the Southern and Western States,* edited by J. D. B. DeBow, 1:365–73. New Orleans: DeBow's Review, 1852.

Mayer, Brantz. *Captain Canot; or Twenty Years of an African Slaver.* New York: Appleton, 1854.

Mayo, Anthony J., and Nitin Nohira. *In Their Time: The Greatest Business Leaders of the Twentieth Century.* Boston: Harvard Business School Publishing, 2005.

McIllvain, Myra Hargrave. *Texas Tales: Stories that Shaped a Landscape and a People.* Santa Fe: Sunstone, 2017.

McKillop, Heather. "Ancient Maya Canoe Navigation and its Implications for Classic to Postclassic Maya Economy and Sea Trade: A View from the South Coast of Belize." *Journal of Caribbean Archaeology, Special Publication No. 3,* (2010): 93–105.

Meed, Douglas V. *The Fighting Texas Navy, 1832–1843.* Plano: Republic of Texas Press, 2001.

Mereness, Newton D., ed. *Travels in the American Colonies.* New York: Macmillan, 1916.

Merington, Marguerite, ed. *The Custer Story: The Life and Intimate Letters of General*

George A. Custer and His Wife Elizabeth. Lincoln, Neb.: Devin-Adair, 1950.

Milanich, Jerald T. *Florida Indians and the Invasion from Europe.* Gainesville: University Press of Florida, 1995.

Miller, James J. *An Environmental History of Northeast Florida.* Gainesville: University Press of Florida, 1998.

Millett, Nathaniel. *The Maroons of Prospect Bluff and Their Quest for Freedom in the Atlantic World.* Gainesville: University Press of Florida, 2013.

"Miscellany." *Army and Navy Chronicle,* August 15, 1839, 109.

Mistovich, Tim S., and Vernon James Knight Jr. "Cultural Resources Survey of Mobile Harbor, Alabama." Report submitted to U.S. Dept. of the Army, Corps of Engineers, Mobile District. Moundville, Ala.: OSM Archaeological Consultants, 1983.

Monzote, Reinaldo Funes. *From Rainforest to Canefield in Cuba: An Environmental History since 1492.* Chapel Hill: University of North Carolina Press, 2008.

Moorehead, Warren K. *The Cahokia Mounds.* Tuscaloosa: University of Alabama Press, 2000.

Morison, Samuel Eliot. *Admiral of the Ocean Sea: A Life of Christopher Columbus.* New York: Milford, 1942.

———. *The European Discovery of America: The Southern Voyages.* Oxford: Oxford University Press, 1974.

———. *History of United States Naval Operations in World War II,* vol. 1, *The Battle of the Atlantic, September 1939–May 1943.* Boston: Little, Brown, 1947.

Morris, John, ed. *Wanderings of a Vagabond: An Autobiography.* New York: Privately printed, 1873.

Morrison, Andrew, ed. *Mobile: The New South.* Mobile, Ala.: Metropolitan and Star, 1887–88.

Morse, Jedidiah. *The American Universal Geography, or a View of the Present State of all the Kingdoms, States and Colonies. Vol. 1.* Boston: Thomas & Andrews, 1812. Morse, Sidney

Edwards. *A System of Geography for the Use of Schools.* New York: Harper & Brothers, 1845.

Mort, Terry. *The Hemingway Patrols: Ernest Hemingway and His Hunt for U-Boats.* New York: Scribner, 2009.

Morton, Michael Quentin. "Beyond Sight of Land: A History of Oil Exploration in the Gulf of Mexico." *GEO ExPro,* June 2016, 60–63.

Moss, Robert F. *Southern Spirits: Four Hundred Years of Drinking in the American South, with Recipes.* Berkeley, Calif.: Ten Speed, 2016.

Munroe, Kirk. "Sponge and Spongers of the Florida Reef." *Scribner's Magazine,* November 1892, 639–50.

National Commission on the BP Deepwater Horizon Oil Spill and Offshore Oil Drilling. *Report to the President. Deep Water: The Gulf Oil Disaster and the Future of Offshore Drilling.* Washington, D.C.: U.S. Government Printing Office, January 2011.

The Navigation of the Gulf of Mexico and Caribbean Sea. Vol. 2. Washington, D.C.: U.S. Government Printing Office, 1902.

Neely, Wayne. *The Great Hurricane of 1780: The Story of the Greatest and Deadliest Hurricane of the Caribbean and the Americas.* Bloomington, Ind.: iUniverse, 2012.

Nevin, David. *The Mexican War.* Alexandria, Va.: Time-Life Books, 1978.

New South Associates. *From Alluvium to Commerce: Waterfront Architecture, Land Reclamation, and Commercial Development in Mobile, Alabama.* Stone Mountain, Ga.: New South Associates, 1995.

New York as It Is. New York: Tanner, 1840.

Nobel, Justin. "Everything Spirals Back Around: New Orleans, the Sea, and Life in Between." *Virginia Quarterly Review* 92, no. 2 (2016): 26–31.

Nobles, Cynthia LeJuene. "Gumbo." In *New Orleans Cuisine: Fourteen Signature Dishes and Their History,* edited by Susan Tucker, 98–115. Baton Rouge: Louisiana State University Press, 2000.

North Tampa Land Company Advertisement. *Popular Mechanics Magazine,* November 1915, 116.

Obadele-Starks, Ernest. *Freebooters and Smugglers: The Foreign Slave Trade in the United States after 1808.* Fayetteville: University of Arkansas Press, 2007.

Ohls, Gary J. "Roots of Tradition: Amphibious Warfare in the Early American Republic." Ph.D. diss., Texas Christian University, 2008.

Olcina, Antonio Gil, and Jorge Olcina Cantos. *Tratado de Climatología.* Sant Vincent del Raspeig: Universitat d'Alacat, 2017.

Oldmixon, John W. *Transatlantic Wanderings.* London: Routledge, 1855.

Olmstead, Frederick Law. *The Cotton Kingdom: A Traveler's Observations on Cotton and Slavery in the American Slave States.* New York: Mason Brothers, 1861.

Ormond, John J., Arthur P. Bagby, and George Goldthwaite, eds. *The Code of Alabama.* Montgomery, Ala.: Brittan & De Wolf, 1852.

Ostram, Thomas P. *United States Revenue and Coast Guard Cutters in Naval Warfare, 1790–1918.* Jefferson, N.C.: McFarland, 2018.

Ownby, Ted, and Charles Reagan Wilson, eds. *The Mississippi Encyclopedia.* Jackson: University Press of Mississippi, 2017.

"Packetarians." *Galaxy,* April 1, 1867, 725–32.

Pagden, Anthony, ed. *Hernan Cortes: Letters from Mexico.* New Haven, Conn.: Yale University Press, 1986.

Paine, Lincoln. *The Sea and Civilization: A Maritime History of the World.* New York: Knopf, 2013.

Panamerican Consultants. "Underwater Remote Sensing Survey Dog River, Mobile County, Alabama." Final Report for U.S. Army Corps of Engineers, February 2001.

Paradise, Viola I. *Child Labor and the Work of Mothers in Oyster and Shrimp Canning Communities on the Gulf Coast.* Washington, D.C.: U.S. Government Printing Office, 1922.

Parkman, Francis. *The Discovery of the Great West.* Boston: Little, Brown, 1870.

Payne, Edward John, ed. *Voyages of Hawkins, Frobisher and Drake: Select Narratives from the Principal Navigations of Haklyut.* Oxford: Clarendon, 1907.

Peck, Douglas T. "The Case for Prehistoric Cultural Contact between the Maya on the Yucatan and the Indians of Florida." *Florida Anthropologist* 51, no. 1 (1998): 3–13.

———. *The Yucatán: From Prehistoric Times to the Great Maya Revolt.* N.p.: Xlibris, 2005.

Pezuela, Don Jacabo de la. *Diccionario Geografico, Estadistico, Historico, de la Isla de Cuba.* Madrid: Imprenta del Establecimiento de Mellado, 1863.

Phalen, William J. *The Consequences of Cotton in Antebellum America.* Jefferson, N.C.: McFarland, 2014.

Phillips, Ulrich B. *Plantation and Frontier Documents: 1649–1863, Illustrative of Industrial History in the Colonial and Antebellum South.* Vol. 1. Cleveland: Clark, 1909.

Pickett, Albert James. *History of Alabama.* Charleston, S.C.: Walker & James, 1851.

Plasencia, Adela Pinet. *La Península de Yucatán en el Archivo General de la Nación.* Mexico City: Universidad Nacional Autónoma de México, 1998.

Power, Tyrone. *Impressions of America, during the Years 1833, 1834, and 1835.* Vol. 2. London: Richard Bentley, 1836.

Prescott, William H. *History of the Conquest of Mexico.* Paris: Baudry's European Library, 1844.

Pugh, Philip R., and Rebeca Gasca. "Siphonophorae (Cnidaria) of the Gulf of Mexico." In *Gulf of Mexico Origins, Waters, and Biota: Volume 1, Biodiversity,* edited by John W. Tunnell Jr., Darryl L. Felder, and Sylvia A. Earle, 395–98. College Station: Texas A&M University Press, 2009.

Quijano, José Antonio Calderón. *Historia de las Fortificaciones de Nueva España.* Madrid: Escuela de Estudios Hispanoamericanos, 1984.

Quirk, Robert E. *An Affair of Honor: Woodrow Wilson and the Occupation of Veracruz.*

Lexington: University of Kentucky Press, 1962.

Rafael, Vicente L. *Contracting Colonialism: Translation and Christian Conversion in Tagalog Society under Early Spanish Rule.* Durham, N.C.: Duke University Press, 1993.

Rangel, Juan José Flores. *Historia de México I.* Mexico City: Cengage Learning, 2010.

Raupp, Jason T. "Fish On: Pensacola's Red Snapper Fishery." *Florida Historical Quarterly* 85, no. 3 (2007): 324–41.

Reed, Alma M. *The Ancient Past of Mexico.* New York: Crown, 1966.

Report of the Officers Constituting the Light House Board Convened under Instructions from the Secretary of the Treasury to Inquire into the Condition of the Light-House Establishment of the United States, under the Act of March 3, 1851. Washington, D.C.: Hamilton, 1852.

Reséndez, Andrés. *A Land So Strange: The Epic Journey of Cabeza de Vaca.* New York: Basic Books, 2007.

Reynolds, Michael. *Hemingway: The Final Years.* New York: Norton, 1999.

Richards, Addison T. "The Rice Lands of the South." *Harper's New Monthly Magazine,* November 1859, 721–38.

Richter, William L. *Historical Dictionary of the Old South.* Plymouth: Scarecrow, 2013.

Robenalt, Jeffrey. *Historic Tales from the Republic of Texas: A Glimpse of Texas Past.* Charleston, S.C.: History, 2013.

Roland, Alex, W. Jeffrey Bolster, and Alexander Keyssar. *The Way of the Ship: America's Maritime History Reenvisioned, 1600–2000.* New York: Wiley, 2008.

Romans, Bernard. *A Concise Natural History of East and West Florida.* New York: For the author, 1775.

Rosen, Harry M., ed. *The Golden Conquistadores.* New York: Bobbs-Merrill, 1960.

Ross, S. L., C. W. Ross, F. Lepine, and R. K. Langtry. "Ixtoc-I Oil Blowout." In *Proceedings of a Symposium on Preliminary Results from the September 1979 Researcher/Pierce Ixtoc-I Cruise: Key Biscayne, Florida, June 9–10, 1980.* Boulder, Colo.: U.S. Dept. of Commerce, National Oceanic and Atmospheric Administration, Office of Marine Pollution Assessment, 1980.

Rothman, Joshua D. *Flush Times and Fever Dreams: A Story of Capitalism and Slavery in the Age of Jackson.* Athens: University of Georgia Press, 2012.

Rowland, Dunbar, *Mississippi: Comprising Sketches of Counties, Towns, Events, Institutions, and Persons, Arranged in Cyclopedic Form.* Atlanta: Southern Historical Publishing Association, 1907.

———, ed. *The Official Letter Books of W. C. C. Claiborne: 1801–1816.* Jackson, Miss.: State Department of Archives and History, 1917.

Ruggles, D. Fairchild, ed. *On Location: Heritage Cities and Sites.* Champaign, Ill.: Springer, 2012.

Russell, William Howard. *My Diary North and South.* Vol. 1. London: Bradbury & Evans, 1863.

Sanders, Randy. "Delivering Demon Rum: Prohibition Era Rumrunning in the Gulf of Mexico." *Gulf Coast Historical Review* 12, no. 1 (1996): 92–113.

Saul, David, ed. *The Illustrated Encyclopedia of Warfare: From Ancient Egypt to Iraq.* New York: DK, 2009.

Saxon, Lyle. *Lafitte the Pirate.* 1930. Reprint, Gretna, La.: Pelican, 2012.

"Scenes in the Suburbs of Matamoros." *Living Age,* August 1846, 275–76.

Schmidly, David J., and Bernd Würsig, "Mammals (Vertebrata: Mammalia) of the Gulf of Mexico." In *Gulf of Mexico Origins, Waters, and Biota: Volume 1, Biodiversity,* edited by John W. Tunnell Jr., Darryl L. Felder, and Sylvia A. Earle, 1343–52. College Station: Texas A&M University Press, 2009.

Schneider, Paul. *Old Man River: The Mississippi River in North American History.* New York: Holt, 2013.

Scott, Loren C. *The Energy Sector: Still a Giant Economic Engine for the Louisiana Economy —An Update.* Baton Rouge: Mid-Continent Oil and Gas Association, 2014.

Scribner's Magazine, December 1916.

Scroggs, William O. *Filibusters and Financiers: The Story of William Walker and His Associates.* New York: Macmillan, 1916.

Sears, Mary, and Daniel Merriman. *Oceanography: The Past.* New York: Springer, 1980.

Semmes, Raphael. *Memoirs of Service Afloat during the War between the States.* Baltimore: Kelly, Piet, 1869.

Shatto, Rahilla Corinne Abbas, "Maritime Trade and Seafaring of the Precolumbian Maya." M.A. thesis, Texas A&M University, 1998.

"The Siege of Pensacola in 1781." In *The Historical Magazine and Notes and Queries Concerning the Antiquities, History, and Biography of America.* Vol. 4. New York: Richardson, 1860.

Sigsbee, Charles D. "Appliances for Deep-Sea Sounding." *Bulletin of the United States National Museum,* no. 27, 580–90. Washington, D.C.: Government Printing Office, 1884.

———. *Deep Sea Sounding and Dredging: A Description and Discussion of the Methods and Appliances Used on Board the Coast and Geodetic Survey Steamer 'Blake.'* Washington, D.C.: Government Printing Office, 1880.

———. "Personal Narrative of the 'Maine,' First Paper." *Century,* November 1898, 74–97.

———. "Personal Narrative of the 'Maine,' Second Paper." *Century,* December 1898, 241–63.

Simons, Norman. "The Pensacola Fortifications." In *Siege! Spain and Britain: The Battle of Pensacola March 9–May 8, 1781,* edited by Valerie Parks, 44–56. Pensacola, Fla.: Pensacola Historical Society, 1981.

Simpson, Lesley Byrd, trans. and ed. *Cortés: The Life of the Conqueror by His Secretary Francisco López de Gómara.* Berkeley: University of California Press, 1964.

Sledge, John. *Cities of Silence: A Guide to Mobile's Historic Cemeteries.* Tuscaloosa: University of Alabama Press, 2002.

———. *The Mobile River.* Columbia: University of South Carolina Press, 2015.

———. *The Pillared City: Greek Revival Mobile.* Athens: University of Georgia Press, 2009.

Sletcher, Michael, ed. *New England.* London: Greenwood, 2004.

Sloan, Edward W. "The Roots of a Maritime Fortune: E. K. Collins and the New York–Gulf Coast Trade, 1821–1848." *Gulf Coast Historical Review* 5, no. 2 (1990): 104–13.

Smith, Aaron. *The Atrocities of the Pirates.* London: Whittaker, 1824.

Smith, Buckingham, trans. *Memoir of Don d'Escalente Fontaneda Respecting Florida, Written in Spain, about the Year 1575.* Washington, D.C., 1854.

Smith, Roger C. "Ships in the Exploration of *La Florida.*" *Gulf Coast Historical Review* 8, no. 1 (1992): 18–29.

Snyder, Robert E. "Gulf Coast Gold: The Natural Sponge." *Gulf Coast Historical Review* 5, no. 2 (1990): 140–51.

Sondhaus, Lawrence. *Naval Warfare, 1815–1914.* London: Routledge, 2001.

———. *Navies in Modern World History.* London: Reaktion Books, 2004.

Sparks, W. H. *The Memories of Fifty Years: Containing Brief Biographical Notices of Distinguished Americans, and Anecdotes of Remarkable Men; Interspersed with Scenes and Incidents Occurring during a Long Life of Observation Chiefly Spent in the Southwest.* Philadelphia: Claxton, Remsen & Haffelfinger, 1870.

Spears, John Randolph. *Captain Nathaniel Brown Palmer: An Old Time Sailor of the Sea.* New York: Macmillan, 1922.

———. *David G. Farragut.* Philadelphia: Jacobs, 1905.

Sprague, John T. *The Origin, Progress, and*

Conclusion of the Florida War. New York: Appleton, 1848.

"Stauter-Built: A Mobile Original." *Alabama Seaport,* Fall 2013, 32–35.

Stephens, John L. *Incidents of Travel in Yucatan.* Vol. 2. New York: Harper & Brothers, 1843.

Stoltz, Joseph F., III. *The Gulf Theater, 1813–1815.* Washington, D.C.: Center of Military History, United States Army, 2014.

"Storms and Weather Warnings. Washington Forecast District." *Monthly Weather Review,* October 1923, 544–45.

Strand, Ginger. *Inventing Niagara: Beauty, Power, and Lies.* New York: Simon & Schuster, 2008.

Surrey, N. M. Miller. *The Commerce of Louisiana during the French Regime, 1699–1763.* 1916. Reprint, Tuscaloosa: University of Alabama Press, 2006.

Swanton, John R. *Indian Tribes of the Lower Mississippi Valley and Adjacent Coast of the Gulf of Mexico.* Washington, D.C.: U.S. Government Printing Office, 1911.

Tallant, Robert. *Mardi Gras . . . as It Was.* 1947. Reprint, Gretna, La.: Pelican, 2007.

Tarver, H. Michael, ed. *The Spanish Empire: An Historical Encyclopedia.* Vol. 1. Santa Barbara, Calif.: ABC-CLIO, 2016.

Temple, William G. "Memoir of the Landing of the United States Troops at Vera Cruz in 1847." *United Service: A Monthly Review of Military and Naval Affairs* 16 (1896): 492–504.

Thomas, Hugh. *Rivers of Gold: The Rise of the Spanish Empire from Columbus to Magellan.* New York: Random House, 2003.

Thomas, Mary Martha. "The Mobile Homefront During the Second World War." *Gulf Coast Historical Review* 1, no. 2 (1986): 55–75.

Thomason, Michael, V. R., ed. *Mobile: The New History of Alabama's First City.* Tuscaloosa: University of Alabama Press, 2001.

"To Make New Orleans Open Lumber Market." *Lumber Trade Journal,* April 1, 1915, 22–23.

Tomlinson, H. L. *The Sea and the Jungle.* New York: Dutton, 1912.

Tonti, Henri de. *Relation of Henri de Tonti Concerning the Explorations of La Salle from 1678 to 1683.* Trans. Melville B. Anderson. Chicago: Caxton Club, 1898.

Tucker, Spencer C., ed. *The Civil War Naval Encyclopedia.* Vol. 1, *A–M.* Santa Barbara, Calif.: ABC-Clio, 2012.

———. *The Encyclopedia of the War of 1812: A Political, Social and Military History.* Vol. 1. Santa Barbara, Calif.: ABC-Clio, 2012.

Turner, Frederick C. *A Border of Blue: Along the Gulf of Mexico from the Keys to the Yucatán.* New York: Holt, 1993.

Twichell, David C. "A Review of Recent Depositional Processes on the Mississippi Fan, Eastern Gulf of Mexico." In *Gulf of Mexico Origin, Waters, and Biota,* vol. 3, *Geology,* edited by Noreen A. Buster and Charles W. Holmes, 141–56. College Station: Texas A&M University Press, 2011.

Ulanski, Stan. *The Gulf Stream: Tiny Plankton, Giant Bluefin, and the Amazing Story of the Powerful River in the Atlantic.* Chapel Hill: University of North Carolina Press, 2008.

U.S. Army Corps of Engineers, *Final Feasibility Report for Sabine-Neches Waterway Channel Improvement Project Southeast Texas and Southwest Louisiana.* Vol. 1. Galveston, Tex.: March 2011.

United States Senate, 31st Congress, 1st Session, Executive Document 57. *Message of the President of the United States, Transmitting Reports from the Several Heads of Department Relative to the Subject of the Resolution of the Senate of the 23rd of May, as to Alleged Revolutionary movements in Cuba.* Washington, D.C.: William M. Belt, 1850.

U.S. War Department. *War of the Rebellion: Official Records of Union and Confederate Navies.* 30 vols. Washington, D.C.: U.S. Government Printing Office, 1894–1922.

Upton, Emory. *The Deepwater Horizon Oil Spill and the Gulf of Mexico Fishing Industry.*

Congressional Research Service, February 11, 2011.

Valdés, Antonio J. *La Historia de la Isla de Cuba, y en especial de la Habana*. Vol. 1. Habana: Oficina de la Cena, 1813.

Van Doren, Mark, ed. *The Travels of William Bartram*. New York: Dover, 1955.

Varnum, Robin. *Álvar Núñez Cabeza de Vaca: American Trailblazer*. Norman: University of Oklahoma Press, 2014.

Vascáno, Antonio. *Ensayo Biográfico del Célebre Navegante y Consumado Cosmógrafo Juan de la Cosa y Descripción é Historia de su Famosa Carta Geográfica*. Madrid: Tipo-Litografía de V. Faure, 1892.

Viele, John. *The Florida Keys*, vol. 3, *The Wreckers*. Sarasota, Fla.: Pineapple, 2001.

Vogel, Robert C. "Jean Laffite, the Baratarians, and the Historical Geography of Piracy in the Gulf of Mexico." *Gulf Coast Historical Review* 5, no. 2 (1990): 62–77.

Walthall, John A. *Prehistoric Indians of the Southeast: Archaeology of Alabama and the Middle South*. Tuscaloosa: University of Alabama Press, 1980.

Ward, Martha. *Voodoo Queen: The Spirited Lives of Marie Laveau*. Jackson: University Press of Mississippi, 2004.

Ware, John D., and Robert R. Rea. *George Gauld: Surveyor and Cartographer of the Gulf Coast*. Gainesville: University Presses of Florida, 1982.

Wasserman, Mark. *Everyday Life and Politics in Nineteenth Century Mexico: Men, Women, and War*. Albuquerque: University of New Mexico Press, 2000.

Weber, David J. *The Spanish Frontier in North America*. New Haven, Conn.: Yale University Press, 1992.

Weddle, Robert S. *Changing Tides: Twilight and Dawn in the Spanish Sea, 1763–1803*. College Station: Texas A&M University Press, 1995.

———. *The French Thorn: Rival Explorers in the Spanish Sea, 1682–1762*. College Station: Texas A&M University Press, 1991.

———. *Spanish Sea: The Gulf of Mexico in North American Discovery, 1500–1685*. College Station: Texas A&M University Press, 1985.

———. *The Wreck of the* Belle, *the Ruin of La Salle*. College Station: Texas A&M University Press, 2001.

Whipple, A. B. C. *The Seafarers: Fighting Sail*. Alexandria, Va.: Time-Life Books, 1978.

Willoughby, Hugh L. *Across the Everglades: A Canoe Journey of Exploration*. Philadelphia: Lippincott, 1904.

Wilson, Robert. *Mexico and Its Religion; with Incidents of Travel in That Country during Parts of the Years 1851–52–53–54*. London: Sampson, Low, 1855.

Winningham, Geoff. *Traveling the Shore of the Spanish Sea: The Gulf Coast of Texas and Mexico*. College Station: Texas A&M University Press, 2010.

Winters, Lisa Ze. *The Mulatta Concubine: Terror, Intimacy, Freedom, and Desire in the Black Transatlantic*. Athens: University of Georgia Press, 2016.

Wood, Michael. *Conquistadores: The Spanish Explorers and the Discovery of the New World*. London: BBC Books, 2000.

Wright, John D. *The Language of the Civil War*. Westport, Conn.: Oryx, 2001.

Wulf, Andrea. *Founding Gardeners: The Revolutionary Generation, Nature, and the Shaping of the American Nation*. New York: Vintage, 2012.

Zakour, Michael J., Nancy B. Mock, and Paul Kadetz, eds. *Creating Katrina, Rebuilding Resilience: Lessons from New Orleans on Vulnerability and Resiliency*. Cambridge, Mass.: Butterworth-Heinemann, 2018.

Websites

"*Bienvenue, Aiokpanchi*, Welcome to Isle de Jean Charles." http://www.isledejeancharles.com. Accessed November 26, 2017.

BP. Deepwater Horizon *Accident Investigation Report*. September 8, 2010. https://www.bp.com/content/dam/bp/pdf/sustainability

/issue-reports/Deepwater_Horizon_Accident_Investigation_Report.pdf.

"Brief History of Destin Florida." http://www.destinfl.com/history. Accessed November 27, 2016.

Carlyle, Ryan. "What Does It Feel Like to Work on an Oil Rig?" https://oilgas.quora.com/What-does-it-feel-like-to-work-on-an-oil-rig. Accessed December 25, 2017.

"Carnival Fantasy." https://www.carnival.com/cruise-ships/carnival-fantasy.aspx. Accessed May 27, 2018.

Cerrillo, Carlos Serrano. "La Navegacion entre los Antiguos Mayas." http://www.academia.edu/4621918/LA_NAVEGACION_ENTRE_LOS_ANTIGUOS_MAYAS. Accessed February 5, 2017.

Chatelain, Christopher. "Gulf Shores Weather." http://www.beachguide.com/blog/gulf-coast/gulf-shores-weather. Accessed January 7, 2017.

Church, Robert, et al. "Archaeological and Biological Analysis of World War II Shipwrecks in the Gulf of Mexico: Artificial Reef Effect in Deep Water." Study Report OCS MMS 2007–015. http://www.data.boem.gov/PI/PDFImages/ESPIS/4/4239.pdf. Accessed November 23, 2017.

Encyclopedia of Alabama. http://www.encyclopediaofalabama.org/article/h-1160. Accessed various dates.

"FDR Fishing, Gulf Port." Posted by FDRLibrary, June 11, 2009. https://www.youtube.com/watch?v=ywOOjxn-TBg&feature=youtu.be.

Flank, Lenny. "The Pastry War: How a French Bakery Caused a War in Mexico." Daily Kos, July 10, 2014. https://www.dailykos.com/stories/2014/7/10/1301627/-The-Pastry-War-How-a-French-Bakery-Caused-a-War-in-Mexico.

Gallagher, John. "Veracruz Port Takes Aim at US Competitors with Expansion." JOC.com, October 18, 2017. https://www.joc.com/port-news/international-ports/mexicos-veracruz-prepares-teu-expansion_20151018.html.

Henry, Devin. "Oil Lobby Pushes for Offshore Drilling in the Eastern Gulf of Mexico." The Hill, May 1, 2017. http://thehill.com/policy/energy-environment/331376-oil-lobby-pushes-for-offshore-drilling-in-the-eastern-gulf-of.

Howard, Brian Clark. "72 Years Later, Snubbed Captain Credited with Downing German U-Boat." National Geographic, December 19, 2014. https://news.nationalgeographic.com/news/2014/12/141217-german-u-boat-u-166-gulf-mexico-archaeology-history/.

Isle de Jean Charles, a film by Emmanuel Vaughn-Lee. https://www.shortoftheweek.com/2014/09/18/isle-de-jean-charles/. Accessed January 21, 2018.

"Journal of Alfred Walke, April and May, 1843." https://www.tsl.texas.gov/exhibits/navy/al_walke-aprmay_1843_1.html. Accessed September 26, 2017.

Keyes, Pam. "Eyewitness Pension Record Testimonies Place Jean Laffite at Battle of New Orleans." Historia Obscura, February 21, 2018. http://www.historiaobscura.com/eyewitness-pension-record-testimonies-place-jean-laffite-at-battle-of-new-orleans/.

Kotkin, Joel. "The Rise of the Third Coast: The Gulf Region's Ascendancy in U.S." Forbes.com, June 23, 2011. http://www.forbes.com/sites/joelkotkin/2011/06/23/the-rise-of-the-third-coast-the-gulf-regions-ascendancy-in-u-s/#626f7e7a2ad7.

Lieber, Ron. "Life on Board a Gulf of Mexico Oil Drilling Platform." Fast Company, September 30, 2000. https://www.fastcompany.com/41051/life-board-gulf-mexico-oil-drilling-platform.

Macko, Stephen. "An Almost Forgotten Oil Spill: Remembering the Ixtoc I Oil Spill in the Gulf of Mexico." Virginia, Fall 2010. http://uvamagazine.org/articles/an_almost_forgotten_oil_spill.

"*Mega Borg*—IMO 7388944." Shipspotting .com. http://www.shipspotting.com/gallery /photo.php?lid=2704539. Accessed December 7, 2017.

Morley, Hugh R. "Veracruz Port Expands to Support Manufacturing Demand." JOC. com, November 14, 2016. https://www.joc .com/port-news/international-ports/ veracruz-port-expands-support-manufac turing-demand_20161114.html.

Mullen, John. "Orange Beach Acquires Piece of Charter Fishing History." OBA Community Website, July 24, 2017. https:// obawebsite.com/oba-news/2017/orange -beach-acquires-piece-of-charter-fishing -history.

Munson, Robert. "Conquistador Clothing." https://www.nps.gov/cabr/learn/history culture/conquistador-clothing.htm. Accessed April 11, 2017.

National Oceanic and Atmospheric Administration, *Deepwater Horizon Oil Spill: Final Programmatic Damage Assessment and Restoration Plan and Final Programmatic Environmental Impact Statement,* October 2015. http://www.gulfspillrestoration.noaa.gov/ sites/default/files/wp-content/uploads/ Front-Matter-and-Chapter-1_Introduction -and-Executive-Summary_508.pdf.

National Wildlife Federation. *Five Years and Counting: Gulf Wildlife in the Aftermath of the Deepwater Horizon Disaster.* https:// www.nwf.org/~/media/PDFs/water/2015 /Gulf-Wildlife-In-the-Aftermath-of-the -Deepwater-Horizon-Disaster_Five-Years -and-Counting.pdf. Accessed December 29, 2017.

Shaer, Matthew. "Ponce De Leon Never Searched for the Fountain of Youth." *Smithsonian,* June 2013. http://www.smithso nianmag.com/history/ponce-de-leon -never-searched-for-the-fountain-of-youth -72629888/.

Skoglund, Nancy Galey. "The *I'm Alone* Case: A Tale from the Days of Prohibition." *University of Rochester Library Bulletin* 33, no. 3 (1968): 1–18. http://rbscp.lib.rochester. edu/1004. Accessed November 14, 2017.

"Spanish Ship *Santísima Trinidad* 1798 (the Largest Warship in the World)." http:// forum.worldofwarships.eu/index.php?/ topic/2120-spanish-ship-santisima-trinidad -1798-the-largest-warship-in-the-world/. Accessed June 4, 2017.

"Trans-Gulf Migration." *Monarch Joint Venture.* http://monarchjointventure.org/news -events/news/trans-gulf-migration. Accessed October 31, 2016.

"Ursa Oil and Gas Field Project." http://www .offshore-technology.com/projects/ursa/. Accessed November 4, 2017.

U.S. Geological Service. *Wetland Change in Coastal Louisiana, 1932–2010.* http://www .conference.ifas.ufl.edu/intecol/presenta tions/018/0140%20B%20Couvillion.pdf. Accessed December 30, 2017.

"Veracruz, Mexico." Encyclopaedia Britannica. https://www.britannica.com/place/ Veracruz-Mexico. Accessed November 20, 2017.

Wilkinson, Jerry. "Marjory Stoneman Douglas." http://www.keyshistory.org/35-hurr -Douglas.html. Accessed January 7, 2017.

Index

PV 11/2019